The
Animal
in You

Roy Feinson

ST. MARTIN'S GRIFFIN  NEW YORK

The
Animal
in
You

WWW.ANIMALINYOU.COM

Design by MAUREEN TROY

Library of Congress Cataloging-in-Publication Data

Feinson, Roy.
    The animal in you / Roy Feinson. — 1st ed.
        p.   cm.
    ISBN 0-312-18040-3
    1. Typology (Psychology)   2. Animals—Psychological aspects.
    I. Title.
    BF698.3.F45   1998
    155.2'6—dc21   97-43744
                                                                  CIP

First St. Martin's Griffin Edition: April 1998

10   9   8   7   6   5   4   3   2   1

TO MY PARENTS MARCIA AND SIDNEY,

The Owl and the Pussycat

Contents

Acknowledgments

Thanks to all those who inspired this work and bravely bared their personalities for analysis.

Special thanks to Philappa *Prairie Dog* Strelitz for her wisdom and guidance, Pam *Penguin* James for her enthusiasm, Kim *Wildcat* Lyell for her inspiration, Jem *Zebra* Martin for his strong-shouldered support, Tamara *Wolf* Palmer for her encouragement, and Joe *Bat* Mozdzen for his insights. Thanks also to Joanne Karney, Jonathan Cullen, Susan Little, Victoria Holland, Dennis Barton, Buzz Busbey, Elisa Marchand, and Nancy McConnell.

A mighty roar of thanks to Peter Miller, the literary *Lion,* and his staff at PMA for guidance and instinctive understanding of the project.

Thanks to the world of knowledge contained in *The International Wildlife Encyclopedia* by Dr. Maurice Burton and Robert Burton of B.P.C. Publishing Ltd.

Finally, my special gratitude to editor Jennifer *Rooster* Enderlin and staff. Without her sensitivity and unwavering support, this project would not have found its spirit.

Introduction

The Relationship Between Man and Animals

Humans are an unusual and highly successful species that spends a great deal of time examining its higher motives and an equal amount of time ignoring its fundamental ones.

—Desmond Morris

Have you ever noticed how people tend to assume animal personalities? We talk of someone being a bear of a man or someone acting like a dog. People we don't care for are weasels, sloths, or sometimes vultures.

Why is there such a strong correlation between human and animal behavior? Are these connections coincidental, or is there a more prosaic explanation? A possible clue lies in nature's need for diversity.

Life consists of an astonishing variety of animal species, each with its own distinct behavior and physical properties. This diversity appears to be an essential component of life, for without it, an ecosystem cannot successfully maintain itself.

At first glance, it would seem that nature would find the most efficient structure for an animal species and duplicate it en masse. However, an ecosystem with a single species cannot survive, and it takes a range of animal species to ensure a healthy habitat. The food chain—or, more accurately, the food web—requires the interaction of predators, prey, burrowing creatures, arboreal animals, and insects to remain stable. It is the interplay among these divergent species that gives rise to enduring and healthy populations.

In a process known as parallel evolution, unrelated animal species separated by vast distances often evolve corresponding behavioral and physical characteristics in order to take advantage of available niches. For example, isolated from the mainland for thousands of years, the marsupial Tasmanian wolf, or *thylacine*, evolved numerous features similar to the North American wolf. Although almost extinct from being hunted, its doglike body, coughing bark, and canine hunting behavior closely parallel that of wolf society, even though they have markedly different ancestries.

A similar process seems to have taken place in human society. Our human species dominates the earth and is essentially a microcosm of nature. The attributes that provide stability in the animal world—aggression, passivity, stealth, skittishness, and so on—serve the same function in our own society. It is no coincidence, therefore, that we mimic these animal behaviors to better survive in a complex and competitive world.

Be True to Thyself

Animals are themselves at all times. A pig always exhibits pure pig behavior and nothing it does is un-piglike. It has found a niche in the scheme of things and, when being a pig, is supremely happy.

We humans are not always this true to our own natures. We struggle to find our niche in this multifaceted society and accept jobs or relationships ill-suited to our personalities. The resulting tensions contribute to our stress and unhappiness.

The goal of this book is to identify your true animal spirit and give you a deeper insight into your authentic nature.

Animal Personalities in Culture

CHINESE CALENDAR

Recognition of the intimate connections between animals and humans dates back tens of thousands of years. The ancient Chinese developed a distinctive calendar system that described twelve animal personalities: Rat, Tiger, Rabbit, Ox, Dragon, Rooster, Snake, Horse, Ram, Pig, Dog, and Monkey. While the precise origins of these animals are unknown, Chinese astrologers considered them to be a reflection of the universe itself.

NATIVE AMERICAN

Native Americans also recognized the intractable bond between humans and animals. Reverence for animals was almost universal among the plains

Indians, who dedicated a great deal of energy to paying tribute to their companions of the prairies.

Spiritual beliefs were formed in large part by their close survival bonds with North American wildlife. Bison were not viewed simply as a food source but were recognized to be an essential element in the grand scheme.

POPULAR CULTURE

Calvin and Hobbes. © Watterson. Distributed by Universal Press Syndicate. Reprinted with permission. All rights reserved.

Contemporary literature also reflects our connections to animals with rich references in language. We refer to people as being bitchy, foxy, slothful, and catty. People work like horses, eat like pigs, and are as stubborn as mules.

George Orwell's classic *Animal Farm* explored this idea to its limits, and today, animal characters dominate the comic pages. The Pulitzer Prize–winning *Maus*, by Art Spiegelman, detailed his father's concentration camp experiences and used animal personalities to depict the drama of the Nazi atrocities; mice were used to portray victims, cats to represent the Germans, frogs the French, and pigs to describe the Poles.

Peanuts, Calvin and Hobbes, and *The Far Side* also provide remarkable insight into the behaviors of their characters. Perhaps the popularity of these cartoons stems from our ability to see our own selves reflected in the animal subjects.

The
Animal
in You

Translating Behavior

The Four Fs

How do we translate human behavior into its corresponding animal personality? When we examine deeply rooted patterns of animal behavior and compare them to our own, certain motifs begin to emerge. The fundamental survival techniques of animals can be summarized by the four **Fs**: feeding, fighting, fleeing, and sex.

The *feeding* technique of a particular animal translates into the career that its corresponding human personality would choose. Bird personalities, for example, prefer jobs that provide a great deal of freedom, while sheep personalities flourish under the direction of a strong dog personality. Bear personas have a need to maintain control of their environment and chafe under the direction of a boss.

The way an animal *fights* is equivalent to the way in which a person controls his or her environment. Carnivorous personalities are assertive and adventurous, while herbivorous personalities tend to be passive and cautious.

The method an animal species uses to *flee* from danger translates into how people protect themselves from each other. Herd animal personalities find refuge in the company of friends and family, while rodent personalities maintain low profiles to avoid danger.

Animals exhibit a variety of approaches in attracting the opposite *sex*. From the brutal display of strength of the wild elk to the seductive display of the peacock, all creatures exert control over their reproductive choices.

Some animal species are monogamous, while others have a variety of mates. An animal's mating habits translate directly into the way that people conduct their sexual relationships. Beaver personalities mate for life, while tiger personalities are solitary and rarely monogamous.

Why Can't We All Just Get Along?

We use the general term *enemy* to describe the relationship of a wolf to a rabbit, but we should recognize that a much deeper relationship exists. In fact, the wolf plays a mutually beneficial role in its prey's survival.

Wolves almost always select an old, weak, or diseased rabbit as a meal, simply because it is easier to catch. There's no point wasting energy in chasing a healthy adult rabbit well equipped to evade capture. This selection process weeds out genetically challenged individuals and keeps the population and gene pool healthy by eliminating diseased animals.

While it seems strange to describe wolves as providing protection for their prey, the wolf also discourages the encroachment of new predators into

the prey's range. The arrival of a new predator in an ecosystem could cause the balance of power to shift dramatically, resulting in the extinction of species lower on the food chain. By aggressively defending their territories against potential competitors, wolves preserve the balance to the benefit of both species. Thus, the prey receives protection and health benefits in exchange for the sacrifice of a few weak, diseased, and old individuals.

A similar deal is struck in human society. Deer personalities may seek protection from a stronger wolf or lion personality. Lion personalities, who are generally successful in business, bargain their services as employers in exchange for the deer's time and hard work.

Toward a More Perfect Union

Trouble can occur when two animal personalities team up without understanding the conflicting nature of their true animal personalities, and the union can struggle for years before the partners recognize the incompatibility of their fundamental natures.

Consider a relationship between a wildcat and fox. Superficially, a connection between these two species seems natural: Both share the same range and a common nocturnal spirit. Equally matched in size, they are both lithe and attractive. However, as a canine personality, the fox is a natural competitor of the cat. Both are carnivorous, and the resulting struggle for control in the relationship causes stress. The fox's natural friendliness chafes against the cat's instinct to maintain distance, and over time these tensions conspire to destroy the relationship. Both people are left to wonder what happened.

Similarly, animal personalities should never form close relationships with their natural predators. If a mouse personality married a cat, the results could be catastrophic. Control issues and spousal abuse would quickly destroy the union.

Just Friends

However, not all herbivore personalities need to avoid predators. A cottontail personality might strike up a friendship with a lion; lions are disinclined to waste energy in chasing elusive, low-calorie rabbits. Although marriage is out of the question, friendships with disparate animal personalities can be quite enduring. In exchange for companionship and loyalty, larger predators provide powerful security. Although the stronger animal personality—in this case, the lion—will dominate these relationships, cottontails are not without their power. With innate cuteness and charm, they control the friendship in subtle but potent ways.

Home on the Range

Animal personalities have an affinity for those species that share their range. The water personality of the dolphin has much in common with the sea lion, and the pastoral nature of sheep gives them an affinity for the grazing deer personalities.

Conversely, animal personalities that live in markedly different environments tend to avoid each other. Birds choose to remain above-land mammal personalities, while the unencumbered lives of the sea creatures make them awkward mates for complex land dwellers. A bat personality wouldn't dream of courting a dolphin personality.

On the other hand, the beaver that lives in a transitional range, intersecting both water and land, is capable of forming relationships with both seagoing and land-based animal personalities.

Trying Each Other on for Size

To ensure a successful union, the physical sizes of animal personalities should be in the range of each other. It makes little sense for a mouse personality to try its luck mating with an elephant (although the results are typically amusing). *Friendships* with incompatibly sized animals are possible, especially when teaming up for symbiotic reasons. Cottontails could serve as a warning system for a larger grazing animal, and some birds form mutually beneficial relationships with crocodiles, by cleaning the teeth of their larger companions in exchange for scraps of food from the crocodile's mouth.

Animal Personality Test

B efore reading further, take the test outlined below. The test, which takes only a few minutes to complete, builds a mathematical model that corresponds to your animal personality.

If you find that your personality matches the winning (or second or third) animal but differs on a few minor points, it may well be that you are a subspecies of that animal. For example, if you tested to be a deer but have a more aggressive personality than represented in those pages, your true personality may well be a stag deer.

Note that people adapt their animal personalities to help cope with the turmoil of everyday life. Therefore, they may modify their animal personalities as changes occur in their lives. A man who was previously a mouse personality might inherit a great deal of money and construct a new animal personality to complement his new lifestyle.

Step 1

Fill out **Score Sheet 1** on page 6, rating yourself on each of the listed attributes as detailed on the following page.

NOTE: Be as honest as you can. You might want to get ratings from people who know you well (secret voting is recommended, for reasons that will become obvious). If none of the descriptions quite matches your personality, simply rate yourself on a scale of 1–5, 1–4, 1–3, or 1–2 as shown.

SCORE SHEET 1	SCORE
PHYSICAL SIZE (1-4)	_____
AGGRESSION (1-5)	_____
GREGARIOUSNESS (1-4)	_____
ATTRACTIVENESS (1-4)	_____
DEPENDABILITY (1-4)	_____
INTELLIGENCE (1-3)	_____
ATHLETIC ABILITY (1-3)	_____
LIFE SUCCESS (1-3)	_____
LOVE OF TRAVEL (1-2)	_____

Physical Size
Score 1: Small and trim
Score 2: Average size
Score 3: Above average size
Score 4: Extra large

Aggression
Score 1: Submissive; prefers not to compete
Score 2: Low key and sensitive; usually puts needs of others first
Score 3: Can be assertive but is usually accommodating
Score 4: Strong-willed and assertive
Score 5: Extremely assertive and competitive

Gregariousness
Score 1: Self-contained; keeps mainly to self and family
Score 2: Prefers the company of small group of friends
Score 3: Popular and outgoing; enjoys socializing
Score 4: Extremely outgoing; wide circle of friends

Attractiveness
Score 1: Ordinary looking, nothing striking
Score 2: Average looking, with some nice attributes
Score 3: Good looking, strong features and sexy
Score 4: Very attractive; turns heads

Dependability
Score 1: Not very dependable or trustworthy
Score 2: Generally honest but sometimes unpredictable
Score 3: Dependable and honest, usually reliable
Score 4: Very dependable and reliable

Intelligence
Score 1: Prefers avoiding intellectual pursuits
Score 2: Intelligent and bright; enjoys reading or debating
Score 3: Very intelligent; loves intellectual challenges

Athletic Ability
Score 1: Generally inactive, but occasionally plays sports
Score 2: Enjoys sports as a recreational tool
Score 3: Extremely athletic, loves physical challenges

Life Success
Score 1: Has potential but struggles to find motivation
Score 2: Reaches most goals set for self
Score 3: Driven to constantly achieve; very successful at work

Love of Travel
Score 1: Homebody; enjoys vacations close to home
Score 2: Loves to travel

Step 2
Score sheet 1 now contains nine numbers. These numbers (in order, from top to bottom) constitute your *key*.

For example, if you had filled in the score sheet as follows:

SCORE SHEET 1	SCORE
PHYSICAL SIZE (1-4)	1
AGGRESSION (1-5)	4
GREGARIOUSNESS (1-4)	1
ATTRACTIVENESS (1-4)	2
DEPENDABILITY (1-4)	4
INTELLIGENCE (1-3)	1
ATHLETIC ABILITY (1-3)	1
LIFE SUCCESS (1-3)	2
LOVE OF TRAVEL (1-2)	2

Your key would be: **141-241-122.** Write this down.

Step 3

Using the numerically ordered tables beginning on page 99, locate your key; your animal personality will be listed next to it.

If more than one animal is listed next to your key, you could be any of these animal personalities. Additional animals are listed in no particular order of importance; read the pages corresponding to each of these animals. One animal, in particular, will fit you best.

NOTE: If your specific key is not listed, use the number directly above where you expected to find it. There will be a down arrow on the number above.

For example, your key is **141-241-122**, and the lookup table shows:

141-
241-121↓Bat
241-211 Mouse, Shrew

Since your actual key does not appear in this listing, you must use the number *above* where you would expect to find your key. Since 241–122 follows 241–121, this means you are a bat.

BABOON

Class: Mammalia
Order: Primates
Related Species: Monkey, Chimpanzee, Orangutan

Because of the *baboon's close relationship to man, researchers have long been drawn to the study of baboon society. Baboon troops consist of females with their young and a few older males, and within the troop, a clearly defined social structure is apparent. Unlike herds of antelope, in which the dominant males must work hard at keeping the herd together, baboons appear to coexist amicably, and there is little indication of coercion.*

When food is abundant, the troops are large and can support many males, but where food is scarce, most troops have only one male. In this way, pregnant females do not have to compete for scarce resources.

The Kung tribe of Southern Africa believe that baboons are able to talk but are careful not to let people hear them, lest they be put to work.

The Human Baboon

Intelligent and shrewd, you are a highly adaptable individual. As a student of the lighter side of life, there is nothing you enjoy more than indulging in complicated practical jokes or an impromptu comedic performance. Your reputation as a clown belies an introspective side glimpsed only by those who know you intimately.

An intensely social animal, you work hard to maintain your large, well-run family. You insist on order in your household and stand for no disagreement from your mate or children. Although you have a tendency to become cantankerous under pressure, these moods are short-lived and harmless.

Although you are rarely aggressive toward members of your own family, you'll never back down from a physical confrontation. When threatened, you are a formidable fighter, and even larger animal personalities think twice before initiating conflict.

Your love for physical contact finds you spending considerable time in social and grooming activities, and you relish giving (and receiving) long, soothing massages. You sometimes spend entire weekends indulging in quiet, relaxing play with your family.

Baboon personalities come in all shapes and sizes but are usually powerfully built, smaller individuals with bright, intelligent eyes. Arguably, you are neither handsome nor beautiful, although your robust personality is engaging and charming. Little value is placed on physical exertion, and you have a tendency to gain weight in later life. Your most noticeable physical characteristic is an elastic and expressive face, and with your animated communication style, you delight in being the center of attention.

Careers

Disdain for physical work leaves you dissatisfied with manual labor unless it contains a strong creative component, and your curious nature makes you perfect for **investigative work** or **journalism**. You function best during the daylight hours, preferring to spend nights quietly in the company of your family.

Ultimately, however, you only find true happiness when performing as a **comedian** or **actor**.

Relationships

Your affinity for a rigid social structure makes you an excellent mate. Children are treated with respect and disciplined gently and intelligently. Considerable care is taken in their education, and you pride yourself on their achievements.

Your desire to be the center of attention sometimes causes friction as you compete with siblings and friends for the spotlight. This struggle for prestige can disrupt the tranquillity of your troop, but disputes are quickly resolved.

You are naturally well suited for relationships with **dog**, **gorilla**, or **fox** personalities. You identify with their gregarious, loyal natures, and your romantic unions are happy and fulfilling. Your cheerful disposition even makes you a good foil for the grumpy **warthog**, but you should avoid larger carnivorous personalities that have little patience for your sometimes disquieting humor.

Famous Baboons
Robin Williams, Jim Carrey, Billy Crystal

Advice for a Baboon
You can't have everything. Where would you put it?

BADGER

Class: Mammalia
Order: Carnivora
Related Species: Wolverine, Weasel, Ferret, Mink

T**he badger is** *a bearlike animal with short, powerful legs and strong claws. Although it is armed with musk glands, like its close relative the skunk, it* relies on its powerful and stocky three-foot-long body to protect itself. Because of their nocturnal habits, they are rarely observed in the wild, although they are common throughout Northern Europe and the United States.

A badger's response to danger can be quite astonishing. When threatened, the hair on its body stands on end so that it suddenly looks twice its normal size. Accompanied by a violent snarling sound, this blustering reaction is enough to frighten off any would-be predator.

The Human Badger

You are closely related to the **weasel** personality and share the same range as your cousin the skunk. What distinguishes you from your relatives is your extraordinary physical and emotional strength and tenacious approach to life's challenges.

A good-looking, small- to medium-size individual, you walk and talk as if you own the world. Your powerfully built body and dominating personality backs down for no one, not even the much larger personality of the lion. You confidently enter the territory of others, and woe betide anyone blocking your path.

Like most carnivores, you stay in shape with regular physical activity and are usually well dressed and precisely groomed. You enjoy all sports, and your competitive nature drives you to the limits of your abilities. Because of your small size, you sometimes feel the need to assert yourself to gain the respect accorded the larger carnivores. Your tendency to bite off more than you can chew often results in an overestimation of your capabilities. With the heart of a **tiger**, your tenacity is both your greatest asset and biggest downfall.

You seldom find time for the finer pleasures of life. Art and literature are considered distracting to your pursuit of resources, and your reading habits are usually confined to light fiction or popular action novels.

Careers

You are almost always successful in business but often find yourself over your head. Your towering ambitions cause you to make sweeping plans without considering the finer details of the exercise. With such an abundance of self-confidence, you sometimes rush headlong into overwhelming situations and are forced to burrow your way out. You don't go down without a struggle, however, and fight to the end.

You are highly regarded as a leader, especially by the smaller animal personalities, but your physical stature limits your political ambitions. However, this doesn't deter you from running races you are destined to lose. Like your cousin the **weasel**, you are an opportunist and sometimes team up in business with the more thoughtful animal personalities to help offset your impetuous nature.

As a **salesperson**, you have few equals. Jobs requiring a high degree of proactive selling are ideally suited for your get-up-and-go personality; as a **manager**, you are somewhat overbearing but fair and rational. You don't exhibit much of an ego, and with your head down, rooting for opportunities, you generate a great deal of respect from your peers.

Relationships

You love to debate, viewing an argument as just another challenge. However, with your black-and-white view of the world, you'll sometimes simply badger your opponents into submission. This quality makes you a difficult mate, and you are best suited for relationships with the more gregarious **dog** or aloof **wildcat**. **Mice, shrews, cottontails**, and other small mammals cannot compete with your aggressive nature and are advised to give you a wide berth.

With the larger, stronger carnivores like the **lion** and **tiger**, you often find common ground for friendship or business liaisons, but romantic relationships rarely fruit due to your high degree of competitiveness.

Famous Badgers

Napoleon Bonaparte, Robert DeNiro, Oliver North

Advice for a Badger

Think big. If you're going after Moby Dick, take along the tartar sauce.

BAT

*Class: **Mammalia***
*Order: **Chiroptera***
*Related Species: **Rat, Mouse***

Because they fly, *bats are often mistaken for birds. However, they are mammals that have chosen to abandon the world of the terrestrial and adopt the nocturnal, airborne envi-ronment in which they thrive.*

Although a number of mammals are able to glide, bats are the only mammal to have achieved real flight.

Highly skilled hunters, bats have been able to infil-trate a variety of geographi-cal niches using all manner of feeding techniques. From the famous bloodsucking vampire to the tiny pollen-eating fruit bat, their nocturnal flappings evoke an image of a mysterious and vaguely repellent rodent on the wing.

The Human Bat

Being an airborne personality, you tend to be vulnerable in the company of ground animals. However, you are not a true bird personality and haven't mastered the art of smooth, controlled flight, so you often appear clumsy in social situations (hence the term *acting batty*). As compensation for your awkwardness, you seem to have a built-in radar that allows you to read the intentions and motivations of others.

Identifying a bat personality is not difficult. Being nocturnal, you come alive at night and prefer dark, nondescript clothing. Underground clubs or dimly lit bars are your favorite haunts, and you *never* have a tan. You are an intelligent, spiritual, active individual and use your full range of senses (other than your poor eyesight) to carefully evaluate every situation.

You have a habit of flitting in and out of social situations. Swooping down to interact with others, you'll quickly fly off to resume your bat life. You tend to be unassertive and aloof, preferring to take flight at the first hint of a confrontation, and seek comfort in your personal space that is decorated in an unusual but comfortable way.

Careers

A sixth sense gives you a number of advantages in your work, and your insightful nature enables you to understand others better than you understand yourself. This intuitiveness makes you an excellent **psychiatrist, psychologist, social worker**, or **palm reader**.

You respond poorly to direction and function best as a sole practitioner in your own business. Preferring to work at night and sleep by day, your job must be flexible enough to accommodate these unusual hours. A creative streak finds you in the **design** and **architectural** fields, and your unique relationship with dark caves makes you a natural **archeologist** or **spelunker**.

Relationships

Although your spiritual side is always on display, you are not overly emotional, and because of your unusual and sometimes awkward approach to life, you sometimes have difficulty finding companions. However, you respond well to anyone who shares your philosophical perspective, and you love spending long hours in conversation. Once you have successfully located a partner, you prove to be both a dependable and committed companion.

Cats and other animal personalities that share your nocturnal spirit, such as **shrews** and **weasels**, make good casual companions. However, their aggressive natures cause trouble for you in marriage.

Your best relationships are with other **bats, penguins, moles**, and **owls**, but you should avoid water mammal personalities that place play over the more serious aspects of life. You are an excellent communicator, and people who have you in their lives are well served in getting to know you well.

Famous Bats

Nostradamus, Gypsy Rose Lee

Advice for a Bat

If originality means eccentricity, so be it.

BEAR

Class: Mammalia
Order: Carnivora
Related Species: Polar Bear, Grizzly Bear

Although bears belong to the order Carnivora, they are actually omnivorous, and their diets vary greatly depending on where they live. Highly adaptable creatures, bears have a range that extends throughout Europe and most of North America, and they are found in both forest and mountainous regions.

Bears are well-armed for conflict. Equipped with sharp, nonretractable claws, their powerfully built bodies are capable of defending against any aggressor. Although they do occasionally attack and kill small deer, their favorite foods are fish and fruit.

The Human Bear

Supporting a bear personality requires a strong physical presence. Along with your gruff, outgoing personality, you are easy to identify by your burly physique and strong demeanor. Your natural confidence and swagger in your gait put others on notice that a bear is present. You require a great deal of personal space, and when you enter a room, the tension level rises.

Being both carnivorous and herbivorous, you exhibit two distinct sides to your personality. Sometimes a strong-willed, aggressive individual that never backs down from a fight, you are also introspective and intensely interested in the world around you. You feel no need to observe social niceties and do whatever is necessary to overcome your opponents in both business and social situations. When threatened, you become very aggressive.

As a youngster you excelled in sports, although your propensity for laziness now relegates you to being an observer and fan. Familiar with the seduction of the couch, your ability to sleep soundly is legendary throughout the animal world.

Careers

Although you are aware and intelligent, you mostly succeed from the sheer force of your personality and are rarely challenged to reach your full intellectual potential. You dominate conversations with your intense single-mindedness, but you are unwilling to argue from a position that you don't truly believe in. This makes you a lousy lawyer.

Your natural leadership qualities combine with your physical prowess to make you an excellent **physical education teacher, martial arts trainer,** or **professional wrestler,** and you could also have a measure of success in **politics** if you were to put your mind to it.

Teaching and **academia** appeal to you, although intellectual laziness prevents you from reaching any great heights in these fields.

Relationships

As a parent you are first-rate. Protective and attentive to the well-being of your children, you provide strong but loving discipline.

You tend to form relationships with animal personalities who don't challenge your status. Your obsession with dominance means that you should avoid marriage with **elephants, lions,** and **giraffes,** who will readily challenge your authority. Although you respect the strength of these animals, they are more appropriate as business associates.

Similarly, although you respect intelligence in others, close relationships with **foxes, owls,** and **bats** can cause problems. Their intellectual pursuits challenge you beyond your zone of comfort. While you tolerate the company of small mammal personalities, such as **cottontails, porcupines,** and **shrews,** your disdain for their passivity results in dysfunctional and disrespectful relationships. Similarly, **deer, sheep,** and **goat** personalities are vulnerable to your temper and aggression.

Dogs, horses, eagles, vultures, and **warthogs** are capable of providing you with the loyalty you crave, and the resulting marriages are usually permanent.

Famous Bears

Teddy Roosevelt, Babe Ruth, Norman Schwarzkopf, Jack Nicklaus

Advice for a Bear

Be unafraid of opposition. Remember, a kite rises against, not with, the wind.

BEAVER

Class: Mammalia
Order: Castoridae
Related Species: Capybara, Cottontail, Rat

The **beaver is** *second in size to the South American capybara as the world's largest rodent. Famous for their engineering talents, beavers are able to cre-*ate advanced damming sys-tems and intricate lodges.

It is arguable, however, whether the beaver's com-plex home-building skills require intelligence or is simply instinct, much as a bird builds a nest. Today, it is generally believed that the beaver's intelligence is over-rated. Contrary to the notion that they purposely fell trees to fall into the water, they are not infre-quently killed by having these trees fall on them.

Beavers live in colonies and mate for life. They are preyed on by all carni-vores of their own weight or more, and away from the protection of their lodge, they are relatively defenseless. Today, the beaver receives protection from human hunting, although some beaver populations have been so successful that control has become necessary.

The Human Beaver

You are the workaholic of the animal world. No animal personality places more emphasis on, nor derives more self-esteem from, career as you do. Organized and structured, your determined attitude spills over into all aspects of your busy life.

You plan for the future almost unconsciously. Decisions made regarding your relationships, career, and family are methodically and practically pre-pared. You are most comfortable at work or ensconced in your fastidiously decorated home, and in your spare time love to busy yourself around the house or tend your precisely manicured lawn. While others are playing, you're usually hard at work.

You are well prepared for any eventuality. Your home is well stocked with spare water, an emergency radio, and survival kits. You're not sure why you spend such energy in securing your home, but you instinctively feel more comfortable when you do.

Beaver personalities come in all shapes and sizes. Generally in good physical condition, you find time to keep fit even with a busy work schedule. A conscientious attitude makes you dependable as a friend, and a commitment from you is like money in the bank. Once you have given your word, you'll follow through, no matter what personal inconveniences you encounter.

Careers

You are an excellent worker and can be found at all levels in the workplace. As a manager you are often frustrated by the lack of motivation in your employees, and friction often results. As a business owner you are typically successful but work equally hard as a low-level employee in a large corporation.

Performing best in unsupervised positions, you excel in jobs that require trustworthiness. This makes you ideal for roles as a **ship's captain, naval officer, judge, accountant,** or **bank manager.** As a **handyperson** you have no equal: If asked to fix a chair, you'll build one from scratch.

Relationships

Once married, you prove to be a committed partner. You mate for life and are an excellent provider, but you tend to neglect your family in lieu of your career.

As a water personality you have a natural affinity for the playful **dolphin** personality. However, monogamous relationships with this animal never fruit because you are a terrestrial mammal at heart. For the same reason, you don't get on well with **roosters, peacocks,** and **bats,** who are too flighty and irreverent for your earnest nature.

Your closest relationships are usually with **sea lion** and **otter** personalities. Your patience enables you to connect with their tricky personalities, and in a committed relationship, they can depend on your fidelity. However, they must always compete with your obsession for work.

Famous Beavers
Jimmy Carter, Alexander Graham Bell

Advice for a Beaver
Don't confuse comfort with happiness.

BISON

Class: Mammalia
Order: Artiodactyla
Related Species: Buffalo, Cow

Some fifty million *bison once roamed the North American plains, but as recently as 1890 fewer than six hundred individuals remained. The near extinction of the bison is attributable to their whole-sale slaughter by European settlers satisfying the demand for meat and hides. The disappearance of the bison also triggered numer-ous Indian wars as the food supply of the Native Americans dwindled.*

Unlike other bovine species, the bison social structure does not support a harem master who monopo-lizes sexual activities. Although there is some fighting among males for mates, peaceful coexistence is the order of the day.

The Human Bison

You are a pragmatic, strong-shouldered individual who excels in the art of compromise. As an herbivorous personality, you are methodical and ded-icated to the pursuit of resources. No one would ever accuse you of being handsome, and you have a plain, placid face that's difficult to remember. Your staid temperament complements your looks.

Although your large frame can handle any physical confrontation, you never go looking for trouble. Keeping a low profile with your head down, you attract as little attention as possible, and your reputation as a methodical plod-der often elicits unkind remarks from jealous associates. As a consequence of this backbiting, your implacable expression sometimes masks a deep-seated inferiority complex.

Closely related to the African buffalo personality, you share its strong aggressive streak. Righteous indignation is a hallmark of your tempera-ment, and you are determined to maintain your status in the workplace hierarchy. You are conservative in most aspects of your life, and your political views reflect your strong sense of moral direction and commitment to family. Fearful of change, you steer clear of radical ideas that might engender change in the societal order.

Stolid and stable, you go about your business with careful deliberation, and your moods are uninspiringly predictable. The only time you will display your emotions is when directly challenged, but even then, your temper is controlled and muted.

As a migratory animal, you love to travel and do so in large, organized groups. You are often seen in popular vacation spots, herding around local landmarks before stampeding off to the next predictable tourist trap.

Careers

With your strong herding instinct, you are adept at group interactions and love participating in committees. You are rarely showy or flashy and prefer to work behind the scenes, and you will usually gain consensus before making definitive decisions.

These attributes make you a fine **accountant, committee leader, manager, politician,** or **banking industry worker.** Your dependability and dedication make you a trustworthy and dependable employee.

Relationships

When you make up your mind with regard to the opposite sex, you come on strong. As an aggressive if clumsy suitor, you ply your limited charms with enthusiasm. However, once in a relationship, you revert to your normal impassive self, and life soon resumes a dull monotony.

Still, you are a dependable partner, protective and attentive to your children, who are well trained in the art of social responsibility. Your best mates include **deer, sable, sheep,** and other pastoral animals, but you should avoid **lions, tigers,** and **bears** at all costs.

Famous Bison
Al Gore, Bob Dole, Gerald Ford

Advice for a Bison
Don't take life so seriously; you're not getting out alive.

COTTONTAIL

Class: Mammalia
Order: Lagamorpha
Related Species: Jackrabbit, Hare

The **cottontail is** *a small rabbit that varies in color from a reddish-brown to dark gray. They are abundant throughout the world and particularly favor brush-covered woodland.*

As an herbivore, the cottontail faces a difficult problem in digesting the coarse twigs and grass that makes up its diet. Unlike other grazing animals, such as goats and sheep which can chew their cud, the cottontail must pass the food through its digestive system twice to ensure complete digestion.

The Human Cottontail

Cottontails get their name from their fluffy snow-white bottoms. You are astoundingly appealing and rely heavily on your soft personality and vulnerable appearance to succeed. Although you are intelligent, you will disguise this characteristic if it interferes with your primary method of survival—cuteness!

Almost all mammal personalities find you attractive, and you need rarely employ your intelligence or personal resources to succeed in your career or relationship.

Unless married, you tend toward being solitary and shy in the company of large groups and you have only a few close friends. You enjoy being outdoors and love going on long hikes to explore nature, particularly in the company of **horses**, **zebras**, **deer**, and **sheep** personalities. Though you are stimulated by wide-open spaces, you choose small, comfortable living areas that are well secured against predators.

Although your first line of defense is to keep a low profile, your senses are extraordinarily well developed. Your large, wide eyes and sensitive ears constantly warn of approaching trouble, and you'll take flight at the first hint of trouble.

Careers

Your quiet, solitary behavior is often mistaken for timidity, but you're actually quite aggressive in your search for resources. You function best in situations that don't involve confrontations, and you are not a natural salesperson. However, with your ability to work well with people, you are suited for careers in **customer support, diplomacy, administrative work,** and **nursing.**

Because you lack the physical strength of larger animal personalities, you must rely on your incomparable social skills to compete in the workplace. Your well-developed senses are helpful in assessing long-term **marketing** plans, and you make a wonderful **advertising** executive.

Like most small-mammal personalities, it is not uncommon for you to strike alliances with **lions, bears,** or **gorillas** as confidantes or aides. In the company of these strong animals, you feel comfortable and safe, proving to be a loyal, trustworthy colleague.

Relationships

You are conscious of your physical charm, and you wring every advantage from it. When attracting a mate, you are inordinately selective and carefully probe the intentions of potential suitors before making a lifelong commitment. During the courtship period, you scamper off at the first sign of infidelity.

Once in a relationship, you breed prodigiously. You love children and feel secure when surrounded by your large family. Strong links to your parents and siblings are carefully maintained, and you are an excellent aunt or uncle, always remembering the appropriate birthdays and anniversaries.

Your best partners include the **horse, gorilla, mole, sheep,** and **deer** personalities.

Famous Cottontails

Marilyn Monroe, Anna Nicole Smith

Advice for a Cottontail

Be an excellent housekeeper: When you get a divorce, keep the house.

CROCODILE

Class: Reptilia
Order: Crocodilia
Related Species: Alligator, Caiman, Gharial

Among the most *feared animals in nature, these cold-blooded creatures are masters of their domain. Adults have no natural enemies and will ruthlessly attack all creatures who enter their realm.*

They are distinguishable from their close relatives the alligators by the shape of their snouts. The size of a crocodile can vary greatly, sometimes reaching lengths of twenty feet.

To assist in their lives in the water, crocodiles will swallow several pounds of stones to help stabilize their bodies. This technique is useful for younger crocodiles who are naturally top heavy and need the weight of the stones to keep them from capsizing.

Crocodiles are unquestionably man-eaters, but it is arguable just how dangerous they are. It seems that most of the killing is only done by a few individuals, while others prefer their regular diet of deer, rodents, and even young crocodiles. Because of their tendency for cannibalism, juvenile crocodiles are always separated from the adults when basking.

The Human Crocodile

You are a lean, tough individual, and your skin is often decorated with scars or tattoos. A natural predator, you attack without subtlety or intelligence, using any weapon at your disposal. Your prey is the unwary individual who has strayed from his environment, and you'll often gang up with others in order to better victimize your prey. You think nothing of using dirty tricks to gain an advantage and have little sense of honor. You have little conscience, compassion, or guiding philosophy save that of survival and self interest.

Living on the fringes of society, you avoid mainstream locales and prefer dimly lit, grimy hotels for your pursuit of food and entertainment. You ply your nefarious crafts by both day and night and are a master of disguise. Your ability to mask your true colors allows you to befriend unsuspecting victims, usurp their resources, and then suddenly disappear.

Careers

You provide a useful service to society by doing jobs that others find too unpleasant, and you are unafraid of breaking the law in your quest to earn a living. With your talent for disguise, you are an excellent **private investigator**, doing deep undercover work that reputable companies shun. Because of your ruthless nature, you are also hired by legitimate businesses as a **bouncer** or **personal bodyguard**.

Some enterprising crocodiles go into their own businesses as **gang members**, **drug dealers**, **hired killers**, and **burglars**, but all too often you find your true calling as a **common thief** or **con man**.

Relationships

As a parent you apply the minimum effort required to ensure your progeny's survival. Your children are encouraged to fend for themselves and must learn life's lessons the hard way. As a strong disciplinarian, you withstand no disrespect from anyone in your family, and your children regard you with fear and respect, while they emulate your street-smart demeanor.

Most others instinctively avoid you, and your social life is usually relegated to uneasy alliances with **hippo** personalities. Sometimes you'll form a mutually rewarding relationship with a bird personality, receiving grooming and personal services in exchange for money.

Although indiscriminate in your search for your mate, you avoid animal personalities larger than yourself, particularly **bears, elephants**, and large cats. From a prospective mate's view, you are an unpredictable and dangerous partner. Your only naturally enduring relationship is with the water-going **snake** personality, who is wary enough to avoid your clutches. As a fellow reptile, the snake empathizes with your cold-blooded nature, and these relationships are tense but long lasting.

Famous Crocodiles

Charles Manson, Ted Bundy, Jeffrey Dahmer, Al Capone

Advice for a Crocodile

Life is war. There are no winners, only survivors.

DEER

Class: Mammalia
Order: Artiodactyla
Related Species: Moose, Springbok

Extremely shy and *wary, most deer spend their time in small herds, constantly surveying their surroundings as they nervously browse on grass and shrubs.*

Male deer sport antlers ranging in size from inch-long stubs to handsome, multi-branched displays. Interestingly enough, reindeer are the only species of deer in which the female also has antlers.

Deer populations in North America are making a comeback. Because of the good press provided by the movie Bambi, *communities are loathe to cull their numbers, and in many western states they have become significant pests and health hazards. Belying their large populations, there are fewer than fifty species of deer left in the world, with the majority found in Asia and South America.*

The Human Deer

The hallmark of your personality is your skittish behavior. This instinct to take flight at the first hint of trouble makes you a difficult and fickle partner, and though you crave close relationships with stronger animals, you are much better suited for friendships with **mountain goats**, **prairie dogs**, and **horses**.

You are active and lithe, with little excess body fat, and you enjoy—and excel at—most athletic pursuits. Your athleticism and grace create a fine first impression, but others find you to be scatter-brained and emotionally taxing. This results in a haphazard love life, and although it might be too callous to describe you as schizophrenic, your behavior *is* difficult to predict. With your propensity to withdraw emotionally for fear of getting hurt, you struggle to settle down.

As a deeply spiritual person with strong religious convictions, you spend much time in the company of like-minded individuals. You're also a habitual people-watcher and enjoy nothing better than quietly ruminating while the world goes by.

The outdoors is where you feel most comfortable, and you appreciate the freedom of wide-open spaces, where your graceful movements and love for dance can express themselves.

Careers

When it comes to your work, you are not known for your stability and change jobs often while looking for a long-term career. Part of this problem is that relationships with your bosses are difficult. Most bosses are larger, predatorial animal personalities, and proximity to **lions, warthogs,** and **bears** makes you nervous. Unless you are a member of a large team of workers, the resulting tensions cause problems.

You are more comfortable when plying your grace as a **dancer** or **actor** but are also content in **social work**, working as a **secretary**, or employed in the **service industry**.

Relationships

Your need to select a strong animal as a partner often results in poor choices for your relationships. Although these unions are repeatedly ill-fated, you never seem to learn your lesson and insist on dating **rhinoceroses, gorillas, tigers,** and **elephants**. While these unions seem to offer the security you crave, they are unbalanced and ultimately result in unsuccessful relationships. Conversely, life with smaller mammals results in insipid and uninspiring unions.

You are better off in the company of other grazing animals, and friendships with **zebras, sable,** and **sheep** are strong and enduring. Your closest relationships are with **mountain goats** and **horses,** and you like to spend hours hiking and exploring in their company. With a great deal of patience from your partner, you make an excellent mate, and when feel secure in your relationship, you are unflinchingly loyal and quickly set about raising a family.

Famous Deer

Elizabeth Taylor, Sean Young

Advice for a Deer

Experience is that marvelous thing that enables you to recognize a mistake when you make it again.

DOG

Class: Mammalia
Order: Carnivora
Related Species: Wolf, Fox

The dog was *probably the first animal to be fully domesticated, and there is evidence of its liaison with man dating back as far as 8000* B.C. *Recent genetic studies, however, indicate that this partnership may go back as far as 100,000 years. Conventional opinion holds that the dog descended from the wolf, although it is possible that its ancestry includes jackals and perhaps a species of wild dog that is now extinct. The breeding of dogs for specific social duties began soon after the dog was domesticated, and by the Bronze Age, at least four types of dogs were common. In more recent times, dogs have been used for guidance for the handicapped and by the military.*

Because of this selective breeding, dogs show enormous variation in size within their species. From a high of the two-hundred-pound St. Bernard to the diminutive four-pound Chihuahua, it is difficult to imagine that these dogs had a recent common ancestor.

The Human Dog

Dog personalities come in all shapes and sizes, and it's difficult to identify your species by physical appearance alone. The best way to recognize a dog is by its dominant trait—gregariousness.

Usually, you are a small- to medium-size individual, who is good-looking and in fine physical shape. Energetic and eager to please, you have an overabundance of energy and spend a great deal of time at play. You are frisky and happy even when hard at work. Demonstrative with people you love, you readily display distaste for those you dislike. Highly tactile with an exceptionally advanced sex drive, you have a reputation of acting like . . . a dog, even with casual acquaintances.

You do not display the characteristically sharp intelligence and aggression of your cousins the **wolf** and **fox**. Instead, you rely on your advanced emotional senses to survive. Sensitive to the feelings of others, you recognize the importance of dominance and submission in the social order and are ready to play your role either way. Sometimes you take the lead, while other times you are happy to tag along to play a more subdued role. You are only secure when your position in the social hierarchy has been clearly defined.

Careers

You take pride in helping others and excel in all aspects of the **service industry**. Some of the world's best restaurants employ dogs as **waiters**. Dedicated to your job, you love to please your boss. Your desire to help others finds you in a wide variety of jobs, including the **medical** and **retail** fields.

You are also comfortable in leadership roles and are capable of owning your own business or being a supervisor in a large company, with **deer** or **sheep** as subordinates. Your strong presence and commanding voice barks clear, concise orders, and you're well liked and respected.

Your intelligent insights and gregarious nature make you a wonderful **salesperson**. People instinctively trust you, and with a concerted effort, you could easily earn a high income.

Relationships

A relationship with a dog personality is a treat. Your effervescence and eagerness to please means that your partner gets a great deal of attention, while your skillful communication ensures a deeply rich love life.

Not everyone enjoys your attentions, however. Members of the cat family find you cloying and suffocating, and these relationships are short lived. You are strongly drawn to the small, passive animal personalities, such as **mice**, **sheep**, and **cottontails**, but these attractions are superficial. Once the chase is over, you quickly lose interest and move on.

Your best unions are with those capable of appreciating the strong, affectionate companionship you provide; **wolves**, **foxes**, and **bears** are your natural soulmates.

Famous Dogs

"Kato" Kaelin, Huey Lewis

Advice for a Dog

Only the lead dog's view ever changes.

DOLPHIN

Class: Mammalia
Order: Cetacea
Related Species: Whale, Porpoise

Dolphins live in *schools containing males and females of all ages. There does not appear to be any particular leader, but males do observe a hierarchical structure based on size. Dolphins are highly social animals and will assist an injured member of the school, raising it to the surface to breathe. This behavior has been reported by injured swimmers who have been helped to safety by these gregarious creatures.*

Dolphins have an insulating layer of blubber, but because they have no sweat glands and are unable to pant, they must dispel their excess heat through their tail flukes and flippers. This is why these parts of their bodies are warmer to the touch. It is believed that dolphins have little or no sense of smell, although their excellent hearing ability and built-in sonar more than compensate for this deficiency.

The Human Dolphin

Characterized by your propensity for play, you are the definitive hedonist and party animal.

Active in physically demanding sports—particularly skiing, scuba diving, and surfing—you gravitate to others who enjoy your fun-seeking philosophy. Your sleek, trim body looks its best on the beach, with only a swimsuit for modesty, and because of your constant activity, you can expect to enjoy a long and healthy life.

Though your large brain is capable of solving almost any problem, your reputation for intelligence is overrated. You place little value in cerebral pursuits, and you avoid mental challenges. Nonetheless, you are able to hold your own in debates, but you avoid discussing weighty philosophical issues, preferring instead to cavort and surf.

You expect nothing from life other than time to enjoy it. As a highly sexual individual, you spend a great deal of time in the pursuit of bodily pleasure, and your aggressive quest for sex sometimes dominates your social interactions.

Generally you are a peaceful and fun-loving individual, almost never displaying open aggression. When accosted, you'll swim away rather than engage in negative behavior. Socially, you crave the company of others and are always on the lookout for friends to join you in recreation. You love to host elaborate parties or social events, and you take your fun seriously.

Careers

You were not designed for manual labor. Your body lacks the skillful hands of the land-mammal personalities and you are a poor tool user. However, your intelligence and social ability give you an advantage in people-oriented careers.

Rarely found in nine-to-five office jobs, your outgoing personality makes you a capable **public relations representative** or **outside salesperson**. Other recommended careers include **professional sports figure, fitness instructor,** and **actor.**

You seem to have a sixth sense. A natural sonar gives you the ability to accurately read the hidden intentions of others by picking up their subtle body language. This talent makes you an ideal **psychologist** or **crime investigator.**

Relationships

Unlike the **sea lion** and **otter,** you are an *exclusive* water personality and have completely isolated yourself from the terrestrial world. Consequently, you only find true comfort in relationships with other water mammals, such as **sea lions** and **otters,** and feel little connection with land-mammal or bird personalities.

You are attracted to those who enhance your quest for play, and you have many casual friends. However, you don't form intimate relationships with anyone who could distract you from life's pleasures, and you particularly avoid the serious-natured **bats, moles, owls,** and **foxes.**

You involve your children in all manner of physical activity, dragging them around in your pursuit of play. As a lover, you are rarely faithful although always passionate and creative.

Famous Dolphins

Burt Reynolds, Dan Marino, David Hasselhoff

Advice for a Dolphin

Don't wait for your ship to come in. Swim out and meet it.

EAGLE

Class: *Aves*
Order: *Falconiformes*
Related Species: *Hawk, Vulture, Falcon*

Perhaps from its *use on the Seal of the United States of America, the eagle has become the most familiar of birds. Most eagles are solitary and only come together in groups when prey is plentiful.*

Eagles take a variety of small animals for food and are not averse to eating carrion. A more spectacular method of feeding is the eagle's habit of robbing ospreys. By constantly harrying an osprey carrying a captured fish, the eagle forces the bird to drop the fish. Sometimes an eagle will grab the fish from the osprey's talons while in flight.

The Human Eagle

Eagle personalities are proud, physically strong, and universally admired for their independent, soaring spirit. Extraordinarily energetic and agile, you are usually in excellent physical condition, since body fat is a luxury that weighs you down and limits your spirit from flying freely.

Sleek and well groomed, your looks are striking. However, you occasionally have a flawed aspect to your appearance—perhaps a bald spot or too large a nose—but you still exude a strong sexual energy that turns heads. You enjoy most outdoor sports and have a particular affinity for extreme sports such as sky diving, rock climbing, or bungee jumping.

Like all bird personalities, you tend to disassociate yourself with the everyday life of land creatures. Hovering above the fray, it is *you* who decides when to come down and socialize. The need to carefully choose your companion is an important component of your personality, and your independence is jealously guarded. More than any other animal, you love to travel and predictably prefer to fly.

Like most bird personalities (with the exception of the **owl**), you tend to be flighty and emotionally jittery, and your high metabolism makes you edgy and unable to remain in one place for long. Instead, you prefer to keep moving for no other reason than the sheer joy of exploration. Rarely alighting to integrate with the locals, you are a consummate voyeur and prefer to people watch with your eagle eyes.

Careers

You do not adjust well to the confines of office work. When you find yourself in this predicament, you are unsettled and perform poorly, unless the work is creative and challenging. Outdoor jobs are coveted, and you enjoy working in the hot sun as a **construction worker**, serving in a natural setting as a **park ranger**, or **piloting** the friendly skies.

The proverbial legal eagle, you also enjoy the creative freedom of **litigation**, **police**, and **detective** work. However, you are truly at your best when **performing** for others. Like the wild eagle whose aerial displays attract a large audience, you are in your element when singing, acting, or telling stories.

Relationships

Your need for freedom makes you a difficult creature to tame, and though you enjoy the challenge of a relationship, you are wary of the confines of commitment. Comfortable with your own company, you find little value in settling down.

When you do form a relationship, though, you mate for life, and your strong nesting instincts require you to find a secure, comfortable place to live. However, if you feel pressured by your mate, you will fly the coop, leaving only turbulence in your wake. Those close to you know that the best way to maintain your friendship is to give you your freedom and provide a comfortable haven for your return.

You are attracted to independent mammal personalities such as the **fox**, **wolf**, and **wildcat**, but your aggressive tendencies sometimes scare them away before strong bonds form. **Mice**, **shrews**, and **moles** should be wary of your powerful personality, and though you share the same aerial spirit as **owls**, they find you to be pushy and unsettled.

Your predilection for the freedom of a mountaintop perch strikes a chord with the **mountain goat**, and you treasure the unique perspective on life that you both share.

Famous Eagles

Madonna, Don Henley, Cher

Advice for an Eagle

Learn to listen. Opportunity sometimes knocks softly, and when it does, invite it in for dinner.

ELEPHANT

Class: Mammalia
Order: Elephantoidea
Related Species: Rock Hyrax, Mammoth

Elephants are the *largest living land animal. All elephants have a communal society that requires an intricate communication system, and a little-known facet of elephant behavior is that they purr. For a long time, naturalists were puzzled by the unusual sound emanating from their stomachs. These loud and low-frequency tummy-rumblings would suddenly stop when someone approached. These sounds have nothing to do with digestion and can be heard over incredibly long distances. The sound acts*

as a signal to the rest of the herd that all is well, and when danger approaches, the sudden silence alerts all.

In addition to these sounds, elephants will trumpet loudly and aggressively. This shrill tone instantly sets all animals on notice that elephants are in the neighborhood.

The Human Elephant

As the largest land-mammal personality, you are a rare individual. If there is any doubt as to whether you are an elephant personality, chances are that you're not.

Your huge persona is both warm and overpowering, and your slow, deliberate movements exude supreme confidence. You are a considerate and spiritual soul. Because of your immunity to attack, you're able to spend the bulk of your time building family relationships and indulging in the philosophical aspects of life.

Slow to anger, you can sometimes exhibit a violent temper, and you use your powerful personality to humble and drive off unwanted intruders. Active during day and night, you take naps whenever the urge strikes you.

As a friend or mate, you are loyal for life, and your devotion is matched only by the **dog** personality. While your loyalty is slower to develop, you'll never forget a friendly face or an act of kindness.

Careers

When you set your mind to something, you don't waver in your commitment until the task is complete. Your intelligence, combined with a formidable personality, gives you a terrific advantage in business and social affairs, while your communication skills make you a first-rate leader. Trustworthy and honest, you always let others know where they stand with regard to your feelings.

Your vocal skills can make you an excellent **singer** or **musician**, and your sober nature aligns you with the classical arts rather than contemporary music. In business, you are usually found in leadership roles as a **business executive** or **company president** and, although highly paid, are never ostentatious with your wealth.

In the top echelons of **political office**, elephant personalities are far more likely to be female. Male elephants are not as predictable as their counterparts, and females are more likely to maintain an even temper.

Relationships

With your incomparable communication skills, you are a great choice for a mate. Sharing your feelings with ease, you expect the same from your partner and are an instinctively protective parent. However, you do have a tendency to be sloppy, so potential mates should be prepared to pick up after you.

Your best partners are **horses, hippos, rhinos, giraffes**, and even the tricky **warthog**. You are advised to steer clear of **mice** and other small mammals, whose skittish behavior can irritate you. **Lion** and **tiger** personalities should also be avoided, as their aggressive natures pose a threat to the stability of your family.

Famous Elephants

Indira Gandhi, Golda Meir, Luciano Pavarotti

Advice for an Elephant

You can tell whether a man is clever by his answers, and whether he is wise by his questions.

FOX

Class: Mammalia
Order: Carnivora
Related Species: Dog, Wolf, Coyote

Foxes are closely related to dogs and jackals and actually comprise a number of distinct species, each with a unique range. Assessing the population of foxes worldwide is difficult, as these animals mainly go about their business at night and are skilled at staying out of sight. During the day they rest in thick brush or in the hollows of trees. They are not particularly fast runners, nor do they have the endurance for a long chase, relying instead on their keen intelligence to make a living.

The fox is the only member of the canine family to routinely climb trees and often escapes danger by running up the trunk of a sturdy tree and navigating overhanging branches.

Foxes sometimes fall prey to coyotes and wolves, but today its main enemy is man: Because of its tree-climbing habit, it is an easy animal to trap.

The Human Fox

You are very much a creature of the night and, along with your **dog** relatives, are the most gregarious of the carnivores. Your agile mind is always active, and although you never intend to harm others, you have developed a reputation for slyness and manipulation. The female of your species is called a vixen for good reason: With her sharp mind and equally sharp tongue, she is best left alone when angry.

You are a fussy eater and feed on a wide range of foods. With an appreciation for the finer things in life, you demand quality in your entertainment, food, and friends. Your love for exploration is mixed with your enjoyment in overcoming challenges, and you're often out climbing mountains or journeying to exotic, forbidden places.

You prefer to be inconspicuous. Flamboyance is usually not your style, and you choose subtlety and cunning over brute strength.

You live in a small, cozy environment, and your house is usually organized and neat. As a hunter personality, you are in good physical shape and enjoy sports that challenge your mind and body.

Careers

You are typically successful in the workplace, but your competitiveness and ambition sometimes makes coworkers feel belittled. You would never deliberately take advantage of others, but your single-mindedness often blinds you to their feelings.

You thrive in your own business and like to surround yourself with family and friends in your ventures. Although you demand consensus in all decisions, you dominate discussions and steer the plans to reflect your own agenda. Competent in a wide range of fields, you are particularly well suited for a career as a **computer programmer, lawyer, doctor,** or **professional chess player.**

Relationships

You are a social animal, and relationships are important to you. Your aura is attractive to others, but you are choosy with whom you form loving relationships. With your strong moral code you should avoid less sophisticated animal personalities, such as **sheep, giraffes,** and **gorillas.** A relationship with a **bat, deer,** or **weasel** can be gratifying, but you tend to challenge them in ways that can alienate the relationship.

As a member of the dog family, you should avoid cats and larger carnivores, although your quick-wittedness and agility provide you immunity from their aggression. Your best mates are **dogs, horses,** and **owls,** but because of your dominating personality, you are incompatible with **cottontails** and other small mammals.

An outstanding parent, you raise your young with affection and care, usually having a large number of children in your litter.

Famous Foxes
Johnny Cochran, Michael J. Fox

Advice for a Fox
The best way to remember your wedding anniversary is to forget it once.

GIRAFFE

Class: Mammalia
Order: Artiodactyla
Related Species: Okapi, Horse, Deer

The tallest animal *in the world, the giraffe tops out at eighteen feet. Living in herds with casual social structures, the females and their offspring live separately from groups of males.*

The thirteenth-century Arabic writings of Zakariya al-Qaswini declared, "The giraffe is produced by the camel mare, the male hyena, and the wild cow," and the mystique surrounding the giraffe persists to this day.

Some observers believe that giraffes never sleep, although it's probable that they do—for about thirty minutes a day. Another puzzle surrounding the giraffe is its unusually large voice box. For a long time it was believed that giraffes were mute, and naturalists are still unsure why such a large voice system rarely gets used.

The Human Giraffe

You are a tall, well-groomed, and proud animal with an unmatched aura of grace. A natural beauty, you take pride in your appearance, and your long graceful legs, narrow neck, and beautiful skin make you the envy of all who cross your path. Being a large game personality, your species is rare. With your proud jaw thrust forward, you stand out in a crowd and strut through life with an imposing confidence. Fastidious about your diet, you select only the choicest and most succulent foods available at the finest restaurants.

You prefer to spend personal time shopping or showing off your latest fashions, and you enjoy being the center of attention. Your aloof behavior is designed to enhance your image, and you could be accused of being too self-conscious. This impressive physical presence contrasts with your untidy and funky living space, and a large apartment or sparsely furnished loft is your preferred living environment.

Intellectually, you're no owl, but then you've never had to rely on your wits to compete. Instead, your graceful presence and charm provide you with a serene and gentle passage through life. When necessary, though, you display a sharp wit and have an engaging sense of humor and ready smile.

Careers

Other than personal possessions that serve to enhance your prestige, you have little need for worldly goods. You have a definite taste for quality and would rather own a few prized possessions than anything at all. Your ambitions are limited to having a comfortable living environment, close friends, and universal admiration.

When and if you work, you're able to make a good living with your physical attributes alone, perhaps as a **model** or **dancer**. Your sense of the aesthetic makes you a natural for the creative arts, including **writing** and **acting**, and as an **athlete** you have no equal on the basketball court.

Relationships

You are particular about the company you keep, and your standards are sometimes too high for your friends to live up to. Occasionally you'll team up with the equally large **elephant** or **rhinoceros** personality, but on a long-term basis, these unions are rarely successful.

You admire the chutzpah of those that have the courage to try their luck in winning your attentions, and you have special relationships with **deer**, **horses**, and **zebras**, sharing long walks and exchanging gossip. You are always the dominant partner in these relationships.

You should avoid **lions** and **tigers** at all costs, since their aggressive personalities tend to upset the harmony of your otherwise uncomplicated existence.

When mated, you usually have only one child and are a casual and permissive parent. Although monogamous, you do not remain in relationships for long and often have multiple marriages.

Famous Giraffes
Cindy Crawford, RuPaul, Michael Jordan

Advice for a Giraffe
Find someone to look up to.

GORILLA

Class: Mammalia
Order: Primates
Related Species: Gibbon, Chimpanzee, Orangutan

Gorillas are the *largest of the great apes, weighing up to six hundred pounds. Living in troops consisting of a single adult male and several females,* gorillas do not defend a particular territory. When two troops do mingle, they generally ignore one another, and fighting between groups is rare.

With the exception of man, gorillas have no natural enemies, although leopards have been known to take the occasional youngster. Probably as intelligent as chimpanzees, gorillas are less volatile in their emotional makeup, belying their savage reputation.

The Human Gorilla

Characterized by an apparent ferocity, your aggressive exterior masks a gentle, loving heart. Your rough demeanor is designed to discourage unwelcome intrusions in your life and is enhanced by the addition of rough clothing or jewelry. Tattoos are sometimes used for added effect. However, it only takes a safe, trusting environment for your inner warmth to emerge.

When threatened, you'll readily display aggressive behavior but will never physically attack. You pay little attention to your physical condition and can even be a bit of a slob. With this tendency to be untidy, you're not one to recycle or pick up after yourself.

Days spent in quiet comfort with close friends suit your nonpredatory nature. Your need to be in control of your environment makes you ill at ease in the presence of larger individuals, such as **elephants**, **bears**, and **rhinoceroses**. Their strong personalities infringe on your privacy.

You are unmotivated by money, and you avoid strenuous physical exertion, preferring to spend your leisure time in play. Drawn to social groups, the classic gorilla scene is a group of Hells Angels revving its bikes, mimicking a gorillalike chest pounding and roaring.

Careers

You are intelligent but not overly motivated. When you were young, you avoided formal learning, and as an adult your intelligence manifests itself as street-smarts. You have the talent and problem-solving skills to be an excellent **mechanic, plumber,** or **repair person**.

Your career, however, takes a backseat to your pursuit of recreational activity, and you'll rarely rise to great heights in business. However, if you're lucky enough to find a job that incorporates fun and physical prowess—such as a **personal trainer** or **professional wrestler**—you could rise to the top of your field.

Your appreciation for the good life stands you in good stead for careers in the **service industry,** including the **hotel** and **restaurant** businesses, and customers appreciate your gruff but can-do attitude.

Relationships

You are capable of forming long-lasting, monogamous relationships, and you enjoy the peace and comfort provided by a large family and close groups of friends. Considered a good mate, you make an effort to provide a secure and comfortable nest. Not overly ambitious, though, you have a tendency to rest on your laurels once you've achieved a desired level of comfort.

Smaller-animal personalities are attracted to your embracing persona and you form lasting bonds with submissive **mice** and **cottontails**. Warm and kind to these "pets," you dominate the relationships and control their duration.

Your personality clashes with the challenging nature of **owls, foxes,** and **moles,** who retard your carefree spirit, and you are at your best in relationships with **baboons, cottontails,** and **dogs**.

Famous Gorillas
Hulk Hogan, Mr. T

Advice for a Gorilla
Dust is not a protective coating for furniture.

HIPPOPOTAMUS

Class: *Mammalia*
Order: *Hippopotamidae*
Related Species: *Pygmy Hippopotamus, Warthog*

Distantly related to *the pig, the hippo is the third-largest land mammal. Its body is hairless except for sparse whiskers on its muzzle, and its skin* exudes an unusual oily pink fluid known as pink sweat, which serves to lubricate its skin.

Hippo society is a matriarchy, and young males are forced to keep their distance from the main group of females, winning reentry only by fighting other males. A baby hippo must show strict obedience or risk the wrath of its mother, who will lash the offending youngster with her head and slash with her tusks.

Hippos feed mainly at night, and their insatiable appetites can severely damage the environment. They spend most of their time in rivers and small inlets where their weight is supported and hidden by the water.

The Human Hippopotamus

Your hippopotamus personality is easy to identify. Of impressive physical bulk, you invariably attempt to disguise your size and ponderous movements. Wallowing in loose-fitting clothes or large tent dresses, your uncomfortable dimensions are the result of a compulsive eating habit. This massive bulk triggers an overwhelming hunger, and your life is centered around food and its preparation.

Traditionally viewed as a jolly fat person, your girth makes you uncomfortable and vulnerable, and your discomfort forces you to withdraw from society. You are rarely seen at clubs or dances.

You carry around a great deal of unrequited anger from hurtful experiences in your youth, and although you're generally peaceful, you are aggressive when provoked. Consequently, others avoid you, further adding to your sense of alienation.

Careers

Food acts as a salve for your loneliness and alienation, and with your intimate knowledge of it, you are an excellent **chef** and **food critic**. Extraordinarily fond of children, you often volunteer for baby-sitting duties, finding solace in the unjudgmental nature of youth. You are the first to bake cookies for the local school.

For some reason, the **IRS** hires hippo personalities in large numbers—probably because of their aggressive and intimidating demeanor when agitated.

Like the **elephant** personality, you have a wonderfully rich voice. The deep resonance produced by your bulk, together with your desire to hide from society, makes you perfect for the role as a **phone receptionist, operator**, or even a **phone sex actor**.

Relationships

Having lived with the pain caused by your weight issues for many years, you have learned to compensate by adopting the jolly exterior that characterizes your species.

You should seek relationships with other river-based animal personalities, such as the **beaver** and **otter**, and might consider a cautiously superficial friendship with a **crocodile**—provided you protect yourself from its predatory instincts.

When you mate, you prefer others of equally oversize dimensions, such as **elephants** and **rhinoceroses**, but are best suited for marriage with water-based animals, such as **sea lions** and **dolphins**. True happiness, though, is most likely to be found in a union with your food-loving soul mate, the **walrus**. Predatory personalities such as **lions**, **eagles**, and **weasels** should be avoided, although you are in no real jeopardy from them.

You are an excellent parent but have a tendency to overdiscipline your children. Nonetheless, they grow up with a strong moral framework and sense of community.

Famous Hippos
Shelly Winters, Julia Child

Advice for a Hippo
Remember that a gourmet is just a glutton with brains.

HORSE

Class: Mammalia
Order: Perissodactyla
Related Species: Zebra, Mule, Donkey

Wild horses live in *large herds on lush plains. Each herd is led by a stallion, and as male colts reach maturity, they are driven to the edges of the herd by the dominant stallion.*

The domestic horse has played an important role in the history of war; the mounted Spanish conquistadors were virtually unstoppable in their conquest of South America.

No one is quite sure when the horse was first domesticated, but it is certain that it was some time before 2000 B.C. The best horses have traditionally been reserved for nobility and are still considered a status symbol.

The Human Horse

Everyone appreciates having a horse in their lives. Strong, capable, and broad-shouldered, you are a popular individual. You are also helpful and unselfish and are known for forming long-lasting friendships. Unlike your cousin the **zebra**, you are warm and approachable, moving gracefully through life and rarely making enemies.

Your strong physique is well maintained by physical activity, and you exude personal charm and confidence. Sometimes, however, others take advantage of your helpful spirit. When this happens, you react with predictable horse behavior—saddling up and running off without a word. Usually, though, a long, solitary walk lets you blow off steam, and you soon resume your good-natured demeanor. Your social skills are at their best during twilight, when you gather with your friends to ruminate and discuss the events of the day.

Long hikes and nature walks are among your favorite pastimes, and your enormous endurance is evident in your talent for long-distance running.

You enjoy all forms of activity, ranging from dancing and swimming to basketball and football, although you prefer team sports to solitary pursuits.

You are well traveled and insist on journeying in comfort. Rather than blazing new trails, like the **fox** and **wildcat** personalities, you prefer to frequent popular tourist destinations, just like your fellow herbivores, the **sheep** and **bison**.

Careers

With confidence in your strength and speed, you are unintimidated by hard physical work. Your stamina makes you a good candidate for any type of manual labor, and you are a dedicated employee. When tasked with a challenging job, you'll champ at the bit to show off your capabilities.

With your gregarious nature, you generally rise to the top in your organization, especially in **sales** and **public relations** positions, but due to your lack of aggression you are not a natural leader. You prefer to slipstream behind others and control events from behind the scenes. If you are to be found in the **political** arena, it is usually in a key advisory position, and you're almost never the person in the limelight.

Relationships

Perhaps because of your wide circle of friends, you don't have a strong desire to commit to a single relationship, preferring the freedom of remaining single. When you do decide to marry, you perform your role in typical horse fashion, proving to be monogamous and consistent, and accept the responsibilities of matrimony with natural good grace. You love children, and your playful, patient nature enables you to spend hours entertaining and teaching.

You are capable of forming a friendship with almost any type of animal personality, including the bad-tempered **warthog** and the wily **weasel**. You are not known as a deep individual, however, and close liaisons with philosophical animals like the **bat, mole, owl**, and **fox** can end in frustration for both parties.

Your best mates are other **horses, zebra, cottontails, sable, dogs**, and **deer**, with whom you share a common love of nature and open spaces.

Famous Horses
Magic Johnson, Tom Selleck

Advice for a Horse
Shoot for the moon. Even if you miss, you'll land among the stars.

LION

Class: Mammalia
Order: Carnivora
Related Species: Tiger, Wildcat, Leopard

With the exception *of the tiger, the lion is the largest member of the cat family and commands enormous respect wherever it is found. Lions were once* common throughout Southern Europe, Asia, and the whole of Africa, but the last lion in Europe died about two thousand years ago. They were exterminated largely because of their perceived threat to man.

Lions live in prides and hunt cooperatively. Each pride is serviced by one or two male lions, whose job it is to protect the territory from marauding hyenas and single male lions. In return, the male lion gets the benefit of feeding first at the lioness' kills.

It is not widely known that lions are not completely carnivorous and will even eat fruit occasionally. They typically eat the entrails of their prey first, taking advantage of the minerals, salts, and vitamins from their victim's last meal.

The Human Lion

You usually have an imposing physical presence. Naturally fit, your powerful physique is attractive, and your full head of hair is usually healthy and glowing. You have no qualms about demonstrating your superiority in financial and physical matters, and you always dress the part. Your car is carefully chosen to reflect your status, and your home and furniture are ostentatious and expensive. As long as others pay you proper tribute and keep a respectful distance, you maintain your celebrated pride.

Since you attack only when hungry, you usually pose no threat to smaller animal personalities—you're interested in larger game. Generally tolerating those beneath you on the food chain, you tend to be condescending and impatient with them.

You usurp a disproportional amount of resources with your extravagant lifestyle, and because of your voracious appetites, society cannot support a great number of your species.

Energetic and strong, you respect strength in others and have no time for subtlety. Your moods are demonstrated with abandon, from yawning in public to growling at impudent inferiors, and you feel no need to follow social etiquette. You're always the first to complain about bad food or service in a restaurant, but you are fair-minded and equitable and are often called to settle disputes of others.

Careers

In business, you prefer to surround yourself with animals beneath you on the food chain, offering leadership, strength, and protection in exchange for loyalty and hard work. You realize that your survival depends on these animals, and you are protective and possessive with your employees. At the end of the day, however, you insist on taking the lion's share of the profits.

You are aggressive, predictable, and dependable. Others always know where they stand with you, and your confidence and leadership abilities make you a successful **CEO, company president, judge,** or **lion tamer**.

Relationships

Lions usually pair for life, and both sexes make very good parents. You personally supervise your children's education and organize your life around their needs. The lioness is a particularly industrious individual: She doesn't hesitate to use her sharp claws to make a point and is more aggressive than her male counterpart. She is usually the breadwinner of the family, and although she brooks no disrespect from others, she will defer to her mate and tolerate his lazy, unresponsive behavior.

You identify with birds of prey and form interesting power-liaisons with submissive **sheep** and **cottontails**, but should avoid **bears, elephants,** and **crocodiles,** whose powerful personalities could challenge your own.

You are particularly susceptible to the wiles of the **snake** and **weasel**, who prey on your vanity. These relationships always end in disaster, with you getting the worst of the affair.

Famous Lions

Ted Turner, Sharon Stone

Advice for a Lion

One is not born, but rather becomes, a lion.

MOLE

Class: Mammalia
Order: Talpidae
Related Species: Shrew, Desman

Moles spend most *of their lives in darkness. Living in underground burrows, they tunnel through tough soil to make their living. Moles are* voracious eaters and can consume more than their own weight in food daily.

They are superbly adapted for their unique underground environment: Strong, curved claws make short shrift of even the toughest soil, and mating, childbirth, and dying all take place deep below the surface.

©Fred Whitehead/Ecostock

The Human Mole

An aura of mystery surrounds you. Probably a result of your affinity for the dark, you don't connect well with the above-ground animal personalities, and your intentions are sometimes misunderstood.

You do, however, have a rich social life with others who share your nocturnal spirit, and you are often found in dimly lit, underground clubs or cafes, enjoying offbeat music and art in the company of **bats** and **owls**. You have a particular affinity for dark poetry and you eschew popular music for alternative.

Physically, you are not an awe-inspiring individual. Your pale skin and plumpish physique are usually accompanied by thick glasses or contacts that compensate for your poor eyesight. However, you are comfortable with your flaccid body and seek companionship with others who appreciate your more philosophical qualities. Shunning contemporary fashions, you prefer dark clothes and retro-styles.

You favor apartment living, furnishing your space with eclectic and interesting designs. Your living space is central to your existence, and you spend a great deal of time entertaining friends or merely hanging out in your den.

When you feel comfortable in the company of others, you reveal an interesting and rich philosophy that's somewhat out of synch with the majority view.

Passive and unassertive, you prefer to retreat at the first sign of confrontation and would rather argue than take physical action. If you were to be found on a rare trip to Disneyworld, your angry tan lines would be a dead giveaway to your mole personality.

Careers

Despite your drab appearance, you have an extremely sharp mind and are an excellent problem solver. As reflected by your determined burrowing through difficult terrain, your approach to problems is straightforward rather than roundabout. When confronted with a difficult issue, you never give up but hack away with dogged determination until the answer is found. This attribute makes you perfect for a job in **engineering, accounting,** or **diagnostic** work of any kind.

With your unique underground perspective on life, you have enormous potential as a **songwriter, poet,** or left-wing **journalist,** and some of the world's finest philosophical **writing** has emanated from moles.

Relationships

By a wide margin you are at your best in the company of other **mole, owl,** or **bat** personalities, finding solace in their philosophical inclinations. Relationships with these creatures are long-lasting and rewarding, but because you have no interest in being in the spotlight, you feel little connection with the gregarious and outgoing natures of the **horse, deer,** and **elephant** personalities.

You are an adequate parent and form strong bonds with your children and mates, spending a great deal of time with your family rather than socializing with others. Being connected so strongly to the ground and other earthy matters, you should avoid bird and water mammal personalities, especially the brightly colored **peacocks** and flamboyant **dolphins.** Similarly, you should stay away from the aggressively inclined **weasels** and **shrews** who share your range.

Famous Moles
Bob Dylan, John Lennon

Advice for a Mole
Occasionally bite off more than you can chew.

MOUNTAIN GOAT

Class: *Mammalia*
Order: *Artiodactyla*
Related Species: *Sheep, Llama*

Mountain goats have *a precarious existence. While their highly evolved hooves make them master of their slippery, dangerous domain, they are* challenged by the sparse vegetation found at these higher elevations. Having found a niche on slopes between two thousand and seventeen thousand feet, they feed mainly on grass and herbs during the summer and leaves in the winter.

Mountain goats are also known as Ibexes, and there are seven distinct species found in Asia, North Africa, and Europe. One advantage to living in such an inhospitable environment is the lack of predators. However, snow leopards and wolves will often claim unwary individuals on the lower elevations.

The Human Mountain Goat

Being a mountain personality makes you very much a loner. Observing the goings-on from your unique perch, you are a consummate voyeur, and when mingling with other terrestrial animal personalities, you feel uncomfortable and vulnerable. After brief forays into their world, you must return to your place of security.

Balance is a critical component of your life, and you are moderate in every facet of your behavior. With conservative family values, your politics are middle of the road, and your even-keeled life has similar characteristics to that of your cousin the **sheep**. However, you have an air of eccentricity about you, and this is reflected in your unusually decorated home.

Careers

Nimble of foot and quick of mind, you are adept at extricating yourself from tricky situations. Usually, though, you're responsible for getting into these predicaments in the first place and have a habit of not learning from your mistakes. Although intelligent, you do not have much in the way of street smarts and could be considered naive. This is probably due to your lack of real-world experience.

A creature of gossip, you subscribe to the rumor mill that includes tabloid magazines and TV shows, in an attempt to better understand the world of the terrestrial personalities. You love to watch soap operas and other shows depicting the tumult of human relationships. With this affinity for intrigue and gossip, you would make a great **movie critic**, **writer**, **hairdresser**, or **journalist**.

Relationships

Your desire to find a mate can lure you from your solitary hideout, and you choose partners with strong personalities that seem to promise protection in an unfriendly world.

However, you often feel pressure to be a permanent relationship and will quickly withdraw if you fail to get a commitment. This behavior can be interpreted as desperation by a potential partner, and some relationships are doomed before they get off the ground.

However, a partner who takes time to understand the nuances of your personality will experience one of the most committed mates in the animal kingdom. You are unconditional with your love, and you'll do anything to make your relationships work. As long as your love is reciprocated, you are generous and faithful.

Although capable of having a relationship with almost any animal personality, you are best suited for marriage with other **mountain goats**, **sheep**, or **deer**. You have a special relationship with the **eagle**, with whom you share a common mountain perspective.

Relationships with **tigers**, **wolves**, **bears**, and **lions** are too unbalanced for your herbivorous nature, and **wildcats** are too aloof and unpredictable to fulfill your emotional needs.

Famous Mountain Goats

Sir Edmund Hillary, Mia Farrow

Advice for a Mountain Goat

Life can only be understood backward, but it must be lived forward.

MOUSE

Class: **Mammalia**
Order: **Rodentia**
Related Species: **Rat, Shrew**

In the United States, *the most commonly seen outdoor mouse is the deer-mouse. These mice are nocturnal, making daylight appearances only when very hungry or under a cover of snow, which allows them to forage.*

Even though they are a favorite on most predators' menus, mice still seem to thrive. With their high reproductive rates and ability to coexist with humans, their populations can sometimes explode with incredible speed. A farmhouse in Australia was recently overrun by hundreds of thousands of mice feeding off a nearby grain field. Even the cats brought in to stem the tide were overwhelmed by the waves of mice, and only poisoning specialists were able to bring the population back to normal.

The Human Mouse

Mice personalities are enormously successful and are well represented throughout cities and suburbs. Living in close proximity to larger animal personalities, you survive by utilizing the resources they consider insignificant, and because of your limited consumption you place very little stress on the environment. You are a quiet, compliant person, and you disappear into your home after work, without ever drawing attention to yourself.

Physically small and emotionally timid, you are unassuming and plain. As a youngster, you were endearingly cute, but in your later years, your smallish features have failed to mature with the rest of your body. As you age, you'll probably evolve into a mousy-haired elder and go quietly about your business.

Adaptability is the key to your success. You make do with anything that life hands you, and you are resourceful with your limited means. Like your cousin the packrat, you discard nothing. Instead, you recycle. Always working on broken appliances, your garage overflows with what appears to be junk, but you see this mess as a treasure trove of valuable goods. Consequently, you are often seen scurrying around swap meets and garage sales, eagerly adding to your collection.

Careers

You are uncomfortable when exposed in the open, and your timidity forces you to keep a low profile. You enjoy the security of numbers and join social organizations like the Rotary Club or the chamber of commerce to enhance your acquisition of resources. Your work environment is always neat and well organized, and you take great care in ensuring that things are always in their correct place. You are a creature of habit and need schedules and routines to make you feel in control.

With your small personality, you find it difficult to compete in the business world. Consequently, you almost never own your own business, relying instead on the abilities of larger animal personalities to lead the way. You are content to function as a cog in the wheel of a large corporation. A dependable worker, you are found as a **customer service representative, factory worker, bank teller**, and **librarian**.

Relationships

In a relationship, you will scurry away at the first sign of a problem. Lacking the communication skills of the social **prairie dogs** and **sheep**, your unions are often based on need rather than love. You identify strongly with the **cottontail** and **shrew** and will even befriend the benign **deer** or **sheep** personality. Marriage should be with an individual able to cope with your shy, withdrawn personality.

Your arch enemy, the **snake**, should be studiously avoided, and you should keep an eye out for the active claws of the **wildcat**, who is disdainful of your introverted and withdrawn behavior.

Famous Mice

By definition, mice are never famous.

Advice for a Mouse

Go out on a limb. That's where the fruit is.

OTTER

Class: Mammalia
Order: Carnivora
Related Species: Weasel, Skunk

This engaging creature *is a master swimmer. Using its tail and hind-quarters as a rudder, the otter is able to maneuver as quickly as the fastest fish and is equally at home on land.*

Otters are nomadic animals, covering up to fifteen miles a day in an effort to find a good fishing hole. Moving rapidly over land by tobogganing over muddy patches, they travel mainly at night to avoid predators.

Because of its characteristic mode of swimming, which reveals a little furry hump, mothers with families in tow are sometimes mistaken for a large sea serpent, giving rise to a number of legends. In fact, President Theodore Roosevelt saw a "monster" on Lake Naivasha in Kenya and fired at the three humps of the swimming beast. Two humps promptly disappeared, but the third was killed—and sent to a New York museum.

The Human Otter

Your otter personality is engaging and charming, and you are living proof that good things come in small packages. For all your inquisitiveness and apparent open-mindedness, you are conservative at heart and hold strong views on how others should behave in social situations. Independent minded, you dislike being tied down and have a powerful need to be financially self-sufficient.

With strong social instincts, you enjoy the company of others and are an adaptable creature, comfortable in the presence of both land and water animal personalities. You are usually the first one to make social plans and get the group moving.

Your love for play finds your agile body involved in all manner of recreational activities, from swimming and in-line skating to dancing. You are very aware of your own body, and you are always well groomed and meticulous about your presentation, with well-manicured nails and perennially pressed clothes.

Careers

Although intelligent and witty, you have a tendency to suffer from self-doubt, and fear of failure can prevent you from living up to your true potential. Still, you are a great problem solver with the ability to spend endless hours on abstract or practical challenges.

As a worker, you are dedicated and capable and always eager for a chance to prove yourself. Your determination makes you a valuable employee, and although you often feel that your contribution is undervalued, you would rather accept lower pay than risk confrontations in your workplace.

Although you are a fine motivator, you avoid taking leadership roles. Instead, you perform well in large groups, with your social skills coming in handy when counseling coworkers through their problems.

Your dexterous hands are useful in a wide range of careers, and you're ideally suited for work in the **engineering**, **design**, **accounting**, and **medical** fields.

Relationships

You are invariably forthright and open about your motives, and you take care in ensuring that boundaries are understood and respected in a relationship. You have little to fear from a union with a predatory animal since you are quick to dissociate yourself from bad relationships.

Sea lions, beavers, and **dolphins** make ideal partners, and you sometimes form interesting unions with the quirky **penguin**. With your highly developed tactile senses, you enjoy cuddling and spending lazy afternoons nuzzling in the arms of your partner.

You are a doting parent and are unafraid of disciplining your children, who respect your fair and open-minded approach to life. Your quick intelligence, active imagination, and *joie de vivre* make you a desirable friend.

Famous Otters

Mary Lou Retton, Scott Hamilton

Advice for an Otter

Never give up. Never ever. Ever!

OWL

Class: Aves
Order: Strigiformes
Related Species: Hawk, Eagle, Osprey

Owls often live in churches and empty houses and are prone to swoop suddenly out of the dark with a ghostly appearance. Their eerie hoots create a mournful backdrop for their spooky behavior, and these sounds are probably responsible for the origin of a number of ghost stories.

Although owls can sometimes be seen by day, they function best at twilight as they patrol their regular routes and swoop down to catch mice and squirrels.

Owls are able to hunt in complete darkness, having evolved a system of "outer ears" hidden under their feathers. By detecting slight differences in the timing of their prey's noises as the sounds strike these asymmetrical ear flaps, owls are able to zero in on their prey by sound alone.

The Human Owl

You are known as a serene, wise observer of human society. Always well groomed, you are a noble individual with elegantly chiseled features bordering on the fine edge of beauty and homeliness. Your large eyes are often framed by handsome eyeglasses.

Dapper and well coordinated, you exude dignity in your bearing. Immaculately groomed, you are never flashy or ostentatious and prefer understated clothing that enhances your serious and thoughtful demeanor.

You've developed quite a reputation for intelligence, but it's really your calm and insightful nature that gives this impression. Instead of an intellectual approach to life, you use your deeper spiritual senses to guide you, and like your nocturnal cohort the **bat**, you have a deeply philosophical bent.

As is typical of bird personalities, you tend to remain above the turmoil of life. On controversial issues you take the moral high ground and have a tendency to be somewhat preachy. Nonetheless, you make a wonderful leader and you inspire others by example.

To the other terrestrial mammal personalities, you are a bit of a mystery. Spending much of your time in solitary pursuits, you like to hole up in a quiet working environment and venture out only when necessary. You are not a playful creature. Only engaging in exercise and sport in order to keep physically fit, you avoid the more gregarious animal personalities like **dogs, dolphins**, and **sea lions**.

You are not without your assertive side however, and you won't hesitate to use your razor-sharp tongue to settle an argument. Never the aggressor in a confrontation, you fight only when your survival or honor is at stake and have no desire for a prolonged or physical struggle. You espouse nonviolence, think logically, and argue persuasively.

Careers

As a wise observer of human nature, you are eminently suited to be a **judge** or **diplomat**. Your trustworthiness and dependability find you in positions of responsibility, perhaps as a **bank manager, head of state**, or **religious leader**. A conscientious worker, you take your responsibilities seriously, and when you accept the burden of public office, you do so with the grace and skill typical of your species.

With an enormous capacity for hard work, you achieve great things in almost any field you choose. This success doesn't always translate into financial rewards but invariably satisfies your need to impart your wisdom to others.

Relationships

In matters of the heart, you are a traditionalist. Even though your owl persona belongs to the bird family, you disdain the aggressive natures of **eagles** and falcons and have absolutely no time for the irreverent **peacock** personality, although you are attracted to the quiet nobility of the **swan**.

The **bat** personality is your natural soul mate. You share a common nocturnal spirit and don't compete for resources. You enjoy the company of small predatory ground personalities, such as **badgers** and **weasels**, but do not share a common range and thus are unable to form close relationships.

Famous Owls

Nelson Mandela, Oprah Winfrey, Abraham Lincoln

Advice for an Owl

Share your wisdom. It's your path to immortality.

PEACOCK

Class: Aves
Order: Phasianidae
Related Species: Turkey, Guinea Fowl

Throughout history, peacocks *have been venerated and admired. The Ancient Greeks made it sacred to Hera, queen of the heavens, and it became* a proud symbol of the Greek empire until the Romans discovered the birds to be mighty tasty when roasted.

Peacocks roost in trees and feed from the ground, eating anything that seems remotely edible. They have been known to kill snakes and small rodents and have even been observed snapping flies and bees from the air. Their *wonderfully distinct plumage serves as a sexual stimulant to potential mates, but it is merely a single component in a rich series of strutting courtship rituals.*

The Human Peacock

You are not overburdened by brains. Beautiful, vain, and irreverent, you derive your self-worth almost entirely from your wardrobe and enchanting beauty. Attracted to superficial qualities in others, the wealth of a potential partner is more important than his or her character. The expensive sportscar of a male peacock has an electric effect on the female of your species.

Perched on top of your lovely neck is a rather small head, decorated by a shock of perfectly coifed hair. Your designer wardrobe is obsessively maintained, and you spend a great deal of time primping before going out to strut your stuff. At heart, you are an exhibitionist who enjoys nothing more than showing off and parading on the beach in skimpy attire. A great deal of money is spent in the pursuit of your beauty, and plastic surgery and body piercings are sometimes used to enhance your appearance. Because you hate to be outshone by others, you keep the company of drab, unassuming companions who high-light your beauty.

Sporting events are fastidiously avoided, but you do spend an inordinate amount of time in the gym, perfecting every aspect of your well-developed body.

Careers

As are a natural primper, you flourish in all facets of the **personal care** business, and you are well suited as a **model, dancer, actor,** or **fitness instructor.**

Because of your love for beautiful objects, you could excel as a **decorator** or **cosmetologist,** while industrious peacocks can even become **architects** and **designers.**

In later life as your beauty dims, you might reexamine your priorities, return to school, and learn a new trade. Most peacocks evolve different animal personalities to better cope with the fading of their luster as middle age approaches.

Relationships

Most animal personalities are in awe of your good looks, but are wary of your superficial nature. This doesn't prevent some from falling prey to your charms, and they are easily bewitched into ill-fated liaisons. This means that you should be careful about your choice of mate. Because most people are only attracted to your physical attributes, you can never quite be sure about the intentions of a prospective suitor. Many peacocks realize this too late in life to avoid a history of painful, failed relationships.

When you form a substantial relationship with a **giraffe** or **deer,** your grace and style makes this quite a majestic union. Although you are a faithful partner, you are destined to be insecure in your marriage, constantly worrying about your mate's fidelity. Your best mate, however, is the proud and life-loving **rooster,** whose ability to handle most social situations and appreciation for the finer things in life makes for an ideal relationship.

The grounded personalities of cats, **foxes, bats,** and **wolves** avoid you, finding you shallow and uninteresting.

Famous Peacocks

Josephine Baker, Liberace, Zsa Zsa Gabor

Advice for a Peacock

Marry someone smarter than you.

PENGUIN

Class: Aves
Order: Sphenisciformes
Related Species: Arctic Tern, Seagull

Like all flightless birds, *penguins reside only in the southern hemisphere. Having found a niche in the wild, frozen wasteland that is Antarctica, most* penguin species move south in winter to breed in the extreme cold. Although conditions are harsh, penguins can form large breeding groups with minimal fear of predators, and they are supremely well adapted for this environment.

Surviving an Antarctic winter takes a great deal of cooperation from the penguins since they huddle together to conserve heat.

As the penguins on the outside of the group begin to get cold, they are allowed by the others to move into the interior of the group and regain body heat.

The Human Penguin

You are an unusual bird! With all the attributes of a bird personality, you have chosen to live life as a terrestrial animal—resulting in a decided conflict in your enigmatic personality. Since penguin emotions tend to be black or white with very little gray, casual acquaintances perceive you to be aggressive and intolerant, while those who know you well experience your sensitive and caring side.

Sometimes, you find it difficult to relate to others, and when life gets too stressful, you tend to withdraw and find solace in your close family and tight circle of friends. This antisocial behavior can alienate coworkers and employers, further exacerbating your reputation as a difficult individual.

Penguins are deceptively intelligent and are particularly animated when intellectually challenged. They excel at word games and puzzles but are modest about their abilities and are generally underestimated by others.

Careers

With your misunderstood personality, you find writing an ideal tool for expressing your true feelings. You have a natural aptitude for languages, and penguin personalities dominate the world of publishing as **writers, editors,** and **journalists**.

With a strong sense of drama you are drawn to the theater and cinema. Unlike the typical bird personality, you avoid the spotlight unless you're able to hide behind the characters you play. Once on stage, you prove to be an excellent **actor**, and your multifaceted personality helps convey a wide range of emotions.

However, your lack of confidence affects your work. You tend to give up on tasks you were otherwise capable of, and often disappoint yourself with your performance. Still, work never dominates your life, and you always put your family first.

Relationships

Those intimate with your penguin personality are impressed by your unswerving loyalty. You are sentimental at heart and always remember anniversaries and birthdays. With a strong compassion for others, you often place their needs ahead of your own, and thus often feel taken advantage of.

In matters of the heart, you connect poorly with other bird personalities, who look down on you because of your terrestrial connections. Mammalian personalities also treat you with suspicion, finding you flighty and unpredictable.

You have much in common with the **bat** personality who shares your out-of-your-element traits. In general, animal personalities that live around water, such as the **otter, walrus,** and **beaver**, make good mates, although **sea lion** personalities are too aggressive for your delicate disposition.

Famous Penguins

Oscar Wilde, Truman Capote, Danny DeVito

Advice for a Penguin

Never answer a question—other than an offer of marriage—by saying yes or no.

PORCUPINE

Class: Rodentia
Order: Hystricidae
Related Species: Rat, Vole

Porcupines are solitary herbivores that spend much of their time in trees in the New World or on the ground in the Old World. Often confused with their distant relative the hedgehog, these animals are highly adapted for self-defense, and when threatened they will rattle their quills in warning, much like rattlesnakes do before striking.

Contrary to popular belief, porcupines do not shoot their quills but instead detach them easily from their bodies and embed them in enemies' skin. The barbed quills work their way into the victim's body, causing painful infections and sometimes death.

The Human Porcupine

Nervous and antisocial, you are a small individual with a remarkable attitude. Your prickly, acerbic personality can make you quite a disagreeable character, and sarcasm and wit are your primary weapons. When you feel uncomfortable or threatened, you become argumentative, reacting to the slightest provocation. With sufficient coaxing it is possible to lure you from your defensive posture, but you always remain on your guard.

Unlike other small mammal personalities, you strike back when threatened. Although your sarcastic barbs aren't meant to cause serious harm, they are hurtful enough to discourage others from risking your wrath. This trait proves difficult for your family, who usually abandon you to your moods. Your reputation as a backstabber is somewhat undeserved, although you have no problem with gossiping about friends and foe alike.

You are generally disinterested in physical activity and move cautiously through life, expending minimal energy in the pursuit of your resources.

Typical of most rodents, you are a thrifty individual who conserves resources for the future, and you are considered to be selfish with your time and money.

Careers

Like other rodent personalities, you are an opportunist and are resourceful and creative in your endeavors. Adept at taking advantage of others' mistakes, you are first to jump on the bandwagon when the opportunity arises. With your consciously minimalistic lifestyle, your financial needs are limited to the bare essentials of living, and your home is unadorned but functional.

An unambiguous loner, you prefer a job that rewards individual effort. You avoid manual labor and work that demands mental concentration. However, if you're lucky enough to find a job that needs your biting tongue, you will perform above the call of duty and are ideally suited for the role as a **collection agent**. Your nocturnal personality is perfect for making late-night calls to delinquent payers.

As a **government bureaucrat** you are without equal. You are the quintessential nonbudging **DMV employee**, delighting in failing people on their driver's license tests.

Relationships

A nocturnal animal, you prefer the safety of your home or small office during the day. Most of your social connections take place at night, when you wander off to seek the companionship of the opposite sex, but your caustic wit and defensive posture tends to put others on their guard. You often return alone.

It can be painful to get close to you, and only those who have earned your trust can endure an intimate relationship. You are comfortable and secure in the company of **mouse** and **mole** personalities but should fastidiously avoid the companionship of the larger carnivores, such as **bears**, **foxes**, and **wolves**.

As the only rodent personality who will accept the presence of **snakes**, you tolerate their company but rarely form intimate unions with these unhappy animals.

Famous Porcupines
Don Rickles, Joan Rivers

Advice for a Porcupine
Wit is treacherous. It is the only weapon that can stab you in the back.

PRAIRIE DOG

Class: Mammalia
Order: Rodentia
Related Species: Mouse, Squirrel, Beaver

Prairie dogs inhabit *the plains of North America and live in large "cities," measuring up to two hundred miles long and containing 400 million prairie dogs. Such large populations require an exceptional social and communication system, and the prairie dogs live in highly organized groups. Recent research has suggested that prairie dogs have a vocabulary more extensive than any other animal except man. With up to five sounds to name predators, prairie dogs also use adjectives to modify these nouns. An approaching man generates a particular alarm call, while a man with a gun elicits a slightly different vocalization.*

Although they live in such vast cities, individuals rarely venture from their individual coteries, which cover about an acre. Since most of the individuals within a coterie are related, their social bonds are very strong. When members of a coterie meet, they exchange ritual kisses: Each nibbles the other, and prolonged mutual grooming begins.

The Human Prairie Dog

You are a lithe, friendly individual and share a number of traits with your rodent cousins, **beavers** and **mice**. With your exceptional communication skills, you are constantly in touch with friends and relatives, ferreting out the latest news and relaying it back to your family.

As a letter writer you are without equal, and it's difficult to lose touch with a prairie dog. Being such a social animal, you are generous and unselfish with your time and find sharing to be a source of pleasure. Your personal life is well organized, and upon this foundation, you confidently tackle life's challenges as you build your successful career.

You derive a great deal of pleasure from nature and return this favor by stepping lightly on the land. You recycle conscientiously and encourage your community to do the same.

You spend most of your recreational time at play with your close friends or large family. Avoiding competitive sports that require physical contact, you prefer group activities that cement social bonding, like card and board games.

You love music and dancing. Outdoor concerts are a special treat, where you draw energy from the crowd under an open sky.

Careers

With your natural empathy and understanding of social interactions, you excel in all niches of the behavioral sciences, including **social work, journalism, teaching**, and **psychology**.

Your well-developed social skills make you suitable for a range of careers that include **sales** or **public relations**. However, your lack of aggression can limit your earning potential.

Like all social animals, you are an excellent observer of human nature, and this combined with your communication skills would make you an excellent **writer** or documentary **filmmaker**.

Relationships

Like most small noncarnivorous personalities you are cautious in your relationships. Wary of strangers, potential mates must be introduced by someone from your large circle of friends. A night on the town is made in the company of your acquaintants, and you avoid singles bars, where predators might lurk.

A relationship with a prairie dog is a special treat. Your ability to communicate openly means that problems are dealt with promptly and honestly. You are compatible with a wide range of potential mates and particularly enjoy the company of the larger grazing animals. In marriage, your best mates are **cottontails, beavers, deer**, and **sheep**.

When a relationship ends, you find it difficult to make a clean break and continue communicating or flirting with previous partners. Consequently, you have quite a number of active friends who are ex-lovers.

You should fastidiously avoid the company of the medium-size predators: **Weasels, wolves, badgers**, and **wildcats** are far too aggressive and selfish for your gentle, kindred spirit.

Famous Prairie Dogs

Rosie O'Donnell, Mary Tyler Moore, Julie Andrews

Advice for a Prairie Dog

The surest way to destroy your enemy is to make him your friend.

RHINOCEROS

Class: Mammalia
Order: Perissodactyla
Related Species: Horse, Tapir

This armor-plated beast *is found in Africa and southeast Asia but is a vanishing breed thanks to extermination by man. An unusual characteristic* of these aggressive, ponderous animals is their tendency to deposit their dung in communal heaps, forming mounds up to twenty feet across and four feet high.

The rhino's horn is made of tubular fibers secreted from the skin of the nose and cemented together. Highly prized as an aphrodisiac in Asia, these horns can attain massive dimensions—the record length for a white rhino's horn is more than five feet.

The Human Rhinoceros

You are a large, looming individual. Muscular and strong, you dominate your environment and you zealously protect your personal space. You only want to be left alone to feed your face. You're peaceful enough if undisturbed, but uninvited guests usually encounter the darker side of your short-tempered persona.

With such a cantankerous personality, your unpopularity is hardly surprising, and your bullying reputation is carefully cultivated to ensure the solitude you crave. You prefer to stay close to home and never go looking for trouble, but when it finds you, you prove to be a dangerous creature with an uncontrollable temper. You won't hesitate to inflict harm on your victim, and your aggressive charges often result in self-injury. With your formidable bulk and tightly wound nature, even the most aggressive carnivorous personalities give you a wide berth.

When not engaged in physical activities, you prefer spending quiet time with your family or taking long walks with close friends. You are proud of your girth and spend a great deal of time bulking up, either in the gym or grazing contentedly at your favorite restaurant.

You have none of the subtlety or intelligence of your **elephant** colleagues, but you do have a gift for smooth talk. Persuasive when making a point, you spice your conversation with curses and colorful language and have little interest in the finer things in life.

For all your faults, however, you have a uniquely engaging charm, and your determination and grit engenders grudging respect from your colleagues.

Careers

Your physical prowess makes you ideal for any job requiring strength or intimidation, and you might excel as a **bouncer, police officer,** or **soldier.** In your younger days, you were in demand as a **professional athlete,** and your combination of speed, strength, and aggression gave you the ability to shine as a **professional wrestler, football player,** or **boxer.**

As a businessperson, however, you are less likely to succeed. You have a tendency to be shortsighted in your planning, and although you sometimes win through intimidation, your lack of foresight ultimately prevents you from achieving the envied financial heights of the **lion, tiger,** and **sable** personalities.

Relationships

Your thick skin proves to be both a boon and a problem in your life. Although impervious to criticism, you tend to be insensitive to the emotional impact of your heavy movements on those close to you. Your insistence on having your way at all times makes life difficult for your mate, who must be wary of your temper.

Although powerfully attracted to the grace of the **deer, horse,** and **sable,** these relationships are typically unbalanced, and stability usually comes in the form of **hippopotamus** and **bison** personalities.

Preferring the companionship of close family members, you see no benefit in maintaining a large circle of friends. In your relationships you are tight-lipped and loyal. Although protective of your children, they are kept at arm's length and don't have to be reminded to avoid your surly and unpredictable moods.

Famous Rhinoceroses

O. J. Simpson, Mike Tyson, Marge Schott

Advice for a Rhinoceros

Being feared provides less security than being loved.

ROOSTER

Class: Aves
Order: Galliformes
Related Species: Peacock, Guinea Fowl

Although it is *uncertain when the domestication of the jungle fowl took place, it is generally thought to have happened around 2500 B.C. in Asia. In the 1920s, observation of roosters and chickens led to the discovery of the pecking order, in which the most dominant bird will peck any other bird without being pecked back. The second most dominant bird also pecks others without reprisal, except for the most dominant. This hierarchy continues until the least dominant bird is pecked by all.*

Although this kind of social structure exists in most mammalian societies, including our own, it is still referred to as the pecking order because of its initial discovery in chickens.

The Human Rooster

You exhibit a decided theatrical streak as you strut your stuff in the latest fashions. Craving attention, your show-off attitude sometimes generates criticism from those close to you, and your need to be the center of attention permeates every aspect of your busy life. When it comes to clothes, furniture, and cars, you only purchase the highest quality items and your excessive spending can land you in financial disarray.

You are in big demand at parties. With a witty repartee and an ability to mix easily, you flirt shamelessly while reveling in the glow of the spotlight. Concerned about how you are perceived by others, you are only happy if people are talking to or about you.

Your active mind is always working on a way to create more drama in your life, and you are creative and determined in your quest. Offsetting your feisty and competitive nature is a secretive and aloof side that manifests itself when you feel insecure. And yet you are a solid friend. Your blunt approach, while sometimes hurtful and tactless, can always be counted on to be honest and frank.

Careers

Your indomitable temperament is suited for any job that rewards self-motivation. Your resilient ego and extroverted nature are perfect for careers in **broadcasting** or **acting**, and your logical approach to problem solving makes you ideal for the **engineering** and **medical** fields.

As a salesperson, you are without equal and can sell anything from real estate to used cars. A hard worker with a keen eye for detail, your creativity and dedication make you a wonderful employee.

As a **manager** or **business owner**, however, you are finicky and picky and tend to alienate subordinates with your unrelenting enthusiasm. You are also not a particularly strong team player, and your perceived self-absorbed and sanctimonious attitude breeds resentment.

Relationships

Your ideal mates include **peacocks**, who are attracted to your strong demeanor and flashy style. You are an incorrigible flirt and although successful in attracting mates, your ego sometimes drives potential partners away. When sufficiently motivated by the right partner, however, you generally find a way to make the relationship work.

As a parent, you are fussy and attentive. Like the proverbial brooding hen, you are involved with every aspect of your children's lives, including their dress and the company they keep. Some even call you overprotective, and although your children might resent your interference, they learn to appreciate your concern as they mature. The more reserved animal personalities, such as **bats**, **bison**, and **moles**, find you to be fussy and bossy, and **snake** and **canine** personalities should be avoided.

Famous Roosters

P. T. Barnum, Dennis Rodman, The Artist Formerly Known as Prince

Advice for a Rooster

Don't count your chickens before they hatch.

SABLE ANTELOPE

Class: Mammalia
Order: Artiodactyla
Related Species: Deer, Giraffe

The sable is *surely the most handsome of all the antelope. With long curving horns, these black-coated animals are so confident of their strength that they* will even take on a lion in defense of their territories. When approaching a water hole, other grazing animals give way to families of up to thirty individual sable, but they are peaceful if left alone. The adult sable has no natural enemies except man.

Particularly magnificent is the giant sable of southern Africa. Although it is an extremely endangered animal, the majority of its population lives safely in the Luando Reserve in Angola.

The Human Sable

A proud and noble demeanor characterizes your sable personality. Gifted with a handsome visage and complemented by immaculate grooming, you find success in almost everything you do. Attractive to the opposite sex and popular with your own, you create a sense of well-being in those who surround you. Dapper in dress and noble in bearing, your tastes and lifestyle are refined and restrained, and you disapprove of flashy or ostentatious behavior in any form.

When life's obstacles are not sufficiently challenging, you set even higher personal goals and, with boundless energy, subject yourself to a vigorous regimen of biking, running, or hiking. Whether tooling around in a sportscar or simply running on the beach, speed holds a special fascination, and you love nothing more than the feel of wind in your hair.

Although you are a popular individual, your intimidating presence and impossibly high standards can create an air of arrogance. Usually unsympathetic to those who cannot keep up with your fast pace, you show little patience for their complaints and have no time for prolonged excuses or debate. Not one to hold a grudge when wronged, you'll sharply rebuke an offender then quickly forgive the transgression.

Careers

In business, you are admired for your excellent negotiating skills and your ability to make courageous decisions, making you well suited for top management. Because of the ease of which you earn money, you tend to be profligate in your spending habits and don't hesitate to spend money on leisure activities.

You fiercely protect your hard earned reputation for integrity, taking pride in your ability to make business deals with just a handshake. You are cautious about giving that trust to others, however, which further aggravates your reputation for taking yourself too seriously.

You have a particular distaste for routine of any kind, and your work must always be demanding and fast paced. As a high-powered **salesperson, stockbroker,** or **manager,** you are consistently in the top echelons of your field and should avoid jobs that have little chance for advancement.

Relationships

As a lover you are adventurous and aggressive. Your sexual prowess is no secret, and your dominant personality is irresistible to the opposite sex. You expect your mate to play a traditionally dutiful role in the relationship which can sometimes fuel resentment. Although you are a terrific provider, your family would sometimes trade your hard-driving perfectionist style for a warmer-hearted, gentler soul.

Particular about the company you keep, you prefer to spend time with other strong, capable personalities, such as **horses, giraffes, zebra,** and **swans.** Attracted to your strength, passion, and dependability, these personalities complement your grace and style.

Famous Sables
Pat Riley, George Washington, Howard Hughes

Advice for a Sable
Don't flaunt your success, but don't apologize for it either.

SEA LION

Class: Mammalia
Order: Pinnipedia
Related Species: Walrus, Seal

Sea lions are *one of the few land mammals that have returned to the sea to eke out a living. Supremely well adapted for life in a rocky, unpredictable environment, they have even evolved "rubber" ribs made from soft cartilage to protect them when swimming around rocks in high seas.*

Like their dolphin companions, sea lions have developed a rudimentary sonar system, but their eyesight is the preferred hunting tool. It is the California sea lion that is commonly seen performing in circuses and animal parks, and the creature's intelligence and social expertise make it a perennial crowd favorite.

The Human Sea Lion

You share a number of characteristics with the **dolphin** personality, including a lazy streak. However, you are not exclusively a creature of the sea and have much in common with more serious and family-oriented land mammals.

A charming and good-looking individual, you are generally in good physical shape. The beach is your natural habitat, and you're often observed swimming, playing volleyball, and enjoying other group activities. Naturally athletic, your sleek body is well maintained by this active lifestyle. Your agile mind is exercised by long hours of debate on issues of a philosophical and spiritual nature. Your lazy disposition, however, can result in conversations that lack substance and logical grounding. You are curious about the universe and pay particular attention to numerology and astrology.

A cheerful disposition belies your hot-tempered core. When you react assertively, it comes in the form of a sharp, barked retort and occasionally even a physical attack. You have no natural enemies, and your slippery persona provides sufficient defense in the event of an attack.

Careers

Your smooth personality is well suited for a wide range of **sales** positions. Whether selling real estate or motor vehicles, you are skillful, enthusiastic, and sincere. Your straightforward, genuine desire to help others shines through in your work, and others instinctively trust you. However, your career can suffer from your lack of motivation, and you are prone to rest on your laurels.

Your irrepressible nature craves the spotlight, and you enjoy performing, telling stories and hogging the attention of your large group of friends. You are well suited for careers in the **performing arts.**

Your aggressive streak serves you well in jobs that require physical and emotional strength, and you're a good fit for a career as a **police officer, air traffic controller, paramedic,** or **lifeguard.**

As an **entrepreneur** with a high level of self-esteem, you confidently plunge into risky business ventures. This confidence is not always warranted, however, and you often find yourself in trouble, both financially and socially. Luckily, your natural buoyancy always helps you keep your head above water.

Relationships

With your outgoing and social nature, you enjoy spending time in the company of a wide variety of mammals, including the gregarious **dog** and **dolphin** personalities. These relationships are generally for purposes of play, and deep unions rarely form. Displaying the herd mentality typical of your species, you surround yourself with friends and family and are secure and complete in their presence. You can be quite selfish in your pursuit for your own enjoyment, and your mate often feels alienated by your apparent lack of commitment.

Relationships with **otter** and **walrus** personalities seem to work well, perhaps because you share their unique aquatic/terrestrial lifestyles. However, your true soul mate is the **beaver;** you complement each other's qualities. You prod the beaver to relax and enjoy life, while the hardworking beaver provides you with the comfort and security your happy-go-lucky personality secretly craves.

Famous Sea Lions
Pamela Anderson Lee, Mark Spitz

Advice for a Sea Lion
If you're not making waves, you're not paddling.

SHEEP

Class: Mammalia
Order: Artiodactyla
Related Species: Mountain Goat, Ibex

Following the dog, *sheep were the first animals to be domesticated, around 10,000 B.C. The domestication of the dog may have made this possible by its* contribution in controlling the first wild herds. No one is quite sure which animal is the ancestor of the domestic sheep, but it is most likely a species that has since become extinct.

Inherent in the sheep's behavior is its instinct to crowd together when threatened. This behavior produces the sheep's distinctive flocking patterns and makes it an ideal farm animal. As grazers, sheep don't just simply take nutrition from the soil. They can actually restore fertility to otherwise sandy or poor lands, and many farmers use them to increase the value of their property.

The Human Sheep

As a sheep personality, your reputation for lack of vision and ambition is well deserved. Nonetheless, you are an enormously successful individual, and you and your ilk are well represented in society. A prime factor in your success is your ability to concentrate on resource acquisition and money making. Preferring to let other animals perform the time-consuming jobs of philosophizing and defending the community, you quietly go about building your family.

Physically, you are nondescript and uninspiring. Dressing conservatively (in wool coats), you draw as little attention to yourself as possible. Largely disinterested in politics—viewing it as time taken from work—you respect the law and never question authority.

Lacking the bulk and strength of larger animal personalities, you are vulnerable to predatory behavior. As a defense mechanism, you utilize your strong herding instinct to compensate. Safety in numbers and the pooling of resources more than make up for your vulnerability, and you flourish accordingly.

You tend to congregate in the suburbs. Proximity to neighbors provides you a sense of communal safety and facilitates shared child-rearing duties. You are conservative in financial and political matters, and your species comprises a significant portion of the proverbial silent majority. Civic-minded, you support your local police, and you send your children to summer camp and to the best schools.

You are, however, susceptible to the whims of the canine personalities, who with their dominance and leadership are able to change the direction of your entire herd. Like most things in life, though, you turn this into your advantage by utilizing the protection and guidance provided by these stronger animals.

Careers

You are a tireless and valued worker with the ability to spend hours on monotonous tasks. Skilled at taking direction, your concentration ability makes you an outstanding **accountant**, **research assistant**, or **secretary**. You are rarely found in leadership roles and would even turn down a promotion if it were to remove you from the safety of the herd.

Relationships

You are insecure when not in a relationship. Without a mate, you surround yourself with family and friends and quietly go about your business. When mated, though, you are a wonderful partner. With a high priority on the well-being of your family, you play an active role in your children's education and maintain strong relationships with your offspring long after they have left home.

Relationships with other **sheep** personalities are stable and comfortable. Sheep almost never argue with each other, preferring to seek consensus and compromise on thorny issues.

Your most enduring relationships are with **deer**, **cottontails**, **mountain goats**, and other pastoral animals. For obvious reasons, you should follow your instincts and avoid liaisons with **lions**, **wolves**, and **wildcats**. **Bats** and **foxes** are too spiritual for your practical nature.

Famous Sheep
The Moral Majority, Clark Kent

Advice for a Sheep
Remember that the difference between a rut and a grave is its depth.

SHREW

Class: *Mammalia*
Order: *Tupaioidea*
Related Species: *Pygmy Shrew, Water Shrew*

The smallest of all mammals, shrews are pound for pound among the most belligerent creatures on earth. Also extremely nervous and sensitive, shrews have been rumored to die from the shock of a loud noise. In reality, they are remarkably resilient and are quite capable of handling the stresses of life near the bottom of the food chain.

Shrews live solitary lives among ground litter or in shallow tunnels. Their high-pitched squeaks suggest that they also use ultrasonics for echolocation, although not to the same degree as bats. Because of their high metabolic rates, shrews are constantly on the hunt for food, and although basically insectivorous, they eat seeds, snails, worms, and even carrion. Although domestic cats will kill shrews, they will not eat them, perhaps because of the musk glands in each flank that emit a foul odor.

The Human Shrew

Slightly built, you are an intelligent and thrifty creature who conserves resources to the point of being miserly. Sharing does not come naturally to you, and you are typically the last to pay your portion at a group dinner. It's not that you're greedy. Rather, you're responding to a compulsive need to save for the future, and in this respect, you are much like your cousin the chipmunk, who takes planning for the future to extremes.

You can be a demanding, high maintenance individual whose obsession for resources dominates your life. Although you have a reputation for being bloodthirsty and vicious, these labels are not entirely accurate. You are rarely aggressive, and your attacks are limited to a shrill verbal assault in the form of incessant whining.

You are constantly working, cleaning, preparing meals, or running errands. You're active at all times of the day and night, and it's rare for you to relax. Others struggle to keep pace with your intense energy level.

Although it appears that you are impervious to criticism, you are actually a sensitive soul who feels deeply wounded by those who misinterpret your motives. However, because you are driven by deep insecurities, you are doomed to persist in your obsessive behavior.

Careers

Because you're constantly on the move, careers that require concentration and sober thinking are unsuitable. You perform best in chaotic jobs and thrive on the unpredictability of disorder, making you a natural **production assistant, circus performer, journalist, wedding organizer**, or **emergency room technician**.

Your predilection for collecting and organizing things would also make you a good **librarian, computer operator**, or **bookkeeper**, while your desire to keep moving makes you suitable for any job requiring **travel** and creativity.

Relationships

A deep relationship with a shrew is difficult. Because of your sharp personality and frantic lifestyle, you have few friends—and this suits you perfectly well. Relationships distract you from your busy day. Occasionally, an encounter with a **mole, mouse**, or **cottontail** will precipitate an enduring friendship, but most creatures are kept at arm's length.

Without the time to take other people's feelings into account, you create a number of enemies as you blaze busily through life. Consequently, you need to be wary of the vicious claws of the feline personalities and the clumsy but powerful canines. Birds of prey and **snakes** are particularly attracted to your hard-earned resources, and you're vulnerable to their aggressive overtures.

As a parent, you place a high value on your family's comfort and security, schlepping your kids around and involving yourself in every aspect of their lives. You have a tendency to be somewhat overbearing and pushy with your children, and this can breed resentment when they reach adulthood.

Famous Shrews

Leona Helmsley, Tammy Faye Baker

Advice for a Shrew

Don't get ulcers. Give them.

SNAKE

Class: *Reptilia*
Order: *Squamata*
Related Species: *Lizard, Skunk*

Snakes have long *been feared and often appear in art and mythology. Although some are dangerously venomous, most are quite harmless and approachable.*

It is difficult to deter-mine which snake is the most dangerous to man, because there are so many factors involved. Those with a very potent poison may not be dangerous because they rarely bite, while others with a less-toxic venom might be more aggressive. Nonetheless, it is generally agreed that the boomslang, mamba, cobra, and krait are contenders for this dubious title.

More interesting is the almost universal revulsion of snakes. Fear of snakes might well be a genetically encoded behavior, and although some people have adopted snakes as pets, these reptiles continue to generate bad press in popular mythology.

The Human Snake

Lacking the defense mechanisms of other animal personalities, you are highly vulnerable as you slink through life in a uniquely lone way. Physically, you are a small and slim individual with sharp, prominent features, and your skittish behavior and well-developed sense of danger steers you clear of aggressive predatory personalities. Shy and suspicious, you constantly check your environment for trouble and keep a low profile in social situations.

Because some snake personalities are aggressive, most people instinctively avoid *all* snakes, and you consequently suffer a number of indignities. As an adolescent, you endured an unfair amount of taunting and abuse, and you've developed a rather vicious way of defending yourself. Reacting suddenly and with as much violence as you can muster, you strike back at the offending party and then quickly slither away. This behavior further adds to your reputation as a yellow-belly and alienates you from your friends even further.

Your reputation as a slimy and deceitful person is due in part to your inability to communicate well. Not the most logical of creatures, your conversational skills can leave others going in circles. This communication problem is exacerbated by a thin, weak voice and an occasional stutter or speech impediment. Combined with your unusual appearance and cold-blooded reputation, you are condemned to search endlessly for friendship and warmth.

Careers

You are not fussy about your choice of jobs. As a cold-blooded personality, you perform best when given warmth and kindness, and you'll accept almost any work—provided you feel secure and wanted. Trust given to you is taken seriously and is generally warranted. However, if you feel distrusted, you live up to your reputation and return the disloyalty. Consequently, you are often relegated to menial jobs in the **fast-food** industry or as unskilled labor as a **factory worker**.

With your intimate connection to the earth and a unique perspective on life, you sometimes find fame by venting your pain as a **writer** or **artist**.

Relationships

Some snake personalities are completely marine and attempt unions with **sea lions** and **dolphins**, while others are strictly terrestrial and try their luck with smaller land creatures, such as **beavers** and **moles**. However, most people don't give you time to form a decent relationship, and rejection is an integral component of your love life.

You seek companionship everywhere but are often forced to settle for second-rate relationships with **crocodiles** or **weasels**. For obvious reasons, you should fastidiously avoid predatory birds, such as **eagles**, **vultures**, and **owls**.

Although you can be clingy and dependent, it is ironic that some animal personalities are attracted to you with Freudian intensity. Irresistibly drawn to your sensual movements and phallic overtones, they offer you warmth and comfort in exchange for excitement and raw animal pleasures.

Famous Snakes

Son of Sam, Woody Allen

Advice for a Snake

A person who trusts nobody is apt to be the person nobody trusts.

SWAN

Class: Aves
Order: Anseriformes
Related Species: Peacock, Eagle

It is thought *that the long, graceful neck of these magnificent birds evolved to facilitate feeding on the bottom of the shallow waters that they frequent.* Unlike most water birds, swans rarely dive and prefer instead to float serenely on the surface.

Despite their weight, swans are excellent fliers. Takeoffs can be a bit of a problem, though, and they must build flying speed by running with their broad webbed feet on a long stretch of water. Like a small aircraft, swans maneuver poorly in flight and often lose their lives by flying into telephone and power lines.

Revered throughout history for their beauty, swans feature prominently in Greek lore, where Zeus disguised himself as a swan to seduce Leda, and in medieval England, where all swans were the property of the king, who issued licenses for their private possession.

The Human Swan

Few animal personalities rival your grace and dignity. Complementing this elegance is a sense of empathy that resonates throughout your social interactions. However, you display the same typical flightiness of the bird personalities as you struggle to find your place in a world dominated by ungainly mammals. As a result, you've developed a reputation for being a bit of a snob, although those intimate with you find you sensitive and understanding.

Supporting a high-profile swan persona requires substantial energy, and your high metabolism can leave you feeling exhausted and drained. When life gets overwhelming, you'll take off and find a tranquil, gentle place to meditate and recharge your batteries before resuming your full life. This unsettled aspect of your personality means that you probably have moved to a different city at least once in your life, or are planning to do so.

Careers

As is typical of bird personalities, you are well traveled. Your experiences have made you a well-rounded and worldly individual who can adapt to almost any career. You have no problem taking direction from a boss and are always looking for input from others. Your career is well integrated into your life, and you have found a good balance in your career and family life.

Because swan personalities are often gangly and awkward as children, they have substantial experience in dealing with difficult people and are well equipped to handle conflicts in the workplace. Their innate empathy makes them ideal **therapists, doctors, nurses,** or **personnel managers.** With their natural beauty they are also well suited for careers in the arts, with a particular affinity for **music, ballet,** and **acting.**

Relationships

You are cautious in your love life and are attracted to the spiritual qualities of **bats, prairie dogs,** and **owls,** but your ideal love match comes in the form of the equally magnificent **sable.** Swan personalities mate for life and are romantic and realistic about their marriages, never taking their partner for granted.

With a strong nesting instinct, you place tremendous emphasis on raising your brood, and your children are always neatly presented and well mannered. However they rarely get a chance to express their independence or spread their wings until they are much older.

Relationships with the larger herbivores, such as **deer, bison,** and **horses,** are solid but unexciting, and you should beware the wiles of the carnivores for they have but one thing on their minds.

Famous Swans

Rudolf Nureyev, Grace Kelly, Florence Nightingale, Winona Ryder

Advice for a Swan

Be like a swan—calm on the surface but always paddling like the dickens underneath.

TIGER

Class: Mammalia
Order: Carnivora
Related Species: Lion, Mountain Lion, Wildcat

The tiger is *a magnificent animal. With its splendid carriage and sinuous grace, it can grow to lengths of more than ten feet and weigh more than five hundred pounds. The tiger is an excellent swimmer but, unlike most members of the cat family, is a poor climber.*

Male and female tigers come together only when the tigress is in heat for a period of a few weeks. During this time the tiger will not tolerate the presence of other males and will fight to the death in order to control the female.

Adult tigers have no natural enemies except man, but they have an unusually high mortality rate from infected wounds caused by porcupine quills.

Although largely protected from human hunting, pressure from civilization and development has kept the tiger population on the verge of extinction.

The Human Tiger

You are a handsome and powerful person. Acutely aware of your charms, you dress the part to the hilt. You move with supreme confidence and are as fierce as your powerfully built frame suggests. Relishing the respect that your dangerous demeanor commands, you use it to your fullest advantage.

Unlike the family oriented **lion**, you are a solitary creature who hates to lie around doing nothing. In this regard you have more in common with **wildcats** and leopards, who are always on the move. Because of this antisocial nature, it can be difficult to discern your true motives, and you are considered unpredictable and enigmatic. You have a strong aversion to routine in your daily life, and your spontaneity and energy infect others who are graced with your presence.

As a nocturnal hunter you are equipped with a great deal of street sense.

Able to read people's motivations and assess situations quickly, you are blunt and to the point, commanding attention with just a whisper or a raise of your eyebrow. You demand respect and command fear.

Careers

Unlike your cat relatives, you enjoy sports of all kinds. With a particular affinity for water sports, you are often seen in the company of **dolphins** and **sea lions** on a casual and socially limited basis.

You dislike small talk in the workplace and expect professionalism from your coworkers, and you demand the highest standards in your business dealings. With your killer instincts, you could be an excellent **trial lawyer** and have no hesitation in using aggression to your advantage. Acutely aware of your ability to intimidate, your single-mindedness enhances your reputation as a force to be reckoned with.

Because of your preference for solitude, however, you are not a natural leader. While perfectly capable of assuming the role of a **CEO**, you prefer the challenges inherent in self-employment. Your businesses are invariably successful and cover a wide range of industries, from **engineering** to **retailing**.

Relationships

Your natural strength and splendid appearance make you a desirable mate. With a need to dominate your partner, your passionate advances can sometimes be too intense for the faint-hearted, and you must choose your lovers wisely. Because of your propensity for solitude, you avoid long-lasting relationships and place little value on fidelity.

In a relationship, you are extremely competitive and hate to lose, sometimes pursuing others just for the thrill of the chase. You are delighted when you can put a **giraffe** on your trophy shelf. Its elegance is becoming to your reputation.

In the company of other cat personalities, you feel connected and happily challenged. Oddly enough, you'll sometimes form a respectful union with an **elephant**, being one of the few animals unintimidated by your gruff exterior. Medium-size herbivore personalities, such as **deer** and **goats**, should keep their distance: You want only one thing from them!

Famous Tigers

F. Lee Bailey, James Bond, Tiger Woods

Advice for a Tiger

Not getting what you want is sometimes a stroke of luck.

VULTURE

Class: Aves
Order: Falconiformes
Related Species: Hawk, Eagle, Falcon

Vultures can soar *effortlessly for hours on their powerful wings, and using their keen eyesight, they can detect carrion from vast distances by watching* the behavior of other animals approaching the carcass.

The vulture's neck is practically naked and comes in handy when thrusting its head deep into the steamy carcass of a freshly killed animal. They are not entirely scavengers, however, and will even hunt small rodents and flamingo chicks.

The Egyptian vulture is one of the few animals that has learned to use tools and is able to smash the tough shells of ostrich eggs by throwing stones at them. It will even make a special trip to find a suitable stone and then sling it repeatedly at the egg with its mouth until it breaks.

The Human Vulture

You are the opportunist of the animal world. Closely related to the hawk and **eagle** personalities, you are a strong and ungainly creature. You are not easy on the eye, and your features are either too small for your face or your head is a little too large for your body. However, you are quite comfortable with your appearance and have a quirkiness that endears you to certain tastes. Unlike most bird personalities, you tend to struggle with your weight, and your clumsy movements lack the grace typical of the **eagle** and **peacock** personalities. You have no inclination to exhibit good manners and never consider the feelings of others in your determined pursuit of resources.

Like most birds of prey, you love to travel. You particularly favor long trips and are always on the lookout for business opportunities. Even when vacationing with your family, you would interrupt your trip if you spied a chance to make money.

Careers

Intellectually, you cannot compete with other predatory personalities and must resort to other means to garner resources. Relying heavily on your keen senses, you have the ability to smell opportunities at a great distance.

You hate to work, preferring to shadow other aggressive characters until opportunities arise. You circle these situations with infinite patience and have an uncanny ability to determine when the moment is ripe. Only when assured of a reward will you swoop in and take control. You can be extremely possessive with your prize and will defend it against all intruders. However, you won't risk injury, and you take flight when the situation becomes volatile.

When others observe you circling, they can be confident that an opportunity is at hand. Always alert to the opportunity to buy or sell, you make an excellent **stockbroker** and trade your services for a percentage of the profits. Your species also earns a living by buying up ailing businesses and selling off their assets to make a quick buck.

With your excellent vision, you are also able to provide far-sighted leadership as a **business adviser**, **lawyer**, or **company director**.

Relationships

You place little value on relationships, and this makes you a perfect partner for the free-flying **eagle**, who shares your aerial perspective on life. You are attracted to the strength of the prey animals such as the **lion, wolf**, and **wild dog**, but these relationships are usually one-sided, and you have no qualms about usurping your mate's resources without giving anything in return. In a divorce, you'll greedily pick over the remains of the estate, and when a relative dies you are the first to arrive at the reading of the will, sometimes descending on the scene before the body is cold.

You are quite comfortable with your antisocial makeup and never try to disguise your true intentions. This honesty, combined with your determined and aggressive nature, makes a relationship with you tiresome but ultimately rewarding.

Famous Vultures

Michael Milken, Charles Keating

Advice for a Vulture

If someone offers you a breath mint, accept it.

WALRUS

Class: Mammalia
Order: Pinnipedia
Related Species: Sea Lion

Walruses congregate in *groups of about a hundred individuals, living primarily in coastal waters and basking on rocks or ice floes. Characterized* by their ponderous, blub-bery bodies, large tusks, and tough reddish brown skin, these magnificent animals are largely protected from man and flourish in the Arctic Circle.

Their tusks are actually elongated canine teeth and serve many functions, including defense, clam digging, and as an aid in pulling their ponderous bulk from the water. Their family name Odobenidae means "walks with teeth."

On land, walruses are able to travel faster than a man can run, and with their formidable bulk and dangerous tusks, these seemingly lazy creatures have earned a great deal of respect from hunters.

The Human Walrus

Your complacent walrus personality slogs through life with little finesse or grace, albeit with a happy-go-lucky air. Thick-skinned and somewhat self-absorbed, you are the classic strong, silent, and stout type, and although not much to look at, your craggy gruff exterior resonates charm and reassurance.

You are unimpressed by money and power. To you, the success of each day is measured in the hours of available leisure time. Consequently, you are knowledgeable about all aspects of domestic beer and televised sports, and even though you wouldn't be caught dead on a playing field, you admire the courage and athleticism of others.

As a creature of comfort, you covet the pleasures of beaches and parks and can be often observed lounging on a sagging chair, displaying your ample girth with pride.

Walruses are not to be trifled with, and as good-natured as you appear, you can be cantankerous and aggressive when slighted. Mostly your bark is worse than your bite, and your big-hearted nature soon reasserts itself. A stubborn streak exhibits itself when your personal comfort is compromised, although being accustomed to large groups of people, you are self-contained and respect the privacy of others. You are happiest when surrounded by the comforts of home and feel little need to travel far afield.

For all your carefree mannerisms, you are dependable and forthright. People are attracted to your consistent and predictable personality, and you can always be counted on to dish out a loan or lend a hand to a friend.

Careers

Although you perceive work to be a complete waste of time, you are a methodical and consistent employee and perform best in jobs demanding reliability and an understanding of the big picture. You function poorly under deadlines and prefer careers that enable you to work at your own pace, particularly as an **engineer**, **government worker**, **food inspector**, or **manager**.

Relationships

Everyone benefits from having a walrus as a grandparent, and you are always willing to give up personal time to spend it in the company of children.

You are, however, decidedly unromantic, and your idea of an anniversary gift is a new microwave to heat hot dogs. Still, you are demonstrative in your own way, expressing affection with great big hugs and small gifts. You make few demands on your mate other than the expectation of a steady supply of food, and you return this attention with loyalty and commitment.

You appreciate the laid-back company of **gorilla** personalities, but a marriage with one of these sloppy creatures would be disastrous, because there would be no one to clean up. **Bears** and **sea lions** are both suitable prospects, but your ideal mate comes in the form of the equally food-loving and water-based **hippopotamus**.

Famous Walruses
Wilford Brimley, Boris Yeltsin

Advice for a Walrus
It's better to rust out than to wear out.

WARTHOG

Class: Mammalia
Order: Artiodactyla
Related Species: Pig, Wild Boar

The warthog is *an odd quadruped. It has a flat, almost concave head orna-mented with four large warts, two razor-sharp curling tusks, and a thick, sinewy neck.*

Warthogs are principally grazers but have been known to take carcasses abandoned by other carni-vores or an animal that has died from natural causes. Its neck is too short for easy feeding on the sparse grass of the African plains, and it is often seen on its knees, grazing and rooting along the dusty veldt.

Warthogs are virtually fearless and have been observed turning the tails on pursuing leopards or ele-phants. Sows with young are particularly bold and do not hesitate to make physi-cal contact with marauding predators.

The Human Warthog

Your strong, aggressive spirit is closely related to the domestic pig and wild boar personalities. Largely self-absorbed, you are primarily concerned with filling your own pocket and stomach.

With a well-deserved reputation as an ill-tempered, pushy individual, you have no style or grace. Little pride is taken in your physical appearance, and you are homely in both personality and countenance. Preferring intim-idation and bluster in achieving your goals, you have no inclination to observe social niceties. Your distaste for etiquette manifests in backbiting and manipulation. However, you can be quite charming when the situation calls for it.

The worst thing that anyone can do is to underestimate your intelli-gence. Your razor-sharp mind is constantly probing for a weakness in your opponent, and you dominate your workplace and family life. You refuse to back down from a confrontation, and only an overwhelming show of force can make you turn and trot arrogantly away.

Your reading habits reflect your personality, and you're more likely to be reading *Winning Through Intimidation* than *The Joys of Butterflies*. Reflected by your unkempt personal living space, your personal life is disorganized and resembles a pigsty. You thrive on clutter and chaos.

Careers

Your active mind is always on the lookout for opportunities, and you are a canny businessperson. You respect strength and loyalty in others, and your excellent negotiating skills stand you in good stead in your business dealings. You persevere until your goals are met, even if it means fighting dirty or breaking the law to do so.

It's common for warthogs to be self-employed. With your strength of character and self-discipline, you are a formidable business adversary. You reward loyalty but have a vindictive streak toward those who cross swords with you. Your temper often overcomes your good judgment.

You would make an excellent **personal injury lawyer, salesperson, merchant, mercenary,** or **poker player,** and even though warthog personalities are almost universally disliked, you are able to succeed by determination alone.

Relationships

The same tenacity displayed in your career is evident in your relentless pursuit for a mate. Your thick skin is impervious to the rebuffs that are integral to your quest.

However, there are some animal personalities that are attracted to your strength and loyalty, and **cottontails, wild dogs, deer,** and **weasels** will occasionally team up with you. As long as they cater to your cranky whims and are fleet of foot, they are immune to your bad temper. Favoring them with protection and guidance, you will, at the first sign of disloyalty, unleash the full fury of your temper and send them scurrying for cover.

Famous Warthogs
Newt Gingrich, Jimmy the Greek

Advice for a Warthog
No one is against you; they are simply for themselves.

WEASEL

Class: Mammalia
Order: Carnivora
Related Species: Skunk, Marten, Polecat, Ferret, Stoat

Weasels and their related species are the world's most widespread carnivores. They are extremely adaptable animals and are found throughout Asia, Europe, North America, and Africa.

Rumor has it that a weasel can make itself small enough to pass through a wedding ring. While this is difficult to prove, it has been shown that its skull can be pulled through a one-inch hole.

The weasel is a relentless killer. Courageous out of all proportion to its size, it is able to bring down a full-grown cottontail three times its own weight. Sometimes weasels will follow larger predators, wait for them to make the kill, then scurry off with a piece of the prey.

The weasel's natural enemies are hawks, foxes, owls, and even domestic cats. Because of its reputation as a chicken killer, man has increasingly contributed to its diminishing numbers in the wild.

The Human Weasel

At first glance you can be quite charming and gracious. Your handsome and dapper appearance readily puts others at ease, but those who fall prey to your charms soon discover the darker, predatorial side to your personality.

A master at disguising your true intentions, you are capable of considerable violence and exploit your opponent's every weakness in achieving your goals. Like your **badger** cousin, your lean, wiry frame is surprisingly powerful, and you're unintimidated by others larger than yourself. You can be a dirty fighter and have no qualms about breaking the law.

Weasels are attracted to unorthodox and chaotic environments. Your quick mind is able to take advantage of rapidly changing situations, and you always emerge with more than your fair share of the booty. You have an uncanny knack for sensing weakness in others, and your most notable characteristic is your inclination for deception. You share the same ambitious streak as your cousin the **beaver**, but your distaste for hard work has you behaving more like your skunk relative, who also resorts to chicanery.

Often you'll team up with more successful animal personalities, gain their trust, and then milk them for all they're worth. These relationships are completely one-sided. Taking what you need, you soon scuttle off to prey on the next victim.

Careers

You'll disguise your intelligence if you believe it to be in your best interest. A natural liar, your earnest persuasions make it difficult to discern your true motives. You have no internal moral struggle with your behavior, since you believe that the end justifies your means. Your talent for manipulation makes you a natural **politician**.

As a **lawyer**, you are the essence of what is wrong with the justice system. Interested only in filling your own pockets, you can be seen on late-night TV touting your personal-injury services. A competent business owner, your success usually comes from not paying taxes or stiffing your creditors.

You love to be the center of attention and toy with the idea of becoming a professional entertainer. However, your love for your craft is secondary to your love for yourself, and you will probably never make it to the top as a performer.

Relationships

You are rarely faithful in your relationships. A male weasel is considerably larger than the female, and domestic violence is not uncommon. In a relationship with a weaker animal personality, you dominate your partner until the relationship self-destructs.

When, using all your charms, you marry a successful and wealthy partner, your instincts are to usurp the union's resources and have no qualms in satisfying every whim, no matter what pain or hardship it causes others.

Still, you are capable of deep romantic feelings and prove to be charming and sexually considerate in long-term relationships with those who don't pass judgment on you. Your ideal partners are **foxes**, **warthogs**, and **shrews**.

Famous Weasels

Mark Fuhrman, Manuel Noriega

Advice for a Weasel

Trust everyone, but cut the cards yourself.

WILDCAT

Class: Mammalia
Order: Carnivora
Related Species: Bobcat, Serval, Lynx

The term wildcat *covers a number of distinct species, including the lynx and the American bobcat. Wildcats move through life with noiseless stealth on padded feet that make no sound. The distinctive tufts of hair on the tips of their ears enhance the animal's extremely sensitive hearing. Its retractable claws make short shrift of its favorite prey—mice, cottontails, and woodchucks.*

The term wildcat has quite a range of meanings. Rather than denoting ferocity, it typically conveys an element of unpredictability. Commonly used in the oil-drilling industry to describe an oil field uncertain to produce results, its origin probably springs from the picture of a bobcat that appeared on money issued by a midwestern bank in the early 1800s. The notes were produced with limited financial backing and became synonymous with risk and uncertainty.

The Human Wildcat

With the exception of the **lion**, all feline personalities are solitary animals that make their way through the world alone. Like most nocturnal creatures, you are deeply spiritual and philosophical. Intensely curious, you often find yourself in tricky situations but have an uncanny ability to land on your feet. Your keen senses and agile body and mind complement your sharp tongue.

When someone wrongs you, you make it your business to even the score. Displaying superb patience, you will even wait years for the right moment. When the occasion comes to strike, you gather all your force and attack. In the face of a ferocious display of hissing and blustering, your surprised victim has little chance of escape.

You are a creature of comfort. You crave attention and choose companions who pamper you, returning their affection only when it suits you.

Exceptional personal hygiene is a hallmark of your personality, and from your hair to your fingernails, you are immaculately groomed. Shopping for clothing or personal-care items spices up long, dreary days.

Careers

As a natural explorer, you disdain staying in one place for long, preferring the freedom of solitary roaming. When traveling, you prefer to remain off the beaten path to seek out exotic locales. This wanderlust makes you ideal for a career as a **travel agent, explorer, mountain climber, researcher,** or **writer.**

Although you are uncomfortable performing in front of large groups, your grace and lithe body make you a natural **dancer** or **gymnast.**

Relationships

It's difficult to really know a cat. Although you make little attempt to disguise your emotions, your communication style is somewhat abstract. You readily display your disgust and boredom as you stalk off to spend solitary time sulking, and you have a habit of disappearing for no particular reason. Usually, however, you return to a place that offers you security and creature comforts.

Close alliances are formed with others who share your eremitic and wandering ways. **Horse** and **deer** personalities are good candidates to be your soul mate, while **gorillas** provide you with much appreciated security.

Canine personalities are your natural enemy. You disdain their stability, loyalty, and willingness to please, but you'll sometimes form an uneasy alliance with the **fox,** who shares your love of exploration. **Cottontails** and other small mammals should avoid your catty nature.

Famous Wildcats

Michelle Pfeiffer, Heather Locklear

Advice for a Wildcat

The cure for boredom is curiosity. There is no cure for curiosity.

WILD DOG

Class: Mammalia
Order: Carnivora
Related Species: Wolf, Domestic Dog

It is believed *that the domestic dog descended not from the wild dog but from the wolf. This is primarily due to differences in social structure between these two* species. Unlike the wolf, which orders its society in a strong hierarchy, wild dogs tend to act as a pack, without any formal social structure. Domestic dogs must accept their role as subordinate to their owners, and since wild dogs are not naturally submissive, they are unsuccessful as pets.

Cooperative hunting is conducted without a dominant animal, and this proves highly effective on long hunts, when each wild dog takes a turn in the lead. This wears down the prey, which succumbs to exhaustion before its eventual disembowelment. After quickly feeding at the site of the kill, the wild dogs make their way back to the den to regurgitate the meal for the benefit of the pups.

The Human Wild Dog

Your wild dog personality has much in common with both the wolf and domestic dog personalities. Sharing an inquisitive and friendly spirit, you exhibit the same exceptional range of social skills. There are, however, some important differences in your makeup. You are very much your own person, and while you respect the rights of others, you tend to be neither a leader nor a follower in your wide social network.

Reliable in a crisis, you are charitable to those in need and have a strong sense of social justice. You are dependable and generous to a fault, but there is a darker side to your character. If you believe that you have been wronged, you'll carry a grudge for a long time and punish the offender by withdrawing your otherwise unconditional support.

Although you are not a natural leader, you are popular and well liked, and your indomitable sense of adventure attracts others who appreciate living on the edge. You were not blessed with a particularly handsome face, but your trim body is well conditioned by your athletic endeavors, and you take pride in your appearance.

As is typical of a carnivorous personality, you love to travel and choose to vacation in stimulating environments where you can expand your understanding of the world. You become restless when you haven't taken a vacation in a while.

Careers

You are a highly principled individual, although it takes time for people to build their trust in you. Employers should provide you with a great deal of freedom since you perform poorly in structured environments. Instead, you prefer working in groups and are attracted to jobs that require collective consensus.

When it comes to stamina, you are without equal, and you are usually the first to arrive and the last to leave the office. You are versatile in your skills, and your sharp mind can adapt to almost any environment, standing you in good stead as a **researcher, engineer, draftsman, architect,** or **academic.** Your ability to think on your feet makes you an excellent **police officer, politician,** or **journalist.**

Relationships

Your easygoing nature is appealing to some, although your high energy level is too intense and overbearing for others. In matters of the heart, you enjoy playing the field, but once married, you prove to be a committed and faithful partner. **Domestic dogs, baboons,** and **warthogs** make compatible mates, while **vultures, lions,** and **snakes** should be specifically avoided.

A doting parent, you are always available to help out with baby-sitting duties. However, you do expect others to do their part. You believe that children should find their own way in life, and you're quick to discipline when the social order has been transgressed.

Famous Wild Dogs

Martina Navratilova, Vladimir Lenin

Advice for a Wild Dog

Make dust. Don't eat it.

WOLF

Class: *Mammalia*
Order: *Carnivora*
Related Species: *Dog, Fox*

No **animal has** *been as misunderstood as the wolf. Cast as a bloodthirsty villain in folklore and children's stories, wolves have enjoyed a special mystique that has engendered fear and respect throughout their range.*

Thought by many to be the ancestor of the domestic dog, wolves were once widespread over Europe, Asia, and North America. Their range was probably wider than any other carnivore, and their success was due in part to their rigidly enforced social structure.

The Human Wolf

Closely related to the domestic dog personality, you are a highly intelligent and courageous individual. Although you share a number of traits with your cousins the coyote and jackal, your unmatched strength and loyalty elevate you to a breed of your own.

You are ruggedly good-looking, and your regal bearing exudes confidence. However, jealousy of your success and a misunderstanding of your doglike nature has added to your dark reputation. Athletic and energetic, you dominate your workplace, and you are both respected for your loyalty and admired for your doggedness. Nothing excites you more than the thrill of a chase, and your legendary powers of endurance contribute to your prosperity.

Careers

You are intensely ambitious and never shy from hard work. Socially adept, you function well in leadership and management roles, as well as in jobs requiring vision and strength of character. Being a natural motivator, your instinctive understanding of group dynamics serves you well in goal-oriented tasks.

As a boss you demand absolute loyalty, and you provide the same allegiance to your employees. Your ability to perform under pressure helps you attain the highest executive levels, and with your strong communication instincts, you maintain a constant stream of notes, letters, and faxes to your coworkers. Your instinctive understanding of the chain of command would make you an excellent **soldier** or **law enforcement officer**.

Relationships

Close familial relationships provide you with a sense of stability. When your family or friends are by your side, you feel all-powerful and there is little you can't accomplish.

You are facially expressive, readily communicate your emotional states with body language, and you work hard at developing your social relationships. Unlike your cousin the **dog** personality, however, you are quick to anger when you sense a threat to the social order. When a confrontation occurs you tend to react suddenly and violently, barking displeasure at offending subordinates. Those close to you know how to avoid your biting tongue until you resume your normal gregarious behavior.

Friendly and generous with those you consider to be peers, you have a tendency to show scant regard to those personalities beneath you on the food chain. **Sheep, deer, cottontails, prairie dogs,** and other small mammal personalities are thus advised to show you appropriate respect or risk being overwhelmed by your aggressive nature.

Bear, dog, and **fox** personalities are typically your best partners. They understand your need for social order, and they follow the same strict hierarchical code, keeping arguments to a minimum and cooperation at a maximum.

You are in great demand as a lover. Your partner gets your undivided attention, and your communication skills ensure a rich and intimate lovelife.

Famous Wolves

Tom Cruise, Hillary Rodham Clinton, Larry King

Advice for a Wolf

Don't be afraid to take big leaps. You can't cross a chasm in two small jumps.

ZEBRA

Class: *Mammalia*
Order: *Perissodactyla*
Related Species: *Horse, Quagga, Donkey*

Zebras are differentiated *from horses and asses by the distinctive stripes on their bodies. Only recently settled was the debate about whether the* zebra's stripes are white on black or black on white. (It has black stripes on a white background.)

Zebras are aggressive and protect themselves and their young when attacked. It is the only herbivore known to use its teeth as a weapon, and a kick from its powerful hindquarters is quite capable of shattering a lion's jaw.

A species of zebra known as the quagga has

quite a sad story. Hunted into extinction by South African settlers in the mid 1800s, it was not until the last quagga was shot that anyone realized that it was even endangered. Zoos requesting replacement animals were shocked to be informed, "We can't seem to find any."

The Human Zebra

In many ways you share the strong, broad-shouldered characteristics of your relative, the **horse**. Being a creature of the wild, however, your emotional makeup tends to be more extreme. You are a powerfully built creature and are always keen to test yourself with all manner of challenges. Favoring sports that demand strength and endurance, you generally avoid activities that require physical contact.

Wild and untamable, you have quite an aggressive streak, and your enormous self-confidence gives you an unusually swaggering gait. Quick to anger, your temper often gets the better of you, and you are considered so volatile that even **lion** personalities will think twice before accosting you. However, you rarely initiate these confrontations and are peaceable and self-contained if left alone.

You have a tendency to view the world in black and white, and you have a strong sense of right and wrong. Unlike your **horse** cousin, you are unwilling to be saddled with the burdens of others and insist that everyone carry his own weight. Your well-defined life philosophy is evident in your relationships, and you are surprised when others don't see things your way. With a penchant for debate, you seek friendships with people who hold diametrically opposed views.

Your enigmatic personality contains a well-hidden dark side, and there are some personal issues you simply refuse to discuss. But when these deeper aspects of your character surface, you prove to be an interested and interesting individual.

Careers

As is typical of herbivorous personalities, you tend to form mixed herds with other grazing animals, and these mutually beneficial friendships even extend to successful business partnerships.

Once your mind is made up, it is difficult to shift your position, which explains your reputation for stubbornness. This reputation is unfair, since your opinions are usually formed after deliberate and logical consideration. Your analytical thinking primes you for careers in **science**, **engineering**, **accounting,** and **football refereeing**.

Your strong sense of justice makes you ideal for careers in the legal system, including **police work** or **law**, while your ability to endure a long race might bring you success in **politics**.

Your love for things tangible makes it unlikely that you'll excel in the arts, and your distaste for physical labor makes you unsuitable for blue-collar jobs.

Relationships

As a friend you are dependable and demonstrative, and you are attracted to the pragmatic aspects of your natural companions—**sheep**, **deer**, **horses**, and **giraffes**. However, when you get together with your perennial enemy, the **lion** personality, sparks are sure to fly.

You struggle with committed and meaningful relationships. You have no reason to commit to a single mate and prefer the freedom of wide-open spaces, where your strength and endurance make you the ruler of the plains.

Famous Zebras
Christopher Darden, Jim McMahon

Advice for a Zebra
The road to success is always under construction.

Lookup Tables

Refer to the Animal
Personality Test on page 5

Lookup Tables

111-

111-111↓ Mole,Snake,Mouse
112-111↓ Mole,Snake,Mouse
113-111↓ Mole,Snake,Mouse
121-111↓ Mole,Mouse,Snake
122-111↓ Mole,Mouse,Snake
123-111↓ Mole,Mouse,Snake
131-111↓ Mouse,Mole
132-111↓ Mouse,Mole
132-132↓ Mouse,Mole,Bat
133-111↓ Mouse,Mole,Bat
141-111↓ Mouse
142-111↓ Mouse
143-111↓ Mouse,Bat
211-111↓ Snake,Mouse
212-111↓ Snake,Mouse
213-111↓ Snake,Mouse
221-111↓ Mouse,Snake
222-111↓ Mouse,Snake
223-111↓ Mouse,Snake,Bat
231-111↓ Mouse,Snake
232-111↓ Mouse,Bat,Snake
233-111↓ Mouse,Bat,Snake
241-111↓ Mouse
242-111 Mouse
243-111↓ Mouse,Bat
311-111↓ Snake,Mouse
312-111↓ Snake,Mouse
313-111↓ Snake,Mouse
321-111↓ Mouse,Snake
322-111↓ Mouse,Snake
323-111↓ Mouse,Snake
331-111↓ Mouse,Snake
332-111↓ Mouse,Bat,Snake
333-111↓ Mouse,Bat,Snake
341-111↓ Mouse
342-111↓ Mouse
343-111↓ Mouse,Bat
411-111↓ Snake,Mouse,Mole
412-111↓ Snake,Mouse,Mole
413-111↓ Snake,Mouse,Mole
413-122↓ Mouse,Bat,Snake
413-131↓ Mouse,Snake,Mole
421-111↓ Mouse,Snake
422-111↓ Mouse,Snake
423-111↓ Mouse,Snake
423-112↓ Mouse,Snake,Bat
431-111↓ Mouse,Cottn
432-111↓ Mouse,Cottn

433-111↓ Mouse,Bat
433-221↓ Mouse,Cottn
441-111↓ Mouse
442-111↓ Mouse
443-111↓ Mouse,Bat

112-

111-111↓ Mole,Snake,Mouse
112-111↓ Mole,Snake,Mouse
113-111↓ Mole,Snake,Mouse
121-111↓ Mole,Mouse,Snake
122-111↓ Mole,Mouse,Snake
123-111↓ Mole,Mouse,Snake
131-111↓ Mouse,Molecc
132-111↓ Mouse,Mole
132-122↓ Mouse,Mole,Bat
133-111↓ Mouse,Bat
133-121 Mouse,Mole
133-122↓ Mouse,Bat
141-111↓ Mouse
142-111↓ Mouse
143-111↓ Mouse,Bat
211-111↓ Snake,Mouse
212-111↓ Snake,Mouse
213-111↓ Snake,Mouse
213-122↓ Mouse,Bat,Snake
221-111↓ Mouse,Snake
222-111↓ Mouse,Snake
223-111↓ Mouse,Snake
223-212↓ Mouse,Snake,Bat
231-111↓ Mouse,Snake
232-111↓ Mouse,Bat,Snake
233-111↓ Mouse,Bat,Snake
241-111↓ Mouse
242-111↓ Mouse
243-111↓ Mouse,Bat
311-111↓ Snake,Mouse
312-111↓ Snake,Mouse
313-111↓ Snake,Mouse
313-122↓ Mouse,Bat,Snake
313-222↓ Mouse,Otter
321-111↓ Mouse,Snake
322-111↓ Mouse,Snake
323-111↓ Mouse,Snake
323-112↓ Mouse,Snake,Bat
323-222↓ Mouse,Otter
331-111↓ Mouse
332-111 Mouse
333-111↓ Mouse,Bat

333-212↓ Mouse,Otter,Bat
341-111↓ Mouse
342-111↓ Mouse
343-111↓ Mouse,Bat,Otter
411-111↓ Cottn,Snake,Mouse
411-332↓ Cottn,Mouse,Deer
412-111↓ Cottn,Snake,Mouse
412-332↓ Cottn,Mouse,Deer
413-111↓ Cottn,Snake,Mouse
413-332↓ Cottn,Mouse,Deer
421-111↓ Cottn,Mouse,Snake
421-332↓ Cottn,Mouse,Swan
422-111↓ Cottn,Mouse,Snake
422-332↓ Cottn,Mouse,Swan
423-111↓ Cottn,Mouse,Snake
423-332↓ Cottn,Mouse,Swan
431-111↓ Cottn,Mouse
431-332↓ Cottn,Mouse,Swan
432-111↓ Cottn,Mouse
432-332↓ Cottn,Mouse,Swan
433-111 Cottn,Mouse
433-332↓ Cottn,Mouse,Swan
441-111↓ Cottn,Mouse
441-332↓ Cottn,Mouse,Swan
442-111↓ Cottn,Mouse
442-332↓ Cottn,Mouse,Swan
443-111 Cottn,Mouse
443-332↓ Cottn,Mouse,Swan

113-

111-111↓ Mole,Snake,Mouse
112-111↓ Mole,Snake,Mouse
113-111↓ Mole,Snake,Mouse
113-132↓ Mole,Mouse,Bat
121-111↓ Mole,Mouse,Snake
122-111↓ Mole,Mouse,Snake
123-111↓ Mole,Mouse,Snake
123-132↓ Mole,Mouse,Bat
131-111↓ Mouse
132-111↓ Mouse
132-121↓ Mouse,Mole
133-111↓ Mouse,Bat
141-111↓ Mouse
142-111↓ Mouse
143-111↓ Mouse,Bat
211-111↓ Snake,Mouse
212-111↓ Snake,Mouse
213-111↓ Snake,Mouse
221-111↓ Mouse,Snake

(113 cont'd)
222-111↓ Mouse,Snake
223-111↓ Mouse,Snake
231-111↓ Mouse,Snake
232-111↓ Mouse,Snake
233-111↓ Mouse,Bat
241-111↓ Mouse
242-111↓ Mouse
243-111↓ Mouse,Bat
311-111↓ Snake,Mouse
312-111↓ Snake,Mouse
313-111↓ Snake,Mouse
313-122↓ Mouse,Bat,Snake
313-212↓ Mouse,Snake,Otter
321-111↓ Mouse,Snake
321-221↓ Mouse,Cottn
322-111↓ Mouse,Snake
322-121↓ Mouse,Snake,Cottn
323-111 Mouse,Snake
323-112↓ Mouse,Snake,Bat
331-111↓ Mouse,Cottn
332-111↓ Mouse,Cottn
332-122↓ Mouse,Cottn,Bat
333-111↓ Mouse,Bat,Otter
333-121 Mouse,Cottn
333-132↓ Mouse,Bat,Otter
333-222↓ Mouse,Otter,Cottn
341-111↓ Mouse
342-111↓ Mouse
342-221↓ Mouse,Cottn
343-111↓ Mouse,Bat
343-122↓ Mouse,Bat,Otter
343-132↓ Mouse,Bat,Pr.Dog
343-222↓ Mouse,Otter
343-232↓ Mouse,Pr.Dog
343-322↓ Mouse,Otter
343-332 Mouse,Pr.Dog
411-111↓ Cottn,Deer
412-111↓ Cottn,Deer
413-111↓ Cottn,Deer
421-111↓ Cottn,Deer
422-111↓ Cottn,Mouse
423-111↓ Cottn,Deer
431-111↓ Cottn,Mouse
432-111↓ Cottn,Mouse
433-111↓ Cottn,Mouse
441-111↓ Cottontail
442-111↓ Cottontail
443-111↓ Cottontail

114-
111-111↓ Mole,Snake,Mouse
112-111↓ Mole,Snake,Mouse
113-111↓ Mole,Snake,Mouse
113-132↓ Mole,Mouse,Bat
121-111↓ Mole,Mouse,Snake
122-111↓ Mole,Mouse,Snake
123-111↓ Mole,Mouse,Snake
123-132↓ Mole,Mouse,Bat
131-111↓ Mouse
132-111↓ Mouse
133-111↓ Mouse,Bat
141-111↓ Mouse
142-111↓ Mouse
143-111↓ Mouse,Bat

143-132↓ Mouse,Bat,Pr.Dog
211-111↓ Snake,Mouse
212-111↓ Snake,Mouse
213-111↓ Snake,Mouse
221-111↓ Mouse,Snake
222-111↓ Mouse,Snake
223-111↓ Mouse,Snake
231-111↓ Mouse
232-111↓ Mouse
233-111↓ Mouse,Bat
241-111↓ Mouse
242-111↓ Mouse
243-111↓ Mouse,Bat
243-132↓ Mouse,Bat,Pr.Dog
311-111↓ Snake,Mouse
312-111↓ Snake,Mouse
313-111↓ Snake,Mouse
313-122↓ Mouse,Bat,Snake
313-132↓ Mouse,Bat,Pr.Dog
313-212↓ Mouse,Snake
313-232↓ Mouse,Pr.Dog
321-111↓ Mouse,Snake
322-111↓ Mouse,Snake
323-111↓ Mouse,Snake
323-112↓ Mouse,Snake,Bat
331-111↓ Mouse
332-111↓ Mouse
332-211↓ Mouse,Cottn
333-111↓ Mouse,Bat
341-111↓ Mouse,Dog
341-332↓ Mouse,Dog,Pr.Dog
342-111↓ Mouse,Dog
342-122↓ Mouse,Dog,Pr.Dog
343-111↓ Mouse,Pr.Dog,Dog
411-111↓ Cottn,Deer,SeaLn
412-111↓ Cottn,Deer,SeaLn
413-111↓ Cottn,Deer,SeaLn
421-111↓ Cottn,Deer
422-111↓ Cottn,Deer
423-111↓ Cottn,Deer
423-322↓ Cottn,Deer,SeaLn
431-111↓ Cottontail
432-111↓ Cottontail
432-221↓ Cottn,Mouse
433-111↓ Cottontail
441-111 Cottontail
442-111↓ Cottn,Dog
442-332↓ Cottn,Pr.Dog,Dog
443-111↓ Cottn,Pr.Dog,Dog

121-
111-111↓ Snake,Bat
112-111↓ Snake,Bat
113-111↓ Snake,Bat
121-111↓ Snake,Bat
121-332↓ Snake,Bat,Mouse
122-111↓ Snake,Bat
122-331↓ Snake,Mouse,Bat
123-111↓ Snake,Bat
131-111↓ Snake,Bat
131-212↓ Snake,Bat,Mouse
132-111 Snake,Bat
132-212↓ Bat,Snake,Mouse
133-111↓ Bat,Snake
133-311↓ Bat,Snake,Mouse

141-111↓ Snake,Bat
141-211↓ Snake,Mouse,Bat
141-232 Bat,Mouse,Beaver
141-311↓ Snake,Mouse,Bat
141-331↓ Mouse,Bat,Beaver
142-111↓ Snake,Bat
142-221↓ Bat,Mouse,Snake
142-231↓ Bat,Mouse,Beaver
142-311↓ Snake,Mouse,Bat
142-331↓ Mouse,Bat,Beaver
143-111↓ Bat,Snake
143-321↓ Bat,Mouse
143-331↓ Bat,Beaver
211-111↓ Snake,Bat
211-332↓ Snake,Bat,Shrew
212-111↓ Snake,Bat
212-332↓ Snake,Bat,Shrew
213-111↓ Snake,Bat
221-111↓ Snake,Bat
221-221↓ Snake,Mouse,Bat
222-111↓ Snake,Bat
222-321↓ Snake,Mouse,Bat
223-111↓ Snake,Bat
231-111↓ Snake,Bat
231-211↓ Snake,Mouse,Bat
232-111 Snake,Bat
232-212↓ Bat,Snake,Mouse
233-111↓ Bat,Snake
233-221↓ Bat,Snake,Mouse
241-111↓ Snake,Bat
241-211↓ Snake,Mouse,Bat
241-232 Bat,Mouse,Beaver
241-311↓ Snake,Mouse,Bat
241-332 Bat,Mouse,Beaver
242-111↓ Snake,Bat,Mouse
242-231↓ Bat,Mouse,Beaver
242-311↓ Snake,Mouse,Bat
242-331↓ Mouse,Bat,Beaver
243-111↓ Bat,Snake
243-221↓ Bat,Mouse,Snake
243-231↓ Bat,Beaver,Mouse
243-311↓ Bat,Snake,Mouse
243-331↓ Bat,Beaver,Mouse
311-111↓ Snake,Bat,Shrew
312-111↓ Snake,Bat
312-322↓ Shrew,Snake,Bat
313-111↓ Snake,Bat
313-212↓ Snake,Bat,Shrew
321-111↓ Snake,Bat
321-221 Snake,Mouse,Cottn
321-222↓ Snake,Bat,Mouse
321-331 Snake,Mouse,Cottn
321-332↓ Snake,Bat,Mouse
322-111↓ Snake,Bat
322-221↓ Snake,Bat,Mouse
322-222 Snake,Bat,Otter
322-231 Snake,Bat,Mouse
322-232↓ Snake,Bat,Otter
322-321 Snake,Mouse,Cottn
322-322 Snake,Bat,Otter
322-331 Snake,Mouse,Cottn
322-332↓ Snake,Bat,Otter
323-111↓ Snake,Bat
323-212↓ Snake,Bat,Otter
331-111↓ Snake,Bat

331-131↓ Snake,Bat,Mouse
331-211 Snake,Mouse,Cottn
331-212 Snake,Bat,Mouse
331-221 Snake,Mouse,Cottn
331-222 Bat,Snake,Mouse
331-231 Mouse,Cottn,Snake
331-232 Bat,Mouse,Cottn
331-311 Snake,Mouse,Cottn
331-312 Snake,Bat,Mouse
331-321 Mouse,Cottn,Snake
331-322 Bat,Mouse,Cottn
331-331 Mouse,Cottn,Snake
331-332 Bat,Mouse,Cottn
332-111 Snake,Bat
332-212↓ Bat,Snake,Otter
332-221 Bat,Snake,Mouse
332-222 Bat,Snake,Otter
332-231 Bat,Mouse,Cottn
332-232 Bat,Otter,Mouse
332-311 Snake,Mouse,Cottn
332-312 Bat,Snake,Otter
332-321 Mouse,Cottn,Bat
332-322 Bat,Otter,Mouse
332-331 Mouse,Cottn,Bat
332-332 Bat,Otter,Mouse
333-111↓ Bat,Snake
333-211↓ Bat,Snake,Otter
333-331↓ Bat,Otter,Mouse
341-111↓ Snake,Bat
341-131↓ Bat,Snake,Mouse
341-211 Snake,Mouse,Cottn
341-212 Bat,Snake,Mouse
341-221↓ Mouse,Cottn,Bat
341-311 Snake,Mouse,Cottn
341-312 Bat,Snake,Mouse
341-321↓ Mouse,Cottn,Bat
342-111 Snake,Bat
342-211↓ Snake,Bat,Mouse
342-221 Bat,Mouse,Cottn
342-222 Bat,Otter,Mouse
342-231 Bat,Mouse,Cottn
342-232 Bat,Beaver
342-311 Snake,Mouse,Cottn
342-312 Bat,Snake,Otter
342-321 Mouse,Cottn,Bat
342-322 Bat,Otter,Mouse
342-331 Mouse,Cottn,Bat
342-332 Bat,Beaver,Otter
343-111↓ Bat,Snake
343-232↓ Bat,Otter,Pr.Dog
411-111↓ Snake,Cottn
411-222↓ Cottn,Shrew,Snake
411-232 Cottn,Shrew,Pcock
411-311↓ Cottn,Snake,Shrew
411-332↓ Cottn,Shrew,Swan
412-111↓ Snake,Cottn
412-232↓ Cottn,Shrew,Snake
412-332↓ Cottn,Shrew,Swan
413-111↓ Snake,Bat
413-121↓ Snake,Cottn,Bat
413-222 Cottn,Bat,Shrew
413-231 Cottn,Snake,Shrew
413-232 Cottn,Bat,Shrew
413-311↓ Cottn,Snake,Shrew
413-332↓ Cottn,Shrew,Swan

421-111↓ Snake,Cottn
421-312↓ Cottn,Swan,Snake
421-322↓ Cottn,Swan,Deer
422-111 Snake,Cottn
422-312↓ Cottn,Swan,Snake
422-322↓ Cottn,Swan,Deer
423-111↓ Snake,Cottn,Bat
423-232 Cottn,Bat,Otter
423-312↓ Cottn,Swan,Snake
423-322↓ Cottn,Swan,Bat
431-111 Cottn,Snake
431-222↓ Cottn,Swan,Bat
432-111 Cottn,Snake,Bat
432-322↓ Cottn,Swan,Bat
433-111↓ Cottn,Bat,Snake
433-322↓ Cottn,Swan,Bat
441-111 Cottn,Snake
441-112↓ Cottn,Bat,Snake
441-312↓ Cottn,Swan
442-111 Cottn,Snake
442-112↓ Cottn,Bat,Snake
442-312↓ Cottn,Swan
443-111↓ Cottn,Bat,Snake
443-222↓ Cottn,Bat,Otter
443-312↓ Cottn,Swan,Bat

122-

111-111↓ Snake,Bat
111-331↓ Snake,Shrew,Cottn
111-332↓ Shrew,Snake,Bat
112-111↓ Snake,Bat
112-332↓ Shrew,Snake,Bat
113-111↓ Snake,Bat
113-222↓ Bat,Snake,Shrew
121-111↓ Snake,Bat
121-322↓ Snake,Bat,Cottn
121-331 Snake,Cottn,Mouse
121-332↓ Snake,Bat,Cottn
122-111↓ Snake,Bat
122-331↓ Snake,Cottn,Mouse
122-332↓ Snake,Bat,Cottn
123-111↓ Snake,Bat
131-111↓ Snake,Bat
131-131↓ Snake,Bat,Cottn
131-211 Snake,Cottn,Mouse
131-212 Snake,Bat,Cottn
131-221 Cottn,Snake,Mouse
131-222 Bat,Cottn,Snake
131-231 Cottn,Mouse,Snake
131-232 Bat,Cottn,Mouse
131-311 Snake,Cottn,Mouse
131-312 Snake,Bat,Cottn
131-321 Cottn,Mouse,Snake
131-322 Bat,Cottn,Mouse
131-331 Cottn,Mouse,Snake
131-332 Bat,Cottn,Mouse
132-111 Snake,Bat
132-212↓ Bat,Snake,Cottn
132-311 Snake,Cottn,Mouse
132-312 Bat,Snake,Cottn
132-321↓ Cottn,Mouse,Bat
133-111↓ Bat,Snake
133-212↓ Bat,Snake,Otter
133-221 Bat,Cottn,Snake
133-222↓ Bat,Otter

133-311↓ Bat,Snake,Cottn
133-321↓ Bat,Cottn,Otter
141-111↓ Snake,Bat
141-131↓ Bat,Beaver,Snake
141-211 Snake,Sheep,Cottn
141-212 Bat,Snake,Sheep
141-221 Sheep,Cottn,Mouse
141-222 Bat,Sheep,Beaver
141-231 Beaver,Sheep,Cottn
141-232 Beaver,Bat,Sheep
141-311 Sheep,Snake,Cottn
141-312 Sheep,Bat,Beaver
141-321 Sheep,Cottn,Mouse
141-322 Sheep,Beaver,Bat
141-331 Beaver,Sheep,Cottn
141-332 Beaver,Sheep,Bat
142-111↓ Snake,Bat
142-131↓ Bat,Beaver,Snake
142-211 Snake,Sheep,Cottn
142-212 Bat,Beaver,Snake
142-221 Sheep,Beaver,Cottn
142-222 Bat,Beaver,Sheep
142-231 Beaver,Sheep,Cottn
142-232 Beaver,Bat
142-311 Sheep,Snake,Cottn
142-312 Beaver,Bat,Sheep
142-321 Sheep,Beaver,Cottn
142-322 Beaver,Bat,Sheep
142-331↓ Beaver,Sheep,Cottn
143-111↓ Bat,Snake
143-131↓ Bat,Beaver
143-211 Bat,Snake,Sheep
143-321↓ Bat,Beaver,Sheep
211-111↓ Snake,Bat,Shrew
212-111↓ Snake,Bat
212-332↓ Shrew,Snake,Bat
213-111↓ Snake,Bat
213-212↓ Snake,Bat,Shrew
221-111↓ Snake,Bat
221-221 Snake,Cottn,Mouse
221-222 Snake,Cottn,Cottn
221-231 Snake,Cottn,Mouse
221-332↓ Snake,Bat,Cottn
222-111↓ Snake,Bat
222-221↓ Snake,Cottn,Bat
222-321 Snake,Cottn,Mouse
222-322 Snake,Bat,Cottn
222-331 Snake,Cottn,Mouse
222-332↓ Snake,Bat,Cottn
223-111↓ Snake,Bat
223-212↓ Snake,Bat,Otter
231-111↓ Snake,Bat
231-121↓ Snake,Bat,Cottn
231-221 Cottn,Snake,Mouse
231-222 Bat,Cottn,Snake
231-231 Cottn,Mouse,Snake
231-232 Bat,Cottn,Mouse
231-311 Snake,Cottn,Mouse
231-312 Snake,Bat,Cottn
231-321 Cottn,Mouse,Snake
231-322 Bat,Cottn,Mouse
231-331 Cottn,Mouse,Snake
231-332 Bat,Cottn,Mouse
232-111 Snake,Bat
232-212↓ Bat,Snake,Cottn

(122 cont'd)

232-232 Bat,Cottn,Otter
232-311 Snake,Cottn,Mouse
232-312 Bat,Snake,Cottn
232-321 Cottn,Mouse,Bat
232-322 Bat,Cottn,Otter
232-331 Cottn,Mouse,Bat
232-332 Bat,Cottn,Otter
233-111↓ Bat,Snake
233-211↓ Bat,Snake,Otter
233-331↓ Bat,Otter,Cottn
241-111↓ Snake,Bat,Sheep
241-131↓ Bat,Beaver,Snake
241-211 Snake,Sheep,Cottn
241-212 Bat,Snake,Sheep
241-221 Sheep,Cottn,Mouse
241-222 Bat,Sheep,Beaver
241-231 Beaver,Sheep,Cottn
241-232 Beaver,Bat,Sheep
241-311 Sheep,Snake,Cottn
241-312 Sheep,Bat,Beaver
241-321 Sheep,Cottn,Mouse
241-322 Sheep,Beaver,Bat
241-331↓ Beaver,Sheep,Cottn
242-111 Snake,Bat,Sheep
242-112 Bat,Snake,Beaver
242-121 Bat,Snake,Sheep
242-122↓ Bat,Beaver,Snake
242-211 Snake,Sheep,Cottn
242-212 Bat,Beaver,Snake
242-221 Sheep,Beaver,Cottn
242-222 Bat,Beaver,Sheep
242-231 Beaver,Sheep,Cottn
242-232 Beaver,Bat,Sheep
242-311 Sheep,Snake,Cottn
242-312 Beaver,Bat,Sheep
242-321 Sheep,Beaver,Cottn
242-322 Beaver,Bat,Sheep
242-331 Beaver,Sheep,Cottn
242-332 Beaver,Bat
243-111↓ Bat,Snake
243-131↓ Bat,Beaver
243-211 Bat,Snake,Sheep
243-212 Bat,Beaver,Otter
243-221 Bat,Snake,Sheep
243-222 Bat,Beaver,Otter
243-231 Beaver,Bat,Sheep
243-232 Beaver,Bat,Otter
243-311 Bat,Sheep,Beaver
243-312 Bat,Beaver,Otter
243-321 Bat,Beaver,Sheep
243-322 Bat,Beaver,Otter
243-331↓ Beaver,Bat,Sheep
311-111↓ Snake,Shrew
311-321↓ Shrew,Cottn,Snake
312-111↓ Snake,Shrew
312-132↓ Shrew,Snake,Bat
312-321↓ Shrew,Cottn,Snake
313-111↓ Snake,Bat,Shrew
313-211↓ Snake,Shrew,Otter
313-232 Shrew,Otter,Bat
313-311↓ Shrew,Snake,Otter
313-331↓ Shrew,Otter,Cottn
321-111↓ Snake,Bat
321-332↓ Cottn,Otter,Snake

322-111↓ Snake,Bat
322-121↓ Snake,Cottn,Bat
322-212↓ Snake,Cottn,Otter
323-111↓ Snake,Bat,Otter
323-211 Snake,Otter,Cottn
323-212 Otter,Snake,Bat
323-221 Otter,Cottn,Snake
323-222↓ Otter,Bat,Cottn
323-311 Snake,Otter,Cottn
323-312 Otter,Snake,Bat
323-321 Otter,Cottn,Snake
323-322↓ Otter,Bat,Cottn
331-111↓ Snake,Cottn,Bat
331-132 Bat,Cottn,Otter
331-211↓ Cottn,Snake,Otter
331-222 Cottn,Otter,Bat
331-231 Cottn,Otter,Mouse
331-232 Cottn,Otter,Bat
331-311 Cottn,Snake
331-322↓ Cottn,Otter,Swan
332-111↓ Snake,Cottn,Bat
332-122 Bat,Cottn,Otter
332-131 Cottn,Bat,Snake
332-132 Bat,Cottn,Otter
332-211 Cottn,Snake,Otter
332-212↓ Cottn,Otter,Bat
332-311 Cottn,Otter,Snake
332-312 Cottn,Otter,Bat
332-321 Cottn,Otter,Mouse
332-322 Cottn,Otter,Bat
332-331 Cottn,Otter,Mouse
332-332 Cottn,Otter,Bat
333-111↓ Bat,Snake,Otter
333-211↓ Otter,Cottn,Bat
341-111↓ Snake,Cottn,Bat
341-132↓ Bat,Cottn,Beaver
341-212↓ Cottn,Dog,Otter
341-232↓ Cottn,Beaver,Dog
341-312↓ Cottn,Dog,Otter
341-332 Cottn,Beaver,Dog
342-111↓ Snake,Cottn,Bat
342-122 Bat,Cottn,Otter
342-131↓ Cottn,Bat,Beaver
342-211 Cottn,Otter,Snake
342-212 Cottn,Otter,Dog
342-221 Cottn,Otter,Sheep
342-222 Cottn,Otter,Dog
342-231 Cottn,Beaver,Otter
342-312↓ Cottn,Otter,Dog
342-331 Cottn,Beaver,Otter
343-111↓ Bat,Otter,Snake
343-121↓ Bat,Otter,Cottn
343-131↓ Bat,Otter,Pr.Dog
343-211↓ Otter,Cottn,Bat
343-231 Otter,Pr.Dog,Cottn
343-232 Otter,Pr.Dog,Beaver
343-311↓ Otter,Cottn,Bat
343-331 Otter,Pr.Dog,Cottn
343-332 Otter,Pr.Dog,Beaver
411-111 Cottn,Snake
411-112↓ Cottn,Snake,Shrew
411-122↓ Cottn,Shrew,Pcock
411-312↓ Cottn,Deer,Shrew
412-111 Cottn,Snake
412-312↓ Cottn,Deer,Shrew

413-111 Cottn,Snake
413-112↓ Cottn,Snake,Shrew
413-232↓ Cottn,Shrew,W.Cat
413-312↓ Cottn,Deer,Shrew
421-111↓ Cottn,Snake
421-312↓ Cottn,Swan,Deer
422-111↓ Cottn,Snake
422-311↓ Cottn,Swan,Deer
423-111 Cottn,Snake
423-112↓ Cottn,Snake,Bat
423-222↓ Cottn,Otter,W.Cat
423-312↓ Cottn,Swan,Deer
431-111↓ Cottn,Swan
432-111↓ Cottn,Swan
433-111 Cottn,Bat
433-132↓ Cottn,Bat,Otter
433-332↓ Cottn,Swan,Otter
441-111↓ Cottn,Swan
442-111↓ Cottn,Swan
443-111↓ Cottn,Bat
443-222↓ Cottn,Otter
443-312↓ Cottn,Swan

123-

111-111↓ Snake,Bat
111-222↓ Snake,Shrew,Cottn
112-111↓ Snake,Bat
112-222↓ Snake,Shrew,Cottn
113-111↓ Snake,Bat
113-221↓ Snake,Bat,Cottn
113-222 Bat,Snake,Shrew
113-231 Snake,Bat,Cottn
113-232↓ Bat,Snake,Shrew
113-321 Snake,Cottn,Bat
113-322 Bat,Snake,Shrew
113-331 Snake,Cottn,Bat
113-332↓ Bat,Shrew,Snake
121-111↓ Snake,Bat
121-332↓ Cottn,Snake,Bat
122-111↓ Snake,Bat
122-332↓ Cottn,Snake,Bat
123-111↓ Snake,Bat
123-231↓ Bat,Snake,Cottn
131-111 Snake,Cottn
131-112↓ Snake,Bat,Cottn
132-111↓ Snake,Bat,Cottn
133-111↓ Bat,Snake
133-121↓ Bat,Snake,Cottn
141-111 Snake,Sheep,Cottn
141-112 Bat,Snake,Sheep
141-121↓ Sheep,Cottn,Bat
141-132 Bat,Sheep,Beaver
141-211 Sheep,Cottn,Snake
141-222↓ Sheep,Cottn,Bat
141-231↓ Sheep,Cottn,Beaver
142-111↓ Snake,Sheep,Bat
142-131↓ Sheep,Bat,Cottn
142-132 Bat,Beaver,Sheep
142-211 Sheep,Cottn,Snake
142-222↓ Sheep,Cottn,Bat
142-231↓ Sheep,Cottn,Beaver
143-111↓ Bat,Snake,Sheep
143-131↓ Bat,Beaver,Sheep
143-221↓ Sheep,Bat,Cottn
143-222↓ Bat,Sheep,Beaver

143-311	Sheep,Cottn,Bat	
143-312	Bat,Sheep,Beaver	
143-321	Sheep,Cottn,Bat	
143-322	Bat,Sheep,Beaver	
143-331	Beaver,Sheep,Cottn	
143-332	Beaver,Bat,Sheep	
211-111↓	Snake,Bat,Shrew	
211-221↓	Snake,Cottn,Shrew	
212-111↓	Snake,Bat	
212-221↓	Snake,Cottn,Shrew	
213-111↓	Snake,Bat	
213-212↓	Snake,Bat,Shrew	
213-221	Snake,Bat,Cottn	
213-222	Bat,Snake,Shrew	
213-231	Snake,Bat,Cottn	
213-232↓	Bat,Shrew,Snake	
213-321	Snake,Cottn,Shrew	
213-322	Bat,Shrew,Snake	
213-331	Snake,Cottn,Shrew	
213-332↓	Bat,Shrew,Snake	
221-111↓	Snake,Bat	
221-212↓	Snake,Cottn,Bat	
221-221	Snake,Cottn,Mouse	
221-332↓	Cottn,Snake,Bat	
222-111↓	Snake,Bat	
222-312↓	Snake,Cottn,Bat	
222-321	Snake,Cottn,Mouse	
222-332↓	Cottn,Snake,Bat	
223-111↓	Snake,Bat	
223-211↓	Snake,Bat,Cottn	
223-212	Snake,Bat,Otter	
223-221	Snake,Bat,Cottn	
223-222	Bat,Snake,Otter	
223-231	Bat,Snake,Cottn	
223-232	Bat,Snake,Otter	
223-311	Snake,Cottn,Bat	
223-312	Snake,Bat,Otter	
223-321	Snake,Cottn,Bat	
223-322	Bat,Snake,Otter	
223-331	Cottn,Bat,Snake	
223-332	Bat,Otter,Cottn	
231-111↓	Snake,Cottn,Bat	
231-211	Cottn,Snake,Mouse	
231-212	Cottn,Snake,Bat	
231-221	Cottn,Snake,Mouse	
231-222	Cottn,Bat,Snake	
231-231	Cottn,Mouse,Snake	
231-232	Cottn,Bat,Mouse	
231-312↓	Cottn,Snake,Bat	
231-321	Cottn,Mouse	
232-111↓	Snake,Bat,Cottn	
232-231	Cottn,Bat,Mouse	
232-232	Cottn,Bat,Otter	
232-311	Cottn,Snake,Mouse	
232-312	Cottn,Bat,Snake	
232-321	Cottn,Mouse,Bat	
232-322	Cottn,Bat,Otter	
232-331	Cottn,Mouse,Bat	
232-332	Cottn,Bat,Otter	
233-111↓	Bat,Snake,Cottn	
233-212↓	Bat,Otter,Cottn	
233-311	Cottn,Bat,Snake	
233-312↓	Bat,Otter,Cottn	
241-111	Snake,Sheep,Cottn	
241-112	Bat,Snake,Sheep	

241-121↓	Sheep,Cottn,Bat	
241-132	Bat,Sheep,Beaver	
241-222↓	Sheep,Cottn,Bat	
241-231	Sheep,Cottn,Beaver	
241-322↓	Sheep,Cottn,Dog	
241-331↓	Sheep,Cottn,Beaver	
242-111↓	Snake,Sheep,Bat	
242-121	Sheep,Bat,Cottn	
242-132	Bat,Beaver,Sheep	
242-211	Sheep,Cottn,Snake	
242-212	Sheep,Cottn,Bat	
242-221	Sheep,Cottn,Beaver	
242-222	Sheep,Cottn,Bat	
242-231↓	Sheep,Cottn,Beaver	
243-111↓	Bat,Snake,Sheep	
243-121↓	Bat,Sheep,Cottn	
243-131	Bat,Beaver,Sheep	
243-132	Bat,Beaver,Pr.Dog	
243-211	Sheep,Bat,Cottn	
243-212	Bat,Sheep,Beaver	
243-221	Sheep,Bat,Cottn	
243-222↓	Bat,Sheep,Beaver	
243-232	Beaver,Bat,Pr.Dog	
243-311	Sheep,Cottn,Bat	
243-312	Bat,Sheep,Beaver	
243-321	Sheep,Cottn,Bat	
243-322	Bat,Sheep,Beaver	
243-331	Beaver,Sheep,Pr.Dog	
243-332	Beaver,Bat,Pr.Dog	
311-111↓	Snake,Shrew	
311-121↓	Snake,Cottn,Shrew	
312-111↓	Snake,Shrew	
312-121↓	Snake,Cottn,Shrew	
313-111↓	Snake,Bat,Shrew	
313-121	Snake,Cottn,Shrew	
313-122	Bat,Shrew,Snake	
313-131	Snake,Cottn,Shrew	
313-132	Bat,Shrew,Snake	
313-211	Snake,Cottn,Shrew	
313-212	Shrew,Snake,Otter	
313-221	Cottn,Shrew,Snake	
313-222↓	Shrew,Otter,Cottn	
313-311	Cottn,Shrew,Snake	
313-312↓	Shrew,Otter,Cottn	
321-111↓	Snake,Cottn	
321-312↓	Cottn,Snake,Deer	
322-111	Snake,Cottn	
322-112↓	Snake,Cottn,Bat	
322-312↓	Cottn,Snake,Deer	
322-322↓	Cottn,Deer,Otter	
323-111	Snake,Cottn,Bat	
323-112	Snake,Bat,Otter	
323-121	Snake,Cottn,Bat	
323-122	Bat,Snake,Otter	
323-131	Cottn,Bat,Snake	
323-132	Bat,Otter,Cottn	
323-211↓	Cottn,Snake,Otter	
323-231↓	Cottn,Otter,Bat	
331-111	Cottn,Snake	
331-112↓	Cottn,Snake,Bat	
331-212↓	Cottn,Otter,Snake	
332-111↓	Cottn,Snake,Bat	
332-122	Cottn,Bat,Otter	
332-131	Cottn,Bat,Snake	
332-132↓	Cottn,Bat,Otter	

333-111	Cottn,Bat,Snake	
333-112↓	Bat,Otter,Cottn	
341-111	Cottn,Snake	
341-221↓	Cottn,Sheep,Dog	
341-332↓	Cottn,Dog,Pr.Dog	
342-111↓	Cottn,Bat,Dog	
342-121	Cottn,Sheep,Dog	
342-122↓	Cottn,Bat,Dog	
342-132	Cottn,Bat,Pr.Dog	
342-211↓	Cottn,Sheep,Dog	
342-231	Cottn,Sheep,Pr.Dog	
342-321↓	Cottn,Sheep,Dog	
342-332	Cottn,Pr.Dog,Dog	
343-111↓	Cottn,Bat,Otter	
343-131	Pr.Dog,Cottn,Bat	
343-132	Bat,Pr.Dog,Otter	
343-212↓	Otter,Cottn,Bat	
343-221↓	Cottn,Otter,Pr.Dog	
411-111↓	Cottn,Pcock	
411-312↓	Cottn,Deer,Pcock	
412-111↓	Cottn,Shrew,Deer	
413-111↓	Cottn,Deer	
421-111↓	Cottn,Snake	
421-322↓	Cottn,Deer,Swan	
422-111↓	Cottn,Snake	
422-332↓	Cottn,Deer,Swan	
423-111↓	Cottn,Snake	
423-122↓	Cottn,Bat	
423-322↓	Cottn,Deer,Swan	
431-111↓	Cottn,Swan	
432-111↓	Cottn,Swan	
433-111↓	Cottn,Bat	
433-312↓	Cottn,Swan	
441-111↓	Cottontail	
442-111↓	Cottontail	
442-312↓	Cottn,Swan	
443-111↓	Cottn,Pr.Dog	

124-

111-111↓	Snake,Bat	
111-232↓	Snake,Shrew,Cottn	
112-111↓	Snake,Bat	
112-322↓	Snake,Shrew,Cottn	
113-111↓	Snake,Bat	
113-231↓	Snake,Bat,Cottn	
113-322	Bat,Snake,Shrew	
113-331	Snake,Cottn,Bat	
113-332↓	Bat,Snake,Baboon	
121-111↓	Snake,Bat	
121-332↓	Cottn,Snake,Bat	
122-111↓	Snake,Bat	
122-332↓	Cottn,Snake,Bat	
123-111↓	Snake,Bat	
123-231↓	Bat,Snake,Cottn	
123-232	Bat,Snake,Baboon	
123-311↓	Snake,Cottn,Bat	
123-332	Bat,Baboon,Cottn	
131-111↓	Snake,Cottn,Bat	
132-111↓	Snake,Bat,Cottn	
133-111↓	Bat,Snake	
133-331↓	Bat,Cottn,Baboon	
141-111	Snake,Sheep,Cottn	
141-112	Bat,Dog,Snake	
141-121	Sheep,Cottn,Dog	
141-122	Bat,Dog,Sheep	

(124 cont'd)
141-131   Sheep,Cottn,Dog
141-132   Bat,Dog,Sheep
141-211↓ Sheep,Cottn,Dog
141-232   Dog,Sheep,Pr.Dog
141-311↓ Sheep,Cottn,Dog
141-332   Dog,Sheep,Pr.Dog
142-111   Snake,Sheep,Bat
142-112   Bat,Dog,Snake
142-121   Sheep,Bat,Cottn
142-122   Bat,Dog,Sheep
142-131   Sheep,Bat,Cottn
142-132   Bat,Pr.Dog,Dog
142-211↓ Sheep,Cottn,Dog
142-231   Sheep,Cottn,Pr.Dog
142-232   Pr.Dog,Dog,Beaver
142-311↓ Sheep,Cottn,Dog
142-331   Sheep,Cottn,Pr.Dog
142-332   Pr.Dog,Dog,Beaver
143-111↓ Bat,Snake,Sheep
143-211↓ Sheep,Bat,Pr.Dog
143-212   Bat,Pr.Dog,Dog
143-221   Sheep,Pr.Dog,Bat
143-222   Bat,Pr.Dog,Dog
143-231   Pr.Dog,Sheep,Beaver
143-232   Pr.Dog,Bat,Beaver
143-311   Sheep,Pr.Dog,Cottn
143-312   Bat,Pr.Dog,Dog
143-321   Sheep,Pr.Dog,Cottn
143-322   Pr.Dog,Bat,Dog
143-331   Pr.Dog,Sheep,Beaver
143-332   Pr.Dog,W.Dog,Beaver
211-111↓ Snake,Bat
211-222↓ Snake,Shrew,Cottn
212-111↓ Snake,Bat
212-222↓ Snake,Shrew,Cottn
213-111↓ Snake,Bat
213-221↓ Snake,Bat,Cottn
213-222   Bat,Snake,Shrew
213-231   Snake,Bat,Cottn
213-232↓ Bat,Snake,Shrew
213-321   Snake,Cottn,Bat
213-322   Bat,Snake,Shrew
213-331   Snake,Cottn,Bat
213-332   Bat,Shrew,Pr.Dog
221-111↓ Snake,Bat
221-332↓ Cottn,Snake,Bat
222-111↓ Snake,Bat
222-332↓ Cottn,Snake,Bat
223-111↓ Snake,Bat
223-221↓ Snake,Bat,Cottn
223-332   Bat,Baboon,Pr.Dog
231-111   Snake,Cottn
231-112↓ Snake,Bat,Cottn
232-111↓ Snake,Bat,Cottn
232-231↓ Cottn,Bat,Mouse
233-111↓ Bat,Snake,Cottn
233-221↓ Bat,Cottn,Otter
233-231   Bat,Cottn,Baboon
233-232   Bat,Baboon,Pr.Dog
233-331↓ Cottn,Bat,Baboon
233-332   Bat,Baboon,Pr.Dog
241-111   Snake,Sheep,Dog
241-112   Dog,Bat,Snake
241-121   Sheep,Dog,Cottn

241-122   Dog,Bat,Sheep
241-131   Sheep,Dog,Cottn
241-132   Dog,Bat,Pr.Dog
241-211   Sheep,Dog,Cottn
241-232   Dog,Pr.Dog,Sheep
241-311   Dog,Pr.Dog,Sheep
241-332   Dog,Pr.Dog,Sheep
242-111   Snake,Sheep,Dog
242-112   Bat,Dog,Snake
242-121↓ Sheep,Dog,Bat
242-131   Sheep,Pr.Dog,Dog
242-132   Bat,Pr.Dog,Dog
242-211   Sheep,Dog,Cottn
242-222↓ Dog,Sheep,Pr.Dog
242-232   Pr.Dog,Dog,Beaver
242-311   Sheep,Dog,Cottn
242-322↓ Dog,Sheep,Pr.Dog
242-332   Pr.Dog,Dog,Beaver
243-111↓ Bat,Snake,Sheep
243-131↓ Pr.Dog,Bat,Sheep
243-211   Sheep,Pr.Dog,Dog
243-212   Bat,Pr.Dog,Dog
243-221   Pr.Dog,Sheep,Dog
243-222↓ Pr.Dog,Bat,Dog
243-311   Sheep,Pr.Dog,Dog
243-312   Pr.Dog,Dog,Bat
243-321   Pr.Dog,Sheep,Dog
243-322   Pr.Dog,Dog,Bat
243-331↓ Pr.Dog,Sheep
311-111↓ Snake,Shrew
311-121↓ Snake,Cottn,Shrew
311-332↓ Shrew,Cottn,Deer
312-111↓ Snake,Shrew
312-121↓ Snake,Cottn,Shrew
312-332↓ Shrew,Cottn,Deer
313-111↓ Snake,Bat,Shrew
313-121   Snake,Cottn,Bat
313-122   Bat,Snake,Shrew
313-131   Snake,Cottn,Bat
313-132   Bat,Shrew,Pr.Dog
313-211↓ Snake,Cottn,Shrew
313-222   Shrew,Cottn,Otter
313-231↓ Cottn,Shrew,Pr.Dog
313-311↓ Cottn,Snake,Shrew
313-321   Cottn,Shrew,Otter
313-332   Shrew,Pr.Dog,Cottn
321-111↓ Snake,Cottn
321-312↓ Cottn,Snake,Deer
322-111   Snake,Cottn
322-312↓ Cottn,Snake,Deer
323-111↓ Snake,Cottn,Bat
323-132   Bat,Pr.Dog,Cottn
323-211↓ Snake,Cottn,Bat
323-222   Cottn,Otter,Bat
323-231   Cottn,Pr.Dog,Otter
323-322↓ Cottn,Otter,Bat
323-332↓ Pr.Dog,Cottn,Otter
331-111   Cottn,Snake
331-112↓ Cottn,Snake,Bat
331-222↓ Cottn,Snake,Dog
332-111↓ Cottn,Snake,Bat
332-122↓ Cottn,Bat,Dog
332-212↓ Cottn,Dog,Otter
332-232↓ Cottn,Pr.Dog,Dog
332-322↓ Cottn,Dog,Otter

333-111   Cottn,Bat,Snake
333-112   Bat,Cottn,Otter
333-131↓ Cottn,Bat,Pr.Dog
333-211↓ Cottn,Otter,Bat
333-231   Cottn,Pr.Dog,Otter
333-322↓ Cottn,Otter,Bat
333-331   Cottn,Pr.Dog,Otter
341-111↓ Dog,Cottn
341-131↓ Dog,Cottn,Pr.Dog
342-111↓ Dog,Cottn,Pr.Dog
343-111   Pr.Dog,Dog,Cottn
343-112   Pr.Dog,Dog,Bat
343-121   Pr.Dog,Dog,Cottn
343-122↓ Pr.Dog,Dog,Bat
343-321↓ Pr.Dog,Dog,Cottn
411-111↓ Cottn,Pcock
411-312↓ Cottn,Deer,Pcock
412-111↓ Cottn,Deer,SeaLn
413-111↓ Cottn,Deer,SeaLn
421-111↓ Cottn,Deer
422-111↓ Cottn,Deer,SeaLn
423-111↓ Cottn,Deer
431-111↓ Cottn,Swan
432-111↓ Cottontail
433-111↓ Cottontail
433-122↓ Cottn,Bat
433-322↓ Cottn,Swan
441-111↓ Cottontail
442-111↓ Cottontail
442-232↓ Cottn,Pr.Dog,Dog
443-111↓ Cottn,Pr.Dog

131-
111-111↓ Snake,Porcp
111-212↓ Snake,Shrew,Porcp
112-111↓ Snake,Porcp
112-122↓ Porcp,Snake,Shrew
113-111   Snake,Porcp
113-112↓ Snake,Porcp,Bat
113-212↓ Snake,Shrew,Porcp
113-222   Shrew,Porcp,Bat
113-231   Shrew,Snake,Porcp
113-232   Shrew,Porcp,Bat
113-312↓ Shrew,Snake,Porcp
113-322   Shrew,Porcp,Bat
113-331   Shrew,Snake,Porcp
113-332   Shrew,Porcp,Bat
121-111↓ Snake,Porcp
122-111↓ Snake,Porcp
122-222↓ Porcp,Snake,Bat
122-231↓ Snake,Porcp,Mouse
122-322   Porcp,Snake,Bat
122-331   Snake,Porcp,Mouse
122-332↓ Porcp,Snake,Bat
123-111↓ Snake,Bat,Porcp
123-232   Bat,Porcp,Otter
123-311↓ Snake,Bat,Porcp
123-322   Bat,Porcp,Otter
123-331   Bat,Snake,Porcp
123-332   Bat,Porcp,Otter
131-111↓ Snake,Bat,Porcp
131-211   Snake,Mouse
131-212   Snake,Bat,Porcp
131-221   Mouse,Snake,Porcp
131-222   Bat,Porcp,Mouse

131-231 Mouse,Snake,Porcp	231-231 Mouse,Snake,Bat	332-231↓ Otter,Mouse,Bat
131-232 Bat,Porcp,Mouse	231-232 Bat,Mouse,Otter	332-232 Otter,Bat,Badger
131-311 Snake,Mouse,Porcp	231-311 Snake,Mouse,Otter	332-311 Otter,Snake,Mouse
131-312 Snake,Mouse,Bat	231-312 Snake,Mouse,Bat	332-312 Otter,Bat
131-321 Mouse,Snake,Porcp	231-321 Mouse,Snake,Otter	332-321 Otter,Mouse,Badger
131-322 Mouse,Bat,Porcp	231-332↓ Mouse,Bat,Otter	332-322 Otter,Bat,Badger
131-331 Mouse,Snake,Porcp	232-111 Snake,Bat,Mouse	332-331 Otter,Badger,Mouse
131-332 Mouse,Bat,Porcp	232-112 Bat,Snake,Otter	332-332 Otter,Badger,Bat
132-111 Snake,Bat,Porcp	232-121 Bat,Snake,Mouse	333-111↓ Otter,Bat,Snake
132-211 Snake,Mouse,Bat	232-122 Bat,Snake,Otter	333-332↓ Otter,Bat,Badger
132-212 Bat,Snake,Porcp	232-131 Bat,Snake,Mouse	341-111↓ Snake,Otter,Bat
132-221 Mouse,Bat,Snake	232-132 Bat,Snake,Otter	341-211 Otter,Snake,Mouse
132-222 Bat,Porcp,Mouse	232-211 Snake,Mouse,Bat	341-212 Otter,Bat
132-231 Mouse,Bat,Snake	232-212 Bat,Snake,Otter	341-221↓ Otter,Mouse
132-232 Bat,Porcp,Mouse	232-221 Mouse,Bat,Snake	341-232 Otter,Bat
132-311↓ Snake,Mouse,Bat	232-222↓ Bat,Otter,Mouse	341-311↓ Otter,Mouse,Snake
132-322 Bat,Mouse,Otter	232-311 Snake,Mouse,Otter	341-331↓ Otter,Badger,Mouse
133-111↓ Bat,Snake	232-312 Bat,Otter,Snake	342-111↓ Snake,Otter,Bat
133-331↓ Bat,Otter,Mouse	232-321↓ Mouse,Otter,Bat	342-211 Otter,Snake,Mouse
141-111 Snake,Bat	233-111↓ Bat,Snake,Otter	342-212↓ Otter,Bat
141-131↓ Bat,Snake,Porcp	233-322 Bat,Otter,Mouse	342-232 Otter,Mouse
141-211↓ Snake,Mouse,Bat	241-111↓ Snake,Bat	342-232↓ Otter,Bat
141-222 Bat,Mouse,Porcp	241-131↓ Bat,Snake,Mouse	342-321↓ Otter,Mouse
141-231 Mouse,Bat,Snake	241-222 Bat,Mouse,Otter	342-331↓ Otter,Badger
141-232 Bat,Mouse,Porcp	241-311 Mouse,Snake,Otter	343-111↓ Otter,Bat
141-311 Mouse,Snake,Bat	241-312↓ Mouse,Bat,Otter	411-111↓ Shrew,Snake
141-332↓ Mouse,Bat,Otter	242-111 Snake,Bat	412-111↓ Shrew,Snake
142-111 Snake,Bat	242-122↓ Bat,Snake,Otter	413-111↓ Shrew,Snake,Otter
142-131↓ Bat,Snake,Porcp	242-131↓ Bat,Snake,Mouse	413-222↓ Shrew,Otter,W.Cat
142-211↓ Snake,Mouse,Bat	242-212 Bat,Otter,Snake	421-111↓ Snake,Cottn
142-222 Bat,Mouse,Otter	242-221↓ Mouse,Bat,Otter	421-122↓ Snake,Cottn,W.Cat
142-231 Mouse,Bat,Beaver	242-311 Mouse,Snake,Otter	421-211↓ Cottn,Snake,Shrew
142-312 Bat,Mouse,Otter	242-312↓ Bat,Otter,Mouse	421-222↓ Cottn,W.Cat,Shrew
142-331 Mouse,Bat,Beaver	243-111 Bat,Snake	421-312↓ Cottn,SeaLn,Shrew
143-111↓ Bat,Snake	243-331↓ Otter,Bat,Mouse	421-322↓ Cottn,W.Cat,SeaLn
143-331↓ Bat,Otter,Mouse	311-111↓ Snake,Shrew	422-111 Snake,Cottn
143-332 Bat,Otter,W.Dog	312-111↓ Snake,Shrew	422-112↓ Snake,Otter,Cottn
211-111↓ Snake,Shrew	313-111↓ Snake,Shrew	422-121 Snake,Cottn,W.Cat
212-111↓ Snake,Shrew,Bat	313-112↓ Shrew,Snake,Bat	422-122 W.Cat,Snake,Otter
213-111↓ Snake,Bat	313-121 Shrew,Snake,Otter	422-131 Cottn,Snake,W.Cat
213-121↓ Snake,Bat,Shrew	313-122 Shrew,Bat,Otter	422-132 W.Cat,Otter,Cottn
213-232 Shrew,Bat,Otter	313-131 Shrew,Snake,Otter	422-211 Cottn,Snake,Otter
213-312↓ Shrew,Snake,Bat	313-132 Shrew,Bat,Otter	422-212↓ Otter,Cottn,W.Cat
213-322 Shrew,Bat,Otter	313-211↓ Shrew,Snake,Otter	422-311 Cottn,Snake,Otter
213-331 Shrew,Snake,Otter	321-111↓ Snake,Bat,Shrew	422-312↓ Otter,Cottn,W.Cat
213-332 Shrew,Bat,Otter	321-212↓ Snake,Shrew,Otter	423-111 Snake,Otter,Cottn
221-111↓ Snake,Bat	321-332 Shrew,Otter,Badger	423-112 Otter,Snake,Bat
221-332↓ Snake,Mouse,Bat	322-111↓ Snake,Bat	423-121 Otter,Snake,Cottn
222-111↓ Snake,Bat	322-211↓ Snake,Otter,Shrew	423-122 Otter,Bat,W.Cat
222-132↓ Snake,Bat,Porcp	322-332 Otter,Shrew,Badger	423-131 Otter,W.Cat,Cottn
222-212 Snake,Bat,Otter	323-111↓ Snake,Otter,Bat	423-132 Otter,W.Cat,Bat
222-221 Snake,Mouse,Bat	323-222 Otter,Bat,Shrew	423-211 Otter,Cottn,Snake
222-222 Snake,Bat,Otter	323-231 Otter,Bat,Snake	423-221↓ Otter,Cottn,W.Cat
222-231 Snake,Mouse,Bat	323-232 Otter,Bat,Shrew	423-311 Otter,Cottn,Snake
222-232 Snake,Bat,Otter	323-312↓ Otter,Snake,Bat	423-331↓ Otter,W.Cat,Cottn
222-311 Snake,Mouse	323-322↓ Otter,Bat,Shrew	431-111 Cottn,Snake
222-312 Snake,Bat,Otter	331-111 Snake,Otter	431-112↓ Cottn,Otter,Snake
222-321 Snake,Mouse,Otter	331-112↓ Snake,Bat,Otter	431-312↓ Cottn,Swan,Otter
222-322 Snake,Bat,Otter	331-211 Otter,Snake,Mouse	432-111 Cottn,Snake,Otter
222-331 Snake,Mouse,Otter	331-212 Otter,Snake,Bat	432-332↓ Otter,Cottn,Swan
222-332↓ Snake,Bat,Otter	331-221↓ Otter,Mouse,Snake	433-111↓ Otter,Cottn,Bat
223-111 Snake,Bat	331-331↓ Otter,Badger,Mouse	441-111↓ Cottn,Snake,Otter
223-112↓ Snake,Bat,Otter	332-111↓ Snake,Otter,Bat	441-312↓ Cottn,Swan,Otter
231-111↓ Snake,Bat,Mouse	332-211 Otter,Snake,Mouse	441-331 Cottn,Sable,Otter
231-222 Bat,Mouse,Otter	332-212 Otter,Bat,Snake	441-332 Sable,Cottn,Swan

(131 cont'd)
442-111 Cottn,Otter,Snake
442-322↓ Otter,Cottn,Swan
442-331↓ Cottn,Otter,Sable
443-111↓ Otter,Cottn,Bat

132-
111-111 Snake,Shrew
111-112↓ Shrew,Snake,Porcp
112-111↓ Snake,Shrew,Porcp
113-111↓ Snake,Shrew
113-112↓ Shrew,Snake,Porcp
113-122 Shrew,Porcp,Bat
113-131 Shrew,Snake,Porcp
113-132 Shrew,Porcp,Bat
113-311↓ Shrew,Snake,Otter
121-111↓ Snake,Porcp
121-212↓ Snake,Porcp,Shrew
121-232 Porcp,Shrew,Otter
121-311↓ Snake,Porcp,Shrew
121-322 Porcp,Shrew,Otter
121-331 Snake,Porcp,Shrew
121-332 Porcp,Shrew,Otter
122-111↓ Snake,Porcp
122-132↓ Porcp,Snake,Bat
122-212↓ Snake,Porcp,Otter
122-232 Porcp,Otter,Shrew
122-311↓ Snake,Otter,Porcp
122-322 Otter,Porcp,Shrew
122-331 Otter,Snake,Porcp
122-332 Otter,Porcp,Shrew
123-111 Snake,Bat
123-112↓ Snake,Bat,Porcp
123-122 Bat,Porcp,Otter
123-131 Bat,Snake,Porcp
123-132 Bat,Porcp,Otter
123-211↓ Snake,Otter,Bat
123-232 Otter,Bat,Porcp
123-311↓ Otter,Snake
123-322↓ Otter,Bat
131-111↓ Snake,Bat,Porcp
131-122 Bat,Porcp,Otter
131-131 Snake,Porcp,Bat
131-132 Bat,Porcp,Otter
131-211 Snake,Otter,Mouse
131-212 Otter,Snake,Bat
131-221 Otter,Mouse,Cottn
131-222 Otter,Bat,Porcp
131-231 Otter,Mouse,Cottn
131-232 Otter,Bat,Porcp
131-311↓ Otter,Snake,Mouse
131-321↓ Otter,Mouse,Cottn
131-331↓ Otter,Badger,Mouse
132-111 Snake,Bat
132-112↓ Bat,Snake,Otter
132-122 Bat,Otter,Porcp
132-131 Bat,Otter,Snake
132-132 Bat,Otter,Porcp
132-211 Otter,Snake,Mouse
132-212 Otter,Bat,Snake
132-221 Otter,Mouse,Cottn
132-222 Otter,Bat
132-231 Otter,Mouse,Cottn
132-232 Otter,Bat
132-311↓ Otter,Snake,Mouse

132-321 Otter,Mouse,Cottn
132-322 Otter,Bat
132-331↓ Otter,Badger,Mouse
133-111↓ Bat,Otter,Snake
141-111↓ Snake,Bat,Otter
141-131↓ Bat,Otter,Beaver
141-211 Otter,Snake,Sheep
141-212 Otter,Bat,Snake
141-221 Otter,Sheep,Mouse
141-222 Otter,Bat,Sheep
141-231 Otter,Beaver,Sheep
141-232 Otter,Beaver,Bat
141-311↓ Otter,Sheep,Mouse
141-322↓ Otter,Sheep,Beaver
141-332 Otter,Beaver,Badger
142-111↓ Snake,Bat,Otter
142-122 Bat,Otter,Porcp
142-131↓ Bat,Beaver,Otter
142-211 Otter,Snake,Sheep
142-212 Otter,Bat,Beaver
142-221 Otter,Sheep,Mouse
142-222 Otter,Bat,Beaver
142-231 Beaver,Otter,Sheep
142-232 Beaver,Otter,Bat
142-311 Otter,Sheep,Mouse
142-312 Otter,Beaver,Bat
142-321 Otter,Sheep,Mouse
142-322 Otter,Beaver,Bat
142-331 Beaver,Otter,Sheep
142-332 Beaver,Otter,Badger
143-111↓ Bat,Otter,Snake
143-231↓ Otter,Beaver,Bat
143-331↓ Otter,Beaver,W.Dog
211-111↓ Snake,Shrew
212-111↓ Snake,Shrew
213-111↓ Snake,Shrew
213-112↓ Shrew,Snake,Bat
213-121 Shrew,Snake,Otter
213-122 Shrew,Bat,Otter
213-131 Shrew,Snake
213-132 Shrew,Bat,Otter
213-211↓ Shrew,Snake,Otter
221-111↓ Snake,Bat
221-122↓ Snake,Bat,Shrew
221-211↓ Snake,Shrew,Otter
221-332 Shrew,Otter,Badger
222-111↓ Snake,Bat,Otter
222-211↓ Snake,Otter,Shrew
222-332 Otter,Shrew,Badger
223-111↓ Snake,Otter,Bat
223-222 Otter,Bat,Shrew
223-231 Otter,Bat,Snake
223-232 Otter,Bat,Shrew
223-312↓ Otter,Snake,Bat
231-111↓ Snake,Otter,Bat
232-111↓ Snake,Otter,Bat
232-221 Otter,Mouse,Cottn
232-222 Otter,Bat
232-231 Otter,Mouse,Cottn
232-232 Otter,Bat,Badger
232-311 Otter,Snake,Mouse
232-312 Otter,Bat,Snake
232-321 Otter,Mouse,Cottn
232-322 Otter,Bat,Badger
232-331 Otter,Badger,Mouse

232-332 Otter,Badger,Bat
233-111↓ Otter,Bat,Snake
233-332↓ Otter,Bat,Badger
241-111↓ Snake,Otter,Bat
241-131↓ Otter,Bat,Beaver
241-221 Otter,Sheep,Mouse
241-222 Otter,Bat
241-231↓ Otter,Beaver,Sheep
241-311↓ Otter,Sheep,Mouse
241-331↓ Otter,Badger,Beaver
242-111↓ Snake,Otter,Bat
242-131↓ Otter,Bat,Beaver
242-221 Otter,Sheep,Mouse
242-222 Otter,Bat,Beaver
242-231 Otter,Beaver,Sheep
242-232 Otter,Beaver,Bat
242-311↓ Otter,Sheep,Mouse
242-331↓ Otter,Beaver,Badger
243-111↓ Otter,Bat,Snake
243-232↓ Otter,Beaver,Bat
311-111↓ Shrew,Snake
312-111↓ Shrew,Snake
313-111↓ Shrew,Otter
321-111↓ Snake,Shrew,Otter
321-221↓ Shrew,Otter,Cottn
321-232 Shrew,Otter,Badger
321-321↓ Shrew,Otter,Cottn
321-322↓ Shrew,Otter,Badger
322-111 Snake,Otter,Shrew
322-231↓ Otter,Shrew,Cottn
322-232 Otter,Shrew,W.Cat
322-311↓ Otter,Shrew,Snake
322-321 Otter,Shrew,Cottn
322-322↓ Otter,Shrew,Badger
323-111 Otter,Snake,Shrew
323-112 Otter,Snake,Bat
323-121 Otter,Snake,Shrew
323-122↓ Otter,Bat,Shrew
323-332↓ Otter,Shrew,Badger
331-111 Otter,Snake,Cottn
331-112 Otter,Snake,Bat
331-121 Otter,Cottn,Snake
331-122 Otter,Bat,Shrew
331-131 Otter,Cottn
331-132 Otter,Bat
331-211↓ Otter,Cottn,Shrew
331-231 Otter,Cottn,Badger
331-232 Otter,Badger,Shrew
331-321↓ Otter,Cottn,Badger
331-322 Otter,Badger,Shrew
331-331↓ Otter,Badger,Cottn
332-111 Otter,Snake,Cottn
332-112 Otter,Bat,Snake
332-331↓ Otter,Badger,Cottn
333-111↓ Otter,Bat
333-332 Otter,Badger
341-111↓ Otter,Snake,Cottn
341-321↓ Otter,Cottn,Badger
342-111↓ Otter,Bat
342-211↓ Otter,Cottn
342-232↓ Otter,Badger,Beaver
343-111↓ Otter,Bat
343-121↓ Otter,Pengn,Bat
411-111↓ Shrew,Pcock
412-111↓ Shrew,Cottn

412-222↓ Shrew,W.Cat
413-111↓ Shrew,Otter
413-222↓ Shrew,Otter,W.Cat
421-111 Cottn,Snake
421-112↓ Cottn,Shrew,Otter
421-122↓ Cottn,W.Cat,Shrew
421-212↓ Cottn,Shrew,Otter
421-222↓ Cottn,W.Cat,Shrew
421-312↓ Cottn,SeaLn,Shrew
421-322↓ Cottn,W.Cat,SeaLn
422-111 Cottn,Snake
422-112↓ Cottn,Otter,W.Cat
423-111 Otter,Cottn,Snake
423-121↓ Otter,Cottn,W.Cat
431-111↓ Cottn,Otter
431-322↓ Cottn,Swan,Otter
432-111↓ Cottn,Otter
432-112↓ Cottn,Otter,W.Cat
432-311↓ Cottn,Otter,Swan
432-331 Cottn,Otter,Badger
432-332↓ Cottn,Otter,Swan
433-111↓ Otter,Cottn
433-332↓ Otter,Cottn,W.Cat
441-111↓ Cottn,Otter
441-312↓ Cottn,Swan,Otter
441-332 Cottn,Sable,Swan
442-111↓ Cottn,Otter
442-332↓ Cottn,Sable,Otter
443-111↓ Otter,Cottn

133-

111-111 Snake,Shrew
111-112↓ Shrew,Snake,Porcp
112-111↓ Snake,Shrew
113-111↓ Snake,Shrew
113-112↓ Shrew,Snake,Porcp
113-122 Shrew,Porcp,Bat
113-131 Shrew,Snake,Porcp
113-132 Shrew,Porcp,Bat
113-311↓ Shrew,Snake,Otter
121-111↓ Snake,Porcp
121-212↓ Snake,Porcp,Shrew
121-221 Snake,Porcp,Cottn
121-222 Porcp,Snake,Shrew
121-231 Snake,Porcp,Cottn
121-232 Porcp,Shrew,Otter
121-311 Snake,Cottn
121-312 Snake,Porcp,Shrew
121-321 Snake,Cottn,Porcp
121-322 Porcp,Shrew,Otter
121-331 Cottn,Snake,Porcp
121-332 Porcp,Shrew,Otter
122-111↓ Snake,Porcp
122-132↓ Porcp,Snake,Bat
122-212 Snake,Porcp,Otter
122-221 Snake,Porcp,Cottn
122-222 Porcp,Otter,Snake
122-231 Snake,Porcp,Cottn
122-232 Porcp,Otter,Shrew
122-311 Snake,Cottn,Otter
122-312 Snake,Otter,Porcp
122-321 Snake,Cottn,Otter
122-322 Otter,Porcp,Shrew
122-331 Cottn,Otter,Snake
122-332 Otter,Porcp,Shrew

123-111 Snake,Bat
123-112↓ Snake,Bat,Porcp
123-122 Bat,Porcp,Otter
123-131 Bat,Snake,Porcp
123-132 Bat,Porcp,Otter
123-312↓ Otter,Snake,Bat
123-332 Otter,Bat,Baboon
131-111 Snake,Cottn
131-112 Snake,Bat,Porcp
131-121 Snake,Cottn,Porcp
131-122 Bat,Porcp,Otter
131-131 Cottn,Snake,Porcp
131-132 Bat,Porcp,Otter
131-211↓ Cottn,Snake,Otter
131-221 Cottn,Otter,Mouse
131-222 Otter,Cottn,Bat
131-231 Cottn,Otter,Mouse
131-232 Otter,Cottn,Bat
131-311 Cottn,Otter,Snake
131-322 Otter,Cottn,Mouse
131-331↓ Cottn,Otter,Badger
132-111 Snake,Bat,Cottn
132-112 Bat,Snake,Otter
132-121 Bat,Snake,Cottn
132-122 Bat,Otter,Porcp
132-131 Bat,Cottn,Otter
132-132 Bat,Otter,Porcp
132-211 Cottn,Otter,Snake
132-212 Otter,Cottn,Bat
132-221 Cottn,Otter,Mouse
132-222 Otter,Cottn,Bat
132-231 Cottn,Otter,Mouse
132-232 Otter,Cottn,Bat
132-311 Cottn,Otter,Snake
132-312 Otter,Cottn,Bat
132-331↓ Cottn,Otter,Badger
133-111↓ Bat,Otter,Snake
133-332↓ Otter,Bat,Baboon
141-111 Snake,Sheep,Cottn
141-112 Bat,Snake,Sheep
141-121 Sheep,Cottn,Bat
141-122 Bat,Sheep,Otter
141-131 Sheep,Cottn,Bat
141-132 Bat,Sheep,Otter
141-211↓ Sheep,Cottn,Otter
141-232 Sheep,Otter,Beaver
141-311↓ Sheep,Cottn,Otter
141-331 Sheep,Cottn,W.Dog
141-332 W.Dog,Sheep,Otter
142-111 Snake,Sheep,Bat
142-112 Bat,Otter,Snake
142-121 Sheep,Bat,Cottn
142-122 Bat,Otter,Sheep
142-131 Sheep,Bat,Cottn
142-132 Bat,Beaver,Otter
142-211↓ Sheep,Cottn,Otter
142-231 Sheep,Cottn,Beaver
142-232 Beaver,Otter,Sheep
142-311↓ Sheep,Cottn,Otter
142-322 Otter,Sheep,W.Dog
142-331 Sheep,W.Dog,Cottn
142-332 W.Dog,Beaver,Otter
143-111↓ Bat,Otter,Snake
143-221↓ Otter,Sheep,Bat
143-231 Otter,Beaver,Sheep

143-232 Otter,Beaver,Bat
143-311 Otter,Sheep,W.Dog
143-312 Otter,W.Dog,Bat
143-321 Otter,W.Dog,Sheep
143-322 Otter,W.Dog,Bat
143-331↓ W.Dog,Otter,Beaver
211-111↓ Snake,Shrew
212-111↓ Snake,Shrew
213-111↓ Snake,Shrew
213-112↓ Shrew,Snake,Bat
213-122 Shrew,Bat,Otter
213-131 Shrew,Snake,Otter
213-132 Shrew,Bat,Otter
213-211↓ Shrew,Snake,Otter
221-111↓ Snake,Bat,Shrew
221-212 Snake,Shrew,Otter
221-221 Snake,Cottn,Shrew
221-222 Shrew,Otter,Snake
221-231 Snake,Cottn,Shrew
221-232 Shrew,Otter,Snake
221-311 Snake,Cottn,Shrew
221-312 Snake,Shrew,Otter
221-321 Snake,Cottn,Shrew
221-322 Shrew,Otter,Snake
221-331 Cottn,Shrew,Otter
221-332 Shrew,Otter,Badger
222-111↓ Snake,Bat,Otter
222-211 Snake,Otter,Cottn
222-212 Snake,Otter,Shrew
222-221 Snake,Otter,Cottn
222-222 Otter,Shrew,Snake
222-231 Otter,Snake,Cottn
222-232 Otter,Shrew,Snake
222-311 Snake,Otter,Cottn
222-312 Otter,Snake,Shrew
222-321 Otter,Snake,Cottn
222-331↓ Otter,Cottn,Shrew
222-332 Otter,Shrew,Badger
223-111↓ Snake,Otter,Bat
223-232↓ Otter,Bat,Baboon
223-311↓ Otter,Snake
223-322↓ Otter,Bat
231-111 Snake,Cottn,Otter
231-112 Snake,Bat,Otter
231-121 Snake,Cottn,Otter
231-122 Bat,Otter,Snake
231-131 Cottn,Otter,Snake
231-132 Bat,Otter,Cottn
231-211 Cottn,Otter,Snake
231-222 Otter,Cottn,Bat
231-231 Cottn,Otter,Mouse
231-232 Otter,Cottn,Bat
231-321↓ Cottn,Otter,Mouse
231-322 Otter,Cottn,Badger
232-111↓ Snake,Otter,Bat
232-131↓ Otter,Bat,Cottn
232-221 Otter,Cottn,Mouse
232-222 Otter,Cottn,Bat
232-231 Otter,Cottn,Mouse
232-232 Otter,Cottn,Bat
232-321↓ Otter,Cottn,Mouse
232-322 Otter,Cottn,Bat
232-331↓ Otter,Cottn,Badger
233-111↓ Otter,Bat,Snake
233-332↓ Otter,Bat,Baboon

(133 cont'd)

241-111	Snake,Sheep,Cottn
241-112	Bat,Otter,Snake
241-121	Sheep,Cottn,Otter
241-122	Bat,Otter,Sheep
241-131	Sheep,Cottn,Otter
241-132	Bat,Otter,Sheep
241-211↓	Sheep,Cottn,Otter
241-232	Otter,Sheep,Beaver
241-311↓	Sheep,Cottn,Otter
241-332	W.Dog,Otter,Badger
242-111	Snake,Sheep,Otter
242-112	Bat,Otter,Snake
242-121↓	Sheep,Otter,Bat
242-132	Bat,Otter,Beaver
242-221↓	Sheep,Otter,Cottn
242-232	Otter,Beaver,Sheep
242-311	Sheep,Otter,Cottn
242-322	Otter,Sheep,W.Dog
243-111↓	Otter,Bat
243-221	Otter,Sheep
243-232↓	Otter,Beaver,Bat
243-332↓	W.Dog,Otter,Beaver
311-111↓	Shrew,Snake
312-111↓	Shrew,Snake
313-111↓	Shrew,Otter
321-111	Snake,Cottn,Shrew
321-112	Snake,Shrew,Otter
321-121	Snake,Cottn,Shrew
321-122	Shrew,Otter,Snake
321-131↓	Cottn,Shrew,Otter
321-332	Shrew,Otter,Badger
322-111	Snake,Otter,Cottn
322-112	Otter,Snake,Shrew
322-121	Otter,Snake,Cottn
322-122	Otter,Shrew,Snake
322-131↓	Otter,Cottn,Shrew
322-332	Otter,Shrew,Badger
323-111	Otter,Snake
323-112↓	Otter,Snake,Bat
323-121	Otter,Snake,Cottn
323-122↓	Otter,Bat,Shrew
323-332↓	Otter,Shrew,Badger
331-111↓	Cottn,Otter,Snake
331-221↓	Cottn,Otter,Shrew
331-322↓	Otter,Cottn,Badger
332-111	Otter,Cottn,Snake
332-312↓	Otter,Cottn,Badger
333-111↓	Otter,Cottn,Bat
341-111↓	Cottn,Otter
341-322↓	Otter,Cottn,Badger
342-111↓	Otter,Cottn
342-331↓	Otter,Cottn,Badger
343-111↓	Otter,Bat
343-221↓	Otter,Cottn
343-232↓	Otter,Pr.Dog,Owl
411-111↓	Shrew,Cottn,Pcock
412-111↓	Shrew,Cottn
413-111↓	Shrew,Cottn,Otter
413-131	Shrew,Cottn,W.Cat
413-132	Shrew,W.Cat,Otter
413-211↓	Shrew,Cottn,Otter
413-231	Shrew,Cottn,W.Cat
413-232	Shrew,W.Cat,Otter
413-311↓	Shrew,Cottn,Otter

413-331	Shrew,Cottn,W.Cat
413-332	Shrew,W.Cat,Otter
421-111↓	Cottn,W.Cat,Shrew
421-322↓	Cottn,SeaLn,Deer
422-111↓	Cottn,W.Cat,Otter
422-332↓	Cottn,SeaLn,W.Cat
423-111	Cottn,Otter
423-332↓	Otter,Cottn,W.Cat
431-111↓	Cottn,Otter
431-322↓	Cottn,Swan,Otter
432-111↓	Cottn,Otter
432-312↓	Cottn,Otter,Swan
433-111	Cottn,Otter
433-322↓	Otter,Cottn,Swan
441-111↓	Cottontail
442-111↓	Cottontail
443-111↓	Cottn,Otter

134-

111-111↓	Snake,Shrew,Porcp
112-111↓	Snake,Shrew
112-112↓	Snake,Shrew,Porcp
113-111↓	Snake,Shrew,Porcp
113-122	Shrew,Porcp,Bat
113-131	Shrew,Snake,Porcp
113-132	Shrew,Porcp,Bat
113-231↓	Shrew,Baboon,Otter
113-331↓	Shrew,Baboon,W.Dog
121-111↓	Snake,Porcp
121-221↓	Snake,Porcp,Cottn
121-222	Porcp,Snake,Shrew
121-231	Snake,Porcp,Cottn
121-232	Porcp,Baboon,Snake
121-311	Snake,SeaLn,Cottn
121-312	SeaLn,Snake,Porcp
121-321	SeaLn,Snake,Cottn
121-322	SeaLn,Porcp
121-331	SeaLn,Cottn,Baboon
121-332	SeaLn,Baboon,Porcp
122-111↓	Snake,Porcp
122-122↓	Porcp,Snake,Bat
122-131	Snake,Porcp,Baboon
122-132↓	Porcp,Snake,Bat
122-212	Snake,Porcp,Otter
122-221	Snake,Porcp,Cottn
122-222	Porcp,Snake,Otter
122-231	Baboon,Snake,Porcp
122-232	Baboon,Porcp,Otter
122-311	Snake,SeaLn,Cottn
122-312	SeaLn,Snake,Porcp
122-321	SeaLn,Snake,Cottn
122-322	SeaLn,Porcp,Otter
122-331	Baboon,SeaLn,Cottn
122-332	Baboon,SeaLn,Porcp
123-111	Snake,Bat
123-112↓	Snake,Bat,Porcp
123-122	Bat,Porcp,Otter
123-131	Baboon,Bat,Snake
123-132	Bat,Baboon,Porcp
123-211	Snake,Otter,Baboon
123-212	Otter,Snake,Bat
123-221↓	Otter,Baboon,Snake
123-332↓	Baboon,Otter,W.Dog
131-111	Snake,Cottn
131-112	Snake,Bat,Porcp

131-121	Snake,Cottn,Porcp
131-122	Bat,Porcp,Snake
131-131	Cottn,Baboon,Snake
131-132	Bat,Baboon,Porcp
131-211↓	Cottn,Snake,Otter
131-221	Cottn,Otter,Mouse
131-222↓	Otter,Cottn,Baboon
131-311	Cottn,Snake,Otter
131-312	Otter,Cottn,Baboon
131-321	Cottn,Otter,Mouse
131-322↓	Otter,Cottn,Baboon
132-111	Snake,Bat,Cottn
132-112	Bat,Snake,Porcp
132-121	Bat,Snake,Cottn
132-122	Bat,Porcp,Otter
132-131	Baboon,Bat,Cottn
132-132	Bat,Baboon,Porcp
132-211	Cottn,Snake,Otter
132-212	Otter,Cottn,Bat
132-221↓	Cottn,Otter,Baboon
132-311	Cottn,Otter,Snake
132-312↓	Otter,Cottn,Baboon
132-332	Baboon,Otter,W.Dog
133-111↓	Bat,Snake,Otter
133-121↓	Bat,Otter,Baboon
133-311↓	Otter,Baboon,Cottn
133-312	Otter,Baboon,Bat
133-321	Otter,Baboon,Cottn
133-332↓	Baboon,Otter,W.Dog
141-111	Snake,Sheep,Cottn
141-112	Bat,Dog,Snake
141-121	Sheep,Cottn,Dog
141-122	Bat,Dog,Sheep
141-131	Sheep,Cottn,Baboon
141-132	Bat,Baboon,W.Dog
141-211	Sheep,Cottn,Dog
141-212	Dog,Sheep,Otter
141-221	Sheep,Cottn,Dog
141-222	Dog,Sheep,W.Dog
141-231	Sheep,W.Dog,Cottn
141-232	W.Dog,Baboon,Dog
141-311	Sheep,W.Dog,Cottn
141-312	W.Dog,Dog,Sheep
141-321	Sheep,W.Dog,Cottn
141-322↓	W.Dog,Dog,Sheep
142-111	Snake,Sheep,Bat
142-112	Bat,Dog,Snake
142-121	Sheep,Bat,Cottn
142-122	Bat,Dog,Sheep
142-131	Sheep,Baboon,Bat
142-132	Bat,Baboon,W.Dog
142-211	Sheep,Cottn,Dog
142-212	Dog,Sheep,Otter
142-221	Sheep,Cottn,Dog
142-222	Dog,W.Dog,Sheep
142-231	W.Dog,Sheep,Baboon
142-232	W.Dog,Baboon,Pr.Dog
142-311	W.Dog,Sheep,Cottn
142-312	W.Dog,Dog,Sheep
142-321	W.Dog,Sheep,Cottn
142-322↓	W.Dog,Dog
143-111↓	Bat,Otter,Snake
143-121↓	Bat,Otter,Baboon
143-131	Baboon,Bat,W.Dog
143-212	Otter,W.Dog,Bat

143-221↓	Otter,W.Dog,Baboon
211-111↓	Snake,Shrew
212-111↓	Snake,Shrew
213-111↓	Snake,Shrew
213-112↓	Shrew,Snake,Bat
213-122	Shrew,Bat,Otter
213-131	Shrew,Snake,Baboon
213-132	Shrew,Bat,Baboon
213-211	Shrew,Snake
213-232↓	Shrew,Baboon,Otter
221-111↓	Snake,Bat
221-132↓	Snake,Bat,Baboon
221-212	Snake,Shrew,Otter
221-221	Snake,Cottn,Shrew
221-222	Snake,Shrew,Otter
221-231	Snake,Cottn,Baboon
221-232	Baboon,Shrew,Otter
221-311	Snake,SeaLn,Cottn
221-312	SeaLn,Snake,Shrew
221-321	SeaLn,Snake,Cottn
221-322	SeaLn,Shrew,Otter
221-331	SeaLn,Cottn,Baboon
221-332	SeaLn,Baboon,Shrew
222-111↓	Snake,Bat,Otter
222-132↓	Snake,Bat,Baboon
222-212	Snake,Otter,Shrew
222-221	Snake,Otter,Cottn
222-222	Otter,Snake,Shrew
222-231	Baboon,Snake,Otter
222-232	Baboon,Otter,Shrew
222-311	Snake,SeaLn,Otter
222-331↓	Baboon,SeaLn,Otter
223-111↓	Snake,Bat,Otter
223-131	Baboon,Bat,Snake
223-132	Bat,Baboon,Otter
223-211	Snake,Otter,Baboon
223-212	Otter,Snake,Bat
223-221↓	Otter,Baboon,Snake
223-312↓	Otter,Baboon,SeaLn
231-111	Snake,Cottn
231-112	Snake,Bat,Otter
231-121	Snake,Cottn,Bat
231-122	Bat,Otter,Snake
231-131	Cottn,Baboon,Snake
231-132	Bat,Baboon,Otter
231-211↓	Cottn,Snake,Otter
231-221	Cottn,Otter,Mouse
231-222↓	Otter,Cottn,Baboon
231-311	Cottn,Otter,Snake
231-312	Otter,Cottn,Baboon
231-321	Cottn,Otter,Mouse
231-322↓	Otter,Cottn,Baboon
231-332	Baboon,Otter,Badger
232-111	Snake,Bat,Otter
232-131	Baboon,Bat,Otter
232-212	Otter,Cottn,Bat
232-221↓	Otter,Cottn,Baboon
233-111↓	Bat,Otter,Snake
233-121↓	Bat,Otter,Baboon
233-332↓	Baboon,Otter,W.Dog
241-111	Snake,Sheep,Dog
241-112	Dog,Bat,Snake
241-121	Sheep,Dog,Cottn
241-122	Dog,Bat,Sheep
241-131	Sheep,Dog,Cottn

241-132	Dog,Bat,Baboon
241-211	Sheep,Dog,Cottn
241-212	Dog,Sheep,Otter
241-221	Sheep,Dog,Cottn
241-222	Dog,Sheep,Otter
241-231	Sheep,Dog,W.Dog
241-232	W.Dog,Dog,Baboon
241-311↓	Sheep,Dog,W.Dog
242-111	Snake,Sheep,Dog
242-112	Bat,Dog,Otter
242-121	Sheep,Dog,Bat
242-122	Bat,Dog,Otter
242-131	Sheep,Baboon,Pr.Dog
242-132	Bat,Baboon,W.Dog
242-211↓	Sheep,Dog,Otter
242-222	Dog,Otter,W.Dog
242-231	W.Dog,Sheep,Baboon
242-232	W.Dog,Baboon,Pr.Dog
242-311	W.Dog,Sheep,Dog
242-312	W.Dog,Dog,Otter
242-321	W.Dog,Sheep,Dog
242-322↓	W.Dog,Dog,Otter
243-111↓	Bat,Otter,Snake
243-121↓	Bat,Otter,Baboon
243-131	Baboon,Pr.Dog,Bat
243-132	Bat,Baboon,W.Dog
243-211	Otter,W.Dog,Baboon
243-212	Otter,W.Dog,Bat
243-221↓	Otter,W.Dog,Baboon
243-231↓	W.Dog,Baboon,Pr.Dog
243-311↓	W.Dog,Otter
311-111↓	Shrew,Snake
312-111↓	Shrew,Snake
313-111↓	Shrew,Snake,Otter
321-111	Snake,Cottn
321-112	Snake,Shrew,Otter
321-121	Snake,Cottn,Shrew
321-122	Shrew,Otter,Snake
321-131	Cottn,Snake,Shrew
321-132	Shrew,Otter,Cottn
321-211	Cottn,Snake,Shrew
321-212↓	Shrew,Otter,Cottn
321-311	SeaLn,Cottn,Shrew
321-312	SeaLn,Shrew,Otter
321-321	SeaLn,Cottn,Shrew
321-322	SeaLn,Shrew,Otter
321-331	SeaLn,Cottn,Shrew
321-332	SeaLn,Shrew,Otter
322-111	Snake,Otter,Cottn
322-112	Snake,Otter,Shrew
322-121	Snake,Otter,Cottn
322-122	Otter,Shrew,Snake
322-131	Otter,Cottn,Snake
322-132	Otter,Shrew,Cottn
322-211	Otter,Cottn,Snake
322-212↓	Otter,Shrew,Cottn
322-311	SeaLn,Otter,Cottn
322-312	SeaLn,Otter,Shrew
322-321	SeaLn,Otter,Cottn
322-322	SeaLn,Otter,Shrew
322-331	SeaLn,Otter,Cottn
322-332	SeaLn,Otter,Shrew
323-111↓	Otter,Snake
323-122↓	Otter,Bat
323-221	Otter,Cottn

323-222↓	Otter,Shrew
323-232↓	Otter,Baboon
323-312↓	Otter,SeaLn
331-111↓	Cottn,Otter,Snake
331-331↓	Cottn,Otter,Badger
332-111↓	Otter,Cottn,Snake
332-322↓	Otter,Cottn,SeaLn
332-331↓	Otter,Cottn,Badger
333-111↓	Otter,Bat
333-132↓	Otter,Bat,Baboon
341-111↓	Dog,Cottn,Otter
341-131	Dog,Cottn,Pr.Dog
341-132	Dog,Pr.Dog,Otter
341-211↓	Dog,Cottn,Otter
341-231	Dog,Cottn,Pr.Dog
341-232	Dog,Pr.Dog,Otter
341-311↓	Dog,Cottn,Otter
341-331	Dog,Cottn,Pr.Dog
341-332	Dog,W.Dog,Pr.Dog
342-111↓	Dog,Otter,Cottn
342-122↓	Dog,Otter,Pr.Dog
342-211↓	Dog,Otter,Cottn
342-222↓	Dog,Otter,Pr.Dog
342-311↓	Dog,Otter,Cottn
342-322	Dog,Otter,W.Dog
342-331↓	Pr.Dog,Dog,W.Dog
343-111↓	Otter,Pr.Dog,Dog
343-312↓	Otter,W.Dog,Pr.Dog
411-111↓	Shrew,Cottn,Pcock
411-212	Shrew,Pcock,SeaLn
411-221	Shrew,Cottn,Pcock
411-222	Shrew,Pcock,SeaLn
411-231	Shrew,Cottn,Pcock
411-232	Shrew,Pcock,SeaLn
411-311	SeaLn,Shrew,Cottn
411-312	SeaLn,Shrew,Pcock
411-321	SeaLn,Shrew,Cottn
411-322	SeaLn,Shrew,Pcock
411-331	SeaLn,Shrew,Cottn
411-332	SeaLn,Shrew,Pcock
412-111↓	Shrew,Cottn,SeaLn
413-111↓	Shrew,Cottn,SeaLn
413-132	Shrew,W.Cat,Cottn
413-211↓	Shrew,Cottn,SeaLn
413-232	Shrew,SeaLn,W.Cat
413-311	SeaLn,Shrew,Cottn
413-312	SeaLn,Dolphin,Shrew
413-321	SeaLn,Shrew,Cottn
413-322	SeaLn,Dolphin,Shrew
413-331	SeaLn,Shrew,Cottn
413-332	SeaLn,Dolphin,Shrew
421-111↓	Cottn,SeaLn
422-111↓	Cottn,SeaLn
422-322↓	SeaLn,Cottn,Dolphin
423-111	Cottn,Otter
423-132↓	Cottn,Otter,W.Cat
423-211↓	Cottn,SeaLn,Otter
423-321↓	SeaLn,Cottn,Dolphin
431-111↓	Cottn,SeaLn
432-111↓	Cottn,Otter
432-322↓	Cottn,SeaLn,Otter
433-111↓	Cottn,Otter
433-332↓	Cottn,Otter,SeaLn
441-111↓	Cottn,SeaLn
442-111↓	Cottn,SeaLn

(134 cont'd)
443-111↓ Cottn,Otter
443-122↓ Cottn,Otter,Pr.Dog
443-322↓ Cottn,Otter,SeaLn
443-331 Cottn,Pr.Dog,Otter

141-
111-111↓ Shrew,Snake
112-111↓ Shrew,Snake
113-111↓ Shrew,Snake
121-111 Snake,Porcp
121-112↓ Snake,Porcp,Shrew
121-311↓ Shrew,Badger,Porcp
122-111 Snake,Porcp
122-331↓ Shrew,Badger,Porcp
123-111↓ Snake,Porcp,Bat
123-132 Porcp,Bat,Shrew
123-211 Snake,Shrew,Porcp
123-222↓ Shrew,Porcp,Bat
123-311 Snake,Shrew,Porcp
123-322 Shrew,Porcp,Bat
123-331↓ Shrew,Badger,Porcp
131-111 Snake,Porcp,Mouse
131-112 Snake,Porcp,Bat
131-121 Porcp,Snake,Mouse
131-122 Porcp,Bat,Snake
131-131 Porcp,Mouse,Snake
131-132 Porcp,Bat,Mouse
131-211 Mouse,Snake,Shrew
131-222↓ Mouse,Shrew,Porcp
131-231↓ Mouse,Badger,Shrew
131-311 Mouse,Snake,Badger
131-312↓ Mouse,Badger,Shrew
132-111↓ Snake,Porcp,Bat
132-131↓ Porcp,Bat,Mouse
132-212 Mouse,Bat,Shrew
132-221 Mouse,Shrew,Porcp
132-222 Mouse,Bat,Shrew
132-231 Mouse,Badger,Shrew
132-232 Mouse,Bat,Badger
132-311 Mouse,Snake,Badger
132-312↓ Mouse,Badger,Shrew
133-111↓ Bat,Snake
133-311↓ Otter,Mouse,Bat
133-322 Bat,Otter,Badger
133-331 Badger,Otter,Mouse
133-332 Badger,Bat,Otter
141-111 Snake,Mouse,Porcp
141-112 Bat,Snake,Porcp
141-121↓ Mouse,Porcp,Bat
141-211 Mouse,Snake,Shrew
141-222↓ Mouse,Shrew,Bat
141-231↓ Mouse,Badger,Shrew
141-322↓ Badger,Mouse,W.Dog
142-111 Snake,Bat,Mouse
142-112 Bat,Snake,Porcp
142-121↓ Bat,Mouse,Porcp
142-211 Mouse,Snake,Shrew
142-212↓ Mouse,Bat,Shrew
142-231 Mouse,Badger,Shrew
142-232 W.Dog,Mouse,Bat
142-311 Mouse,Badger,Shrew
142-312↓ W.Dog,Mouse,Badger
143-111↓ Bat,Snake
143-211 Bat,Otter,Mouse

143-212 Bat,Otter,W.Dog
143-221 Bat,Otter,Mouse
143-222↓ Bat,Otter,W.Dog
143-311 W.Dog,Otter,Mouse
143-312 W.Dog,Bat,Otter
143-321 W.Dog,Otter,Mouse
143-322 W.Dog,Bat,Otter
143-331↓ W.Dog,Badger
211-111↓ Shrew,Snake
212-111↓ Shrew,Snake
213-111↓ Shrew,Snake
221-111↓ Snake,Shrew
222-111↓ Snake,Shrew
222-331↓ Shrew,Badger,Mouse
223-111 Snake,Bat
223-112↓ Snake,Bat,Shrew
223-211 Snake,Shrew,Otter
223-212 Shrew,Snake,Bat
223-221 Shrew,Snake,Otter
223-222↓ Shrew,Bat,Otter
223-311↓ Shrew,Snake,Otter
223-322 Shrew,Otter,Bat
223-331↓ Shrew,Badger,Otter
231-111 Snake,Mouse
231-112 Snake,Bat,Shrew
231-121 Snake,Mouse,Bat
231-122 Bat,Shrew,Snake
231-131 Mouse,Snake,Bat
231-132 Bat,Shrew,Mouse
231-211 Mouse,Snake,Shrew
231-222↓ Shrew,Mouse,Bat
231-231↓ Mouse,Badger,Shrew
232-111 Snake,Bat,Mouse
232-112 Bat,Snake,Shrew
232-121 Bat,Snake,Mouse
232-122 Bat,Shrew,Snake
232-131 Bat,Mouse,Snake
232-132 Bat,Shrew
232-211 Mouse,Snake,Shrew
232-212 Shrew,Mouse,Bat
232-221 Mouse,Shrew,Otter
232-222 Shrew,Mouse,Bat
232-231↓ Mouse,Badger,Shrew
233-111↓ Bat,Snake,Otter
233-211↓ Otter,Bat,Mouse
233-212 Bat,Otter,Shrew
233-221 Otter,Bat,Mouse
233-222 Bat,Otter,Shrew
233-231 Otter,Bat,Mouse
233-232 Bat,Otter,Badger
233-311 Otter,Mouse,Bat
233-312 Otter,Bat,Badger
233-321 Otter,Mouse,Bat
233-322 Bat,Otter,Badger
233-331 Badger,Otter,Mouse
233-332 Badger,Otter,Bat
241-111 Snake,Mouse,Bat
241-112 Bat,Snake,Shrew
241-121↓ Bat
241-211 Mouse,Shrew
241-222↓ Shrew,Mouse,Bat
241-231↓ Mouse,Badger,Shrew
241-331↓ Badger,Mouse,W.Dog
242-111 Snake,Bat,Mouse
242-112 Bat,Snake,Shrew

242-121 Bat,Mouse,Snake
242-131↓ Bat,Mouse,Shrew
242-211 Mouse,Shrew,Snake
242-212 Shrew,Mouse,Bat
242-221 Mouse,Shrew,Otter
242-222 Shrew,Mouse,Bat
242-231 Mouse,Badger,Shrew
242-232 Badger,Shrew,W.Dog
242-311 Mouse,Badger,Shrew
242-312 Badger,Shrew,W.Dog
242-321 Mouse,Badger,Shrew
242-322 Badger,W.Dog,Shrew
242-331↓ Badger,W.Dog,Mouse
243-111↓ Bat,Snake,Otter
243-211↓ Otter,Bat,Mouse
243-212 Bat,Otter,Shrew
243-221 Otter,Bat,Mouse
243-222↓ Bat,Otter,W.Dog
243-311 Otter,W.Dog,Mouse
243-312 W.Dog,Otter,Bat
243-321 W.Dog,Otter,Mouse
243-322 W.Dog,Otter,Bat
243-331↓ W.Dog,Badger,Otter
311-111↓ Shrew
312-111↓ Shrew
313-111↓ Shrew,Snake
321-111↓ Shrew,Snake
321-232↓ Shrew,Badger
322-111↓ Shrew,Snake
322-231↓ Shrew,Badger
323-111↓ Shrew,Snake,Otter
323-322↓ Shrew,Otter,Badger
331-111 Shrew,Snake,Otter
331-131↓ Shrew,Badger,Otter
331-211 Shrew,Otter,Mouse
331-212↓ Shrew,Otter,Badger
332-111 Shrew,Snake,Otter
332-112↓ Shrew,Otter,Bat
332-212↓ Shrew,Otter,Badger
333-111↓ Otter,Bat,Shrew
333-332↓ Badger,Otter,Shrew
341-111 Shrew,Snake,Otter
341-112 Shrew,Otter,Bat
341-121 Shrew,Otter,Mouse
341-122 Shrew,Otter,Bat
341-131↓ Shrew,Badger,Otter
341-211 Shrew,Otter,Mouse
341-212↓ Shrew,Otter,Badger
342-111 Shrew,Otter,Snake
342-112↓ Shrew,Otter,Bat
342-131↓ Shrew,Badger,Otter
342-211 Shrew,Otter,Mouse
342-212↓ Shrew,Otter,Badger
343-111↓ Otter,Bat,Shrew
343-231↓ Otter,Badger,Shrew
343-331↓ Badger,Otter,W.Dog
411-111↓ Shrew
412-111↓ Shrew
413-111↓ Shrew,Snake
421-111↓ Shrew,Snake
421-321↓ Shrew,Badger
422-111↓ Shrew,Snake
422-331↓ Shrew,Badger
423-111↓ Shrew,Snake,Otter
423-331↓ Shrew,Badger,Otter

431-111	Shrew,Cottn,Snake
431-112↓	Shrew,Otter,Cottn
431-131	Shrew,Cottn,Badger
431-132	Shrew,Badger,Otter
431-211↓	Shrew,Cottn,Otter
431-231	Badger,Shrew,Cottn
431-232	Badger,Shrew,Otter
431-311	Badger,Shrew,Cottn
431-312	Badger,Shrew,Otter
431-321↓	Badger,Shrew,Cottn
432-111↓	Shrew,Cottn,Otter
432-131	Shrew,Cottn,Badger
432-132	Shrew,Badger,Otter
432-211↓	Shrew,Cottn,Otter
432-231	Badger,Shrew,Cottn
432-232	Badger,Shrew,Otter
432-311	Badger,Shrew,Cottn
432-312	Badger,Shrew,Otter
432-321	Badger,Shrew,Cottn
432-322↓	Badger,Shrew,Otter
433-111	Otter,Shrew,Cottn
433-112	Otter,Bat,Shrew
433-121	Otter,Shrew,Cottn
433-122	Otter,Bat,Shrew
433-131	Otter,Shrew,Cottn
433-132	Otter,Bat,Shrew
433-231↓	Otter,Badger,Shrew
441-111↓	Shrew,Cottn,Otter
441-131	Shrew,Cottn,Badger
441-132	Shrew,Badger,Otter
441-211↓	Shrew,Cottn,Otter
441-231	Badger,Shrew,Cottn
441-232	Badger,Shrew,Otter
441-311	Badger,Shrew,Cottn
441-312	Badger,Shrew,Otter
441-321	Badger,Shrew,Cottn
441-322↓	Badger,Shrew,Otter
442-111↓	Shrew,Cottn,Otter
442-131	Shrew,Cottn,Badger
442-132	Shrew,Badger,Otter
442-211↓	Shrew,Cottn,Otter
442-231	Badger,Shrew,Cottn
442-232	Badger,Shrew,Otter
442-311	Badger,Shrew,Cottn
442-312	Badger,Shrew,Otter
442-321	Badger,Shrew,Cottn
442-322↓	Badger,Shrew,Otter
443-111	Otter,Shrew,Cottn
443-112	Otter,Bat,Shrew
443-121	Otter,Shrew,Cottn
443-122	Otter,Bat,Shrew
443-131	Otter,Shrew,Cottn
443-132	Otter,Bat,Shrew
443-332↓	Badger,Otter,W.Dog

142-

111-111↓	Shrew
112-111↓	Shrew
113-111↓	Snake,Shrew,Porcp
121-111↓	Snake,Shrew,Porcp
121-331↓	Shrew,Badger
122-111↓	Snake,Shrew,Porcp
122-321↓	Shrew,Badger
123-111	Snake,Shrew,Porcp
123-122	Shrew,Porcp,Bat

123-131	Shrew,Porcp,Otter
123-132	Shrew,Porcp,Bat
123-331↓	Shrew,Badger,Otter
131-111	Snake,Shrew,Porcp
131-122	Shrew,Porcp,Bat
131-131↓	Shrew,Badger,Porcp
131-211	Shrew,Mouse,Otter
131-212	Shrew,Otter,Badger
131-221	Shrew,Mouse,Otter
131-222	Shrew,Otter,Badger
131-231	Badger,Shrew,Mouse
131-232	Badger,Shrew,Otter
131-311	Badger,Shrew,Mouse
131-312	Badger,Shrew,Otter
131-321	Badger,Shrew,Mouse
131-322↓	Badger,Shrew,Otter
132-111	Snake,Shrew,Otter
132-112	Shrew,Bat,Otter
132-121	Shrew,Otter,Porcp
132-122	Shrew,Bat,Otter
132-131	Shrew,Badger,Otter
132-132	Shrew,Bat,Badger
132-221↓	Shrew,Otter,Mouse
132-222↓	Shrew,Otter,Badger
133-111	Otter,Bat,Snake
133-222↓	Otter,Shrew,Bat
133-332↓	Badger,Otter,W.Dog
141-111	Shrew,Snake,Mouse
141-112	Shrew,Bat,Otter
141-121	Shrew,Mouse,Otter
141-122	Shrew,Bat,Otter
141-131	Shrew,Badger,Mouse
141-132	Shrew,Badger,W.Dog
141-211	Shrew,Mouse,Otter
141-212	Shrew,Otter,Badger
141-221	Shrew,Mouse,Otter
141-222	Shrew,Otter,Badger
141-231↓	Badger,Shrew,W.Dog
142-111	Shrew,Snake,Otter
142-112↓	Shrew,Bat,Otter
142-131	Shrew,Badger,Otter
142-132	Shrew,W.Dog,Bat
142-211	Shrew,Otter,Mouse
142-212	Shrew,Otter,W.Dog
142-221	Shrew,Otter,Mouse
142-222	Shrew,Otter,W.Dog
142-231↓	Badger,Shrew,W.Dog
143-111↓	Otter,Bat,Shrew
143-131↓	Otter,W.Dog,Bat
143-211↓	Otter,W.Dog,Shrew
143-321↓	W.Dog,Otter,Badger
211-111↓	Shrew
212-111↓	Shrew
213-111↓	Shrew,Snake
221-111↓	Shrew,Snake
221-232↓	Shrew,Badger
222-111↓	Shrew,Snake
222-231↓	Shrew,Badger
223-111↓	Shrew,Snake,Otter
223-322↓	Shrew,Otter,Badger
231-111↓	Shrew,Snake,Otter
231-122	Shrew,Otter,Bat
231-212↓	Shrew,Otter,Badger
232-111	Shrew,Snake,Otter
232-112↓	Shrew,Otter,Bat

232-131↓	Shrew,Badger,Otter
232-211	Shrew,Otter,Mouse
232-212↓	Shrew,Otter,Badger
233-111↓	Otter,Bat,Shrew
233-332↓	Badger,Otter,Shrew
241-111	Shrew,Snake,Otter
241-112	Shrew,Otter,Bat
241-121	Shrew,Otter,Mouse
241-122	Shrew,Otter,Bat
241-131↓	Shrew,Badger,Otter
241-211	Shrew,Otter,Mouse
241-212↓	Shrew,Otter,Badger
241-232	Badger,Shrew,W.Dog
241-311	Badger,Shrew,Otter
241-312↓	Badger,Shrew,W.Dog
242-111	Shrew,Otter,Snake
242-112↓	Shrew,Otter,Bat
242-131↓	Shrew,Badger,Otter
242-232	Badger,Shrew,W.Dog
242-311	Badger,Shrew,Otter
242-312↓	Badger,Shrew,W.Dog
243-111↓	Otter,Bat,Shrew
243-131↓	Otter,W.Dog,Bat
243-212↓	Otter,Shrew,W.Dog
243-231↓	Otter,W.Dog,Badger
311-111↓	Shrew
312-111↓	Shrew
313-111↓	Shrew
321-111↓	Shrew
321-231↓	Shrew,Badger
322-111↓	Shrew,Snake
322-132↓	Shrew,Badger
323-111↓	Shrew,Otter
323-312↓	Shrew,Otter,Badger
331-111↓	Shrew,Otter
331-122↓	Shrew,Otter,Badger
332-111	Shrew,Otter
332-112↓	Shrew,Otter,Badger
333-111	Otter,Shrew
333-122↓	Otter,Shrew,Bat
333-221↓	Otter,Shrew,Badger
341-111↓	Shrew,Otter
341-131↓	Shrew,Badger,Otter
342-111↓	Shrew,Otter
342-131↓	Shrew,Badger,Otter
342-332	Badger,Shrew,Wolf
343-111↓	Otter,Shrew
343-222↓	Otter,Shrew,Badger
343-331↓	Badger,Otter,W.Dog
411-111↓	Shrew
412-111↓	Shrew
413-111↓	Shrew
421-111↓	Shrew
421-331↓	Shrew,Badger
422-111↓	Shrew,Cottn
422-222	Shrew,W.Cat
422-231	Shrew,Cottn
422-232↓	Shrew,W.Cat,Badger
423-111↓	Shrew,Otter
423-331↓	Shrew,Badger,Otter
431-111	Cottn,Shrew
431-112↓	Shrew,Cottn,Otter
431-131↓	Cottn,Shrew,Badger
431-211	Cottn,Shrew,Otter
431-232↓	Badger,Shrew,Cottn

(142 cont'd)

432-111↓ Cottn,Shrew,Otter
432-131 Cottn,Shrew,Badger
432-132 Shrew,Badger,Otter
432-211↓ Cottn,Shrew,Otter
432-231 Cottn,Badger,Shrew
432-232 Badger,Shrew,Otter
432-311 Cottn,Badger,Shrew
432-312 Badger,Shrew,Otter
432-321 Badger,Cottn,Shrew
432-322 Badger,Shrew,Otter
432-331 Badger,Cottn
432-332 Badger,Shrew
433-111↓ Otter,Cottn,Shrew
433-231 Otter,Cottn,Badger
433-232 Otter,Badger,Shrew
433-311 Otter,Cottn,Badger
433-312 Otter,Badger,Shrew
433-321 Otter,Badger,Cottn
433-322 Otter,Badger,Shrew
433-331↓ Badger,Otter,Cottn
441-111 Cottn,Shrew,Otter
441-132 Shrew,Badger,Cottn
441-211 Cottn,Shrew,Otter
441-232↓ Badger,Shrew,Cottn
442-111↓ Cottn,Shrew,Otter
442-131 Cottn,Shrew,Badger
442-132 Shrew,Badger,Otter
442-211↓ Cottn,Shrew,Otter
442-231 Cottn,Badger,Shrew
442-232 Badger,Shrew,Otter
442-311 Cottn,Badger,Shrew
442-312 Badger,Shrew,Otter
442-321 Badger,Cottn,Shrew
442-322 Badger,Shrew,Otter
442-331↓ Badger,Cottn
443-111↓ Otter,Cottn,Shrew
443-231 Otter,Cottn,Badger
443-232 Otter,Badger,Shrew
443-311 Otter,Cottn,Badger
443-312 Otter,Badger,Shrew
443-321 Otter,Badger,Cottn
443-322 Otter,Badger,Shrew
443-331 Badger,Otter,Cottn
443-332 Badger,Otter,W.Dog

143-

111-111↓ Shrew
112-111↓ Shrew
113-111↓ Snake,Shrew,Porcp
121-111↓ Snake,Shrew,Porcp
121-321↓ Shrew,Badger
122-111↓ Snake,Shrew,Porcp
122-331↓ Shrew,Badger
123-111 Snake,Shrew,Porcp
123-122 Shrew,Porcp,Bat
123-131 Shrew,Porcp,Otter
123-132 Shrew,Porcp,Bat
123-321↓ Shrew,Otter,Badger
123-331↓ Shrew,Badger,W.Dog
131-111 Snake,Shrew,Porcp
131-122 Shrew,Porcp,Bat
131-131↓ Shrew,Badger,Porcp
131-211 Shrew,Mouse,Cottn
131-212 Shrew,Otter

131-221 Shrew,Mouse,Cottn
131-222 Shrew,Otter,Badger
131-231 Badger,Shrew,Mouse
131-232 Badger,Shrew,Otter
131-311 Badger,Shrew,Mouse
131-312 Badger,Shrew,Otter
131-321↓ Badger,Shrew,Mouse
132-111 Snake,Shrew,Otter
132-112 Shrew,Bat,Otter
132-121 Shrew,Otter,Porcp
132-122 Shrew,Bat,Otter
132-131 Shrew,Badger,Otter
132-132 Shrew,Bat,Badger
132-211 Shrew,Otter,Mouse
132-212 Shrew,Otter,Badger
132-221 Shrew,Otter,Mouse
132-222↓ Shrew,Otter,Badger
133-111 Otter,Bat,Snake
133-222↓ Otter,Shrew,Bat
133-231 Otter,Badger,Shrew
133-232 Otter,W.Dog,Badger
133-311 Otter,Badger,Shrew
133-312↓ Otter,W.Dog,Badger
141-111 Shrew,Snake,Sheep
141-112 Shrew,Bat,W.Dog
141-121 Shrew,Sheep,Mouse
141-122 Shrew,W.Dog,Bat
141-131 W.Dog,Shrew,Sheep
141-132 W.Dog,Shrew,Badger
141-211 Shrew,Sheep,W.Dog
141-212 Shrew,W.Dog,Otter
141-221 Shrew,Sheep,W.Dog
141-222 Shrew,W.Dog,Otter
141-332↓ W.Dog,Badger,Wolf
142-111 Shrew,Snake,Sheep
142-112 Shrew,Bat,W.Dog
142-121 Shrew,Sheep,W.Dog
142-122 Shrew,W.Dog,Bat
142-131 W.Dog,Shrew,Sheep
142-132 W.Dog,Shrew,Bat
142-211 Shrew,W.Dog,Sheep
142-212 W.Dog,Shrew,Otter
142-221 W.Dog,Shrew,Sheep
142-222 W.Dog,Shrew,Otter
142-231↓ W.Dog,Badger,Shrew
143-111↓ Otter,Bat,W.Dog
143-211↓ W.Dog,Otter,Shrew
211-111↓ Shrew
212-111↓ Shrew
213-111↓ Shrew,Snake
221-111↓ Shrew,Snake
221-331↓ Shrew,Badger
222-111↓ Shrew,Snake
222-232↓ Shrew,Badger
223-111↓ Shrew,Snake,Otter
223-331↓ Shrew,Badger,Otter
223-332 Shrew,Badger,W.Dog
231-111 Shrew,Snake,Otter
231-131↓ Shrew,Badger,Otter
232-111 Shrew,Snake,Otter
232-112↓ Shrew,Otter,Bat
232-212↓ Shrew,Otter,Badger
232-332 Badger,Shrew,W.Dog
233-111↓ Otter,Bat,Shrew
233-231↓ Otter,Badger,Shrew

233-322 Otter,Badger,W.Dog
241-111 Shrew,Snake,Sheep
241-112 Shrew,Otter,Bat
241-121 Shrew,Sheep,Otter
241-122 Shrew,Otter,W.Dog
241-131 Shrew,W.Dog,Badger
241-212 Shrew,W.Dog,Otter
241-221 Shrew,Sheep,W.Dog
241-222 Shrew,W.Dog,Otter
241-231↓ W.Dog,Badger,Shrew
241-331↓ W.Dog,Badger,Wolf
242-111 Shrew,Otter,Snake
242-112 Shrew,Otter,Bat
242-121 Shrew,Otter,Sheep
242-122 Shrew,Otter,W.Dog
242-131↓ W.Dog,Shrew,Badger
242-211↓ Shrew,Otter,W.Dog
242-332↓ W.Dog,Badger,Wolf
243-111↓ Otter,Bat,W.Dog
243-211↓ Otter,W.Dog,Shrew
311-111↓ Shrew
312-111↓ Shrew
313-111↓ Shrew
321-111↓ Shrew
322-111↓ Shrew,Badger
323-111↓ Shrew,Otter
323-321↓ Shrew,Otter,Badger
331-111↓ Shrew,Otter
331-131↓ Shrew,Badger,Otter
331-211 Shrew,Otter,Cottn
331-212↓ Shrew,Otter,Badger
332-111↓ Shrew,Otter,Cottn
332-122↓ Shrew,Otter,Badger
332-211 Shrew,Otter,Cottn
332-212↓ Shrew,Otter,Badger
333-111↓ Otter,Shrew
333-221↓ Otter,Shrew,Badger
341-111↓ Shrew,Otter,Cottn
341-131↓ Shrew,Badger,Otter
341-132 Shrew,Badger,Wolf
341-221↓ Shrew,Otter,Badger
341-231↓ Badger,Shrew,Wolf
342-111↓ Shrew,Otter,Cottn
342-212↓ Shrew,Otter,Badger
342-232 Badger,Shrew,Wolf
342-311 Badger,Shrew,Otter
342-332↓ Badger,Wolf,W.Dog
343-111↓ Otter,Shrew
343-131↓ Otter,Shrew,W.Dog
343-231↓ Otter,W.Dog,Badger
411-111↓ Shrew
412-111↓ Shrew
413-111↓ Shrew,Cottn
421-111↓ Shrew,Cottn
421-331↓ Shrew,Cottn,Badger
422-111↓ Shrew,Cottn
422-331↓ Shrew,Cottn,Badger
423-111↓ Shrew,Cottn,Otter
423-132 Shrew,Otter,W.Cat
423-211↓ Shrew,Cottn,Otter
423-232 Shrew,Otter,W.Cat
423-311↓ Shrew,Cottn,Otter
423-331 Shrew,Cottn,Badger
423-332 Shrew,Badger,Otter
431-111↓ Cottn,Shrew

431-322↓ Cottn,Badger,Shrew
432-111↓ Cottn,Shrew,Otter
432-322↓ Cottn,Badger,Shrew
433-111 Cottn,Otter
433-312↓ Otter,Cottn,Badger
441-111↓ Cottn,Shrew
441-322↓ Cottn,Badger,Shrew
441-331↓ Cottn,Badger,Wolf
442-111↓ Cottn,Shrew,Otter
442-132↓ Cottn,Shrew,Badger
442-212↓ Cottn,Shrew,Otter
442-322↓ Cottn,Badger,Shrew
442-331↓ Cottn,Badger,Wolf
443-111 Cottn,Otter
443-312↓ Otter,Cottn,W.Dog
443-321 Cottn,Otter,Badger
443-322 Cottn,Otter,W.Dog
443-331 Cottn,Badger,W.Dog
443-332 W.Dog,Badger,Otter

144-

111-111↓ Shrew
112-111↓ Shrew
113-111↓ Shrew,W.Dog
121-111↓ Snake,Shrew,Porcp
121-331↓ Shrew,Badger,W.Dog
121-332 Shrew,W.Dog,Eagle
122-111↓ Snake,Shrew,Porcp
122-232 Shrew,W.Dog
122-311 Shrew,Snake
122-322↓ Shrew,W.Dog,Eagle
122-331 W.Dog,Shrew,Badger
122-332 W.Dog,Shrew,Eagle
123-111 Snake,Shrew,Porcp
123-122 Shrew,Porcp,Bat
123-131↓ Baboon,Shrew,W.Dog
123-211 Shrew,Snake,Otter
123-212↓ Shrew,Otter,W.Dog
123-231↓ W.Dog,Baboon,Shrew
123-311↓ W.Dog,Shrew,Otter
131-111 Snake,Shrew,Porcp
131-122 Shrew,Porcp,Bat
131-131 Shrew,Baboon,Porcp
131-132 Shrew,Baboon,W.Dog
131-211 Shrew,Mouse,Cottn
131-212 Shrew,Otter,W.Dog
131-221 Shrew,Mouse,Cottn
131-222 Shrew,W.Dog,Otter
131-231↓ Badger,W.Dog,Shrew
132-111 Snake,Shrew,Porcp
132-112 Shrew,Bat,Snake
132-121↓ Shrew,Porcp,Bat
132-131↓ Baboon,W.Dog,Shrew
132-211 Shrew,Otter,Mouse
132-212 Shrew,Otter,W.Dog
132-221 Shrew,Otter,Mouse
132-222 Shrew,W.Dog,Otter
132-231↓ W.Dog,Baboon,Badger
132-311↓ W.Dog,Badger,Shrew
132-331↓ W.Dog,Badger,Baboon
133-111 Bat,Otter,Snake
133-112↓ Bat,Otter,Baboon
133-131↓ Baboon,W.Dog,Bat
133-321↓ W.Dog,Otter,Baboon
141-111↓ W.Dog,Snake,Shrew

141-121↓ W.Dog,Shrew,Sheep
142-111↓ W.Dog,Snake,Shrew
143-111↓ Wild Dog
211-111↓ Shrew
212-111↓ Shrew
213-111↓ Snake,Shrew
221-111↓ Snake,Shrew
221-331↓ Shrew,Badger,Eagle
222-111 Snake,Shrew
222-331↓ Shrew,Badger,W.Dog
222-332 Shrew,W.Dog,Eagle
223-111 Snake,Shrew,Otter
223-122 Shrew,Otter,Bat
223-131↓ Shrew,Baboon,W.Dog
223-222↓ Shrew,Otter,W.Dog
223-231 Shrew,W.Dog,Baboon
223-312↓ W.Dog,Shrew,Otter
231-111 Snake,Shrew,Otter
231-131↓ Shrew,Badger,Baboon
231-221↓ Shrew,Otter,Mouse
231-222 Shrew,Otter,Badger
231-231↓ Badger,Shrew,W.Dog
232-111 Snake,Shrew,Otter
232-112↓ Shrew,Otter,Bat
232-131 Shrew,Baboon,Badger
232-132 Shrew,Baboon,W.Dog
232-211 Shrew,Otter,Mouse
232-212 Shrew,Otter,W.Dog
232-221 Shrew,Otter,Mouse
232-222 Shrew,Otter,W.Dog
232-231↓ Badger,W.Dog,Shrew
233-111 Otter,Bat,Snake
233-112↓ Otter,Bat,Baboon
233-131↓ Baboon,W.Dog,Otter
241-111↓ W.Dog,Shrew,Snake
242-111↓ W.Dog,Shrew
243-111↓ Wild Dog
311-111↓ Shrew
312-111↓ Shrew
313-111↓ Shrew
321-111↓ Shrew
321-331↓ Shrew,Badger,Eagle
322-111↓ Shrew,Eagle,Badger
323-111↓ Shrew,Otter
323-331↓ Shrew,Badger,Eagle
331-111↓ Shrew,Otter,Cottn
331-131↓ Shrew,Badger,Otter
331-221↓ Shrew,Otter,Cottn
331-222↓ Shrew,Otter,Badger
332-111↓ Shrew,Otter,Cottn
332-131↓ Shrew,Badger,Otter
332-211 Shrew,Otter,Cottn
332-212 Shrew,Otter,Badger
332-221 Shrew,Otter,Cottn
332-222↓ Shrew,Otter,Badger
333-111↓ Otter,Shrew
333-231↓ Otter,Badger,Shrew
333-232 Otter,Badger,W.Dog
333-311 Otter,Badger,Shrew
333-312↓ Otter,Badger,W.Dog
341-111↓ Shrew,Dog,Otter
341-122 Shrew,Dog,W.Dog
341-131↓ W.Dog,Shrew,Badger
341-211↓ Shrew,Dog,W.Dog
341-231↓ W.Dog,Badger,Shrew

341-322↓ W.Dog,Badger,Wolf
342-111 Shrew,Otter,Dog
342-112↓ Shrew,Otter,W.Dog
342-131↓ W.Dog,Shrew,Badger
342-211↓ Shrew,W.Dog,Otter
342-322↓ W.Dog,Badger
343-111↓ Otter,W.Dog,Shrew
411-111↓ Shrew
412-111↓ Shrew
413-111↓ Shrew,Cottn,SeaLn
421-111↓ Shrew,Cottn,SeaLn
422-111↓ Shrew,Cottn,SeaLn
423-111↓ Shrew,Cottn,Otter
423-132 Shrew,Otter,W.Cat
423-211 Shrew,Cottn,SeaLn
423-212 Shrew,SeaLn,Otter
423-221 Shrew,Cottn,SeaLn
423-222 Shrew,SeaLn,Otter
423-231 Shrew,Cottn,SeaLn
423-232 Shrew,SeaLn,Otter
423-311 SeaLn,Shrew,Cottn
423-312 SeaLn,Dolphin,Shrew
423-321 SeaLn,Shrew,Cottn
423-322 SeaLn,Dolphin,Shrew
423-331 SeaLn,Shrew,Cottn
423-332 SeaLn,Dolphin,Shrew
431-111↓ Cottn,Shrew
431-232↓ Cottn,Badger,Shrew
431-312↓ Cottn,SeaLn,Badger
432-111↓ Cottn,Shrew
432-232↓ Cottn,Badger,Shrew
432-322↓ Cottn,SeaLn,Badger
433-111 Cottn,Otter
433-232↓ Otter,Cottn,Badger
433-311 Cottn,Otter,SeaLn
433-332 Badger,Otter,W.Dog
441-111↓ Cottn,Shrew
441-132↓ Cottn,Shrew,W.Dog
441-232↓ Cottn,W.Dog,Badger
441-312↓ Cottn,W.Dog,SeaLn
441-322↓ Cottn,W.Dog,Badger
441-332 W.Dog,Badger,Wolf
442-111↓ Cottn,Shrew,Otter
442-132↓ Cottn,W.Dog,Shrew
442-212↓ Cottn,Shrew,Otter
442-222↓ Cottn,Shrew,W.Dog
442-232↓ Cottn,W.Dog,Badger
442-312 Cottn,W.Dog,SeaLn
442-321 Cottn,W.Dog,Badger
443-111 Cottn,Otter
443-122↓ Otter,Cottn,W.Dog
443-132 W.Dog,Otter,Pr.Dog
443-211↓ Cottn,Otter,W.Dog

151-

111-111↓ Croc,Shrew
111-231↓ Croc,Shrew,Badger
112-111↓ Croc,Shrew
112-231↓ Croc,Shrew,Badger
113-111↓ Croc,Warthg
113-321↓ Croc,Warthg,Shrew
113-331↓ Badger,Croc,Warthg
121-111 Croc,Porcp,Badger
121-112 Croc,Porcp,Warthg
121-132↓ Badger,Porcp,Warthg

(151 cont'd)
121-211↓ Croc,Badger,Warthg
122-111↓ Croc,Porcp,Warthg
122-121↓ Porcp,Warthg,Badger
122-211↓ Croc,Badger,Warthg
123-111↓ Warthg,Croc
123-121↓ Warthg,Porcp
123-311↓ Warthg,Badger,Croc
131-111↓ Badger,Croc,Porcp
132-111   Badger,Croc,Porcp
132-112↓ Badger,Croc,Warthg
133-111↓ Warthg,Badger,Croc
141-111↓ Badger,Croc
142-111↓ Badger,Croc
143-111↓ Badger,Warthg,Croc
211-111↓ Shrew,Badger
212-111↓ Shrew,Badger
213-111↓ Shrew,Badger
221-111↓ Badger,Snake,Shrew
222-111↓ Badger,Snake,Shrew
223-111↓ Badger,Snake,Shrew
223-122↓ Badger,Shrew,Warthg
231-111↓ Badger
232-111↓ Badger
233-111↓ Badger
241-111↓ Badger
242-111↓ Badger
243-111↓ Badger
311-111↓ Shrew,Badger
312-111↓ Shrew,Badger
313-111↓ Shrew,Badger
321-111↓ Badger,Shrew
322-111↓ Badger,Shrew
323-111↓ Badger,Shrew
331-111↓ Badger
332-111↓ Badger
333-111↓ Badger,Otter
341-111↓ Badger
342-111↓ Badger
343-111↓ Shrew,Badger
411-111↓ Shrew,Badger
412-111↓ Shrew,Badger
413-111↓ Shrew,Badger
421-111↓ Badger,Shrew
422-111↓ Badger,Shrew
423-111↓ Badger,Shrew
431-111↓ Badger
432-111↓ Badger
433-111↓ Badger
441-111↓ Badger
442-111↓ Badger
443-111↓ Badger

152-
111-111↓ Croc,Shrew
111-231↓ Croc,Shrew,Badger
112-111↓ Croc,Shrew
112-231↓ Croc,Shrew,Badger
113-111↓ Croc,Warthg
113-321↓ Croc,Warthg,Shrew
113-331↓ Badger,Croc,Warthg
121-111↓ Croc,Badger,Warthg
122-111↓ Croc,Warthg,Badger
123-111↓ Warthg,Croc
123-311↓ Warthg,Badger,Croc

131-111↓ Badger,Croc
132-111↓ Badger,Croc
132-112↓ Badger,Croc,Warthg
133-111↓ Warthg,Badger,Croc
141-111↓ Badger,Croc
142-111↓ Badger,Croc
143-111↓ Badger,Warthg,Croc
211-111↓ Shrew,Badger
212-111↓ Shrew,Badger
213-111↓ Shrew,Badger
221-111↓ Badger,Shrew
222-111↓ Badger,Shrew
223-111↓ Badger,Shrew
231-111↓ Badger
232-111↓ Badger
233-111↓ Badger
241-111↓ Badger
242-111↓ Badger
243-111↓ Badger
311-111↓ Shrew,Badger
312-111↓ Shrew,Badger
313-111↓ Shrew,Badger
321-111↓ Badger,Shrew
322-111↓ Badger,Shrew
323-111↓ Badger,Shrew
331-111↓ Badger
332-111↓ Badger
333-111↓ Badger,Otter
341-111↓ Badger
342-111↓ Badger
343-111↓ Shrew,Badger
411-111↓ Shrew,Badger
412-111↓ Shrew,Badger
413-111↓ Shrew,Badger
421-111↓ Badger,Shrew
422-111↓ Badger,Shrew
423-111↓ Badger,Shrew
431-111↓ Badger
432-111↓ Badger
433-111↓ Badger
441-111↓ Badger
442-111↓ Badger
443-111↓ Badger

153-
111-111↓ Croc,Shrew
111-231↓ Croc,Shrew,Badger
112-111↓ Croc,Shrew
112-231↓ Croc,Shrew,Badger
113-111↓ Croc,Warthg
113-321↓ Croc,Warthg,Shrew
113-331↓ Badger,Croc,Warthg
121-111↓ Croc,Badger,Warthg
122-111↓ Croc,Warthg,Badger
123-111↓ Warthg,Croc
123-311↓ Warthg,Badger,Croc
131-111↓ Badger,Croc
132-111↓ Badger,Croc
132-112↓ Badger,Croc,Warthg
133-111↓ Warthg,Badger,Croc
141-111↓ Badger,Croc
142-111↓ Badger,Croc
143-111↓ Badger,Warthg,Croc
211-111↓ Shrew,Badger
212-111↓ Shrew,Badger

213-111↓ Shrew,Badger
221-111↓ Badger,Shrew
222-111↓ Badger,Shrew
223-111↓ Badger,Shrew
231-111↓ Badger
232-111↓ Badger
233-111↓ Badger
241-111↓ Badger
242-111↓ Badger
243-111↓ Badger
311-111↓ Shrew,Badger
312-111↓ Shrew,Badger
313-111↓ Shrew,Badger
321-111↓ Badger,Shrew
322-111↓ Badger,Shrew
323-111↓ Badger,Shrew
331-111↓ Badger
332-111↓ Badger
333-111↓ Badger,Otter
341-111↓ Badger
342-111↓ Badger
343-111↓ Shrew,Badger
411-111↓ Shrew,Badger
412-111↓ Shrew,Badger
413-111↓ Shrew,Badger
421-111↓ Badger,Shrew
422-111↓ Badger,Shrew
423-111↓ Badger,Shrew
431-111↓ Badger
432-111↓ Badger
433-111↓ Badger
441-111↓ Badger
442-111↓ Badger
443-111↓ Badger

154-
111-111↓ Croc,Shrew
111-231↓ Croc,Shrew,Badger
112-111↓ Croc,Shrew
112-231↓ Croc,Shrew,Badger
113-111↓ Croc,Warthg
113-321↓ Croc,Warthg,Shrew
113-331↓ Badger,Croc,Warthg
121-111↓ Croc,Badger,Warthg
122-111↓ Croc,Warthg,Badger
123-111↓ Warthg,Croc
123-311↓ Warthg,Badger,Croc
131-111↓ Badger,Croc
132-111↓ Badger,Croc
132-112↓ Badger,Croc,Warthg
133-111↓ Warthg,Badger,Croc
141-111↓ Badger,Croc
142-111↓ Badger,Croc,W.Dog
143-111↓ W.Dog,Badger,Warthg
211-111↓ Shrew,Badger
212-111↓ Shrew,Badger
213-111↓ Shrew,Badger
221-111↓ Badger,Shrew
222-111↓ Badger,Shrew
223-111↓ Badger,Shrew
231-111↓ Badger
232-111↓ Badger
233-111↓ Badger
241-111↓ Badger
242-111↓ Badger,W.Dog

243-111↓ Badger,W.Dog
311-111↓ Shrew,Badger
312-111↓ Shrew,Badger
313-111↓ Shrew,Badger
321-111↓ Badger,Shrew
322-111↓ Badger,Shrew
323-111↓ Badger,Shrew
331-111↓ Badger
332-111↓ Badger
333-111↓ Badger
341-111↓ Badger
342-111↓ Badger
343-111↓ Badger
411-111↓ Shrew,Badger
412-111↓ Shrew,Badger
413-111↓ Shrew,Badger
421-111↓ Badger,Shrew
422-111↓ Badger,Shrew
423-111↓ Badger,Shrew
431-111↓ Badger
432-111↓ Badger
433-111↓ Badger
441-111↓ Badger
442-111↓ Badger
443-111↓ Badger

211-

111-111↓ Mole
112-111↓ Mole
113-111↓ Mole
121-111↓ Mole
122-111↓ Mole
123-111↓ Mole
131-111↓ Mole,Mouse
132-111↓ Mole,Mouse
133-111↓ Mole,Mouse
141-111↓ Mole,Mouse
141-332↓ Mole,Mouse,Beaver
142-111↓ Mole,Mouse
142-332↓ Mole,Beaver,Mouse
143-111↓ Mole,Mouse
143-322↓ Mole,Mouse,Beaver
211-111↓ Mole,Mouse,MGoat
212-111↓ Mole,Mouse,MGoat
213-111↓ Mole,Mouse,MGoat
221-111↓ Mole,Mouse,MGoat
222-111↓ Mole,Mouse,MGoat
223-111↓ Mole,Mouse,MGoat
231-111↓ Mole,Mouse
232-111↓ Mole,Mouse
233-111↓ Mole,Mouse
241-111↓ Mouse,Mole
242-111↓ Mouse,Mole
243-111↓ Mouse,Mole,Beaver
311-111↓ Mole,Mouse,MGoat
312-111↓ Mole,Mouse,MGoat
313-111↓ Mole,Mouse,MGoat
321-111↓ Mole,Mouse
322-111↓ Mole,Mouse,MGoat
323-111↓ Mole,Mouse
331-111↓ Mole,Mouse
331-312↓ Mouse,Swan
332-111↓ Mole,Mouse
332-322↓ Mouse,Swan,Mole
333-111 Mole,Mouse

333-132↓ Mole,Mouse,Bat
333-312↓ Mouse,Swan
341-111 Mouse,Mole
341-122↓ Mouse,Mole,Dog
341-131↓ Mouse,Mole,Beaver
341-212↓ Mouse,Dog,Mole
341-232↓ Mouse,Beaver,Dog
341-312↓ Mouse,Dog,Swan
341-332↓ Mouse,Beaver,Dog
342-111 Mouse,Mole
342-122↓ Mouse,Mole,Dog
342-131↓ Mouse,Mole,Beaver
342-211 Mouse,Mole,Dog
342-212↓ Mouse,Dog,Beaver
342-231↓ Mouse,Beaver,Pr.Dog
343-111 Mouse,Mole,Pengn
343-112 Mouse,Mole,Pr.Dog
343-121 Mouse,Mole,Pengn
343-122 Pr.Dog,Mouse,Mole
343-131↓ Pr.Dog,Beaver,Mouse
411-111↓ Mole,Pcock
411-232↓ Mole,Pcock,Swan
411-311 Deer,Swan,Mole
411-312 Swan,Deer,Pcock
411-321 Deer,Swan,Mole
411-322 Swan,Deer,Pcock
411-331 Deer,Swan,Mole
411-332 Swan,Deer,Pcock
412-111↓ Mole,Swan,Deer
412-222↓ Mole,W.Cat,Swan
412-311 Deer,Swan,Mole
412-332 Swan,Deer,W.Cat
413-111↓ Mole,W.Cat
413-232↓ W.Cat,Mole,Swan
413-311 Deer,Swan,Mole
413-312 Swan,Deer,W.Cat
413-321 Deer,Swan,Mole
413-322 Swan,Deer,W.Cat
413-331 Deer,Swan,Mole
413-332 Swan,Deer,W.Cat
421-111↓ Mole,Swan,Deer
421-232 Mole,Swan,W.Cat
421-331↓ Swan,Deer,Mole
422-111↓ Mole,Swan,Mouse
422-212↓ Mole,Swan,Deer
422-222↓ Mole,Swan,W.Cat
422-331↓ Swan,Deer,Mole
423-111↓ Mole,W.Cat
423-212↓ Mole,Swan,W.Cat
423-321↓ Swan,Deer,Mole
423-322 Swan,Deer,W.Cat
423-331 Swan,Deer,Mole
423-332 Swan,Deer,W.Cat
431-111 Mole,Mouse
431-132↓ Mole,Swan,Mouse
432-111 Mole,Mouse
432-132↓ Mole,Swan,Mouse
433-111 Mole,Mouse
433-122↓ Mole,Swan,Mouse
433-132 Mole,Swan,W.Cat
433-231↓ Swan,Mouse,Mole
441-111↓ Mole,Mouse,Swan
441-212 Swan,Mouse,Dog
441-221 Swan,Mouse,Mole
441-222 Swan,Mouse,Dog

441-231↓ Swan,Mouse,Mole
442-111↓ Mole,Mouse,Swan
442-132 Swan,Mole,Beaver
442-211 Swan,Mouse,Mole
442-212 Swan,Mouse,Dog
442-221 Swan,Mouse,Mole
442-222 Swan,Mouse,Dog
442-231 Swan,Mouse,Beaver
442-232 Swan,Beaver,Sable
442-331↓ Swan,Sable,Mouse
443-111 Mole,Pengn,Mouse
443-112 Swan,Mole,Pr.Dog
443-121 Mole,Pengn,Mouse
443-122 Swan,Pr.Dog,Mole
443-131 Pr.Dog,Mole,Pengn
443-132 Pr.Dog,Beaver,Swan
443-211↓ Swan,Mouse,Pr.Dog
443-231↓ Pr.Dog,Beaver,Swan
443-321↓ Swan,Mouse
443-331↓ Swan,Pr.Dog,Sable

212-

111-111↓ Mole
112-111↓ Mole
113-111↓ Mole
121-111↓ Mole
122-111↓ Mole
123-111↓ Mole
131-111↓ Mole,Mouse
132-111↓ Mole,Mouse
133-111↓ Mole,Mouse
141-111↓ Mole,Beaver
141-222↓ Mole,Sheep,Beaver
141-321 Mole,Sheep,Mouse
141-322↓ Mole,Sheep,Beaver
142-111↓ Mole,Beaver
142-212↓ Mole,Beaver,Sheep
142-311 Mole,Sheep,Mouse
142-312↓ Mole,Beaver,Sheep
143-111↓ Mole,Beaver
143-212↓ Beaver,Mole,Sheep
211-111↓ Mole,Mouse,MGoat
212-111↓ Mole,Mouse,MGoat
212-332↓ Mole,Mouse,Beaver
213-111↓ Mole,Beaver
213-331↓ Mole,Mouse,Beaver
221-111↓ Mole,Mouse,MGoat
222-111↓ Mole,Mouse,MGoat
222-232↓ Mole,Mouse,Beaver
223-111↓ Mole,Mouse,MGoat
223-232↓ Mole,Beaver,Mouse
231-111↓ Mole,Mouse
231-332 Mouse,Beaver
232-111↓ Mole,Mouse
232-222↓ Mouse,Mole,Beaver
233-111 Mole,Mouse
233-122↓ Mole,Mouse,Bat
233-131↓ Mole,Mouse,Beaver
241-111 Sheep,Mouse,Mole
241-112 Sheep,Beaver,Mouse
241-121 Sheep,Mouse,Mole
241-122↓ Sheep,Beaver,Mouse
242-111 Sheep,Mouse,Mole
242-211↓ Sheep,Mouse,Beaver
243-111↓ Sheep,Beaver,Mouse

(212 cont'd)

311-111↓ Mole,Pcock
311-311 Mole,Deer,Mouse
311-312 Deer,Mole,Swan
311-321 Mole,Deer,Mouse
311-322 Deer,Mole,Swan
311-331 Mole,Deer,Mouse
311-332↓ Deer,Mole,Swan
312-111↓ Mole,W.Cat
312-311 Mole,Deer,Mouse
312-312 Deer,Mole,Swan
312-321 Mole,Deer,Mouse
312-322 Deer,Mole,Swan
312-331 Mole,Deer,Mouse
312-332↓ Deer,Mole,Swan
313-111↓ Mole,W.Cat
313-232↓ Mole,W.Cat,Pr.Dog
313-311 Mole,Deer,Mouse
313-312 Deer,Mole,Swan
313-321 Mole,Deer,Mouse
313-322 Deer,Mole,Swan
313-331 Mole,Deer,Mouse
313-332↓ Deer,W.Cat,Mole
321-111↓ Mole,Mouse
321-311↓ Mole,Mouse,Deer
321-312 Deer,Swan,Mole
321-321 Mole,Mouse,Deer
321-322 Deer,Swan,Mole
321-331 Mole,Mouse,Deer
321-332↓ Deer,Swan,Mole
322-111↓ Mole,Mouse
322-232↓ Mole,Mouse,W.Cat
322-311 Mole,Mouse,Deer
322-312 Deer,Swan,Mole
322-321 Mole,Mouse,Deer
322-322 Deer,Swan,Mole
322-331 Mole,Mouse,Deer
322-332↓ Deer,Swan,Mole
323-111↓ Mole,Mouse
323-222↓ Mole,W.Cat,Mouse
323-232 Mole,W.Cat,Pr.Dog
323-311 Mole,Mouse,Deer
323-312 Deer,Swan,Mole
323-321 Mole,Mouse,Deer
323-322 Deer,Swan,Mole
323-331 Mole,Mouse,Deer
323-332 Deer,Swan,W.Cat
331-111↓ Mole,Mouse
331-311 Mouse,Swan
332-111↓ Mole,Mouse
332-212↓ Mouse,Swan,Mole
332-232↓ Mouse,Beaver,Swan
333-111 Mole,Mouse
333-122↓ Mole,Mouse,Bat
333-131 Mole,Mouse,Pr.Dog
333-132 Mole,Pr.Dog,Beaver
333-212↓ Mouse,Swan,Mole
333-222 Mouse,Swan,Pr.Dog
333-231↓ Mouse,Pr.Dog,Beaver
333-311 Mouse,Swan
333-332 Swan,Pr.Dog,Beaver
341-111 Sheep,Dog,Mouse
341-112 Dog,Sheep,Beaver
341-121 Sheep,Dog,Mouse
341-122↓ Dog,Sheep,Beaver

341-132 Beaver,Dog,Pr.Dog
341-211 Sheep,Dog,Mouse
341-212 Dog,Sheep,Beaver
341-221 Sheep,Dog,Mouse
341-222↓ Dog,Sheep,Beaver
341-232 Beaver,Dog,Pr.Dog
341-311 Sheep,Dog,Mouse
341-312 Dog,Swan,Sheep
341-321 Sheep,Dog,Mouse
341-322 Dog,Swan,Sheep
341-331 Beaver,Sheep,Dog
341-332 Beaver,Dog,Pr.Dog
342-111 Sheep,Dog,Pengn
342-112↓ Dog,Beaver,Sheep
342-131 Beaver,Sheep,Pr.Dog
342-132 Beaver,Pr.Dog,Dog
342-211 Sheep,Dog,Mouse
342-212↓ Dog,Beaver,Sheep
342-231 Beaver,Sheep,Pr.Dog
342-232 Beaver,Pr.Dog,Dog
342-311 Sheep,Dog,Mouse
342-312 Dog,Beaver,Swan
342-321 Sheep,Dog,Beaver
342-322 Dog,Beaver,Swan
342-331 Beaver,Sheep,Pr.Dog
342-332 Beaver,Pr.Dog,Dog
343-111 Pengn,Sheep,Pr.Dog
343-211↓ Sheep,Pr.Dog,Beaver
343-212 Pr.Dog,Beaver,Dog
343-221↓ Pr.Dog,Beaver,Sheep
343-312 Pr.Dog,Beaver,Dog
343-321 Pr.Dog,Beaver,Sheep
343-322↓ Pr.Dog,Beaver,Dog
411-111 Mole,Pcock
411-132↓ Pcock,Mole,W.Cat
411-211↓ Pcock,Deer,Swan
412-111↓ Mole,Deer,W.Cat
412-211 Deer,Swan,Mole
412-212↓ Deer,Swan,W.Cat
413-111↓ W.Cat,Mole,Deer
413-321↓ Deer,Swan,W.Cat
421-111↓ Mole,Swan,Deer
421-132 Mole,Swan,W.Cat
421-221↓ Swan,Deer,Mole
421-222 Swan,Deer,W.Cat
421-231↓ Swan,Deer,Mole
422-111↓ Mole,Swan,Deer
422-132↓ W.Cat,Mole,Swan
422-211 Swan,Deer,Mole
422-212↓ Swan,Deer,W.Cat
423-111 Mole,W.Cat
423-132↓ W.Cat,Mole,Swan
423-211↓ Swan,Deer,W.Cat
431-111↓ Swan,Mole,Cottn
432-111↓ Swan,Mole,Cottn
432-232↓ Swan,W.Cat
432-321↓ Swan,Deer
433-111↓ Swan,Mole,Cottn
433-131↓ Swan,Mole,W.Cat
441-111↓ Swan,Dog,Sheep
441-131↓ Swan,Dog,Beaver
441-231↓ Swan,Dog,Sable
442-111↓ Swan,Dog,Sheep
442-131↓ Swan,Beaver,Pr.Dog
442-221↓ Swan,Dog,Sheep

442-231 Swan,Beaver,Pr.Dog
442-232↓ Swan,Beaver,Sable
443-111↓ Pengn,Swan,Pr.Dog
443-131 Pr.Dog,Pengn,Beaver
443-132 Pr.Dog,Beaver,Swan
443-211↓ Swan,Pr.Dog,Dog
443-231↓ Pr.Dog,Beaver,Swan
443-331↓ Swan,Pr.Dog,Sable

213-

111-111↓ Mole
112-111↓ Mole
113-111↓ Mole
121-111↓ Mole
122-111↓ Mole
123-111↓ Mole
131-111↓ Mole,Mouse
132-111↓ Mole,Mouse
133-111↓ Mole,Mouse
133-332 Mole,Beaver
141-111↓ Mole,Sheep
141-222↓ Sheep,Mole,Beaver
142-111↓ Mole,Sheep
142-222↓ Sheep,Mole,Beaver
143-111 Mole,Sheep
143-122↓ Mole,Sheep,Beaver
143-331↓ Beaver,Sheep,Pr.Dog
211-111↓ Mole,Mouse,MGoat
211-312↓ Mole,Deer,Mouse
212-111↓ Mole,Mouse,MGoat
212-312↓ Mole,Deer,Mouse
213-111↓ Mole,Beaver
213-311 Mole,Mouse,MGoat
213-312↓ Mole,Deer,Mouse
213-332↓ Mole,Deer,Beaver
221-111↓ Mole,Mouse
221-311↓ Mole,Mouse,MGoat
221-312↓ Mole,Deer,Mouse
222-111↓ Mole,Mouse,MGoat
222-312↓ Mole,Deer,Mouse
223-111↓ Mole,Mouse
223-232↓ Mole,Beaver,Mouse
223-311 Mole,Mouse,MGoat
223-312↓ Mole,Deer,Mouse
223-332 Mole,Deer,Beaver
231-111↓ Mole,Mouse
231-332↓ Mouse,Sheep,Beaver
232-111↓ Mole,Mouse
232-132↓ Mole,Mouse,Beaver
232-211↓ Mouse,Sheep,Mole
232-332↓ Mouse,Beaver,Sheep
233-111 Mole,Mouse
233-132↓ Mole,Beaver,Mouse
233-211↓ Mouse,Sheep,Mole
233-231 Mouse,Beaver,Sheep
233-232 Beaver,Mouse,Baboon
233-332↓ Mouse,Sheep,Beaver
233-332 Beaver,Mouse,Baboon
241-111↓ Sheep,Dog
241-332↓ Sheep,Beaver,Dog
242-111↓ Sheep,Beaver,Dog
242-221 Sheep,Beaver,Mouse
242-222 Sheep,Beaver,Dog
242-231 Sheep,Beaver,Mouse
242-232↓ Beaver,Sheep,Pr.Dog

243-111↓ Sheep,Beaver
243-322↓ Sheep,Beaver,Pr.Dog
311-111↓ Mole,Pcock
311-331↓ Deer,Mole,Pcock
312-111↓ Mole,Deer
312-232↓ Mole,Deer,W.Cat
313-111↓ Mole,Pr.Dog
313-222↓ Mole,Deer,Pr.Dog
321-111↓ Mole,Mouse,Deer
322-111↓ Mole,Mouse,Deer
323-111↓ Mole,Pr.Dog
323-211 Mole,Mouse,Deer
323-212 Mole,Deer,Pr.Dog
323-221 Mole,Mouse,Deer
323-222 Mole,Deer,Pr.Dog
323-231 Mole,Pr.Dog,Mouse
323-321↓ Deer,Mole,Mouse
323-331↓ Deer,Pr.Dog,Mole
331-111 Mole,Mouse
331-132↓ Mole,Mouse,Dog
331-211 Mouse,Sheep,Mole
331-212 Mouse,Dog,Swan
331-221 Mouse,Sheep,Mole
331-222 Mouse,Dog,Swan
331-231 Mouse,Sheep,Mole
331-232 Mouse,Dog,Swan
331-311↓ Mouse,Swan,Deer
332-111 Mole,Mouse
332-132↓ Mole,Mouse,Pr.Dog
332-211 Mouse,Sheep,Mole
332-212 Mouse,Dog,Swan
332-221 Mouse,Sheep,Mole
332-222 Mouse,Dog,Swan
332-231 Mouse,Sheep,Mole
332-232 Mouse,Pr.Dog,Dog
332-311↓ Mouse,Swan,Deer
333-111 Mole,Mouse
333-112↓ Mole,Pr.Dog,Mouse
333-211 Mouse,Sheep,Pr.Dog
333-212 Pr.Dog,Mouse,Dog
333-221 Mouse,Pr.Dog,Sheep
333-222 Pr.Dog,Mouse,Dog
333-231 Pr.Dog,Mouse,Beaver
333-232 Pr.Dog,Fox
333-311 Mouse,Swan,Deer
333-312 Swan,Deer,Pr.Dog
333-321 Mouse,Swan,Pr.Dog
333-322 Swan,Pr.Dog,Deer
333-331 Pr.Dog,Mouse,Swan
333-332 Pr.Dog,Swan,Fox
341-111 Sheep,Dog
341-332↓ Dog,Pr.Dog,Sheep
342-111 Sheep,Dog
342-122↓ Dog,Sheep,Pr.Dog
342-132 Pr.Dog,Dog,Beaver
342-222↓ Dog,Sheep,Pr.Dog
342-232 Pr.Dog,Dog,Beaver
342-322↓ Dog,Sheep,Pr.Dog
342-332 Pr.Dog,Dog,Beaver
343-111↓ Sheep,Pr.Dog,Dog
343-131↓ Pr.Dog,Beaver
343-211↓ Sheep,Pr.Dog,Dog
343-231 Pr.Dog,Beaver,Sheep
343-232 Pr.Dog,Beaver,Dog
343-311↓ Sheep,Pr.Dog,Dog

343-331↓ Pr.Dog,Beaver
411-111↓ Pcock,Mole,Deer
412-111↓ Mole,Deer,Pcock
412-231↓ Deer,Pcock,W.Cat
413-111↓ Mole,Deer,W.Cat
413-222↓ Deer,W.Cat,Swan
421-111 Mole,Deer,Cottn
421-112 Deer,Mole,Swan
421-121 Mole,Deer,Cottn
421-122 Deer,Mole,Swan
421-131 Mole,Deer,Cottn
421-132↓ Deer,Mole,Swan
422-111 Mole,Deer,Cottn
422-112 Deer,Mole,Swan
422-121 Mole,Deer,Cottn
422-122 Deer,Mole,W.Cat
422-221↓ Deer,Swan,Cottn
422-222↓ Deer,Swan,W.Cat
423-111 Mole,Deer,Cottn
423-112↓ Deer,W.Cat,Mole
423-221↓ Deer,W.Cat,Swan
431-111 Cottn,Swan,Mole
431-112 Swan,Deer,Cottn
431-121 Cottn,Swan,Mole
431-122 Swan,Deer,Cottn
431-131 Cottn,Swan,Mole
431-132↓ Swan,Deer,Cottn
432-111 Cottn,Swan,Mole
432-112 Swan,Deer,Cottn
432-121 Cottn,Swan,Mole
432-122 Swan,Deer,Cottn
432-131 Cottn,Swan,Mole
432-132↓ Swan,Deer,Cottn
433-111 Cottn,Swan,Mole
433-112 Swan,Deer,Cottn
433-121 Cottn,Swan,Mole
433-122 Swan,Deer,Cottn
433-131 Cottn,Swan,Pr.Dog
433-132 Swan,W.Cat,Pr.Dog
433-231↓ Swan,Cottn,Deer
441-111 Dog,Swan,Cottn
441-112 Dog,Swan
441-121 Dog,Sheep,Cottn
441-122 Dog,Swan,Sheep
441-131 Dog,Sheep,Pr.Dog
441-132 Dog,Swan,Pr.Dog
441-211↓ Dog,Sheep,Swan
441-232 Swan,Dog,Pr.Dog
441-311↓ Dog,Swan,Deer
441-331↓ Swan,Sable,Dog
442-111 Dog,Sheep,Cottn
442-112 Dog,Swan,Sheep
442-121 Dog,Sheep,Cottn
442-122 Dog,Swan,Pr.Dog
442-131 Pr.Dog,Dog,Sheep
442-132 Pr.Dog,Dog,Swan
442-211↓ Dog,Sheep,Swan
442-222 Swan,Dog,Pr.Dog
442-231 Pr.Dog,Dog,Sheep
442-232 Swan,Pr.Dog,Dog
442-311↓ Swan,Dog,Deer
442-331↓ Swan,Sable,Pr.Dog
443-111 Pr.Dog,Dog,Pengn
443-112 Pr.Dog,Dog,Swan
443-121 Pr.Dog,Dog,Pengn

443-122↓ Pr.Dog,Dog,Swan
443-211 Pr.Dog,Dog,Sheep
443-212 Pr.Dog,Swan,Dog
443-221 Pr.Dog,Dog,Sheep
443-222↓ Pr.Dog,Swan,Dog

214-

111-111↓ Mole
112-111↓ Mole
113-111↓ Mole
121-111↓ Mole
122-111↓ Mole
123-111↓ Mole
131-111↓ Mole,Mouse
132-111↓ Mole,Mouse
133-111↓ Mole,Baboon
133-232↓ Mole,Baboon,Pr.Dog
141-111 Mole,Sheep
141-132↓ Mole,Dog,Sheep
141-232 Dog,Sheep,Pr.Dog
141-311 Sheep,Dog,Mole
141-332 Dog,Sheep,Pr.Dog
142-111 Mole,Sheep
142-122↓ Mole,Dog,Sheep
142-132 Mole,Pr.Dog,Dog
142-211↓ Sheep,Mole,Dog
142-231 Sheep,Mole,Pr.Dog
142-232 Pr.Dog,Dog,Beaver
142-321↓ Sheep,Dog,Mole
142-322↓ Dog,Sheep,Pr.Dog
142-332 Pr.Dog,Dog,Beaver
143-111 Mole,Sheep,Pr.Dog
143-112 Mole,Pr.Dog,Dog
143-121 Mole,Sheep,Pr.Dog
143-122 Mole,Pr.Dog,Dog
143-131 Pr.Dog,Mole,Sheep
143-132 Pr.Dog,Mole,Beaver
143-211 Sheep,Pr.Dog,Mole
143-212 Pr.Dog,Dog,Sheep
143-221 Sheep,Pr.Dog,Mole
143-222 Pr.Dog,Dog,Sheep
143-231↓ Pr.Dog,Sheep,Beaver
143-311↓ Sheep,Pr.Dog,Dog
143-331↓ Pr.Dog,Sheep,Beaver
211-111↓ Mole,Dog
211-222↓ Mole,Dog,Mouse
211-311 Mole,Mouse,MGoat
211-312 Mole,Deer,SeaLn
211-321 Mole,Mouse,Deer
211-322 Mole,Deer,SeaLn
211-331 Mole,Mouse,Deer
211-332↓ Mole,Deer,SeaLn
212-111↓ Mole,Dog
212-232↓ Mole,Pr.Dog,Dog
212-311 Mole,Mouse,MGoat
212-312 Mole,Deer,SeaLn
212-321 Mole,Mouse,Deer
212-322 Mole,Deer,SeaLn
212-331 Mole,Mouse,Deer
212-332↓ Mole,Deer,SeaLn
213-111↓ Mole,Pr.Dog,Baboon
213-212↓ Mole,Pr.Dog,Baboon
213-222↓ Mole,Pr.Dog,Baboon
213-311 Mole,Mouse,MGoat
213-312 Mole,Dolphin,Deer

(214 cont'd)

213-321 Mole,Mouse,Pr.Dog
213-322 Mole,Pr.Dog,Dolphin
213-331↓ Pr.Dog,Mole,Baboon
221-111↓ Mole,Mouse
221-232↓ Mole,Mouse,Dog
221-311 Mole,Mouse,MGoat
221-312 Mole,Deer,SeaLn
221-321 Mole,Mouse,Deer
221-322 Mole,Deer,SeaLn
221-331 Mole,Mouse,Deer
221-332↓ Mole,Deer,SeaLn
222-111↓ Mole,Mouse
222-232↓ Mole,Baboon,Mouse
222-311 Mole,Mouse,MGoat
222-312 Mole,Deer,SeaLn
222-321 Mole,Mouse,Deer
222-322 Mole,Deer,SeaLn
222-331 Mole,Mouse,Deer
222-332↓ Mole,Deer,Baboon
223-111↓ Mole,Baboon,Pr.Dog
223-211 Mole,Mouse
223-212 Mole,Baboon,Pr.Dog
223-221 Mole,Mouse,Baboon
223-222↓ Mole,Baboon,Pr.Dog
223-311 Mole,Mouse,MGoat
223-312 Mole,Dolphin,Deer
223-321 Mole,Mouse,Baboon
223-322↓ Baboon,Mole,Pr.Dog
231-111 Mole,Mouse
231-132↓ Mole,Mouse,Dog
231-211 Mouse,Sheep,Mole
231-212 Mouse,Dog,Sheep
231-221 Mouse,Sheep,Mole
231-222 Mouse,Dog,Sheep
231-231 Mouse,Sheep,Mole
231-232 Mouse,Dog,Baboon
231-311↓ Mouse,Sheep,Dog
231-332 Mouse,Dog,Baboon
232-111 Mole,Mouse
232-122↓ Mole,Mouse,Dog
232-131↓ Mole,Mouse,Baboon
232-211 Mouse,Sheep,Mole
232-212 Mouse,Dog,Sheep
232-221 Mouse,Sheep,Mole
232-222 Mouse,Dog,Sheep
232-231 Mouse,Baboon,Sheep
232-232 Baboon,Mouse,Pr.Dog
232-311↓ Mouse,Sheep,Dog
232-331 Mouse,Baboon,Sheep
232-332 Baboon,Mouse,Pr.Dog
233-111 Mole,Mouse,Baboon
233-112 Mole,Baboon,Pr.Dog
233-121 Mole,Mouse,Baboon
233-122↓ Baboon,Mole,Pr.Dog
233-211 Mouse,Baboon,Sheep
233-212↓ Baboon,Pr.Dog,Mouse
233-311 Mouse,Baboon,Sheep
233-312↓ Baboon,Pr.Dog,Mouse
241-111 Sheep,Dog
241-332↓ Dog,Pr.Dog,Sheep
242-111 Sheep,Dog
242-122↓ Dog,Sheep,Pr.Dog
242-132 Pr.Dog,Dog,Beaver
242-222↓ Dog,Sheep,Pr.Dog

242-232 Pr.Dog,Dog,Beaver
242-322↓ Dog,Sheep,Pr.Dog
242-332 Pr.Dog,Dog,Beaver
243-111↓ Sheep,Pr.Dog,Dog
243-232 Pr.Dog,Dog,Beaver
243-311↓ Sheep,Pr.Dog,Dog
311-111↓ Mole,Dog,Pcock
311-132 Mole,Dog,Pr.Dog
311-211↓ Mole,Dog,Pcock
311-231 Mole,Dog,Pr.Dog
311-232 Dog,Pr.Dog,Pcock
311-311↓ Deer,SeaLn,Dog
312-111↓ Mole,Dog
312-132↓ Mole,Pr.Dog,Dog
312-211 Mole,Dog,Deer
312-232 Pr.Dog,Dog,Mole
312-311↓ Deer,SeaLn,Dog
312-331↓ Deer,SeaLn,Pr.Dog
313-111↓ Mole,Pr.Dog,Dog
313-311 Deer,SeaLn,Pr.Dog
313-312 Dolphin,Deer,SeaLn
313-321 Pr.Dog,Deer,SeaLn
313-332↓ Pr.Dog,Dolphin,Deer
321-111↓ Mole,Dog
321-132↓ Mole,Dog,Pr.Dog
321-211 Mole,Dog,Mouse
321-212 Dog,Mole,Deer
321-221 Mole,Dog,Mouse
321-222 Dog,Mole,Deer
321-231↓ Mole,Dog,Pr.Dog
321-311↓ Deer,SeaLn,Dog
322-111↓ Mole,Dog
322-132↓ Mole,Pr.Dog,Dog
322-211 Mole,Dog,Mouse
322-212 Dog,Mole,Deer
322-221 Mole,Dog,Mouse
322-222 Dog,Mole,Deer
322-231↓ Mole,Pr.Dog,Dog
322-311↓ Deer,SeaLn,Dog
322-331↓ Deer,SeaLn,Pr.Dog
323-111↓ Mole,Pr.Dog,Dog
323-311 Deer,SeaLn,Pr.Dog
323-312 Dolphin,Deer,SeaLn
323-321 Pr.Dog,Deer,SeaLn
323-332↓ Pr.Dog,Dolphin,Deer
331-111↓ Dog,Mole,Mouse
331-131↓ Dog,Mole,Pr.Dog
331-231↓ Dog,Pr.Dog,Mouse
331-322 Dog,Swan
331-331↓ Dog,Pr.Dog,Mouse
332-111↓ Dog,Mole,Mouse
332-131↓ Pr.Dog,Dog,Mole
332-231↓ Dog,Pr.Dog,Mouse
332-312 Dog,Swan
332-331↓ Pr.Dog,Dog,Mouse
332-332 Pr.Dog,Dog,Swan
333-111↓ Pr.Dog,Dog,Mole
333-232↓ Pr.Dog,Dog,Baboon
341-111↓ Dog,Pr.Dog
342-111↓ Dog,Pr.Dog
343-111↓ Pr.Dog,Dog
411-111 Pcock,Mole,Deer
411-112 Pcock,Deer,SeaLn
411-121 Pcock,Mole,Deer
411-122 Pcock,Deer,SeaLn

411-131 Pcock,Mole,Deer
411-132↓ Pcock,Deer,SeaLn
412-111 Mole,Deer,SeaLn
412-112 Deer,SeaLn,Pcock
412-121 Mole,Deer,SeaLn
412-122 Deer,SeaLn,Pcock
412-131↓ Mole,Deer,SeaLn
413-111↓ Mole,Deer,SeaLn
413-112 Dolphin,Deer,SeaLn
413-121 Mole,Deer,SeaLn
413-122 Dolphin,Deer,SeaLn
413-131 Pr.Dog,Mole,Deer
413-132 Pr.Dog,Dolphin,Deer
413-211↓ Deer,SeaLn,Dolphin
413-231 Deer,SeaLn,Pr.Dog
413-232↓ Dolphin,Deer,SeaLn
421-111↓ Mole,Deer,SeaLn
422-111↓ Mole,Deer,SeaLn
422-332↓ Deer,SeaLn,Swan
423-111 Mole,Deer,SeaLn
423-112 Dolphin,Deer,SeaLn
423-121 Mole,Deer,SeaLn
423-122 Dolphin,Deer,SeaLn
423-131 Pr.Dog,Mole,Deer
423-132 Pr.Dog,Dolphin,Deer
423-211↓ Deer,SeaLn,Dolphin
423-231 Deer,SeaLn,Pr.Dog
423-232↓ Dolphin,Deer,SeaLn
431-111 Cottn,Dog,Swan
431-112 Swan,Dog,Deer
431-121 Cottn,Dog,Swan
431-122 Swan,Dog,Deer
431-131 Cottn,Dog,Swan
431-132 Swan,Dog,Pr.Dog
431-211 Cottn,Swan,Dog
431-212 Swan,Dog,Deer
431-221 Cottn,Swan,Dog
431-222 Swan,Dog,Deer
431-231 Cottn,Swan,Dog
431-232 Swan,Dog,Deer
431-311↓ Swan,Deer,SeaLn
432-111 Cottn,Dog,Swan
432-112 Swan,Dog,Deer
432-121 Cottn,Dog,Swan
432-122 Swan,Dog,Deer
432-131 Cottn,Pr.Dog,Dog
432-132 Swan,Pr.Dog,Dog
432-211 Cottn,Swan,Dog
432-212 Swan,Dog,Deer
432-221 Cottn,Swan,Dog
432-222 Swan,Dog,Deer
432-231 Cottn,Swan,Pr.Dog
432-232 Swan,Pr.Dog,Dog
432-311↓ Swan,Deer,SeaLn
433-111 Cottn,Pr.Dog,Dog
433-112 Swan,Pr.Dog,Dog
433-121 Pr.Dog,Cottn,Dog
433-122 Pr.Dog,Swan,Dog
433-211↓ Cottn,Swan,Pr.Dog
433-212 Swan,Pr.Dog,Dolphin
433-221 Pr.Dog,Cottn,Swan
433-222 Swan,Pr.Dog,Dolphin
433-231↓ Pr.Dog,Cottn,Swan
433-311 Swan,Deer,SeaLn
433-312 Swan,Dolphin,Deer

433-321 Swan,Deer,SeaLn
433-322 Swan,Dolphin,Deer
433-331 Swan,Pr.Dog,Deer
433-332 Swan,Pr.Dog,Dolphin
441-111↓ Dog,Pr.Dog
441-331↓ Dog,Pr.Dog,Swan
442-111↓ Dog,Pr.Dog
442-312↓ Dog,Swan,Pr.Dog
443-111↓ Pr.Dog,Dog
443-322↓ Pr.Dog,Dog,Swan

221-

111-111↓ Porcp,Mole,Snake
111-311↓ MGoat,Porcp,Mole
112-111↓ Porcp,Mole,Snake
112-311↓ MGoat,Porcp,Mole
113-111↓ Porcp,Mole,Snake
113-311↓ MGoat,Porcp,Mole
113-332 Porcp,Mole,Beaver
121-111↓ Porcp,Mole,Snake
121-321↓ MGoat,Porcp,Mole
122-111↓ Porcp,Mole,Snake
122-211↓ MGoat,Porcp,Mole
123-111↓ Porcp,Mole,Snake
123-132↓ Porcp,Mole,Bat
123-211 MGoat,Porcp,Mole
123-232 Porcp,Mole,Beaver
123-321↓ MGoat,Porcp,Mole
123-332 Porcp,Mole,Beaver
131-111↓ Porcp,Mole,Snake
131-231↓ Porcp,Mole,MGoat
131-232 Porcp,Beaver,Mole
131-321↓ MGoat,Porcp,Mole
131-332 Porcp,Beaver,Mole
132-111 Porcp,Mole,Snake
132-132↓ Porcp,Mole,Bat
132-211 MGoat,Porcp,Mole
132-231↓ Porcp,Mole,Beaver
132-311↓ MGoat,Porcp,Mole
132-322 Porcp,MGoat,Beaver
132-331↓ Beaver,Porcp,Mole
133-111↓ Porcp,Mole,Bat
133-211 MGoat,Porcp,Mole
133-212 Bat,Porcp,MGoat
133-221 Porcp,Mole,Bat
133-222 Bat,Porcp,Beaver
133-231 Beaver,Porcp,Mole
133-232 Beaver,Bat,Porcp
133-311 MGoat,Porcp,Mole
133-312 MGoat,Bat,Porcp
133-321 MGoat,Porcp,Mole
133-322 Bat,Porcp,Beaver
133-331 Beaver,Porcp,Mole
133-332 Beaver,Bat,Porcp
141-111 Sheep,Porcp,Mole
141-112 Porcp,Sheep,Beaver
141-121 Sheep,Porcp,Mole
141-122↓ Porcp,Beaver,Sheep
141-211 Sheep,Beaver,MGoat
142-111↓ Sheep,Beaver,Porcp
143-111↓ Beaver,Sheep,Bat
143-112 Beaver,Bat,Porcp
143-121 Beaver,Sheep,Bat
143-122↓ Beaver,Bat,Porcp
143-211↓ Beaver,Sheep

211-111 Snake,MGoat
211-112↓ Snake,MGoat,Vultre
211-121 Snake,MGoat,Porcp
211-122 Vultre,Snake,MGoat
211-131 Snake,MGoat,Porcp
211-132 Vultre,Porcp,Snake
211-211↓ MGoat,Snake
211-332↓ MGoat,Pcock,Beaver
212-111 Snake,MGoat
212-112↓ Snake,MGoat,Vultre
212-121 Snake,MGoat,Porcp
212-122 Vultre,Snake,MGoat
212-131 Snake,MGoat,Porcp
212-132 Vultre,Porcp,Snake
212-222↓ MGoat,Vultre,Snake
212-232↓ MGoat,Beaver,Vultre
212-332 MGoat,Beaver,Deer
213-111 Snake,MGoat
213-112↓ Snake,MGoat,Bat
213-122 Bat,Vultre,Snake
213-131 Snake,MGoat,Bat
213-132 Bat,Vultre,Porcp
213-211↓ MGoat,Snake
213-332↓ Beaver,MGoat,Bat
221-111 Snake,MGoat
221-112↓ Snake,MGoat,Porcp
221-232 MGoat,Beaver,Porcp
221-311↓ MGoat,Snake
221-322↓ MGoat,Deer
221-332 MGoat,Beaver
222-111 Snake,MGoat
222-112↓ Snake,MGoat,Porcp
222-231 MGoat,Snake,Beaver
222-232 MGoat,Beaver,Porcp
222-322↓ MGoat,Deer,Snake
222-331 MGoat,Beaver,Snake
222-332 MGoat,Beaver,Deer
223-111↓ Snake,MGoat,Bat
223-132 Bat,Porcp,Beaver
223-212↓ MGoat,Snake,Bat
223-222↓ MGoat,Bat,Beaver
223-312↓ MGoat,Snake,Bat
223-332↓ Beaver,MGoat,Bat
231-111↓ Snake,MGoat,Bat
231-132 Bat,Beaver,Porcp
231-211 MGoat,Snake,Sheep
231-212 MGoat,Snake,Bat
231-221 MGoat,Sheep,Snake
231-222 MGoat,Bat,Beaver
231-231 MGoat,Beaver,Sheep
231-232↓ Beaver,MGoat,Bat
231-322↓ MGoat,Beaver,Sheep
232-111↓ Snake,MGoat,Bat
232-131 Beaver,Bat,Snake
232-132 Bat,Beaver,Porcp
232-211 MGoat,Snake,Sheep
232-212 MGoat,Bat,Snake
232-221 MGoat,Sheep,Beaver
232-222 MGoat,Beaver,Bat
232-231 Beaver,MGoat,Sheep
232-232 Beaver,Bat,MGoat
232-311 MGoat,Snake
232-312 MGoat,Beaver,Bat
232-321 MGoat,Sheep,Beaver
232-322 MGoat,Beaver,Bat

232-331 Beaver,MGoat,Sheep
232-332 Beaver,MGoat,Bat
233-111↓ Bat,Snake,MGoat
233-131↓ Bat,Beaver,Snake
233-211 MGoat,Bat,Snake
233-212↓ Bat,MGoat,Beaver
241-111 Sheep,Beaver
241-211↓ Sheep,Beaver,MGoat
242-111↓ Sheep,Beaver,Snake
242-112 Beaver,Sheep,Bat
242-121 Sheep,Beaver,Dog
242-211↓ Sheep,Beaver,MGoat
243-111↓ Beaver,Sheep,Bat
243-131 Beaver,Sheep,Pr.Dog
243-132 Beaver,Bat,Pr.Dog
243-211 Beaver,Sheep,MGoat
243-321↓ Beaver,Sheep,Pr.Dog
311-111↓ Snake,MGoat,Pcock
311-122 Pcock,Weasel,Vultre
311-131 Pcock,Snake,MGoat
311-132 Pcock,Weasel,Vultre
311-312↓ MGoat,Pcock,Deer
312-111 Snake,MGoat
312-112↓ Snake,MGoat,Weasel
312-122 Weasel,Vultre,Snake
312-131 Snake,MGoat,Weasel
312-132 Weasel,Vultre,Porcp
312-211 MGoat,Snake
312-222↓ Weasel,MGoat,Pcock
312-312↓ MGoat,Deer,Weasel
312-322 Deer,Weasel,Swan
312-331 MGoat,Deer,Weasel
312-332 Deer,Weasel,Swan
313-111 Snake,MGoat
313-112↓ Snake,MGoat,Bat
313-122 Bat,Weasel,Vultre
313-131 Snake,MGoat,Bat
313-132 Bat,W.Cat,Weasel
313-222↓ Weasel,MGoat,W.Cat
313-231 MGoat,Weasel,Pr.Dog
313-232 W.Cat,Weasel,Pr.Dog
313-311↓ MGoat,Deer,Weasel
313-322 Deer,Weasel,Swan
313-331 MGoat,Deer,Weasel
313-332 Deer,W.Cat,Weasel
321-111↓ Snake,MGoat
321-121↓ Snake,MGoat,Porcp
321-212↓ MGoat,Snake,Swan
321-222↓ MGoat,Swan,Deer
322-111 Snake,MGoat
322-112↓ Snake,MGoat,Porcp
322-212↓ MGoat,Snake,Swan
322-221 MGoat,Snake,Deer
322-222 MGoat,Swan,W.Cat
322-231 MGoat,Snake,Beaver
322-232 MGoat,W.Cat,Beaver
322-311 MGoat,Deer,Snake
322-312↓ MGoat,Swan,Deer
323-111↓ Snake,MGoat,Bat
323-132 Bat,W.Cat
323-212↓ MGoat,Snake,Bat
323-222 MGoat,Bat,W.Cat
323-231 MGoat,Pr.Dog,Beaver
323-232 W.Cat,Pr.Dog,Beaver
323-311↓ MGoat,Swan,Deer

(221 cont'd)

323-332	Swan,Deer,W.Cat
331-111	Snake,MGoat
331-112↓	Snake,MGoat,Bat
331-122	Bat,Swan,Dog
331-131	Snake,MGoat,Bat
331-132	Bat,Swan,Beaver
331-211	MGoat,Snake,Swan
331-212↓	MGoat,Swan,Dog
331-231	Swan,MGoat,Beaver
331-232	Swan,Beaver,Dog
331-311↓	Swan,MGoat
331-322↓	Swan,Deer
332-111↓	Snake,MGoat,Bat
332-122	Bat,Swan,Dog
332-131	Beaver,Bat,Snake
332-132	Bat,Beaver,Swan
332-211	MGoat,Snake,Swan
332-212↓	MGoat,Swan,Dog
332-231	Beaver,Swan,MGoat
332-232	Beaver,Swan,Pr.Dog
332-312↓	Swan,MGoat,Deer
332-331	Swan,Beaver,MGoat
332-332	Swan,Beaver,Deer
333-111↓	Bat,Snake,MGoat
333-121↓	Bat,Pengn,Snake
333-131↓	Bat,Pr.Dog,Beaver
333-211	MGoat,Bat,Snake
333-212↓	Bat,MGoat,Swan
333-222	Bat,Swan,Pr.Dog
333-231↓	Pr.Dog,Beaver,Bat
333-311↓	Swan,MGoat,Bat
333-322	Swan,Bat,Pr.Dog
333-331↓	Swan,Pr.Dog,Beaver
341-111	Dog,Sheep,Pengn
341-112↓	Dog,Sheep,Beaver
341-311↓	Dog,Sheep,Swan
341-321	Dog,Sheep,Beaver
341-322	Dog,Swan,Beaver
341-331	Beaver,Dog,Sheep
341-332	Beaver,Dog,Pr.Dog
342-111↓	Dog,Sheep,Beaver
342-131↓	Beaver,Pr.Dog,Dog
342-211↓	Dog,Sheep,Beaver
342-231↓	Beaver,Pr.Dog,Dog
342-311	Dog,Sheep,Beaver
342-312	Dog,Beaver,Swan
342-321	Dog,Sheep,Beaver
342-322	Dog,Beaver,Swan
342-331↓	Beaver,Pr.Dog,Dog
343-111↓	Pengn,Pr.Dog,Beaver
343-332↓	Pr.Dog,Beaver,Dog
411-111↓	Pcock,Swan,Deer
412-111	Pcock,Snake,MGoat
412-112	Pcock,Swan,W.Cat
412-121	Pcock,W.Cat,Deer
412-122	Pcock,W.Cat,Swan
412-131	Pcock,W.Cat,Deer
412-132	W.Cat,Pcock,Swan
412-211↓	Pcock,Deer,Swan
412-222	Pcock,Swan,W.Cat
412-231	Pcock,W.Cat,Deer
412-232	W.Cat,Pcock,Swan
412-311	Deer,Swan,Pcock
412-332	Swan,Deer,W.Cat
413-111	Pcock,W.Cat,Snake
413-112	W.Cat,Pcock,Swan
413-121	W.Cat,Pcock,Deer
413-122	W.Cat,Pcock,Swan
413-211↓	Pcock,Deer,W.Cat
413-212	W.Cat,Swan,Pcock
413-221	W.Cat,Pcock,Deer
413-222	W.Cat,Swan,Pcock
413-231	W.Cat,Pcock,Deer
413-232	W.Cat,Swan,Pcock
413-322↓	Swan,Deer,W.Cat
421-111	Snake,Swan,MGoat
421-112↓	Swan,Deer,Pcock
421-122↓	Swan,Deer,W.Cat
421-211	Swan,Deer,MGoat
421-212↓	Swan,Deer,Pcock
421-332↓	Swan,Deer,W.Cat
422-111	Snake,Swan,MGoat
422-112↓	Swan,W.Cat,Deer
423-111	W.Cat,Snake,Swan
423-211↓	Swan,Deer,W.Cat
431-111↓	Swan,Cottn
431-311↓	Swan,Deer
432-111↓	Swan,Cottn
432-231↓	Swan,Cottn,W.Cat
432-311↓	Swan,Deer
433-111↓	Swan,Cottn,Bat
433-122	Swan,Bat,W.Cat
433-131	Swan,W.Cat,Cottn
433-132↓	Swan,W.Cat,Bat
433-221↓	Swan,Cottn,W.Cat
433-311↓	Swan,Deer
441-111↓	Swan,Dog,Sheep
441-231↓	Swan,Dog,Beaver
441-232↓	Swan,Sable,Dog
442-111↓	Swan,Dog,Sheep
442-131↓	Swan,Beaver,Pr.Dog
442-222↓	Swan,Dog,Beaver
442-231	Swan,Beaver,Pr.Dog
442-332↓	Swan,Sable,Beaver
443-111↓	Pengn,Swan,Pr.Dog
443-131	Pr.Dog,Beaver,Pengn
443-132	Pr.Dog,Beaver,Swan
443-211↓	Swan,Pr.Dog,Dog
443-231↓	Pr.Dog,Beaver,Swan
443-331↓	Swan,Pr.Dog,Sable

222-

111-111	Porcp,Mole,Snake
111-112↓	Porcp,Vultre,Mole
111-211↓	MGoat,Porcp,Pcock
111-221	Porcp,Pcock,Swan
111-222	Porcp,Pcock,Vultre
111-231	Porcp,Pcock,Mole
111-232	Porcp,Pcock,Vultre
111-311	MGoat,Pcock,Porcp
111-331	Pcock,Porcp,Mole
111-332	Pcock,Porcp,Deer
112-111	Porcp,Mole,Snake
112-112↓	Porcp,Vultre,Mole
112-211	MGoat,Porcp,Mole
112-212	Porcp,MGoat,Vultre
112-221	Porcp,Mole,MGoat
112-222	Porcp,Vultre,Mole
112-231	Porcp,Mole,Beaver
112-232	Porcp,Beaver,Vultre
112-311↓	MGoat,Porcp,Deer
112-321	MGoat,Porcp,Mole
112-322	Porcp,Deer,Vultre
112-331	Beaver,Porcp,Mole
112-332	Beaver,Porcp,Deer
113-111	Porcp,Mole,Snake
113-112↓	Porcp,Vultre,Mole
113-131	Porcp,Mole,Beaver
113-132	Porcp,Vultre,Mole
113-211	MGoat,Porcp,Mole
113-212	Porcp,MGoat,Vultre
113-221	Porcp,Mole,MGoat
113-222	Porcp,Beaver,Vultre
113-231↓	Beaver,Porcp,Mole
113-311	MGoat,Porcp,Mole
113-312	MGoat,Porcp,Deer
113-321	MGoat,Porcp,Mole
113-322	Porcp,Deer,Beaver
113-331	Beaver,Porcp,Mole
113-332	Beaver,Porcp,Deer
121-111↓	Porcp,Mole,Snake
121-211↓	MGoat,Porcp,Mole
121-232	Porcp,Beaver,Mole
121-311↓	MGoat,Porcp,Deer
121-321	MGoat,Porcp,Mole
121-322	Porcp,Deer,MGoat
121-331	Porcp,Mole,MGoat
121-332	Porcp,Deer,Beaver
122-111↓	Porcp,Mole,Snake
122-131↓	Porcp,Mole,Beaver
122-211	MGoat,Porcp,Mole
122-231↓	Porcp,Mole,Beaver
122-311↓	MGoat,Porcp,Deer
122-321	MGoat,Porcp,Mole
122-322	Porcp,Deer,MGoat
122-331	Beaver,Porcp,Mole
122-332	Beaver,Porcp,Deer
123-111↓	Porcp,Mole,Snake
123-122↓	Porcp,Mole,Bat
123-131↓	Porcp,Mole,Beaver
123-211	MGoat,Porcp,Mole
123-222	Porcp,Beaver,Mole
123-311↓	MGoat,Porcp,Deer
123-321	MGoat,Porcp,Mole
123-322	Porcp,Deer,Beaver
123-331	Beaver,Porcp,Mole
123-332	Beaver,Porcp,Deer
131-111↓	Porcp,Mole,Sheep
131-131↓	Porcp,Mole,Beaver
131-211↓	Sheep,MGoat,Porcp
131-221	Sheep,Porcp,Mole
131-222↓	Sheep,Porcp,Beaver
131-312↓	Sheep,MGoat,Beaver
131-322↓	Sheep,Beaver,Porcp
132-111	Porcp,Mole,Sheep
132-112	Porcp,Mole,Beaver
132-121	Porcp,Mole,Sheep
132-122	Porcp,Mole,Beaver
132-212	Beaver,Sheep,Porcp
132-311	Sheep,MGoat,Beaver
132-322↓	Beaver,Sheep,Porcp
133-111	Porcp,Mole,Bat
133-112	Bat,Porcp,Beaver
133-121	Porcp,Mole,Bat

133-122	Bat,Porcp,Beaver
133-131	Beaver,Porcp,Mole
133-132	Beaver,Bat,Porcp
133-211	Sheep,Beaver,MGoat
133-212	Beaver,Bat,Sheep
133-221	Beaver,Sheep,Porcp
133-222↓	Beaver,Bat,Sheep
133-232	Beaver,Baboon,Bat
133-311↓	Sheep,Beaver,MGoat
141-111↓	Sheep,Beaver
142-111↓	Sheep,Beaver
143-111↓	Sheep,Beaver
211-111	Snake,MGoat,Vultre
211-131↓	Vultre,Pcock,Snake
211-212↓	Pcock,MGoat,Vultre
211-221	Pcock,MGoat,Sheep
211-222	Pcock,Vultre,Weasel
211-231	Pcock,MGoat,Beaver
211-232	Pcock,Vultre,Beaver
211-331↓	Pcock,MGoat,Deer
211-332	Pcock,Deer,Beaver
212-111↓	Snake,MGoat,Vultre
212-122	Vultre,Weasel,Snake
212-131↓	Vultre,Beaver,Snake
212-211	MGoat,Snake,Sheep
212-212	MGoat,Vultre,Weasel
212-221	MGoat,Sheep,Vultre
212-222	Vultre,Weasel,MGoat
212-231	Beaver,MGoat,Sheep
212-232	Beaver,Vultre,Weasel
212-311↓	MGoat,Deer,Weasel
212-321	MGoat,Deer,Sheep
212-322	Deer,Weasel,Vultre
212-331	Beaver,MGoat,Deer
212-332	Beaver,Deer,Weasel
213-111↓	Snake,MGoat,Vultre
213-211↓	MGoat,Vultre,Beaver
213-221	MGoat,Beaver,Sheep
213-222	Beaver,Vultre,Weasel
213-312↓	MGoat,Deer,Beaver
213-322	Deer,Beaver,Weasel
213-331↓	Beaver,MGoat,Deer
221-111	Snake,MGoat,Sheep
221-112	Snake,MGoat,Porcp
221-121	Snake,MGoat,Sheep
221-122	Snake,MGoat,Porcp
221-131	Snake,MGoat,Beaver
221-132	Beaver,Porcp,Snake
221-211↓	MGoat,Snake,Sheep
221-222↓	MGoat,Sheep,Beaver
221-321↓	MGoat,Deer,Sheep
221-332	Deer,Beaver,MGoat
222-111	Snake,MGoat,Sheep
222-112	Snake,MGoat,Porcp
222-121	Snake,MGoat,Sheep
222-122↓	Snake,MGoat,Beaver
222-132	Beaver,Porcp,Snake
222-211	MGoat,Snake,Sheep
222-212	MGoat,Snake,Beaver
222-221↓	MGoat,Sheep,Beaver
222-311	MGoat,Deer,Sheep
222-312	MGoat,Deer,Beaver
222-321	MGoat,Deer,Sheep
222-322↓	Deer,MGoat,Beaver
223-111↓	Snake,MGoat,Bat

223-122	Bat,Beaver,Snake
223-211	MGoat,Snake,Sheep
223-212	MGoat,Beaver,Snake
223-221	MGoat,Beaver,Sheep
223-222	Beaver,MGoat,Bat
223-231	Beaver,MGoat,Sheep
223-232	Beaver,W.Cat,Baboon
223-311	MGoat,Deer,Sheep
223-312↓	MGoat,Deer,Beaver
223-332	Beaver,Deer,W.Cat
231-111↓	Sheep,Snake,MGoat
231-121	Sheep,Beaver,Snake
231-132↓	Beaver,Sheep,Bat
231-211↓	Sheep,MGoat,Beaver
231-322↓	Sheep,Beaver,Deer
232-111	Sheep,Snake,MGoat
232-112↓	Beaver,Bat,Sheep
232-211↓	Sheep,MGoat,Beaver
233-111↓	Bat,Sheep,Beaver
233-211	Sheep,Beaver,MGoat
233-212↓	Beaver,Bat,Sheep
233-231	Beaver,Sheep,Baboon
233-232	Beaver,Baboon,Pr.Dog
233-311	Sheep,Beaver,MGoat
233-331	Beaver,Sheep,Baboon
233-332	Beaver,Baboon,Pr.Dog
241-111↓	Sheep,Beaver,Dog
242-111↓	Sheep,Beaver,Dog
243-111	Sheep,Beaver,Pengn
243-112	Beaver,Sheep,Pr.Dog
243-121	Beaver,Sheep,Pengn
243-211↓	Sheep,Beaver,Pr.Dog
311-111	Pcock,Snake,MGoat
311-122↓	Pcock,Weasel,Vultre
311-222↓	Pcock,Weasel,Deer
311-311	Pcock,Deer,MGoat
311-332↓	Pcock,Deer,Weasel
312-111	Snake,MGoat,Weasel
312-112↓	Weasel,Vultre,Pcock
312-211↓	MGoat,Weasel,Pcock
312-221↓	Weasel,Pcock,Deer
312-232	Weasel,Pcock,W.Cat
312-311	Deer,MGoat,Weasel
312-312↓	Deer,Weasel,Swan
313-111	Snake,MGoat,Weasel
313-112	Weasel,Vultre,Snake
313-121↓	Weasel,Vultre,W.Cat
313-131	Weasel,Pr.Dog,Beaver
313-132	W.Cat,Weasel,Vultre
313-211↓	MGoat,Weasel,Pcock
313-221↓	Weasel,W.Cat,Pcock
313-231	Weasel,Pr.Dog,Beaver
313-232	W.Cat,Weasel,Pr.Dog
313-311	Deer,MGoat,Weasel
313-312↓	Deer,Weasel,Swan
313-331	Deer,Weasel,Pr.Dog
313-332	Deer,W.Cat,Weasel
321-111	Snake,MGoat
321-112↓	Snake,MGoat,Deer
321-122	Deer,Swan,Pcock
321-131	Snake,MGoat,Deer
321-132	W.Cat,Deer,Swan
321-211	MGoat,Deer,Snake
321-212↓	MGoat,Deer,Swan
321-232	Deer,Swan,W.Cat

321-311↓	Deer,Swan,MGoat
322-111↓	Snake,MGoat,Deer
322-122	W.Cat,Deer,Swan
322-131	Beaver,W.Cat,Snake
322-132	W.Cat,Beaver,Deer
322-211	MGoat,Deer,Snake
322-212	MGoat,Deer,Swan
322-231↓	Deer,Beaver,W.Cat
322-311↓	Deer,Swan,MGoat
322-322	Deer,Swan,W.Cat
322-331	Deer,Swan,Beaver
322-332	Deer,Swan,W.Cat
323-111	Snake,MGoat,Pengn
323-112	Snake,MGoat,Bat
323-121	W.Cat,Pengn,Snake
323-122	W.Cat,Bat,Pr.Dog
323-131↓	Pr.Dog,Beaver,W.Cat
323-211↓	MGoat,Deer,W.Cat
323-222	W.Cat,Beaver,Swan
323-231↓	Pr.Dog,Beaver,W.Cat
323-311↓	Deer,Swan,MGoat
323-321↓	Deer,Swan,W.Cat
323-331	Deer,Swan,Pr.Dog
323-332	Deer,Swan,W.Cat
331-111	Sheep,Snake,Swan
331-112↓	Swan,Dog,Sheep
331-131	Beaver,Sheep,Swan
331-132	Swan,Beaver,Dog
331-211	Swan,Sheep,MGoat
331-212↓	Swan,Dog,Sheep
331-231	Swan,Beaver,Sheep
331-232	Swan,Beaver,Dog
331-331↓	Swan,Deer,Beaver
332-111	Sheep,Snake,Swan
332-112	Swan,Dog,Beaver
332-121	Sheep,Swan,Dog
332-122	Swan,Dog,Beaver
332-131	Beaver,Sheep,Swan
332-132	Beaver,Swan,Pr.Dog
332-211	Swan,Sheep,MGoat
332-212	Swan,Beaver,Dog
332-221	Swan,Sheep,Dog
332-222	Swan,Dog,Beaver
332-231	Beaver,Swan,Sheep
332-232	Beaver,Swan,Pr.Dog
332-331↓	Swan,Beaver,Deer
333-111	Pengn,Bat,Sheep
333-112	Bat,Swan,Pr.Dog
333-121	Pengn,Bat,Pr.Dog
333-122	Bat,Pr.Dog,Beaver
333-131	Pr.Dog,Beaver,Pengn
333-132	Pr.Dog,Beaver,Bat
333-211	Swan,Sheep,Pr.Dog
333-212↓	Swan,Pr.Dog,Beaver
333-321↓	Swan,Pr.Dog,Beaver
333-331↓	Swan,Pr.Dog,Beaver
341-111	Sheep,Dog
341-112↓	Dog,Sheep,Beaver
341-132	Beaver,Dog,Pr.Dog
341-211	Sheep,Dog,Beaver
341-232	Beaver,Dog,Pr.Dog
341-311↓	Sheep,Dog,Swan
341-321	Sheep,Dog,Beaver
341-322	Dog,Swan,Sheep
341-331	Beaver,Sheep,Dog

(222 cont'd)

341-332 Beaver,Dog,Pr.Dog
342-111↓ Sheep,Dog,Beaver
342-131 Beaver,Sheep,Pr.Dog
342-132 Beaver,Pr.Dog,Dog
342-211↓ Sheep,Dog,Beaver
342-231 Beaver,Sheep,Pr.Dog
342-232 Beaver,Pr.Dog,Dog
342-311 Sheep,Dog,Beaver
342-312 Dog,Beaver,Swan
342-321 Sheep,Dog,Beaver
342-322 Dog,Beaver,Swan
342-331 Beaver,Sheep,Pr.Dog
342-332 Beaver,Pr.Dog,Dog
343-111 Pengn,Sheep,Pr.Dog
343-112↓ Pr.Dog,Beaver,Pengn
343-211 Sheep,Pr.Dog,Beaver
343-212 Pr.Dog,Beaver,Dog
343-221 Pr.Dog,Beaver,Sheep
343-222 Pr.Dog,Beaver,Dog
343-231 Pr.Dog,Beaver,Sheep
343-232 Pr.Dog,Beaver,Dog
343-311 Sheep,Pr.Dog,Beaver
343-312 Pr.Dog,Beaver,Dog
343-321 Pr.Dog,Beaver,Sheep
343-322 Pr.Dog,Beaver,Dog
343-331 Pr.Dog,Beaver,Sheep
343-332 Pr.Dog,Beaver,Dog
411-111↓ Pcock,Deer
411-311↓ Pcock,Deer,Swan
412-111 Pcock,Deer
412-112↓ Pcock,Deer,Swan
412-121↓ Pcock,Deer,W.Cat
412-211↓ Pcock,Deer,Swan
412-231↓ Pcock,Deer,W.Cat
412-311↓ Deer,Swan,Pcock
413-111↓ Pcock,W.Cat,Deer
413-321↓ Deer,Swan,W.Cat
421-111↓ Swan,Deer,Pcock
421-131↓ Swan,Deer,W.Cat
421-211↓ Swan,Deer,Pcock
421-231↓ Swan,Deer,W.Cat
422-111↓ Swan,Deer,W.Cat
423-111↓ W.Cat,Swan,Deer
431-111↓ Swan,Cottn
432-111↓ Swan,Cottn,Deer
432-131↓ Swan,Cottn,W.Cat
432-211↓ Swan,Cottn,Deer
432-232 Swan,W.Cat
432-311↓ Swan,Deer
433-111 Swan,Cottn
433-131↓ Swan,W.Cat,Cottn
433-132 Swan,W.Cat,Pr.Dog
433-211↓ Swan,Cottn,Deer
433-231↓ Swan,W.Cat,Cottn
433-311↓ Swan,Deer
441-111↓ Swan,Dog,Sheep
441-131↓ Swan,Dog,Beaver
441-232↓ Swan,Sable,Dog
442-111↓ Swan,Dog,Sheep
442-122 Swan,Dog,Beaver
442-131↓ Swan,Beaver,Pr.Dog
442-211 Swan,Dog,Sheep
442-212 Swan,Dog,Beaver
442-221 Swan,Dog,Sheep

442-222 Swan,Dog,Beaver
442-231 Swan,Beaver,Pr.Dog
442-232↓ Swan,Beaver,Sable
443-111↓ Pengn,Swan,Pr.Dog
443-131 Pr.Dog,Beaver,Pengn
443-132 Pr.Dog,Beaver,Swan
443-211↓ Swan,Pr.Dog,Dog
443-231 Pr.Dog,Beaver,Swan
443-331↓ Swan,Pr.Dog,Sable

223-

111-111 Porcp,Mole,Pcock
111-112 Porcp,Pcock,Vultre
111-121 Porcp,Mole,Pcock
111-122 Porcp,Pcock,Vultre
111-131 Porcp,Mole,Pcock
111-132 Porcp,Pcock,Vultre
111-211 Pcock,MGoat,Sheep
111-221↓ Pcock,Sheep,Porcp
111-331↓ Pcock,Deer,Sheep
112-111 Porcp,Mole,Snake
112-112↓ Porcp,Vultre,Mole
112-211 MGoat,Sheep,Porcp
112-212 Porcp,MGoat,Pcock
112-221 Sheep,Porcp,Mole
112-222 Porcp,Pcock,Sheep
112-231 Sheep,Porcp,Mole
112-232 Porcp,Beaver,Pcock
112-311 MGoat,Deer,Sheep
112-312 Deer,MGoat,Pcock
112-321 Deer,Sheep,Pcock
112-322 Deer,Pcock,Porcp
112-331 Deer,Sheep,Beaver
112-332 Deer,Beaver,Pcock
113-111 Porcp,Mole,Snake
113-112↓ Porcp,Vultre,Mole
113-131 Porcp,Mole,Beaver
113-132 Porcp,Vultre,Mole
113-211↓ MGoat,Sheep,Porcp
113-221 Sheep,Porcp,Mole
113-222↓ Porcp,Sheep,Beaver
113-232 Beaver,Porcp,Baboon
113-311 MGoat,Deer,Sheep
113-312 Deer,MGoat,Porcp
113-321 Deer,Sheep,MGoat
113-322 Deer,Porcp
113-331 Deer,Beaver,Sheep
113-332 Deer,Beaver,Porcp
121-111↓ Porcp,Mole,Snake
121-131↓ Porcp,Mole,Sheep
121-211↓ MGoat,Sheep,Porcp
121-221 Sheep,Porcp,Mole
121-222 Porcp,Sheep,Deer
121-231 Sheep,Porcp,Mole
121-232 Porcp,Sheep,Deer
121-311 MGoat,Deer,Sheep
121-312 Deer,MGoat,Porcp
121-321 Deer,Sheep,MGoat
121-331↓ Deer,Sheep,Porcp
122-111↓ Porcp,Mole,Snake
122-121↓ Porcp,Mole,Sheep
122-211↓ MGoat,Sheep,Porcp
122-221 Sheep,Porcp,Mole
122-222 Porcp,Sheep,Deer
122-231 Sheep,Porcp,Mole

122-232 Porcp,Beaver,Sheep
122-311 MGoat,Deer,Sheep
122-312 Deer,MGoat,Porcp
122-321 Deer,Sheep,MGoat
122-322 Deer,Porcp,Sheep
122-331 Deer,Sheep,Beaver
122-332 Deer,Beaver,Porcp
123-111↓ Porcp,Mole,Snake
123-131↓ Porcp,Mole,Beaver
123-211↓ MGoat,Sheep,Porcp
123-221 Sheep,Porcp,Mole
123-222↓ Porcp,Sheep,Beaver
123-232 Beaver,Porcp,Baboon
123-311 MGoat,Deer,Sheep
123-312 Deer,MGoat,Porcp
123-321 Deer,Sheep,MGoat
123-322 Deer,Porcp
123-331 Deer,Beaver,Sheep
123-332 Deer,Beaver,Baboon
131-111 Sheep,Porcp,Mole
131-232↓ Sheep,Beaver,Porcp
131-332↓ Sheep,Beaver,Deer
132-111 Sheep,Porcp,Mole
132-122↓ Porcp,Sheep,Beaver
132-211 Sheep,MGoat
132-232↓ Beaver,Sheep,Baboon
132-332↓ Beaver,Sheep,Deer
133-111 Sheep,Porcp,Mole
133-112 Bat,Porcp,Sheep
133-121 Sheep,Porcp,Mole
133-122 Bat,Porcp,Sheep
133-131 Beaver,Sheep,Baboon
133-132 Beaver,Baboon,Bat
133-322↓ Sheep,Beaver,Baboon
141-111↓ Sheep,Beaver
141-212↓ Sheep,Dog,Beaver
142-111↓ Sheep,Beaver
142-332↓ Beaver,Sheep,Pr.Dog
143-111↓ Sheep,Beaver
143-122↓ Sheep,Beaver,Pr.Dog
211-111 Pcock,Snake,MGoat
211-131↓ Pcock,Vultre,Sheep
211-211↓ Pcock,MGoat,Sheep
211-331↓ Pcock,Deer,Sheep
212-111↓ Snake,MGoat,Vultre
212-121 Vultre,Sheep,Snake
212-122 Vultre,Pcock,Sheep
212-131 Vultre,Sheep,Beaver
212-132 Vultre,Beaver,Pcock
212-211↓ MGoat,Sheep,Pcock
212-222 Pcock,Sheep,Vultre
212-231↓ Sheep,Beaver,Pcock
212-311 MGoat,Deer,Sheep
212-312 Deer,MGoat,Pcock
212-321↓ Deer,Sheep,Pcock
212-331 Deer,Sheep,Beaver
212-332 Deer,Beaver,Pcock
213-111↓ Snake,MGoat,Vultre
213-121↓ Vultre,Sheep,Snake
213-131 Beaver,Vultre,Sheep
213-132 Vultre,Beaver,Pr.Dog
213-212↓ MGoat,Sheep,Vultre
213-221 Sheep,MGoat,Beaver
213-222 Sheep,Beaver,Vultre
213-231 Beaver,Sheep,Pr.Dog

213-232 Beaver,Pr.Dog,Baboon	312-122 Pcock,Weasel,Vultre	331-312 Swan,Deer,Dog
213-311↓ MGoat,Deer,Sheep	312-131 Pcock,Weasel,Deer	331-321 Swan,Deer,Sheep
213-331 Deer,Beaver,Sheep	312-132 Pcock,Weasel,Vultre	331-322 Swan,Deer,Dog
213-332 Deer,Beaver,Pr.Dog	312-211 Pcock,Deer,MGoat	331-331 Swan,Deer,Sheep
221-111↓ Snake,MGoat,Sheep	312-322↓ Deer,Pcock,Weasel	331-332 Swan,Deer,Dog
221-132 Sheep,Beaver,Deer	313-111 Pcock,Snake,MGoat	332-111 Sheep,Dog,Cottn
221-211 MGoat,Sheep,Snake	313-112 Pcock,Weasel,Vultre	332-112 Dog,Sheep,Swan
221-212 MGoat,Sheep,Deer	313-121 Pcock,Weasel,Pr.Dog	332-121 Sheep,Dog,Cottn
221-332↓ Deer,Sheep,Beaver	313-122 Pcock,Weasel,Vultre	332-122 Dog,Sheep,Swan
222-111↓ Snake,MGoat,Sheep	313-131 Pr.Dog,Pcock,Weasel	332-131 Sheep,Pr.Dog,Dog
222-131 Sheep,Beaver,Snake	313-132 Pr.Dog,Pcock,W.Cat	332-132 Pr.Dog,Dog,Beaver
222-132 Beaver,Sheep,Deer	313-211 Pcock,Deer,MGoat	332-211 Sheep,Dog,Cottn
222-211 MGoat,Sheep,Snake	313-212↓ Pcock,Deer,Weasel	332-212 Dog,Swan,Sheep
222-212 MGoat,Sheep,Deer	313-231↓ Pr.Dog,Pcock,Deer	332-221 Sheep,Dog,Cottn
222-231 Sheep,Beaver,MGoat	321-111 Snake,MGoat,Deer	332-222 Dog,Swan,Sheep
222-232 Beaver,Sheep,Deer	321-112 Deer,Pcock,Dog	332-231 Sheep,Pr.Dog,Dog
222-311 MGoat,Deer,Sheep	321-121 Deer,Sheep,Pcock	332-232 Pr.Dog,Dog,Beaver
222-331↓ Deer,Sheep,Beaver	321-122 Deer,Pcock,Dog	332-311 Swan,Deer,Sheep
223-111 Snake,MGoat,Sheep	321-131 Deer,Sheep,Pcock	332-312 Swan,Deer,Dog
223-112 Snake,MGoat,Bat	321-132 Deer,Pcock,Dog	332-321 Swan,Deer,Sheep
223-121 Sheep,Snake,MGoat	321-211 Deer,MGoat,Sheep	332-322 Swan,Deer,Dog
223-122 Bat,Sheep,Beaver	321-212 Deer,Pcock,Dog	332-331 Swan,Deer,Sheep
223-131 Beaver,Sheep,Baboon	321-221 Deer,Sheep,Pcock	332-332 Swan,Deer,Pr.Dog
223-132 Beaver,Baboon,Pr.Dog	321-222 Deer,Pcock,Dog	333-111 Sheep,Pr.Dog,Dog
223-211 MGoat,Sheep,Snake	321-231 Deer,Sheep,Pcock	333-112 Pr.Dog,Dog,Horse
223-212 MGoat,Sheep,Deer	321-232 Deer,Pcock,Dog	333-121 Pr.Dog,Sheep,Dog
223-221 Sheep,MGoat,Beaver	321-311↓ Deer,Swan,MGoat	333-122 Pr.Dog,Dog,Horse
223-222 Sheep,Beaver,Deer	322-111 Snake,MGoat,Deer	333-131 Pr.Dog,Beaver,Sheep
223-231 Beaver,Sheep,Baboon	322-112 Deer,Dog,Snake	333-132 Pr.Dog,Fox,Beaver
223-232 Beaver,Baboon,Pr.Dog	322-121 Deer,Sheep,Dog	333-211 Sheep,Pr.Dog,Dog
223-311 MGoat,Deer,Sheep	322-122 Deer,Dog,W.Cat	333-212 Pr.Dog,Dog,Horse
223-322↓ Deer,Sheep,Beaver	322-131 Deer,Sheep,Pr.Dog	333-221 Pr.Dog,Sheep,Dog
223-332 Deer,Beaver,Baboon	322-132 Deer,Pr.Dog,Dog	333-222 Pr.Dog,Dog,Horse
231-111 Sheep,Snake,MGoat	322-211 Deer,MGoat,Sheep	333-231 Pr.Dog,Beaver,Sheep
231-132↓ Sheep,Beaver,Dog	322-212 Deer,Dog,MGoat	333-232 Pr.Dog,Fox,Beaver
231-212↓ Sheep,Dog,MGoat	322-221 Deer,Sheep,Dog	333-311 Swan,Deer,Sheep
231-232↓ Sheep,Beaver,Dog	322-222 Deer,Dog,Swan	333-312↓ Swan,Deer,Pr.Dog
231-311 Sheep,MGoat,Deer	322-231 Deer,Sheep,Pr.Dog	341-111 Sheep,Dog
231-322↓ Sheep,Deer,Dog	322-232 Deer,Pr.Dog,Dog	341-312↓ Dog,Sheep,Swan
231-331↓ Sheep,Beaver,Deer	322-311↓ Deer,Swan,MGoat	341-321↓ Sheep,Dog,Pr.Dog
232-111 Sheep,Snake,MGoat	323-111 Snake,MGoat,Deer	342-111 Sheep,Dog,Pr.Dog
232-122↓ Sheep,Beaver,Dog	323-112 Deer,Pr.Dog,Dog	342-132 Pr.Dog,Dog,Beaver
232-131 Sheep,Beaver,Baboon	323-121 Pr.Dog,Deer,Sheep	342-211 Sheep,Dog,Pr.Dog
232-222↓ Sheep,Beaver,Dog	323-132↓ Pr.Dog,W.Cat,Deer	342-232 Pr.Dog,Dog,Beaver
232-231 Sheep,Beaver,Baboon	323-211 Deer,MGoat,Sheep	342-311 Sheep,Dog,Pr.Dog
232-312↓ Sheep,Deer,Beaver	323-212 Deer,Pr.Dog,Dog	342-332 Pr.Dog,Dog,Beaver
233-111↓ Sheep,Bat,Beaver	323-221 Deer,Pr.Dog,Sheep	343-111↓ Sheep,Pr.Dog,Dog
233-131 Beaver,Sheep,Baboon	323-222 Deer,Pr.Dog,W.Cat	343-131 Pr.Dog,Beaver,Sheep
233-132 Beaver,Baboon,Pr.Dog	323-231 Pr.Dog,Deer,Beaver	343-132 Pr.Dog,Beaver,Dog
233-211 Sheep,Beaver,MGoat	323-232 Pr.Dog,Deer,W.Cat	343-211↓ Sheep,Pr.Dog,Dog
233-212↓ Sheep,Beaver,Baboon	323-311 Deer,Swan,MGoat	343-231 Pr.Dog,Beaver,Sheep
233-311 Sheep,Beaver,MGoat	323-312 Deer,Swan,Dolphin	343-232 Pr.Dog,Beaver,Dog
233-312 Sheep,Beaver,Deer	323-321↓ Deer,Swan,Pr.Dog	343-311↓ Sheep,Pr.Dog,Dog
233-321↓ Sheep,Beaver,Baboon	331-111 Sheep,Dog,Cottn	343-331 Pr.Dog,Beaver,Sheep
241-111 Sheep,Dog	331-112 Dog,Sheep,Swan	343-332 Pr.Dog,Beaver,Dog
241-122↓ Sheep,Dog,Beaver	331-121 Sheep,Dog,Cottn	411-111↓ Pcock,Deer
242-111↓ Sheep,Beaver,Dog	331-122 Dog,Sheep,Swan	411-332↓ Pcock,Deer,Swan
242-131↓ Sheep,Beaver,Pr.Dog	331-131↓ Sheep,Dog,Pr.Dog	412-111↓ Pcock,Deer
242-322↓ Sheep,Beaver,Dog	331-211 Sheep,Dog,Cottn	412-222↓ Pcock,Deer,Swan
242-331↓ Sheep,Beaver,Pr.Dog	331-212 Dog,Swan,Sheep	412-231↓ Pcock,Deer,W.Cat
243-111↓ Sheep,Beaver,Pr.Dog	331-221 Sheep,Dog,Cottn	412-311↓ Deer,Pcock,Swan
311-111↓ Pcock,Deer	331-222 Dog,Swan,Sheep	413-111↓ Pcock,Deer
312-111 Pcock,Snake,MGoat	331-231 Sheep,Dog,Pr.Dog	413-121↓ Pcock,Deer,W.Cat
312-112 Pcock,Weasel,Vultre	331-232 Dog,Swan,Pr.Dog	413-312↓ Deer,Swan,Pcock
312-121 Pcock,Weasel,Deer	331-311 Swan,Deer,Sheep	421-111 Deer,Pcock,Cottn

(223 cont'd)

421-112	Deer,Pcock,Swan
421-121	Deer,Pcock,Cottn
421-122	Deer,Pcock,Swan
421-131	Deer,Pcock,Cottn
422-111↓	Deer,Cottn,Swan
422-112	Deer,Swan,W.Cat
422-121	Deer,Cottn,Swan
422-122	Deer,Swan,W.Cat
422-131	Deer,W.Cat,Cottn
422-132	Deer,W.Cat,Swan
422-211	Deer,Swan,Cottn
422-212	Deer,Swan,W.Cat
422-221	Deer,Swan,Cottn
422-222↓	Deer,Swan,W.Cat
423-111	Deer,Cottn
423-112	Deer,W.Cat,Swan
423-121	Deer,W.Cat,Cottn
423-122	Deer,W.Cat,Swan
423-131	Deer,W.Cat,Cottn
423-132	W.Cat,Deer,Swan
423-211	Deer,Swan,Cottn
423-212↓	Deer,Swan,W.Cat
431-111↓	Cottn,Swan,Deer
432-111↓	Cottn,Swan,Deer
433-111↓	Cottn,Swan,Deer
433-131	Cottn,Swan,Pr.Dog
433-132	Swan,Pr.Dog,W.Cat
433-211↓	Swan,Cottn,Deer
433-232	Swan,Deer,Pr.Dog
433-331↓	Swan,Deer,Cottn
441-111	Dog,Sheep,Cottn
441-112	Dog,Swan,Sheep
441-121	Dog,Sheep,Cottn
441-122	Dog,Swan
441-131	Dog,Sheep,Pr.Dog
441-132	Dog,Swan,Pr.Dog
441-211↓	Dog,Sheep,Swan
441-232	Swan,Dog,Pr.Dog
441-311↓	Swan,Dog,Deer
441-332	Swan,Sable,Dog
442-111	Dog,Sheep,Cottn
442-112	Dog,Swan,Sheep
442-121	Dog,Sheep,Cottn
442-122	Dog,Swan,Pr.Dog
442-131	Pr.Dog,Dog,Sheep
442-132	Pr.Dog,Dog,Swan
442-211↓	Dog,Sheep,Swan
442-222	Swan,Dog,Pr.Dog
442-231	Pr.Dog,Dog,Sheep
442-232	Swan,Pr.Dog,Dog
442-311↓	Swan,Dog,Deer
442-331	Swan,Pr.Dog,Dog
442-332	Swan,Sable,Pr.Dog
443-111	Pr.Dog,Dog,Sheep
443-112	Pr.Dog,Dog,Swan
443-121	Pr.Dog,Dog,Sheep
443-132↓	Pr.Dog,Dog,Beaver
443-211	Pr.Dog,Dog,Sheep
443-212	Pr.Dog,Swan,Dog
443-221	Pr.Dog,Dog,Sheep
443-222	Pr.Dog,Swan,Dog
443-231	Pr.Dog,Dog,Beaver
443-232	Pr.Dog,Swan,Dog
443-332	Pr.Dog,Swan,Sable

224-

111-111↓	Porcp,Mole,Pcock
111-211↓	Pcock,MGoat,Sheep
111-231↓	Pcock,Sheep,Porcp
111-311	Pcock,MGoat,Deer
111-312	Pcock,Deer,SeaLn
111-321	Pcock,Deer,Sheep
111-322	Pcock,Deer,SeaLn
111-331	Pcock,Deer,Sheep
111-332	Pcock,Deer,SeaLn
112-111	Porcp,Mole,Snake
112-112	Porcp,Mole,Vultre
112-121	Porcp,Mole,Sheep
112-122	Porcp,Mole,Vultre
112-131	Porcp,Mole,Sheep
112-132	Porcp,Mole,Vultre
112-211	MGoat,Sheep,Porcp
112-212	Porcp,MGoat,Pcock
112-221	Sheep,Porcp,Mole
112-222	Porcp,Pcock,Dog
112-231	Sheep,Porcp,Mole
112-232	Porcp,Baboon,Pr.Dog
112-311	MGoat,Deer,Sheep
112-312	Deer,SeaLn,MGoat
112-321	Deer,Sheep,SeaLn
112-322	Deer,SeaLn,Pcock
112-331	Deer,Sheep,SeaLn
112-332	Deer,SeaLn,Baboon
113-111	Porcp,Mole,Snake
113-112	Porcp,Mole,Vultre
113-121	Porcp,Mole,Sheep
113-122	Porcp,Mole,Vultre
113-131	Porcp,Mole,Baboon
113-132	Porcp,Baboon,Pr.Dog
113-211	MGoat,Sheep,Porcp
113-212	Porcp,Baboon,Pr.Dog
113-221	Sheep,Baboon,Pr.Dog
113-222	Baboon,Pr.Dog,Porcp
113-231	Baboon,Pr.Dog,Sheep
113-232	Baboon,Pr.Dog,Beaver
113-311	MGoat,Deer,Sheep
113-312	Deer,Dolphin,SeaLn
113-321	Deer,Sheep,Baboon
113-322	Deer,Dolphin,Baboon
113-331↓	Baboon,Pr.Dog,Deer
121-111↓	Porcp,Mole,Snake
121-131↓	Porcp,Mole,Sheep
121-211	MGoat,Sheep,Porcp
121-212	Porcp,MGoat,Dog
121-221	Sheep,Porcp,Mole
121-222	Porcp,Dog,Sheep
121-231	Sheep,Porcp,Mole
121-232	Porcp,Baboon,Dog
121-311	MGoat,Deer,Sheep
121-312	Deer,SeaLn,MGoat
121-321	Deer,Sheep,SeaLn
121-322	Deer,SeaLn,Dog
121-331	Deer,Sheep,SeaLn
121-332	Deer,SeaLn,Baboon
122-111↓	Porcp,Mole,Snake
122-131↓	Porcp,Mole,Sheep
122-132	Porcp,Mole,Baboon
122-211	MGoat,Sheep,Porcp
122-212	Porcp,MGoat,Dog
122-221	Sheep,Porcp,Mole

122-222	Porcp,Dog,Sheep
122-231	Sheep,Baboon,Porcp
122-232	Baboon,Porcp,Pr.Dog
122-311	MGoat,Deer,Sheep
122-312	Deer,SeaLn,MGoat
122-321	Deer,Sheep,SeaLn
122-322	Deer,SeaLn,Dog
122-331	Deer,Sheep,Baboon
122-332	Deer,Baboon,SeaLn
123-111	Porcp,Mole,Snake
123-112↓	Porcp,Mole,Baboon
123-211	MGoat,Baboon,Sheep
123-212	Baboon,Porcp,Pr.Dog
123-221	Baboon,Sheep,Pr.Dog
123-222↓	Baboon,Pr.Dog,Porcp
123-311	MGoat,Deer,Baboon
123-312	Deer,Dolphin,Baboon
123-321	Baboon,Deer,Sheep
123-322	Baboon,Deer,Dolphin
123-331↓	Baboon,Pr.Dog,Deer
131-111↓	Sheep,Dog,Porcp
131-131	Sheep,Baboon,Dog
131-132	Baboon,Dog,Porcp
131-222↓	Dog,Sheep,Baboon
131-322↓	Dog,Sheep,Deer
131-331↓	Sheep,Baboon,Dog
132-111↓	Sheep,Dog,Porcp
132-131	Sheep,Baboon,Pr.Dog
132-132	Baboon,Pr.Dog,Dog
132-212↓	Dog,Sheep,Baboon
132-231	Sheep,Baboon,Pr.Dog
132-232	Baboon,Pr.Dog,Dog
132-312↓	Dog,Sheep,Baboon
132-331	Sheep,Baboon,Pr.Dog
132-332	Baboon,Pr.Dog,Dog
133-111	Baboon,Sheep,Pr.Dog
133-112	Baboon,Pr.Dog,Bat
133-121↓	Baboon,Sheep,Pr.Dog
133-212	Baboon,Pr.Dog,Dog
133-221	Baboon,Sheep,Pr.Dog
133-232↓	Baboon,Pr.Dog,Beaver
133-311	Baboon,Sheep,Pr.Dog
133-312	Baboon,Pr.Dog,Dog
133-321	Baboon,Sheep,Pr.Dog
133-322↓	Baboon,Pr.Dog,Dog
141-111	Sheep,Dog
141-332↓	Dog,Sheep,Pr.Dog
142-111	Sheep,Dog
142-122↓	Dog,Sheep,Pr.Dog
142-132	Pr.Dog,Dog,Beaver
142-212↓	Dog,Sheep,Pr.Dog
142-232	Pr.Dog,Dog,Beaver
142-322↓	Dog,Sheep,Pr.Dog
142-332	Pr.Dog,Dog,Beaver
143-111↓	Sheep,Pr.Dog,Dog
143-131↓	Pr.Dog,Sheep,Beaver
143-211↓	Sheep,Pr.Dog,Dog
143-231	Pr.Dog,Sheep,Beaver
143-232	Pr.Dog,Beaver,Dog
143-311↓	Sheep,Pr.Dog,Dog
143-331	Pr.Dog,Sheep,Beaver
143-332	Pr.Dog,W.Dog,Beaver
211-111	Pcock,Snake,MGoat
211-112	Pcock,Vultre,Dog
211-121	Pcock,Sheep,Dog

211-122	Pcock,Vultre,Dog	
211-131	Pcock,Sheep,Dog	
211-132	Pcock,Vultre,Dog	
211-211	Pcock,MGoat,Sheep	
211-231↓	Pcock,Sheep,Dog	
211-311	Pcock,MGoat,Deer	
211-312	Pcock,Deer,SeaLn	
211-321	Pcock,Deer,Sheep	
211-322	Pcock,Deer,SeaLn	
211-331	Pcock,Deer,Sheep	
211-332	Pcock,Deer,SeaLn	
212-111	Snake,MGoat,Sheep	
212-112	Vultre,Dog,Snake	
212-121	Sheep,Dog,Vultre	
212-122	Vultre,Dog,Pcock	
212-131	Sheep,Pr.Dog,Dog	
212-132	Vultre,Pr.Dog,Dog	
212-211	MGoat,Sheep,Dog	
212-212	Dog,MGoat,Pcock	
212-221↓	Sheep,Dog,Pcock	
212-231	Sheep,Pr.Dog,Dog	
212-232	Pr.Dog,Dog,Baboon	
212-311	MGoat,Deer,Sheep	
212-312	Deer,SeaLn,Dog	
212-321	Deer,Sheep,SeaLn	
212-322	Deer,SeaLn,Dog	
212-331	Deer,Sheep,SeaLn	
212-332	Deer,SeaLn,Pr.Dog	
213-111	Snake,MGoat,Sheep	
213-112	Vultre,Pr.Dog,Dog	
213-121	Pr.Dog,Sheep,Baboon	
213-122↓	Pr.Dog,Vultre,Baboon	
213-211	MGoat,Sheep,Pr.Dog	
213-212	Pr.Dog,Dog,Baboon	
213-221	Pr.Dog,Sheep,Baboon	
213-222↓	Pr.Dog,Baboon,Dog	
213-311	MGoat,Deer,Sheep	
213-312	Deer,Dolphin,Pr.Dog	
213-321	Pr.Dog,Deer,Sheep	
213-322	Pr.Dog,Deer,Dolphin	
213-331↓	Pr.Dog,Baboon,Deer	
221-111	Snake,MGoat,Sheep	
221-112	Dog,Snake,MGoat	
221-131↓	Sheep,Dog,Baboon	
221-132	Dog,Baboon,Pr.Dog	
221-211↓	MGoat,Sheep,Dog	
221-222	Dog,Sheep,Deer	
221-231	Sheep,Dog,Baboon	
221-232	Dog,Baboon,Pr.Dog	
221-311	MGoat,Deer,Sheep	
221-312	Deer,SeaLn,Dog	
221-321	Deer,Sheep,SeaLn	
221-322	Deer,SeaLn,Dog	
221-331	Deer,Sheep,SeaLn	
221-332	Deer,SeaLn,Dog	
222-111	Snake,MGoat,Sheep	
222-112	Dog,Snake,MGoat	
222-121	Sheep,Dog,Snake	
222-122	Dog,Sheep,Baboon	
222-131	Sheep,Baboon,Pr.Dog	
222-132	Baboon,Pr.Dog,Dog	
222-211↓	MGoat,Sheep,Dog	
222-222	Dog,Sheep,Deer	
222-231	Sheep,Baboon,Pr.Dog	
222-232	Baboon,Pr.Dog,Dog	

222-311	MGoat,Deer,Sheep	
222-312	Deer,SeaLn,Dog	
222-321	Deer,Sheep,SeaLn	
222-322	Deer,SeaLn,Dog	
222-331	Deer,Sheep,Baboon	
222-332	Deer,Baboon,SeaLn	
223-111	Snake,MGoat,Baboon	
223-112	Baboon,Pr.Dog,Dog	
223-121	Baboon,Pr.Dog,Sheep	
223-122↓	Baboon,Pr.Dog,Dog	
223-211	MGoat,Baboon,Sheep	
223-212	Baboon,Pr.Dog,Dog	
223-221	Baboon,Pr.Dog,Sheep	
223-222	Baboon,Pr.Dog,Dog	
223-231	Baboon,Pr.Dog,Sheep	
223-232	Baboon,Pr.Dog,Dog	
223-311	MGoat,Deer,Baboon	
223-312	Deer,Dolphin,Baboon	
223-332↓	Baboon,Pr.Dog,Deer	
231-111	Sheep,Dog	
231-322↓	Dog,Sheep,Deer	
231-331	Sheep,Dog,Baboon	
231-332	Dog,Baboon,Pr.Dog	
232-111	Sheep,Dog	
232-112↓	Dog,Sheep,Baboon	
232-131	Sheep,Baboon,Pr.Dog	
232-132	Baboon,Pr.Dog,Dog	
232-211	Sheep,Dog,MGoat	
232-212	Dog,Sheep,Baboon	
232-231	Sheep,Baboon,Pr.Dog	
232-232	Baboon,Pr.Dog,Dog	
232-312↓	Dog,Sheep,Baboon	
232-331	Sheep,Baboon,Pr.Dog	
232-332	Baboon,Pr.Dog,Dog	
233-111	Baboon,Sheep,Pr.Dog	
233-112	Baboon,Pr.Dog,Dog	
233-121	Baboon,Pr.Dog,Sheep	
233-122	Baboon,Pr.Dog,Dog	
233-131	Baboon,Pr.Dog,Sheep	
233-132	Baboon,Pr.Dog,Dog	
233-211	Baboon,Sheep,Pr.Dog	
233-212	Baboon,Pr.Dog,Dog	
233-221	Baboon,Pr.Dog,Sheep	
233-222	Baboon,Pr.Dog,Dog	
233-231	Baboon,Pr.Dog,Sheep	
233-232	Baboon,Pr.Dog,Dog	
233-311	Baboon,Sheep,Pr.Dog	
233-312	Baboon,Pr.Dog,Dog	
233-321	Baboon,Pr.Dog,Sheep	
233-322	Baboon,Pr.Dog,Dog	
233-331	Baboon,Pr.Dog,Sheep	
233-332	Baboon,Pr.Dog,W.Dog	
241-111	Sheep,Dog	
241-312↓	Dog,Sheep,Pr.Dog	
242-111↓	Sheep,Dog,Pr.Dog	
243-111↓	Sheep,Pr.Dog,Dog	
243-132	Pr.Dog,Dog,Beaver	
243-211↓	Sheep,Pr.Dog,Dog	
243-232	Pr.Dog,Dog,Beaver	
243-311↓	Sheep,Pr.Dog,Dog	
243-332	Pr.Dog,W.Dog,Dog	
311-111↓	Pcock,Dog	
311-311↓	Pcock,Deer,SeaLn	
312-111↓	Dog,Pcock,Snake	
312-121↓	Dog,Pcock,Pr.Dog	

312-211↓	Dog,Pcock,Deer	
312-231↓	Pr.Dog,Dog,Pcock	
312-311↓	Deer,SeaLn,Dog	
312-331↓	Deer,SeaLn,Pr.Dog	
313-111↓	Pr.Dog,Dog,Horse	
313-311	Deer,Pr.Dog,SeaLn	
313-312	Deer,Dolphin,Pr.Dog	
313-321	Pr.Dog,Deer,SeaLn	
313-332↓	Pr.Dog,Deer,Dolphin	
321-111↓	Dog,Deer	
321-131↓	Dog,Pr.Dog	
321-212↓	Dog,Deer,SeaLn	
321-231↓	Dog,Pr.Dog,Deer	
321-311↓	Deer,SeaLn,Dog	
322-111↓	Dog,Pr.Dog,Deer	
322-211	Dog,Deer,MGoat	
322-212	Dog,Deer,SeaLn	
322-221↓	Dog,Deer,Pr.Dog	
322-311↓	Deer,SeaLn,Dog	
322-331↓	Deer,SeaLn,Pr.Dog	
323-111↓	Pr.Dog,Dog,Horse	
323-131↓	Pr.Dog,Dog,Baboon	
323-211↓	Pr.Dog,Dog,Horse	
323-231↓	Pr.Dog,Dog,Baboon	
323-311	Deer,Pr.Dog,SeaLn	
323-312	Deer,Dolphin,Pr.Dog	
323-321	Pr.Dog,Deer,SeaLn	
323-322	Pr.Dog,Deer,Dolphin	
323-331	Pr.Dog,Deer,SeaLn	
323-332	Pr.Dog,Deer,Dolphin	
331-111↓	Dog,Pr.Dog,Sheep	
331-312↓	Dog,Swan,Deer	
331-332↓	Dog,Pr.Dog,Swan	
332-111	Dog,Pr.Dog,Sheep	
332-112	Dog,Pr.Dog,Horse	
332-121	Dog,Pr.Dog,Sheep	
332-122	Dog,Pr.Dog,Horse	
332-131	Pr.Dog,Dog,Sheep	
332-132	Pr.Dog,Dog,Baboon	
332-211	Dog,Pr.Dog,Sheep	
332-212	Dog,Pr.Dog,Horse	
332-221	Dog,Pr.Dog,Sheep	
332-222	Dog,Pr.Dog,Horse	
332-231	Pr.Dog,Dog,Sheep	
332-232	Pr.Dog,Dog,Baboon	
332-311	Dog,Pr.Dog,Deer	
332-312	Dog,Swan,Pr.Dog	
332-321	Dog,Pr.Dog,Deer	
332-322	Dog,Pr.Dog,Swan	
332-331	Pr.Dog,Dog,Deer	
332-332	Pr.Dog,Dog,Swan	
333-111↓	Pr.Dog,Dog,Horse	
333-131↓	Pr.Dog,Dog,Baboon	
333-211↓	Pr.Dog,Dog,Horse	
333-231↓	Pr.Dog,Dog,Baboon	
333-311↓	Pr.Dog,Dog,Horse	
333-331↓	Pr.Dog,Dog,Baboon	
341-111↓	Dog,Sheep,Pr.Dog	
342-111↓	Dog,Pr.Dog,Sheep	
343-111↓	Pr.Dog,Dog,Sheep	
411-111↓	Pcock,Deer	
411-311↓	Pcock,Deer,SeaLn	
412-111↓	Pcock,Deer,SeaLn	
413-111	Pcock,Deer,SeaLn	
413-112	Pcock,Deer,Dolphin	

(224 cont'd)

413-121	Pcock,Deer,SeaLn
413-122	Pcock,Deer,Dolphin
413-131↓	Pcock,Pr.Dog,Deer
413-211	Pcock,Deer,SeaLn
413-212	Pcock,Deer,Dolphin
413-221	Pcock,Deer,SeaLn
413-222	Pcock,Deer,Dolphin
413-231	Pcock,Deer,Pr.Dog
413-232	Pcock,Deer,Dolphin
413-311↓	Deer,SeaLn,Dolphin
421-111↓	Deer,Pcock,SeaLn
421-311↓	Deer,SeaLn,Swan
422-111	Deer,SeaLn,Cottn
422-112	Deer,SeaLn,Swan
422-121	Deer,SeaLn,Cottn
422-122	Deer,SeaLn,Swan
422-131	Deer,SeaLn,Cottn
422-132	Deer,SeaLn,W.Cat
422-211	Deer,SeaLn,Cottn
422-212	Deer,SeaLn,Swan
422-221	Deer,SeaLn,Cottn
422-222	Deer,SeaLn,Swan
422-231	Deer,SeaLn,Cottn
422-232↓	Deer,SeaLn,Swan
423-111↓	Deer,SeaLn,Dolphin
423-131	Pr.Dog,Deer,SeaLn
423-132	Pr.Dog,Deer,Dolphin
423-211↓	Deer,SeaLn,Dolphin
423-231	Deer,Pr.Dog,SeaLn
423-232	Deer,Dolphin,Pr.Dog
423-311↓	Deer,SeaLn,Dolphin
431-111	Cottn,Dog,Swan
431-112	Swan,Dog,Deer
431-121	Cottn,Dog,Swan
431-122	Swan,Dog,Deer
431-131	Cottn,Dog,Swan
431-132	Swan,Dog,Pr.Dog
431-211	Cottn,Swan,Dog
431-212	Swan,Dog,Deer
431-221	Cottn,Swan,Dog
431-222	Swan,Dog,Deer
431-231	Cottn,Swan,Dog
431-232	Swan,Dog,Deer
431-311↓	Swan,Deer,SeaLn
432-111	Cottn,Dog,Swan
432-112	Swan,Dog,Deer
432-121	Cottn,Dog,Swan
432-122	Swan,Dog,Deer
432-131	Cottn,Pr.Dog,Dog
432-132	Swan,Pr.Dog,Dog
432-211	Cottn,Swan,Dog
432-212	Swan,Dog,Deer
432-221	Cottn,Swan,Dog
432-222	Swan,Dog,Deer
432-231	Cottn,Swan,Pr.Dog
432-232	Swan,Pr.Dog,Dog
432-311↓	Swan,Deer,SeaLn
433-111	Cottn,Pr.Dog,Dog
433-112	Swan,Pr.Dog,Dog
433-121	Pr.Dog,Cottn,Dog
433-122	Pr.Dog,Swan,Dog
433-131	Pr.Dog,Cottn
433-132	Pr.Dog,Swan,Dog
433-211	Cottn,Swan,Pr.Dog

433-212	Swan,Pr.Dog,Dog
433-221	Pr.Dog,Cottn,Swan
433-222	Swan,Pr.Dog,Dog
433-231	Pr.Dog,Cottn,Swan
433-232	Pr.Dog,Swan,Dog
433-311	Swan,Deer,SeaLn
433-312	Swan,Deer,Dolphin
433-321	Swan,Deer,SeaLn
433-322	Swan,Deer,Dolphin
433-331↓	Swan,Pr.Dog,Deer
441-111↓	Dog,Pr.Dog
441-212↓	Dog,Pr.Dog,Swan
441-221	Dog,Pr.Dog,Sheep
441-322↓	Dog,Swan,Pr.Dog
442-111↓	Dog,Pr.Dog
442-222↓	Dog,Pr.Dog,Swan
442-231	Pr.Dog,Dog,Sheep
442-232↓	Pr.Dog,Dog,Swan
443-111↓	Pr.Dog,Dog
443-311↓	Pr.Dog,Dog,Swan

231-

111-111↓	Porcp,Croc
112-111↓	Porcp,Mole
112-211↓	Porcp,Croc
112-221↓	Porcp,Mole
113-111↓	Porcp,Croc
121-111↓	Porcp,MGoat,Mole
122-111↓	Porcp,MGoat
123-111↓	Porcp,MGoat,Mole
131-111↓	Porcupine
132-111↓	Porcupine
132-121↓	Porcp,Mole
132-211↓	Porcp,MGoat
133-111↓	Porcp,Baboon
141-111↓	Porcp,Sheep
141-311↓	Porcp,Sheep,Beaver
142-111↓	Porcp,Beaver
142-311↓	Porcp,Sheep,Beaver
142-322	Porcp,Beaver,W.Dog
142-331	Beaver,Porcp,Sheep
142-332	Beaver,Porcp,W.Dog
143-111↓	Porcp,Pengn
143-312↓	W.Dog,Porcp,Beaver
211-111↓	Porcp,Vultre,Snake
211-121↓	Porcp,Vultre,Weasel
211-211	MGoat,Weasel,Porcp
211-212↓	Weasel,Vultre,Porcp
211-312↓	Weasel,MGoat,Vultre
211-321	Weasel,MGoat,Porcp
211-322	Weasel,Vultre,Porcp
211-331	Weasel,Porcp,Pcock
211-332	Weasel,Vultre,Porcp
212-111	Porcp,Vultre,Snake
212-112	Vultre,Porcp,Weasel
212-211	MGoat,Weasel,Porcp
212-212↓	Weasel,Vultre,Porcp
212-311	MGoat,Weasel,Porcp
212-312	Weasel,MGoat,Vultre
212-321	Weasel,MGoat,Porcp
212-322↓	Weasel,Vultre,Porcp
213-111↓	Porcp,Vultre,Snake
213-121↓	Porcp,Vultre,Weasel
213-211	MGoat,Weasel,Porcp
213-212↓	Weasel,Vultre,Porcp

213-312↓	Weasel,MGoat,Vultre
213-321	Weasel,MGoat,Porcp
213-322	Weasel,Vultre,Porcp
213-331	Weasel,Porcp,W.Cat
213-332	Weasel,W.Cat,Vultre
221-111↓	Porcp,Snake,MGoat
222-111↓	Porcp,Snake,MGoat
222-232↓	Porcp,W.Cat,MGoat
223-111↓	Porcp,Snake,MGoat
223-122	Porcp,Bat
223-131	Porcp,Baboon
223-132	Porcp,Bat,W.Cat
223-211	Porcp,Snake
223-212↓	Porcp,MGoat,W.Cat
223-231↓	Porcp,Baboon,W.Cat
223-321↓	MGoat,Porcp,W.Cat
223-331↓	Baboon,Porcp,W.Cat
231-111↓	Porcp,Snake,MGoat
231-122↓	Porcp,Bat
231-211	MGoat,Porcp
231-232	Porcp,Baboon,Beaver
231-321↓	MGoat,Porcp,Sheep
231-322↓	Porcp,MGoat,Baboon
231-332	Porcp,Baboon,Beaver
232-111	Porcp,Snake,MGoat
232-112↓	Porcp,Bat,Snake
232-131	Porcp,Baboon,Beaver
232-132	Porcp,Bat,Baboon
232-211	MGoat,Porcp,Snake
232-212	Porcp,MGoat,Bat
232-221↓	Porcp,MGoat,Baboon
232-231↓	Porcp,Baboon,Beaver
232-321↓	MGoat,Porcp,Baboon
232-331↓	Baboon,Beaver,Porcp
233-111	Porcp,Bat,Snake
233-112	Bat,Porcp,Baboon
233-121	Porcp,Bat,Pengn
233-122↓	Bat,Porcp,Baboon
233-211	MGoat,Baboon,Porcp
233-212↓	Bat,Baboon,Porcp
233-231	Baboon,Beaver,Porcp
233-232	Baboon,Beaver,Bat
233-311	MGoat,Baboon,Otter
233-312	Baboon,MGoat,Bat
233-321	Baboon,Otter,MGoat
233-322	Baboon,Bat,Otter
233-332↓	Baboon,W.Dog,Beaver
241-111↓	Sheep,Pengn,Porcp
241-122	Porcp,Beaver,Sheep
241-131	Beaver,Sheep,Pengn
241-322↓	Beaver,Sheep,W.Dog
241-332	Beaver,W.Dog,Sable
242-111	Pengn,Sheep,Beaver
242-112	Beaver,Pengn,Porcp
242-121	Pengn,Sheep,Beaver
242-122	Beaver,Pengn,Porcp
242-131	Beaver,Pengn,Sheep
242-132	Beaver,Pengn,Porcp
242-221↓	Sheep,Beaver,Pengn
242-222	Beaver,Sheep,Dog
242-331↓	Beaver,Sheep,W.Dog
242-332	Beaver,W.Dog,Sable
243-111↓	Pengn,Beaver,Bat
243-121	Pengn,Beaver,Sheep
243-132↓	Beaver,Pengn,Owl

243-221↓ Pengn,Beaver,Sheep
243-222↓ Beaver,Pengn,Owl
243-232 Beaver,Owl,W.Dog
243-311 Beaver,Pengn,W.Dog
243-332↓ W.Dog,Beaver,Owl
311-111 Weasel,Porcp,Pcock
311-112 Weasel,Vultre,Porcp
311-121 Weasel,Porcp,Pcock
311-122 Weasel,Vultre,Porcp
311-131 Weasel,Porcp,Pcock
311-132 Weasel,Vultre,Porcp
311-311↓ Weasel,Pcock,MGoat
312-111↓ Weasel,Porcp,Vultre
312-211 Weasel,MGoat,Shrew
312-212 Weasel,Shrew,Vultre
312-221↓ Weasel,Shrew,W.Cat
313-111↓ Weasel,Porcp,Vultre
313-131 Weasel,Porcp,W.Cat
313-222↓ Weasel,W.Cat,Shrew
313-311↓ Weasel,MGoat
313-322↓ Weasel,W.Cat
321-111↓ Porcp,Snake,MGoat
321-212↓ Porcp,MGoat,W.Cat
321-222 Porcp,W.Cat,Weasel
321-231 W.Cat,Porcp,MGoat
321-232 W.Cat,Porcp,Weasel
321-312↓ SeaLn,MGoat,Porcp
321-321 SeaLn,MGoat,W.Cat
321-322↓ W.Cat,SeaLn,Porcp
321-332 W.Cat,SeaLn,Eagle
322-111 Porcp,Snake,MGoat
322-211↓ MGoat,Porcp,W.Cat
322-222 W.Cat,Porcp,Weasel
322-231 W.Cat,Porcp,MGoat
322-232 W.Cat,Porcp,Weasel
322-311↓ MGoat,SeaLn,W.Cat
322-322↓ W.Cat,SeaLn,Porcp
322-332 W.Cat,SeaLn,Eagle
323-111 Porcp,Snake,Pengn
323-211↓ MGoat,W.Cat,Porcp
323-221↓ W.Cat,Porcp,Otter
323-232 W.Cat,Porcp,Fox
323-311 MGoat,W.Cat,SeaLn
323-312↓ W.Cat,Dolphin,SeaLn
331-111↓ Porcp,Snake,MGoat
331-121↓ Porcp,Pengn
331-132 Porcp,W.Cat
331-211 MGoat,Porcp,Otter
331-212 Porcp,MGoat,Swan
331-221 Porcp,MGoat,W.Cat
331-222 Porcp,W.Cat,Swan
331-231 W.Cat,Porcp,Otter
331-232 W.Cat,Porcp,Swan
331-311↓ Swan,MGoat,SeaLn
331-331↓ Swan,W.Cat,Sable
332-111 Porcp,Pengn,Snake
332-112 Porcp,Pengn,Bat
332-121↓ Porcp,Pengn,W.Cat
332-211 MGoat,Porcp,Otter
332-212↓ W.Cat,Porcp,Otter
332-311↓ Swan,MGoat,Otter
332-321↓ Swan,W.Cat,Otter
332-332↓ Swan,W.Cat,Sable
333-111 Pengn,Otter
333-112↓ Pengn,Bat,Otter

333-121 Pengn,Otter,Porcp
333-122 Pengn,Bat,Otter
333-131 Pengn,Otter,Baboon
333-132 Pengn,Fox,Bat
333-211 Otter,Pengn,MGoat
333-212↓ Otter,W.Cat,Pengn
333-222 Otter,W.Cat,Fox
333-231 Otter,Baboon,Fox
333-232 Fox,W.Cat,Otter
333-311 Otter,Swan,Pengn
333-312↓ Otter,Swan,W.Cat
333-331 Otter,Baboon,Fox
333-332 Fox,W.Cat,Otter
341-111↓ Pengn,Dog
341-132↓ Pengn,Beaver,Dog
341-211 Pengn,Dog,Sheep
341-222↓ Dog,Pengn,Beaver
341-232 Beaver,Sable,Dog
341-311 Dog,Sheep,Pengn
341-312 Sable,Dog,Wolf
341-321 Sable,Dog,Sheep
341-322 Sable,Wolf,Dog
341-331↓ Sable,Wolf,Beaver
342-111↓ Pengn,Dog
342-132↓ Pengn,Beaver,Owl
342-211 Pengn,Dog,Sheep
342-212 Dog,Pengn,Beaver
342-221 Pengn,Dog,Sheep
342-222 Dog,Pengn,Beaver
342-231 Beaver,Pengn,Owl
342-232 Beaver,Owl,Sable
342-311 Pengn,Dog,Sheep
342-312 Sable,Dog,Wolf
342-321 Pengn,Sable,Dog
342-322 Sable,Wolf,Dog
342-331↓ Sable,Beaver,Wolf
343-111↓ Pengn,Owl
343-212↓ Pengn,Owl,Pr.Dog
343-232 Owl,Pr.Dog,Beaver
343-322↓ Owl,Pengn,W.Dog
343-331 Owl,Pengn,Pr.Dog
343-332 Owl,W.Dog,Pr.Dog
411-111↓ Pcock,W.Cat
412-111↓ Pcock,W.Cat,Weasel
412-312↓ W.Cat,SeaLn,Pcock
413-111↓ W.Cat,Pcock,Weasel
413-311↓ W.Cat,SeaLn,Dolphin
421-111↓ W.Cat,Porcp,Pcock
421-232↓ W.Cat,Pcock,SeaLn
421-311↓ SeaLn,Swan,W.Cat
422-111 W.Cat,Porcp
422-112↓ W.Cat,Porcp,SeaLn
422-311↓ SeaLn,W.Cat,Swan
423-111↓ W.Cat,Dolphin
423-311↓ W.Cat,SeaLn,Dolphin
431-111↓ Swan,W.Cat,Porcp
431-232↓ W.Cat,Swan,Sable
431-322↓ Swan,W.Cat,Sable
431-332 Swan,W.Cat,Sable
432-111↓ W.Cat,Swan,Porcp
432-231↓ W.Cat,Swan,Sable
432-311↓ Swan,SeaLn,W.Cat
432-331↓ Swan,W.Cat,Sable
433-111↓ W.Cat,Pengn,Swan
433-321↓ Swan,W.Cat,SeaLn

433-332↓ W.Cat,Swan,Sable
441-111↓ Pengn,Sable,Swan
442-111↓ Pengn,Sable,Swan
442-122↓ Sable,Pengn,W.Cat
442-211 Sable,Swan,Pengn
442-212↓ Sable,Swan,W.Cat
443-111↓ Pengn,W.Cat
443-212↓ Sable,Pengn,W.Cat
443-231 Sable,Pengn,Owl
443-232 Sable,W.Cat,Owl
443-321↓ Sable,Swan,Pengn

232-

111-111↓ Porcp,Vultre,Croc
111-231↓ Porcp,Vultre,Pcock
111-321↓ Porcp,Croc,Pcock
112-111↓ Porcp,Vultre,Croc
112-321↓ Porcp,Croc,Weasel
113-111↓ Porcp,Vultre,Croc
113-232 Porcp,Vultre,Warthg
113-321↓ Porcp,Croc,Weasel
113-322 Porcp,Croc,Warthg
113-331 Porcp,Croc,Weasel
113-332↓ Porcp,Warthg,Croc
121-111↓ Porcupine
122-111↓ Porcupine
122-211↓ Porcp,MGoat
122-232↓ Porcp,W.Cat
123-111↓ Porcp,Warthg
123-221↓ Porcp,Warthg,W.Cat
123-231 Porcp,Baboon,Warthg
123-322↓ Porcp,Warthg,W.Cat
123-331 Porcp,Baboon,Warthg
123-332↓ Porcp,Warthg,W.Cat
131-111↓ Porcp,Baboon
132-111↓ Porcp,Sheep
132-231↓ Porcp,Baboon,Beaver
133-111↓ Porcp,Baboon
133-222↓ Porcp,Baboon,Warthg
133-231↓ Baboon,Porcp,Beaver
133-311↓ Porcp,Baboon,Warthg
133-331 Baboon,Porcp,Beaver
133-332 Baboon,W.Dog,Porcp
141-111 Sheep,Porcp,Pengn
141-112 Porcp,Sheep,Beaver
141-121 Sheep,Porcp,Pengn
141-122↓ Porcp,Sheep,Beaver
141-331↓ Beaver,Sheep,W.Dog
141-332 Beaver,W.Dog,Sable
142-111 Sheep,Porcp,Pengn
142-112 Porcp,Beaver,Sheep
142-121 Sheep,Porcp,Pengn
142-322↓ Beaver,Sheep,W.Dog
143-111 Pengn,Sheep,Porcp
143-112 Pengn,Porcp,Beaver
143-121↓ Pengn,Beaver,Sheep
143-231 Beaver,Sheep,Owl
143-232 Beaver,W.Dog,Owl
143-311↓ Sheep,Beaver,W.Dog
211-111 Vultre,Weasel
211-132↓ Vultre,Weasel,Pcock
212-111↓ Vultre,Weasel,Porcp
212-211↓ Weasel,Vultre,MGoat
212-212↓ Weasel,Vultre,Shrew
212-332↓ Weasel,Vultre,W.Cat

(232 cont'd)

213-111	Vultre,Weasel
213-322↓	Weasel,Vultre,W.Cat
221-111	Porcp,Snake,MGoat
221-122↓	Porcp,Vultre,W.Cat
221-212↓	Porcp,MGoat,W.Cat
221-222	Porcp,W.Cat,Weasel
221-231	W.Cat,Porcp,Baboon
221-232	W.Cat,Porcp,Rooster
221-312↓	SeaLn,MGoat,Porcp
221-321	SeaLn,MGoat,W.Cat
221-322↓	W.Cat,SeaLn,Porcp
221-332	W.Cat,SeaLn,Eagle
222-111	Porcp,Snake,MGoat
222-112↓	Porcp,Vultre,W.Cat
222-211↓	MGoat,Porcp,W.Cat
222-222	W.Cat,Porcp,Weasel
222-231↓	W.Cat,Porcp,Baboon
222-311↓	MGoat,SeaLn,W.Cat
222-322	W.Cat,SeaLn,Porcp
222-331↓	W.Cat,Baboon,SeaLn
223-111	Porcp,Snake,Pengn
223-112	Porcp,W.Cat,Vultre
223-121	Porcp,W.Cat,Pengn
223-122	Porcp,W.Cat,Vultre
223-131↓	Baboon,Porcp,W.Cat
223-211	MGoat,W.Cat,Baboon
223-212↓	W.Cat,Baboon,Porcp
223-231	Baboon,W.Cat,Beaver
223-312	W.Cat,Dolphin,Baboon
223-321	W.Cat,Baboon,SeaLn
223-322	W.Cat,Baboon,Dolphin
223-331	Baboon,W.Cat,Beaver
223-332	W.Cat,Baboon,W.Dog
231-111	Porcp,Sheep,Snake
231-112	Porcp,Vultre
231-121	Porcp,Sheep,Pengn
231-122	Porcp,Vultre,Baboon
231-131↓	Porcp,Baboon,Beaver
231-211	Sheep,MGoat,Porcp
231-212↓	Sheep,Porcp,Baboon
231-232	Baboon,Beaver,W.Cat
231-311	Sheep,MGoat,Baboon
231-312	Sheep,Baboon,SeaLn
231-321	Sheep,Baboon,Beaver
231-332	Baboon,Beaver,Wolf
232-111	Porcp,Pengn,Sheep
232-112	Porcp,Vultre,Baboon
232-121	Porcp,Pengn,Sheep
232-122	Porcp,Baboon,Vultre
232-131↓	Baboon,Beaver,Porcp
232-211	Sheep,MGoat,Baboon
232-212	Baboon,Beaver,W.Cat
232-221	Sheep,Baboon,Beaver
232-222	Baboon,Beaver,W.Cat
232-231	Baboon,Beaver,Sheep
232-232	Baboon,Beaver,W.Cat
232-311	Sheep,MGoat,Baboon
232-312	Baboon,Beaver,W.Cat
232-321	Sheep,Baboon,Beaver
232-322	Baboon,Beaver,W.Cat
232-331	Baboon,Beaver,Sheep
232-332	Baboon,Beaver,W.Cat
233-111	Pengn,Baboon,Otter
233-112	Baboon,Pengn,Bat

233-121	Pengn,Baboon,Otter
233-122	Baboon,Pengn,Bat
233-131	Baboon,Pengn,Beaver
233-132	Baboon,Beaver,Fox
233-211	Baboon,Otter,Pengn
233-212	Baboon,Otter,Beaver
233-221	Baboon,Otter,Pengn
233-222	Baboon,Otter,Beaver
233-231↓	Baboon,Beaver,Fox
233-311	Baboon,Otter,Sheep
233-312	Baboon,Otter,W.Dog
233-321	Baboon,Otter,Beaver
233-322	Baboon,Otter,W.Dog
233-331↓	Baboon,Beaver,W.Dog
241-111↓	Sheep,Pengn,Beaver
241-212	Sheep,Beaver,Dog
241-221	Sheep,Beaver,Pengn
241-331↓	Beaver,Sheep,Wolf
241-332	Beaver,Wolf,W.Dog
242-111↓	Pengn,Sheep,Beaver
242-212	Beaver,Sheep,Dog
242-221	Sheep,Beaver,Pengn
242-321↓	Sheep,Beaver,W.Dog
243-111↓	Pengn,Sheep,Beaver
243-122↓	Pengn,Beaver,Owl
243-212	Beaver,Pengn,Sheep
243-231	Beaver,Owl,Pengn
243-232	Beaver,Owl,W.Dog
243-311	Sheep,Beaver,Pengn
243-312	W.Dog,Beaver,Sheep
243-331	Beaver,W.Dog,Owl
311-111↓	Weasel,Pcock,Vultre
311-332↓	Weasel,Pcock,Shrew
312-111↓	Weasel,Vultre,Shrew
312-122↓	Weasel,Vultre,W.Cat
312-211	Weasel,Shrew,Pcock
312-212	Weasel,Shrew,Vultre
312-221	Weasel,Shrew,W.Cat
312-312↓	Weasel,Shrew,Pcock
312-321↓	Weasel,Shrew,W.Cat
313-111	Weasel,Vultre
313-112↓	Weasel,Vultre,W.Cat
313-211↓	Weasel,Shrew,Vultre
321-111↓	Porcp,Weasel,W.Cat
321-211	Weasel,W.Cat,Pcock
321-232	W.Cat,Rooster,Weasel
321-311	SeaLn,Zebra,Deer
321-312↓	SeaLn,Zebra,W.Cat
322-111↓	W.Cat,Porcp,Weasel
322-132	W.Cat,Rooster,Porcp
322-211	W.Cat,Weasel,MGoat
322-231↓	W.Cat,Weasel,Rooster
322-311	SeaLn,W.Cat,Zebra
323-111	Pengn,W.Cat,Otter
323-132	W.Cat,Fox,Pengn
323-211	W.Cat,Otter,Pengn
323-212	W.Cat,Otter,Weasel
323-221	W.Cat,Otter,Pengn
323-222	W.Cat,Otter,Weasel
323-231↓	W.Cat,Fox,Otter
323-311↓	W.Cat,SeaLn,Dolphin
323-331	W.Cat,SeaLn,Fox
323-332	W.Cat,Fox,Dolphin
331-111↓	Pengn,Porcp,Otter
331-121	Pengn,W.Cat,Porcp

331-132	W.Cat,Pengn,Rooster
331-211	Otter,Swan,Weasel
331-212↓	Swan,Otter,W.Cat
331-231	W.Cat,Otter,Baboon
331-232	W.Cat,Swan,Rooster
331-322↓	Swan,W.Cat,SeaLn
331-331↓	Swan,Wolf,W.Cat
332-111↓	Pengn,Otter,W.Cat
332-212	W.Cat,Otter,Swan
332-221	W.Cat,Otter,Pengn
332-222	W.Cat,Otter,Swan
332-231	W.Cat,Otter,Baboon
332-232	W.Cat,Otter,Fox
332-311	Swan,Otter,SeaLn
332-312↓	Swan,W.Cat,Otter
332-331↓	Swan,W.Cat,Wolf
333-111	Pengn,Otter
333-112↓	Pengn,Otter,W.Cat
333-131	Pengn,Fox,Otter
333-132	Fox,Pengn,W.Cat
333-211	Otter,Pengn,W.Cat
333-212	Otter,W.Cat,Fox
333-221	Otter,Pengn,W.Cat
333-222	Otter,W.Cat,Fox
333-231	Fox,Otter,Baboon
333-232	Fox,W.Cat,Otter
333-311	Otter,Swan,Pengn
333-312↓	Otter,Swan,W.Cat
333-331	Fox,Otter,Baboon
333-332	Fox,W.Cat,Otter
341-111↓	Pengn,Dog
341-121↓	Pengn,Sheep,Dog
341-132↓	Pengn,Beaver,Dog
341-211↓	Pengn,Sheep,Dog
341-231	Pengn,Beaver,Sheep
341-232	Beaver,Wolf,Sable
341-311	Sheep,Dog,Pengn
341-312	Wolf,Sable,Dog
341-321	Sheep,Wolf,Sable
341-322	Wolf,Sable,Dog
341-331↓	Wolf,Sable,Beaver
342-111	Pengn,Sheep
342-112	Pengn,Dog,Beaver
342-121	Pengn,Sheep
342-122	Pengn,Dog,Beaver
342-131↓	Pengn,Beaver,Owl
342-211	Pengn,Sheep,Dog
342-212	Dog,Pengn,Beaver
342-221	Pengn,Sheep,Dog
342-222	Dog,Pengn,Beaver
342-231	Beaver,Pengn,Owl
342-232	Beaver,Owl,Wolf
342-311	Pengn,Sheep,Dog
342-312	Wolf,Sable,Dog
342-321	Pengn,Sheep,Wolf
342-322	Wolf,Sable,Dog
342-331↓	Wolf,Sable,Beaver
343-111↓	Pengn,Owl
343-312↓	Owl,Pengn,W.Dog
343-321	Pengn,Owl,Pr.Dog
343-322	Owl,Pengn,W.Dog
343-331	Pengn,Owl,Pr.Dog
343-332	Owl,W.Dog,Pr.Dog
411-111↓	Pcock,W.Cat
411-321↓	Pcock,SeaLn,W.Cat

412-111↓ Pcock,W.Cat,Weasel
412-312 Pcock,W.Cat,SeaLn
413-111↓ W.Cat,Pcock,Weasel
413-311↓ W.Cat,SeaLn,Dolphin
421-111↓ W.Cat,Pcock,SeaLn
421-311 SeaLn,Swan,Deer
421-312↓ SeaLn,Swan,W.Cat
422-111↓ W.Cat,SeaLn
422-311↓ SeaLn,W.Cat,Swan
423-111↓ W.Cat,SeaLn,Dolphin
431-111↓ Swan,W.Cat,Pcock
431-321↓ Swan,SeaLn,W.Cat
431-331↓ Swan,W.Cat,Sable
432-111 W.Cat,Swan,Cottn
432-112↓ W.Cat,Swan,SeaLn
432-331↓ Swan,W.Cat,Sable
433-111↓ W.Cat,Pengn,Swan
433-311↓ Swan,W.Cat,SeaLn
433-312 Swan,W.Cat,Dolphin
433-321 Swan,W.Cat,SeaLn
433-322 Swan,W.Cat,Dolphin
433-331↓ W.Cat,Swan,Sable
441-111 Pengn,Sable
441-112↓ Sable,Swan,Pengn
442-111↓ Pengn,Sable,Swan
442-121↓ Pengn,Sable,W.Cat
442-211 Sable,Swan,Pengn
442-212↓ Sable,Swan,W.Cat
443-111↓ Pengn,W.Cat,Owl
443-131↓ Pengn,Owl,Sable
443-212↓ Sable,Pengn,W.Cat
443-231 Sable,Owl,Pengn
443-232 Sable,Owl,W.Cat
443-321↓ Sable,Swan,Pengn
443-322 Sable,Swan,W.Cat
443-331↓ Sable,Owl,Swan

233-

111-111↓ Porcp,Vultre,Croc
111-131↓ Porcp,Vultre,Pcock
111-211↓ Croc,Pcock,Porcp
111-232↓ Pcock,Porcp,Vultre
111-311↓ Croc,Pcock,Porcp
112-111↓ Porcp,Vultre,Croc
112-321↓ Porcp,Croc,Weasel
113-111↓ Porcp,Vultre,Croc
113-231↓ Porcp,Baboon,Vultre
113-321↓ Porcp,Croc,Weasel
113-322 Porcp,Croc,Warthg
113-331 Porcp,Baboon,Croc
113-332↓ Porcp,Baboon,Warthg
121-111↓ Porcp,SeaLn
122-111↓ Porcp,Baboon
122-232↓ Porcp,Baboon,W.Cat
122-322 Porcp,SeaLn,Deer
123-111↓ Porcp,Baboon
123-212↓ Porcp,Warthg,Baboon
123-312 Porcp,Warthg,Dolphin
123-321↓ Porcp,Baboon,Warthg
131-111↓ Porcp,Sheep
131-311↓ Porcp,Sheep,Baboon
132-111↓ Porcp,Sheep
132-221↓ Porcp,Sheep,Baboon
133-111↓ Porcp,Baboon
133-232↓ Baboon,Porcp,Fox

133-311 Baboon,Porcp,Sheep
133-312↓ Baboon,Porcp,W.Dog
141-111↓ Sheep,Porcp
141-331↓ Sheep,W.Dog,Beaver
141-332 W.Dog,Sheep,Wolf
142-111 Sheep,Porcp
142-122↓ Sheep,Porcp,Beaver
142-232↓ Beaver,Sheep,W.Dog
143-111 Sheep,Pengn
143-112↓ Sheep,Pengn,Porcp
143-121↓ Sheep,Pengn,Beaver
143-132 Beaver,Owl,Baboon
143-212↓ Sheep,Beaver,W.Dog
143-221 Sheep,Beaver,Owl
143-222 Sheep,Beaver,W.Dog
143-231 Beaver,Sheep,Owl
143-232 Beaver,W.Dog,Owl
143-312↓ W.Dog,Sheep,Beaver
143-332 W.Dog,Beaver,Owl
211-111↓ Vultre,Pcock,Weasel
212-111 Vultre,Weasel
212-132↓ Vultre,Weasel,Porcp
212-211↓ Weasel,Vultre,Pcock
213-111↓ Vultre,Weasel
213-122↓ Vultre,Weasel,Porcp
213-131↓ Vultre,Baboon,Weasel
213-211↓ Weasel,Vultre,Pcock
213-221↓ Weasel,Vultre,Baboon
213-311 Weasel,Vultre,SeaLn
213-312 Weasel,Vultre,Dolphin
213-321 Weasel,Vultre,Baboon
213-322 Weasel,Vultre,Dolphin
213-331↓ Baboon,Weasel,W.Dog
221-111 Porcp,Snake,MGoat
221-122↓ Porcp,Vultre,Pcock
221-131↓ Porcp,Baboon,Rooster
221-211 MGoat,Sheep,Pcock
221-212 Pcock,Porcp,MGoat
221-221 Sheep,Pcock,Porcp
221-222 Pcock,Porcp,W.Cat
221-231 Baboon,Rooster,Sheep
221-232 Rooster,Baboon,W.Cat
221-311 SeaLn,MGoat,Deer
221-312 SeaLn,Deer,Pcock
221-321 SeaLn,Deer,Sheep
221-322 SeaLn,Deer,Pcock
221-331 SeaLn,Baboon,Eagle
221-332 SeaLn,Eagle,Rooster
222-111 Porcp,Snake,MGoat
222-112 Porcp,Vultre,W.Cat
222-121 Porcp,Vultre,Sheep
222-122 Porcp,Vultre,MGoat
222-131↓ Porcp,Baboon,W.Cat
222-211 MGoat,Sheep,Porcp
222-212 W.Cat,Porcp,MGoat
222-221 Sheep,W.Cat,Baboon
222-222 W.Cat,Baboon,Porcp
222-231↓ Baboon,W.Cat,Rooster
222-311 SeaLn,MGoat,Deer
222-312 SeaLn,Deer,W.Cat
222-321 SeaLn,Deer,Sheep
222-322 SeaLn,Deer,W.Cat
222-331↓ Baboon,SeaLn,W.Cat
223-111 Porcp,Baboon,Snake
223-112 Porcp,Baboon,W.Cat

223-211 Baboon,MGoat,W.Cat
223-212 Baboon,W.Cat,Porcp
223-221 Baboon,W.Cat,Sheep
223-222↓ Baboon,W.Cat,Fox
223-311↓ Baboon,SeaLn,Dolphin
223-322 Baboon,Dolphin,W.Cat
223-331↓ Baboon,W.Dog,W.Cat
231-111 Sheep,Porcp,Baboon
231-222↓ Baboon,Sheep,Pcock
231-231↓ Baboon,Sheep,Beaver
231-311↓ Sheep,Baboon,SeaLn
231-332 Baboon,Wolf,W.Dog
232-111↓ Sheep,Baboon,Porcp
232-131 Baboon,Sheep,Beaver
232-132 Baboon,Beaver,Porcp
232-211 Sheep,Baboon,MGoat
232-212↓ Baboon,Sheep,Beaver
232-311 Sheep,Baboon,SeaLn
232-332 Baboon,W.Dog,Beaver
233-111 Baboon,Pengn,Sheep
233-112 Baboon,Fox,Pengn
233-121 Baboon,Pengn,Sheep
233-122↓ Baboon,Fox,Pengn
233-211 Baboon,Sheep,Otter
233-212 Baboon,Fox,Otter
233-312↓ Baboon,W.Dog,Fox
233-321 Baboon,W.Dog,Sheep
233-322↓ Baboon,W.Dog,Fox
241-111↓ Sheep,Dog
241-121↓ Sheep,Pengn,Dog
241-222↓ Sheep,Dog,Baboon
241-232↓ Sheep,Beaver,Wolf
241-312↓ Sheep,Wolf,W.Dog
242-111↓ Sheep,Pengn,Beaver
242-132 Beaver,Sheep,Owl
242-211↓ Sheep,Beaver,Owl
242-231 Sheep,Beaver,Owl
242-232↓ Beaver,Sheep,W.Dog
242-332 W.Dog,Beaver,Wolf
243-111↓ Pengn,Sheep,Owl
243-131 Pengn,Owl,Beaver
243-132 Owl,Beaver,Baboon
243-211 Sheep,Pengn,Owl
243-212 Sheep,Owl,Beaver
243-221 Sheep,Owl,Pengn
243-222↓ Owl,Sheep,Beaver
243-232 Owl,Beaver,W.Dog
243-311 Sheep,W.Dog,Owl
243-331↓ W.Dog,Owl,Beaver
311-111 Pcock,Weasel
311-332↓ Pcock,Weasel,SeaLn
312-111↓ Weasel,Pcock,Vultre
312-211↓ Weasel,Pcock,Shrew
312-222↓ Weasel,Pcock,W.Cat
312-311↓ Weasel,Pcock,SeaLn
313-111↓ Weasel,Vultre,Pcock
313-122↓ Weasel,Vultre,W.Cat
313-212↓ Weasel,Pcock,W.Cat
313-311↓ Weasel,SeaLn,Dolphin
313-322 Weasel,Dolphin,W.Cat
313-331 Weasel,W.Cat,SeaLn
313-332 Weasel,W.Cat,Dolphin
321-111 Pcock,Porcp,Weasel
321-112↓ Pcock,Porcp,W.Cat
321-122↓ Pcock,W.Cat,Rooster

(233 cont'd)

321-211	Pcock,SeaLn,Weasel
321-212↓	Pcock,SeaLn,W.Cat
321-231↓	Rooster,Pcock,W.Cat
321-311↓	SeaLn,Deer,Pcock
321-331	SeaLn,Eagle,Deer
321-332	SeaLn,Eagle,Rooster
322-111	W.Cat,Porcp,Weasel
322-112↓	W.Cat,Porcp,Rooster
322-211	W.Cat,SeaLn,Weasel
322-212↓	W.Cat,SeaLn,Rooster
322-311↓	SeaLn,Deer,W.Cat
322-331↓	SeaLn,W.Cat,Eagle
323-111	Pengn,W.Cat,Otter
323-112↓	W.Cat,Fox,Pengn
323-131↓	W.Cat,Fox,Baboon
323-211	W.Cat,SeaLn,Otter
323-212	W.Cat,Fox,Dolphin
323-221	W.Cat,Fox,Baboon
323-222	W.Cat,Fox,Dolphin
323-231↓	W.Cat,Fox,Baboon
323-311	SeaLn,Dolphin,Deer
323-312	Dolphin,SeaLn,W.Cat
323-331	W.Cat,SeaLn,Fox
323-332	W.Cat,Fox,Dolphin
331-111	Pengn,Sheep,Pcock
331-112	Pcock,Dog,Pengn
331-121	Pengn,Sheep,Pcock
331-122	Pcock,Dog,W.Cat
331-131	Baboon,Pengn,Rooster
331-132	Rooster,Baboon,Fox
331-211	Sheep,Pcock,Dog
331-212	Pcock,Dog,SeaLn
331-221	Sheep,Pcock,Dog
331-222	Pcock,Dog,W.Cat
331-231	Baboon,Rooster,Sheep
331-232	Rooster,Baboon,Fox
331-311↓	SeaLn,Swan,Deer
331-331↓	Wolf,SeaLn,Swan
332-111	Pengn,Sheep,Dog
332-112	Pengn,Dog,W.Cat
332-121	Pengn,Sheep,W.Cat
332-122	W.Cat,Pengn,Fox
332-131	Baboon,Pengn,Fox
332-132	Fox,Baboon,W.Cat
332-211	Sheep,Dog,Otter
332-212	Dog,W.Cat,Otter
332-221	Sheep,W.Cat,Dog
332-222	W.Cat,Fox,Dog
332-231	Baboon,Fox,W.Cat
332-331	Wolf,Baboon,SeaLn
332-332	Wolf,Fox,Baboon
333-111	Pengn,Otter,Horse
333-112	Fox,Pengn,Otter
333-121	Pengn,Fox,Baboon
333-132	Fox,Baboon,Owl
333-211↓	Otter,Horse,Fox
333-221↓	Fox,Baboon,Otter
333-231↓	Fox,Baboon,Owl
333-311↓	Otter,Horse,Fox
333-321↓	Fox,Baboon,Otter
333-331↓	Fox,Baboon,Owl
341-111↓	Pengn,Sheep,Dog
341-132	Dog,Owl,Wolf
341-211	Sheep,Dog,Pengn

341-212	Dog,Sheep,Wolf
341-221	Sheep,Dog,Pengn
341-222↓	Dog,Sheep,Wolf
341-332	Wolf,Sable,Dog
342-111↓	Pengn,Sheep,Dog
342-122	Pengn,Dog,Owl
342-131	Pengn,Owl,Sheep
342-132	Owl,Pr.Dog,Pengn
342-211	Sheep,Dog,Pengn
342-212	Dog,Sheep,Owl
342-221	Sheep,Dog,Pengn
342-222	Dog,Owl,Sheep
342-231	Owl,Sheep,Pr.Dog
342-232	Owl,Wolf,Pr.Dog
342-311↓	Sheep,Dog,Wolf
342-322	Wolf,Dog,Owl
342-331	Wolf,Owl,Sheep
342-332	Wolf,Owl,Sable
343-111	Pengn,Owl
343-112↓	Pengn,Owl,Pr.Dog
343-211	Pengn,Owl,Sheep
343-212↓	Owl,Pr.Dog,Pengn
343-311	Owl,Pengn,Sheep
343-312	Owl,W.Dog,Pr.Dog
343-321	Owl,Pengn,Pr.Dog
343-322↓	Owl,W.Dog,Pr.Dog
411-111↓	Pcock,SeaLn
412-111↓	Pcock,W.Cat
412-211↓	Pcock,W.Cat,SeaLn
412-311↓	Pcock,SeaLn,Deer
412-331↓	Pcock,SeaLn,W.Cat
413-111↓	Pcock,W.Cat
413-211↓	Pcock,W.Cat,SeaLn
413-212	Pcock,W.Cat,Dolphin
413-221	Pcock,W.Cat,SeaLn
413-222	W.Cat,Pcock,Dolphin
413-231	W.Cat,Pcock,SeaLn
413-232	W.Cat,Pcock,Dolphin
413-311	SeaLn,Dolphin,Pcock
413-322↓	Dolphin,W.Cat,SeaLn
421-111↓	Pcock,SeaLn,W.Cat
421-332↓	SeaLn,Deer,W.Cat
422-111↓	W.Cat,SeaLn,Deer
423-111↓	W.Cat,SeaLn,Dolphin
423-311	SeaLn,Dolphin,Deer
423-312↓	Dolphin,SeaLn,W.Cat
431-111	Pcock,Cottn,Swan
431-112	Pcock,Swan,W.Cat
431-121	Pcock,Cottn,W.Cat
431-122	Pcock,W.Cat,Swan
431-131	Pcock,W.Cat,Cottn
431-132	W.Cat,Pcock,Swan
431-211	Pcock,Swan,SeaLn
431-222↓	Swan,Pcock,W.Cat
431-311↓	Swan,SeaLn,Deer
432-111	W.Cat,Cottn,Swan
432-112	W.Cat,Swan,SeaLn
432-121	W.Cat,Cottn,Swan
432-122	W.Cat,Sable,Swan
432-131	W.Cat,Cottn,Swan
432-132	W.Cat,Swan,SeaLn
432-311↓	Swan,SeaLn,Deer
432-331↓	Swan,SeaLn,W.Cat
433-111	W.Cat,Pengn,Cottn
433-112	W.Cat,Swan,Dolphin

433-121	W.Cat,Pengn,Cottn
433-122	W.Cat,Swan,Dolphin
433-131	W.Cat,Fox,Pengn
433-132	W.Cat,Fox,Swan
433-211	W.Cat,Swan,SeaLn
433-212	W.Cat,Swan,Dolphin
433-221	W.Cat,Swan,SeaLn
433-222	W.Cat,Swan,Dolphin
433-231↓	W.Cat,Fox,Swan
433-311↓	Swan,SeaLn,Dolphin
433-322	Swan,Dolphin,W.Cat
433-331	W.Cat,Swan,SeaLn
433-332	W.Cat,Swan,Dolphin
441-111	Pengn,Pcock,Dog
441-112	Pcock,Dog,Sable
441-121	Pengn,Pcock,Dog
441-122	Sable,Pcock,Dog
441-131	Sable,Pengn,Pcock
441-132↓	Sable,Pcock,Dog
441-212	Sable,Swan,Pcock
441-221	Sable,Pcock,Dog
441-222	Sable,Swan,Pcock
441-231	Sable,Pcock,Dog
441-232	Sable,Wolf,Swan
441-311↓	Sable,Swan,SeaLn
441-332	Sable,Wolf,Swan
442-111	Pengn,Dog
442-112↓	Pengn,Dog,Sable
442-121	Pengn,Dog,Sheep
442-122	Sable,Pengn,Dog
442-131	Pengn,Sable,Owl
442-132	Sable,Owl,W.Cat
442-211	Dog,Sable,Sheep
442-212	Sable,Swan,Dog
442-221	Sable,Dog,Sheep
442-222	Sable,Swan,Dog
442-231↓	Sable,Owl,W.Cat
442-311↓	Sable,Swan,SeaLn
442-331↓	Sable,Wolf,Swan
443-111↓	Pengn,Owl
443-122↓	Pengn,Owl,W.Cat
443-131↓	Pengn,Owl,Pr.Dog
443-212	Owl,Sable,Pr.Dog
443-221	Owl,Pengn,Pr.Dog
443-222	Owl,W.Cat,Sable
443-231↓	Owl,Pr.Dog,Sable
443-311↓	Sable,Swan,Owl
443-331↓	Sable,Owl,Pr.Dog

234-

111-111↓	Porcp,Vultre,Pcock
111-231↓	Pcock,Porcp,Baboon
111-311↓	SeaLn,Pcock,Croc
111-321↓	SeaLn,Pcock,Porcp
112-111↓	Porcp,Vultre
112-212↓	Porcp,Croc,Vultre
112-221	Porcp,Croc,SeaLn
112-222	Porcp,Vultre,Croc
112-232↓	Porcp,Baboon,Vultre
112-322↓	SeaLn,Porcp,Dolphin
112-331↓	SeaLn,Baboon,Porcp
113-111↓	Porcp,Vultre
113-132↓	Porcp,Baboon,Vultre
113-211↓	Porcp,Croc,Baboon
113-311	SeaLn,Dolphin,Croc

113-322 Dolphin,Baboon,SeaLn
113-332↓ Baboon,W.Dog,Dolphin
121-111↓ Porcp,SeaLn
121-331↓ SeaLn,Baboon,Porcp
122-111 Porcp,Baboon
122-321↓ SeaLn,Porcp,Baboon
123-111↓ Porcp,Baboon
123-311↓ Baboon,SeaLn,Dolphin
123-332 Baboon,W.Dog,Dolphin
131-111↓ Porcp,Baboon
131-311↓ Baboon,SeaLn,Porcp
131-322↓ Baboon,SeaLn,W.Dog
132-111↓ Porcp,Baboon,Walrus
132-322↓ Baboon,SeaLn,W.Dog
133-111↓ Baboon,Porcp
133-312↓ Baboon,W.Dog
141-111 Sheep,Dog,Porcp
141-132 Baboon,W.Dog,Dog
141-222↓ Dog,Sheep,W.Dog
141-231 Sheep,W.Dog,Baboon
141-232 W.Dog,Baboon,Dog
141-311↓ Sheep,W.Dog,Dog
142-111 Sheep,Dog
142-112↓ Dog,Sheep,Porcp
142-121 Sheep,Dog,Baboon
142-132 Baboon,W.Dog,Pr.Dog
142-212↓ Dog,Sheep,W.Dog
142-231 W.Dog,Sheep,Baboon
142-232 W.Dog,Baboon,Pr.Dog
142-311↓ W.Dog,Sheep,Dog
143-111↓ Baboon,Sheep,W.Dog
143-112 Baboon,W.Dog,Pr.Dog
143-121 Baboon,W.Dog,Sheep
143-122↓ Baboon,W.Dog,Pr.Dog
143-211 W.Dog,Baboon,Sheep
143-212 W.Dog,Baboon,Pr.Dog
143-221 W.Dog,Baboon,Sheep
143-222↓ W.Dog,Baboon,Pr.Dog
211-111↓ Pcock,Vultre,Weasel
211-131↓ Pcock,Vultre,Baboon
211-222 Pcock,Weasel,Vultre
211-231↓ Pcock,Baboon
211-331↓ SeaLn,Pcock,Eagle
212-111↓ Vultre,Weasel
212-131↓ Vultre,Baboon,Weasel
212-211↓ Weasel,SeaLn,Vultre
212-221 Weasel,SeaLn,Baboon
212-222 Weasel,Vultre,SeaLn
212-231 Baboon,Weasel,SeaLn
212-232 Baboon,Weasel,Vultre
212-311↓ SeaLn,Weasel,Eagle
212-331↓ SeaLn,Baboon,Eagle
213-111↓ Vultre,Baboon,Weasel
213-211 Baboon,Weasel,SeaLn
213-212↓ Baboon,Dolphin,Weasel
213-311↓ SeaLn,Dolphin,Baboon
213-332↓ Baboon,W.Dog,Dolphin
221-111 Porcp,Baboon,Walrus
221-112 Porcp,Baboon,SeaLn
221-121 Baboon,Porcp,Walrus
221-122↓ Baboon,Porcp,SeaLn
221-322↓ SeaLn,Eagle,Baboon
222-111 Baboon,Porcp,Walrus
222-112 Baboon,Porcp,SeaLn
222-121 Baboon,Porcp,Walrus

222-132↓ Baboon,Porcp,SeaLn
222-211 Baboon,SeaLn,MGoat
222-212 Baboon,SeaLn,Dolphin
222-221 Baboon,SeaLn,Sheep
222-222↓ Baboon,SeaLn,Eagle
222-311↓ SeaLn,Baboon,Dolphin
222-321↓ SeaLn,Baboon,Eagle
223-111↓ Baboon,Horse
223-211↓ Baboon,SeaLn,Horse
223-212↓ Baboon,Dolphin,SeaLn
223-331 Baboon,W.Dog,SeaLn
223-332 Baboon,W.Dog,Dolphin
231-111 Baboon,Walrus,Sheep
231-112 Baboon,Walrus,Dog
231-121 Baboon,Walrus,Sheep
231-122↓ Baboon,Walrus,Dog
231-221↓ Baboon,Sheep,Dog
231-222↓ Baboon,Dog,SeaLn
231-311 Baboon,SeaLn,Sheep
231-312 Baboon,SeaLn,W.Dog
231-321 Baboon,SeaLn,Sheep
231-332↓ Baboon,W.Dog,SeaLn
232-111 Baboon,Walrus,Sheep
232-112 Baboon,Walrus,Dog
232-121 Baboon,Walrus,Sheep
232-122↓ Baboon,Walrus,Dog
232-211 Baboon,Sheep,Dog
232-212 Baboon,Dog,Horse
232-221↓ Baboon,Sheep,Dog
232-311↓ Baboon,SeaLn,W.Dog
233-111↓ Baboon,Horse
233-311↓ Baboon,W.Dog,Horse
241-111 Sheep,Dog
241-212↓ Dog,Sheep,W.Dog
241-332 W.Dog,Dog,Baboon
242-111 Sheep,Dog
242-112↓ Dog,Sheep,Baboon
242-131 Sheep,Baboon,Pr.Dog
242-132 Baboon,W.Dog,Pr.Dog
242-211↓ Sheep,Dog,W.Dog
242-231 W.Dog,Sheep,Baboon
242-232 W.Dog,Baboon,Pr.Dog
242-311↓ W.Dog,Sheep,Dog
242-331 W.Dog,Sheep,Baboon
242-332 W.Dog,Baboon,Pr.Dog
243-111 Pengn,Baboon,Sheep
243-112 Baboon,W.Dog,Pr.Dog
243-121 Baboon,Pr.Dog,Pengn
243-122↓ Baboon,W.Dog,Pr.Dog
243-211 W.Dog,Baboon,Sheep
243-212↓ W.Dog,Baboon,Pr.Dog
243-311 W.Dog,Baboon,Sheep
243-312↓ W.Dog,Baboon,Pr.Dog
311-111↓ Pcock,Weasel
311-232↓ Pcock,Weasel,SeaLn
311-331↓ SeaLn,Pcock,Eagle
312-111 Weasel,Pcock,SeaLn
312-112 Weasel,Pcock,Vultre
312-121 Weasel,Pcock,SeaLn
312-122 Weasel,Pcock,Vultre
312-131 Weasel,Pcock,SeaLn
312-132 Weasel,Pcock,Vultre
312-312↓ SeaLn,Weasel,Dolphin
312-321 SeaLn,Weasel,Pcock
312-322↓ SeaLn,Weasel,Eagle

313-111 Weasel,SeaLn,Horse
313-112 Weasel,Dolphin,Vultre
313-121 Weasel,Baboon,SeaLn
313-122 Weasel,Dolphin,Vultre
313-131↓ Baboon,Weasel,Pr.Dog
313-211↓ Weasel,SeaLn,Dolphin
313-231 Baboon,Weasel,Pr.Dog
313-232 Baboon,Dolphin,Weasel
313-321↓ SeaLn,Dolphin,Weasel
313-332 Dolphin,SeaLn,Eagle
321-111↓ SeaLn,Pcock,Dog
321-131 SeaLn,Baboon,Eagle
321-132↓ SeaLn,Eagle,Rooster
321-212↓ SeaLn,Pcock,Dog
321-222 SeaLn,Eagle,Pcock
321-231 SeaLn,Eagle,Baboon
321-232↓ SeaLn,Eagle,Rooster
321-332↓ SeaLn,Eagle,Dolphin
322-111↓ SeaLn,Dog,Horse
322-121 SeaLn,Dog,Baboon
322-122 SeaLn,W.Cat,Dog
322-131↓ Baboon,SeaLn,Eagle
322-211 SeaLn,Dog,Horse
322-212 SeaLn,Dolphin,Dog
322-221 SeaLn,Dog,Baboon
322-222 SeaLn,Eagle,Dolphin
322-231↓ SeaLn,Baboon,Eagle
322-311↓ SeaLn,Dolphin,Eagle
323-111 Horse,Baboon,SeaLn
323-112 Horse,Dolphin,Baboon
323-121 Baboon,Horse,SeaLn
323-122 Baboon,Horse,Dolphin
323-131↓ Baboon,Pr.Dog,Horse
323-211↓ SeaLn,Horse,Dolphin
323-221 Baboon,SeaLn,Horse
323-222 Dolphin,Baboon,SeaLn
323-231 Baboon,Pr.Dog,SeaLn
323-232 Baboon,Dolphin,Pr.Dog
323-311 SeaLn,Dolphin,Horse
323-322 Dolphin,SeaLn,Eagle
323-331 SeaLn,Dolphin,Baboon
323-332 Dolphin,SeaLn,Eagle
331-111↓ Dog,Horse,Baboon
331-131↓ Baboon,Dog,Pr.Dog
331-211↓ Dog,SeaLn,Horse
331-221↓ Dog,SeaLn,Baboon
331-322 SeaLn,Dog,Eagle
331-331↓ SeaLn,Baboon,Eagle
332-111↓ Dog,Horse,Baboon
332-131↓ Baboon,Pr.Dog,Dog
332-211↓ Dog,Horse,Baboon
332-221↓ Baboon,Pr.Dog,Dog
332-311↓ SeaLn,Dog,Horse
332-321↓ SeaLn,Dog,Baboon
332-331↓ Baboon,SeaLn,Eagle
333-111 Horse,Baboon,Pengn
333-112↓ Horse,Baboon,Pr.Dog
333-311 Horse,Baboon,SeaLn
333-312 Horse,Dolphin,Baboon
333-321 Baboon,Horse,SeaLn
333-322 Baboon,Horse,Dolphin
333-331 Baboon,Pr.Dog,Horse
333-332 Baboon,W.Dog,Pr.Dog
341-111↓ Dog,Pr.Dog,Sheep
341-232↓ Dog,Pr.Dog,Wolf

(234 cont'd)

341-321   Dog,Pr.Dog,Sheep
341-322   Dog,Wolf,W.Dog
341-331   Dog,Pr.Dog,Wolf
341-332   Dog,Wolf,W.Dog
342-111↓ Dog,Pengn,Pr.Dog
342-132↓ Pr.Dog,Dog,Owl
342-232↓ Pr.Dog,Dog,W.Dog
343-111↓ Pengn,Pr.Dog,Dog
343-122   Pr.Dog,Dog,Owl
343-131   Pr.Dog,Owl,Pengn
343-132↓ Pr.Dog,Owl,Dog
343-232   Pr.Dog,Owl,W.Dog
343-311↓ Pr.Dog,Dog,W.Dog
343-331   Pr.Dog,W.Dog,Owl
411-111↓ Pcock,SeaLn
412-111↓ Pcock,SeaLn
412-122↓ Pcock,SeaLn,W.Cat
412-211↓ SeaLn,Pcock,Dolphin
412-231↓ SeaLn,Pcock,W.Cat
412-311↓ SeaLn,Pcock,Dolphin
413-111   SeaLn,Dolphin,Pcock
413-132   Dolphin,W.Cat,SeaLn
413-211   SeaLn,Dolphin,Pcock
413-332↓ Dolphin,SeaLn,W.Cat
421-111   SeaLn,Pcock
421-132↓ SeaLn,Pcock,W.Cat
421-211↓ SeaLn,Pcock,Dolphin
421-231↓ SeaLn,Pcock,W.Cat
422-111↓ SeaLn,Dolphin,W.Cat
423-111↓ SeaLn,Dolphin,W.Cat
431-111↓ SeaLn,Pcock
431-212↓ SeaLn,Pcock,Swan
431-221   SeaLn,Pcock,Cottn
431-232↓ SeaLn,Pcock,W.Cat
431-311↓ SeaLn,Swan,Dolphin
432-111↓ SeaLn,Dolphin,W.Cat
432-121   SeaLn,W.Cat,Cottn
432-122   SeaLn,W.Cat,Dolphin
432-131   SeaLn,W.Cat,Baboon
432-132   SeaLn,W.Cat,Dolphin
432-211   SeaLn,Dolphin,Cottn
432-212   SeaLn,Dolphin,Swan
432-221↓ SeaLn,Dolphin,W.Cat
432-332↓ SeaLn,Dolphin,Swan
433-111   SeaLn,Dolphin,Horse
433-122   Dolphin,SeaLn,W.Cat
433-131   Baboon,SeaLn,Dolphin
433-132   Dolphin,Baboon,W.Cat
433-211   SeaLn,Dolphin,Horse
433-222   Dolphin,SeaLn,W.Cat
433-231   SeaLn,Dolphin,Baboon
433-312   Dolphin,SeaLn,Swan
433-331   SeaLn,Dolphin,Baboon
441-111↓ Dog,Pr.Dog
441-132↓ Dog,Pr.Dog,Sable
441-231↓ Dog,Pr.Dog,SeaLn
441-232   Dog,Pr.Dog,Sable
441-312↓ SeaLn,Dog,Sable
442-111↓ Dog,Pengn
442-122↓ Dog,Pr.Dog,SeaLn
442-131   Pr.Dog,Dog,Pengn
442-132   Pr.Dog,Dog,Sable
442-212↓ Dog,SeaLn,Pr.Dog
442-232   Pr.Dog,Dog,Sable

442-312↓ SeaLn,Dog,Sable
442-331   SeaLn,Sable,Pr.Dog
443-111↓ Pengn,Pr.Dog,Dog
443-122   Pr.Dog,Dog,Owl
443-131   Pr.Dog,Owl,Pengn
443-132↓ Pr.Dog,Owl,Dog
443-212   Pr.Dog,Dog,Dolphin
443-221↓ Pr.Dog,Dog,Owl
443-311   SeaLn,Dolphin,Pr.Dog
443-332   Pr.Dog,W.Dog,Sable

241-

111-111↓ Porcp,Croc
111-212↓ Croc,Porcp,Weasel
112-111↓ Porcp,Croc
112-212↓ Croc,Porcp,Weasel
113-111↓ Porcp,Croc
113-212↓ Croc,Porcp,Weasel
113-232   Porcp,Weasel,Warthg
113-311↓ Croc,Weasel,Porcp
113-322   Croc,Weasel,Warthg
113-331   Weasel,Croc,Porcp
113-332   Weasel,Warthg,Croc
121-111↓ Porcp,Mole
121-311↓ Porcp,Croc
122-111↓ Porcp,Mole
122-211↓ Porcp,Mole,Croc
122-212   Porcp,Croc,Warthg
122-221   Porcp,Mole
122-222   Porcp,Warthg
122-231   Porcp,Mole
122-232↓ Porcp,Warthg
122-312↓ Porcp,Croc
123-111↓ Porcp,Warthg
123-331↓ Porcp,Warthg,W.Dog
131-111↓ Porcp,Croc
131-332↓ Porcp,W.Dog
132-111↓ Porcp,Mole
132-222↓ Porcp,Warthg
132-311↓ Porcp,Croc
132-331↓ Porcp,W.Dog
133-111↓ Porcp,Warthg
133-231↓ Porcp,Warthg,W.Dog
141-111↓ Porcp,W.Dog,Croc
141-231↓ W.Dog,Porcp,Wolf
142-111↓ Porcp,W.Dog
142-211↓ Porcp,W.Dog,Sheep
142-222↓ Porcp,W.Dog,Beaver
142-312↓ W.Dog,Wolf,Porcp
143-111↓ Porcp,Pengn,W.Dog
143-132   W.Dog,Porcp,Beaver
143-211↓ W.Dog,Porcp,Warthg
211-111↓ Weasel,Vultre
212-111↓ Weasel,Vultre,Shrew
212-121   Weasel,Shrew,Porcp
212-122↓ Weasel,Shrew,Vultre
212-211↓ Weasel,Shrew,Croc
213-111↓ Weasel,Vultre
213-212↓ Weasel,Shrew
221-111↓ Porcp,Snake,MGoat
221-211↓ MGoat,Weasel,Porcp
221-222↓ Weasel,Porcp,Rooster
221-311   Zebra,MGoat,Weasel
221-312↓ Zebra,Weasel,Porcp
221-331   Zebra,Eagle,Weasel

222-111   Porcp,Snake,MGoat
222-132↓ Porcp,Weasel,Rooster
222-211↓ MGoat,Weasel,Porcp
222-222↓ Weasel,Porcp,Rooster
222-311   Zebra,MGoat,Weasel
222-312↓ Zebra,Weasel,Porcp
222-331   Zebra,Eagle,Weasel
223-111↓ Porcp,Snake,MGoat
223-211↓ MGoat,Weasel,Porcp
223-231   Weasel,Porcp,Rooster
223-232   Weasel,Rooster,W.Dog
223-311   Zebra,MGoat,Weasel
223-312↓ Zebra,Weasel,W.Dog
223-331↓ W.Dog,Zebra,Eagle
231-111   Porcp,Hippo,Snake
231-112   Porcp,Weasel
231-121   Porcp,Hippo
231-122   Porcp,Weasel
231-131   Porcp,Hippo
231-132   Porcp,Weasel,Rooster
231-211↓ MGoat,Weasel,Porcp
231-221   Weasel,Porcp,Hippo
231-222↓ Weasel,Porcp,Rooster
231-311   Zebra,MGoat,Weasel
231-312↓ Zebra,Weasel,W.Dog
231-331   W.Dog,Wolf,Zebra
231-332   W.Dog,Wolf,Eagle
232-111   Porcp,Hippo,Snake
232-122↓ Porcp,Weasel,Hippo
232-132   Porcp,Weasel,Rooster
232-211↓ MGoat,Weasel,Porcp
232-221   Weasel,Porcp,Hippo
232-222↓ Weasel,Porcp,W.Dog
232-232   W.Dog,Weasel,Rooster
232-311   Zebra,MGoat,Weasel
232-312↓ Zebra,W.Dog,Weasel
232-332   W.Dog,Wolf,Eagle
233-111   Porcp,Hippo,Bat
233-112   Porcp,Bat,Weasel
233-121   Porcp,Hippo,Bat
233-122   Porcp,Bat,Baboon
233-131↓ Baboon,Porcp,W.Dog
233-211   MGoat,Weasel,W.Dog
233-212↓ W.Dog,Weasel,Baboon
233-231↓ W.Dog,Baboon,Lion
241-111   Pengn,Sheep,Porcp
241-112   Porcp,W.Dog,Pengn
241-121   Pengn,Sheep,Porcp
241-122   W.Dog,Porcp,Wolf
241-131   W.Dog,Wolf,Pengn
241-132   W.Dog,Porcp,Wolf
241-211   Sheep,W.Dog,Wolf
241-212   W.Dog,Wolf,Weasel
241-221   W.Dog,Sheep,Wolf
241-222↓ W.Dog,Wolf,Beaver
241-311↓ W.Dog,Wolf,Sheep
242-111   Pengn,Sheep,W.Dog
242-112   W.Dog,Pengn,Porcp
242-121   Pengn,W.Dog,Sheep
242-122↓ W.Dog,Pengn,Beaver
242-132   W.Dog,Beaver,Wolf
242-211   W.Dog,Sheep,Beaver
242-212   W.Dog,Wolf,Beaver
242-221   W.Dog,Sheep,Beaver

242-222↓ W.Dog,Wolf,Beaver
243-111↓ Pengn,W.Dog
243-222↓ W.Dog,Beaver
311-111↓ Weasel,Shrew
312-111↓ Weasel,Shrew
313-111↓ Weasel,Shrew
321-111↓ Weasel,Porcp
321-122↓ Weasel,Porcp,Rooster
321-212↓ Weasel,Zebra,Rooster
321-232 Weasel,Rooster,Eagle
321-312↓ Zebra,Weasel,Eagle
322-111 Weasel,Porcp
322-112↓ Weasel,Porcp,Rooster
322-211 Weasel,Zebra,Shrew
322-212↓ Weasel,Zebra,Rooster
322-232 Weasel,Rooster,Eagle
322-312↓ Zebra,Weasel,Eagle
323-111↓ Weasel,Porcp
323-121↓ Weasel,Porcp,W.Cat
323-131 Weasel,Rooster,Porcp
323-132 Weasel,Rooster,W.Cat
323-212↓ Weasel,Zebra,W.Cat
323-222↓ Weasel,W.Cat,Rooster
323-312↓ Zebra,Weasel,Eagle
331-111↓ Weasel,Porcp,Hippo
331-122↓ Weasel,Porcp,Rooster
331-211↓ Weasel,Zebra
331-231↓ Weasel,Rooster,Wolf
331-311↓ Zebra,Weasel,Wolf
331-331↓ Wolf,Zebra,Eagle
332-111↓ Weasel,Porcp,Pengn
332-122↓ Weasel,Porcp,Rooster
332-222↓ Weasel,Rooster,Zebra
332-231↓ Weasel,Rooster,Wolf
332-311↓ Zebra,Weasel,Wolf
332-331↓ Wolf,Zebra,Eagle
333-111 Pengn,Weasel,Otter
333-132 Lion,Weasel,Rooster
333-211 Weasel,Otter,Pengn
333-212↓ Weasel,Otter,Lion
333-231↓ Lion,Weasel,Rooster
333-311↓ Zebra,Weasel,W.Dog
333-331↓ W.Dog,Lion,Wolf
341-111↓ Pengn,Wolf,Weasel
341-332 Wolf,W.Dog
342-111↓ Pengn,Wolf,Weasel
342-132↓ Wolf,Pengn,W.Dog
342-211 Wolf,Pengn,Weasel
342-212 Wolf,Weasel,W.Dog
342-221 Wolf,Pengn,Weasel
342-222↓ Wolf,Weasel,W.Dog
343-111↓ Pengn,W.Dog,Owl
343-222↓ W.Dog,Wolf,Pengn
343-232 W.Dog,Wolf,Owl
343-321↓ W.Dog,Wolf,Pengn
411-111↓ Weasel,Pcock
411-222↓ Weasel,Pcock,Shrew
412-111↓ Weasel,W.Cat,Shrew
413-111↓ Weasel,W.Cat
421-111↓ Weasel,W.Cat,Porcp
421-211 Weasel,W.Cat,SeaLn
421-231↓ W.Cat,Weasel,Rooster
421-311 SeaLn,Zebra,Weasel
421-312↓ SeaLn,Zebra,W.Cat
422-111↓ W.Cat,Weasel,Porcp

422-232↓ W.Cat,Weasel,Rooster
422-311 SeaLn,W.Cat,Zebra
423-111↓ W.Cat,Weasel
423-311↓ W.Cat,SeaLn,Dolphin
423-331↓ W.Cat,Tiger
431-111↓ Weasel,W.Cat,Swan
431-321↓ Swan,SeaLn,W.Cat
431-331↓ Swan,W.Cat,Sable
432-111↓ W.Cat,Weasel,Swan
432-321↓ Swan,W.Cat,SeaLn
432-331↓ Swan,W.Cat,Tiger
433-111↓ W.Cat,Pengn,Weasel
433-131↓ W.Cat,Tiger
433-211↓ W.Cat,Swan,Weasel
433-311↓ Swan,Tiger,W.Cat
441-111 Pengn,Sable
442-111↓ Pengn,Sable,Wolf
442-122↓ Sable,Pengn,W.Cat
442-131 Pengn,Sable,Wolf
442-132 Sable,Wolf,W.Cat
442-211 Sable,Wolf,Pengn
442-212↓ Sable,Wolf,Swan
443-111↓ Pengn,W.Cat
443-212↓ Sable,Pengn,W.Cat
443-222 W.Cat,Sable,Wolf
443-231 Sable,Pengn,Wolf
443-232↓ Sable,Wolf,W.Dog

242-

111-111↓ Croc,Weasel,Porcp
112-111↓ Croc,Weasel
112-112↓ Croc,Weasel,Porcp
113-111↓ Croc,Weasel,Porcp
113-122 Croc,Weasel,Warthg
113-131 Weasel,Croc,Porcp
113-212↓ Croc,Weasel,Warthg
121-111↓ Porcp,Croc
121-211↓ Croc,Porcp,Warthg
121-231 Porcp,Warthg,Weasel
121-232 Porcp,Warthg,Rooster
121-311↓ Croc,Porcp,Warthg
121-332 Warthg,Porcp,Eagle
122-111 Porcp,Croc
122-112↓ Porcp,Croc,Warthg
122-232 Warthg,Porcp,Rooster
122-311↓ Croc,Warthg,Porcp
122-332↓ Warthg,Porcp,Eagle
123-111 Porcp,Warthg
123-112↓ Warthg,Porcp,Croc
123-331↓ Warthg,W.Dog
131-111↓ Porcp,Croc
131-211↓ Croc,Porcp,Warthg
131-232↓ Porcp,Warthg,Rooster
131-311↓ Croc,Porcp,Warthg
131-322 Warthg,Porcp,W.Dog
131-331 W.Dog,Wolf,Porcp
131-332 W.Dog,Wolf,Warthg
132-111↓ Porcp,Croc
132-211↓ Croc,Porcp,Warthg
132-232 Warthg,Porcp,W.Dog
132-311↓ Croc,Warthg,Porcp
132-321↓ Warthg,Porcp,W.Dog
132-331↓ W.Dog,Warthg,Wolf
133-111 Porcp,Warthg

133-132↓ Warthg,Porcp,Baboon
133-211↓ Warthg,Croc
133-222↓ Warthg,Porcp,W.Dog
133-231↓ Warthg,W.Dog,Baboon
133-311↓ Warthg,W.Dog,Croc
141-111 Porcp,Sheep,Pengn
141-112 Porcp,Croc,W.Dog
141-121 Porcp,Sheep,Pengn
141-131↓ W.Dog,Porcp,Beaver
141-132 W.Dog,Porcp,Wolf
141-211 Sheep,Croc,W.Dog
141-212 W.Dog,Croc,Wolf
141-221↓ Sheep,W.Dog,Wolf
141-231↓ W.Dog,Wolf,Beaver
141-311↓ W.Dog,Wolf,Sheep
142-111 Porcp,Pengn,Sheep
142-112 Porcp,W.Dog,Croc
142-121 Porcp,Pengn,Sheep
142-122↓ Porcp,W.Dog,Beaver
142-211 W.Dog,Sheep,Croc
142-212 W.Dog,Croc,Wolf
142-221 W.Dog,Sheep,Beaver
142-222↓ W.Dog,Wolf,Beaver
143-111 Pengn,W.Dog,Porcp
143-122↓ W.Dog,Pengn,Warthg
143-131↓ W.Dog,Pengn,Beaver
211-111↓ Weasel,Vultre,Shrew
212-111↓ Weasel,Shrew,Vultre
213-111↓ Weasel,Vultre,Shrew
213-332↓ Weasel,W.Dog,Shrew
221-111 Weasel,Porcp,Hippo
221-112↓ Weasel,Porcp,Rooster
221-232↓ Rooster,Weasel,Eagle
221-312↓ Zebra,Weasel,Eagle
221-332 Eagle,Rooster,Zebra
222-111 Weasel,Porcp,Hippo
222-112↓ Weasel,Porcp,Rooster
222-212↓ Weasel,Rooster,Zebra
222-232 Rooster,Weasel,Eagle
222-312↓ Zebra,Weasel,Eagle
222-332 Eagle,Rooster,Zebra
223-111↓ Weasel,Porcp,Warthg
223-131 Weasel,Rooster,Baboon
223-132 Rooster,Weasel,W.Cat
223-212↓ Weasel,Warthg,Rooster
223-231 Weasel,Rooster,W.Dog
223-322 Zebra,W.Dog,Weasel
223-331 W.Dog,Zebra,Eagle
223-332 W.Dog,Eagle,Rooster
231-111 Hippo,Weasel
231-122↓ Weasel,Hippo,Porcp
231-131↓ Hippo,Weasel,Rooster
231-222 Weasel,Rooster,Zebra
231-231 Weasel,Rooster,Wolf
231-322 Zebra,Wolf,Weasel
231-331 Wolf,W.Dog,Zebra
231-332 Wolf,W.Dog,Eagle
232-111 Hippo,Weasel
232-112↓ Weasel,Hippo,Porcp
232-131↓ Hippo,Weasel,Rooster
232-212 Weasel,Rooster,Zebra
232-221 Weasel,Hippo,Rooster
232-222↓ Weasel,Rooster,W.Dog
232-311↓ Zebra,Weasel,W.Dog
232-322↓ W.Dog,Zebra,Wolf

(242 cont'd)

232-332	W.Dog,Wolf,Eagle
233-111	Hippo,Pengn,Weasel
233-112	Weasel,Baboon,W.Dog
233-121	Hippo,Pengn,Baboon
233-122	Baboon,W.Dog,Weasel
233-131	Baboon,W.Dog,Hippo
233-132	Baboon,W.Dog,Lion
233-211	Weasel,W.Dog,Baboon
233-231↓	W.Dog,Baboon,Lion
233-321↓	W.Dog,Baboon,Zebra
233-331↓	W.Dog,Baboon,Wolf
241-111	Pengn,Sheep,Hippo
241-112	Wolf,W.Dog,Pengn
241-121	Pengn,Sheep,Hippo
241-122↓	Wolf,W.Dog,Pengn
241-132	Wolf,W.Dog,Beaver
241-211↓	Sheep,Wolf,W.Dog
241-231↓	Wolf,W.Dog,Beaver
241-311↓	Wolf,W.Dog,Sheep
242-111	Pengn,Sheep,W.Dog
242-112	W.Dog,Pengn,Wolf
242-121	Pengn,Sheep,W.Dog
242-122	W.Dog,Wolf,Pengn
242-131	W.Dog,Beaver,Pengn
242-132	W.Dog,Wolf,Beaver
242-211	W.Dog,Sheep,Wolf
242-212	W.Dog,Wolf,Beaver
242-221	W.Dog,Sheep,Wolf
242-331↓	W.Dog,Wolf,Beaver
243-111	Pengn,W.Dog
243-122↓	W.Dog,Pengn,Beaver
243-212	W.Dog,Beaver,Wolf
243-221	W.Dog,Pengn,Beaver
243-222↓	W.Dog,Beaver,Wolf
311-111↓	Weasel,Shrew
312-111↓	Weasel,Shrew
313-111↓	Weasel,Shrew
321-111↓	Weasel,Rooster,Shrew
321-132↓	Rooster,Weasel,Eagle
321-211↓	Weasel,Zebra,Rooster
321-232	Rooster,Weasel,Eagle
321-312↓	Zebra,Weasel,Eagle
321-332	Eagle,Rooster,Zebra
322-111↓	Weasel,Rooster,Shrew
322-122↓	Weasel,Rooster,W.Cat
322-212↓	Weasel,Rooster,Zebra
322-232	Rooster,Weasel,Eagle
322-311↓	Zebra,Weasel,Eagle
322-332	Eagle,Rooster,Zebra
323-111↓	Weasel,Rooster,W.Cat
323-212↓	Weasel,Rooster,Zebra
323-222↓	Weasel,Rooster,W.Cat
323-312↓	Zebra,Weasel,Eagle
323-332	Eagle,Rooster,Zebra
331-111	Weasel,Hippo
331-212↓	Weasel,Rooster,Zebra
331-231	Weasel,Rooster,Wolf
331-322	Zebra,Wolf,Weasel
331-331	Wolf,Zebra,Eagle
331-332	Wolf,Eagle,Rooster
332-111	Weasel,Pengn,Hippo
332-112	Weasel,Rooster,Shrew
332-121	Weasel,Pengn,Rooster
332-122	Weasel,Rooster,W.Cat

332-131	Weasel,Rooster,Pengn
332-132	Rooster,Weasel,Wolf
332-211↓	Weasel,Zebra,Rooster
332-231	Weasel,Rooster,Wolf
332-322	Zebra,Wolf,Weasel
332-331	Wolf,Zebra,Eagle
332-332	Wolf,Eagle,Rooster
333-111	Pengn,Weasel,Otter
333-132	Lion,Rooster,Weasel
333-211	Weasel,Otter,Pengn
333-212↓	Weasel,Otter,Lion
333-231↓	Lion,Weasel,Rooster
333-311↓	Zebra,Weasel,W.Dog
333-322	Zebra,W.Dog,Wolf
333-331↓	W.Dog,Wolf,Lion
341-111	Pengn,Wolf
341-221↓	Wolf,Weasel,Pengn
341-222↓	Wolf,Weasel,W.Dog
342-111↓	Pengn,Wolf,Weasel
342-132	Wolf,Pengn,W.Dog
342-211	Wolf,Pengn,Weasel
342-212	Wolf,Weasel,W.Dog
342-221	Wolf,Pengn,Weasel
342-222	Wolf,Weasel,W.Dog
342-231↓	Wolf,W.Dog,Pengn
343-111↓	Pengn,W.Dog,Owl
343-211↓	Pengn,W.Dog,Wolf
343-231↓	W.Dog,Wolf,Owl
343-321↓	W.Dog,Wolf,Pengn
343-322↓	W.Dog,Wolf,Owl
411-111↓	Weasel,Pcock
411-322↓	Weasel,Pcock,Shrew
412-111↓	Weasel,Shrew,W.Cat
413-111↓	Weasel,W.Cat
421-111↓	Weasel,W.Cat,Pcock
421-131↓	W.Cat,Weasel,Rooster
421-211	Weasel,W.Cat,SeaLn
421-232	W.Cat,Rooster,Weasel
421-311	SeaLn,Zebra,Weasel
421-312↓	SeaLn,Zebra,W.Cat
422-111↓	W.Cat,Weasel
422-122↓	W.Cat,Weasel,Rooster
422-211↓	W.Cat,Weasel,SeaLn
422-231↓	W.Cat,Weasel,Rooster
422-311	SeaLn,W.Cat,Zebra
423-111↓	W.Cat,Weasel
423-231↓	W.Cat,Weasel,Rooster
423-311↓	W.Cat,SeaLn,Dolphin
423-331	W.Cat,Tiger,SeaLn
423-332	W.Cat,Tiger,Dolphin
431-111	Weasel,W.Cat,Swan
431-132	W.Cat,Rooster,Weasel
431-211↓	Swan,Weasel,W.Cat
431-322↓	Swan,W.Cat,SeaLn
431-331↓	Swan,Wolf,W.Cat
432-111↓	W.Cat,Weasel,Swan
432-132	W.Cat,Rooster
432-211↓	W.Cat,Swan,Weasel
432-232	W.Cat,Swan,Rooster
432-331↓	Swan,SeaLn,W.Cat
432-331↓	Swan,W.Cat,Tiger
433-111↓	W.Cat,Pengn,Weasel
433-131↓	W.Cat,Tiger
433-211	W.Cat,Swan,Weasel
433-212↓	W.Cat,Swan,Tiger

433-231↓	W.Cat,Tiger,Lion
433-311↓	Swan,Tiger,W.Cat
441-111↓	Pengn,Wolf,Sable
442-111↓	Pengn,Wolf,Sable
442-132	Wolf,Sable,W.Cat
442-211	Wolf,Sable,Pengn
442-212	Wolf,Sable,Swan
442-232↓	Wolf,Sable,W.Cat
442-332↓	Wolf,Sable,W.Dog
443-111↓	Pengn,W.Cat
443-132↓	Pengn,Owl,Wolf
443-211↓	Pengn,Wolf,Sable
443-221	Pengn,Wolf,W.Cat
443-222	Wolf,W.Cat,Sable
443-231	Wolf,Sable,Owl
443-232↓	Wolf,Sable,W.Dog

243-

111-111↓	Croc,Weasel,Porcp
112-111↓	Croc,Weasel
113-111↓	Croc,Weasel,Porcp
113-122	Croc,Weasel,Warthg
113-131	Weasel,Croc,Porcp
113-132↓	Weasel,Warthg,Croc
113-331	Weasel,Croc,Warthg
113-332	W.Dog,Weasel,Warthg
121-111↓	Porcp,Rooster
121-211↓	Croc,Porcp,Warthg
121-222↓	Porcp,Warthg,Rooster
121-311↓	Croc,Porcp,Warthg
121-321	Porcp,Warthg,Eagle
121-332	Eagle,Rooster,W.Dog
122-111↓	Porcp,Croc,Warthg
122-132↓	Porcp,Rooster,Warthg
122-211↓	Croc,Porcp,Warthg
122-222↓	Warthg,Porcp,Rooster
122-311↓	Croc,Warthg,Porcp
122-321↓	Warthg,Porcp,Eagle
122-331↓	Eagle,Rooster,W.Dog
123-111	Porcp,Warthg
123-132↓	Warthg,Porcp,Rooster
123-212↓	Warthg,Croc,Porcp
123-232	Warthg,W.Dog,Rooster
123-311↓	Warthg,Croc,W.Dog
131-111↓	Porcp,Croc
131-132	Porcp,Rooster
131-211↓	Croc,Porcp,Warthg
131-222	Porcp,Warthg,Rooster
131-231↓	Rooster,Porcp,W.Dog
131-311	Croc,W.Dog,Porcp
131-312	W.Dog,Croc,Wolf
131-321	W.Dog,Wolf,Porcp
131-322	W.Dog,Wolf,Warthg
131-331↓	W.Dog,Wolf,Eagle
132-111↓	Porcp,Croc
132-132↓	Porcp,Rooster,Baboon
132-211↓	Croc,Porcp,Warthg
132-221	Porcp,Warthg,W.Dog
132-232	W.Dog,Rooster,Baboon
132-311↓	W.Dog,Croc,Warthg
132-321↓	W.Dog,Wolf,Warthg
133-111	Porcp,Warthg,Baboon
133-132↓	Baboon,W.Dog,Warthg
141-111↓	Sheep,Porcp,W.Dog
141-122	W.Dog,Wolf,Porcp

141-211↓ Sheep,W.Dog,Wolf
142-111↓ Sheep,W.Dog,Porcp
142-122 W.Dog,Wolf,Porcp
142-211↓ W.Dog,Sheep,Wolf
143-111↓ W.Dog,Pengn,Sheep
211-111↓ Weasel,Vultre,Shrew
211-231↓ Weasel,Shrew,Rooster
211-332 Weasel,Eagle,Rooster
212-111 Weasel,Shrew
212-112↓ Weasel,Vultre,Shrew
212-131 Weasel,Shrew,Rooster
212-132 Weasel,Rooster,Vultre
212-231↓ Weasel,Shrew,Rooster
212-331↓ Weasel,Eagle,Shrew
212-332↓ Weasel,Eagle,Rooster
213-111↓ Weasel,Vultre,Shrew
213-231↓ Weasel,Shrew,Rooster
213-332↓ Weasel,W.Dog,Eagle
221-111 Weasel,Rooster,Porcp
221-222↓ Rooster,Weasel,Eagle
221-311 Zebra,Weasel,Eagle
221-312↓ Eagle,Zebra,Rooster
221-332↓ Eagle,Rooster,Wolf
222-111 Weasel,Rooster,Porcp
222-212↓ Rooster,Weasel,Eagle
222-311 Zebra,Weasel,Eagle
222-312↓ Eagle,Zebra,Rooster
222-331↓ Eagle,Rooster,W.Dog
223-111 Weasel,Rooster,Porcp
223-112 Rooster,Weasel,Warthg
223-121↓ Rooster,Weasel,Baboon
223-131↓ Rooster,Baboon,W.Dog
223-211 Weasel,Rooster,W.Dog
223-311 W.Dog,Zebra,Weasel
223-312↓ W.Dog,Eagle,Zebra
223-322↓ W.Dog,Eagle,Rooster
231-111↓ Hippo,Weasel,Rooster
231-131 Rooster,Hippo,Baboon
231-132 Rooster,Baboon,Wolf
231-211 Weasel,Rooster,Sheep
231-212 Rooster,Weasel,Wolf
231-221 Rooster,Weasel,Sheep
231-222 Rooster,Weasel,Wolf
231-231↓ Rooster,Wolf,W.Dog
231-311 Wolf,W.Dog,Zebra
231-312↓ Wolf,W.Dog,Eagle
232-111↓ Hippo,Weasel,Rooster
232-122 Rooster,Weasel,Baboon
232-131 Rooster,Baboon,Hippo
232-132 Rooster,Baboon,W.Dog
232-211 Weasel,Rooster,W.Dog
232-231↓ Rooster,W.Dog,Baboon
232-311 W.Dog,Wolf,Zebra
232-312↓ W.Dog,Wolf,Eagle
233-111 Baboon,W.Dog,Hippo
233-322↓ W.Dog,Baboon,Wolf
241-111↓ Sheep,Wolf,W.Dog
242-111 Sheep,W.Dog,Pengn
242-112↓ W.Dog,Wolf,Sheep
242-132 W.Dog,Wolf,Beaver
242-211↓ W.Dog,Sheep,Wolf
243-111↓ W.Dog,Pengn,Sheep
243-122↓ W.Dog,Pengn,Owl
243-132 W.Dog,Owl,Wolf
243-211 W.Dog,Sheep

243-231↓ W.Dog,Wolf,Owl
311-111↓ Weasel,Shrew
311-131 Weasel,Shrew,Rooster
311-322↓ Weasel,Shrew,Eagle
311-332 Weasel,Eagle,Rooster
312-111↓ Weasel,Shrew
312-131↓ Weasel,Shrew,Rooster
312-331↓ Weasel,Eagle,Shrew
312-332 Weasel,Eagle,Rooster
313-111↓ Weasel,Shrew
313-131↓ Weasel,Shrew,Rooster
313-322↓ Weasel,Shrew,Eagle
313-332↓ Weasel,Eagle,Rooster
321-111 Weasel,Rooster
321-211↓ Weasel,Rooster,Zebra
321-212↓ Rooster,Weasel,Eagle
321-311 Zebra,Weasel,Eagle
321-312↓ Eagle,Zebra,Rooster
321-332 Eagle,Rooster,Wolf
322-111 Weasel,Rooster
322-112↓ Rooster,Weasel,Shrew
322-122↓ Rooster,Weasel,Eagle
322-211 Weasel,Rooster,Zebra
322-212↓ Rooster,Weasel,Eagle
322-311 Zebra,Weasel,Eagle
322-312↓ Eagle,Zebra,Rooster
322-332 Eagle,Rooster,Wolf
323-111 Weasel,Rooster
323-122↓ Rooster,Weasel,W.Cat
323-131↓ Rooster,Weasel,Lion
323-211 Weasel,Rooster,Zebra
323-212 Rooster,Weasel,Eagle
323-221 Rooster,Weasel,Lion
323-222 Rooster,Weasel,Eagle
323-231 Rooster,Weasel,Lion
323-232 Rooster,Eagle,Weasel
323-311 Zebra,Weasel,Eagle
323-312↓ Eagle,Zebra,Rooster
323-331↓ Eagle,Rooster,W.Dog
331-111 Weasel,Rooster,Bear
331-131↓ Rooster,Wolf,Weasel
331-232 Rooster,Wolf,Eagle
331-311 Wolf,Zebra,Weasel
331-312↓ Wolf,Eagle,Zebra
331-322↓ Wolf,Eagle,Rooster
332-111 Weasel,Rooster,Bear
332-122 Rooster,Weasel,Wolf
332-131↓ Rooster,Lion,Wolf
332-211 Weasel,Rooster,Wolf
332-311 Wolf,Zebra,Weasel
332-312↓ Wolf,Eagle,Zebra
332-322↓ Wolf,Eagle,Rooster
333-111 Pengn,Lion,Weasel
333-112 Lion,Rooster,Weasel
333-121 Lion,Pengn,Rooster
333-122↓ Lion,Rooster,Fox
333-211↓ Lion,Weasel,Rooster
333-222↓ Lion,Rooster,Fox
333-311↓ W.Dog,Wolf,Lion
341-111↓ Wolf,Pengn,Sheep
341-222↓ Wolf,W.Dog
342-111↓ Pengn,Wolf,Sheep
342-122↓ Wolf,Pengn,W.Dog
342-132 Wolf,W.Dog,Owl
342-211 Wolf,W.Dog,Sheep

342-212 Wolf,W.Dog,Dog
342-231↓ Wolf,W.Dog,Owl
343-111↓ Pengn,W.Dog,Owl
343-132 W.Dog,Owl,Wolf
343-211 W.Dog,Wolf,Pengn
343-312↓ W.Dog,Wolf,Owl
411-111↓ Pcock,Weasel
412-111↓ Weasel,Pcock
413-111↓ Weasel,W.Cat
413-232↓ Weasel,W.Cat,Rooster
413-311↓ Weasel,SeaLn,Dolphin
413-322 Weasel,Dolphin,W.Cat
413-331 Weasel,W.Cat,SeaLn
413-332 Weasel,W.Cat,Dolphin
421-111 Pcock,Weasel,SeaLn
421-112↓ Pcock,W.Cat,Rooster
421-212↓ SeaLn,Pcock,W.Cat
421-222↓ W.Cat,SeaLn,Rooster
421-322↓ SeaLn,Deer,W.Cat
421-331↓ SeaLn,Eagle,Rooster
422-111 W.Cat,Weasel,SeaLn
422-132↓ W.Cat,Rooster,Weasel
422-211 W.Cat,SeaLn,Weasel
422-212↓ W.Cat,SeaLn,Rooster
422-311↓ SeaLn,Deer,W.Cat
422-331↓ SeaLn,W.Cat,Eagle
423-111 W.Cat,Weasel,SeaLn
423-112↓ W.Cat,Dolphin,Rooster
423-211↓ W.Cat,SeaLn,Dolphin
423-231 W.Cat,Rooster,SeaLn
423-232 W.Cat,Rooster,Dolphin
423-311↓ SeaLn,Dolphin,W.Cat
431-111 Pcock,Weasel,SeaLn
431-112↓ Pcock,W.Cat,Rooster
431-211↓ SeaLn,Pcock,Swan
431-221 SeaLn,Pcock,W.Cat
431-222 W.Cat,SeaLn,Swan
431-231↓ Rooster,W.Cat,Wolf
431-311 SeaLn,Swan,Deer
431-312↓ SeaLn,Swan,Wolf
432-111 W.Cat,Weasel,SeaLn
432-131↓ W.Cat,Rooster,Lion
432-132 W.Cat,Rooster,Wolf
432-211↓ W.Cat,SeaLn,Swan
432-231↓ W.Cat,Rooster,Wolf
432-311 SeaLn,Swan,Deer
432-312↓ SeaLn,Swan,Wolf
433-111 W.Cat,Pengn,Lion
433-112 W.Cat,Lion,Dolphin
433-131↓ W.Cat,Lion,Rooster
433-211 W.Cat,SeaLn,Lion
433-212 W.Cat,Dolphin,SeaLn
433-221 W.Cat,Lion,SeaLn
433-222 W.Cat,Lion,Dolphin
433-231↓ W.Cat,Lion,Tiger
433-311 SeaLn,Dolphin,Swan
433-322 Dolphin,W.Cat,Tiger
433-331↓ Tiger,Wolf,W.Cat
441-111 Wolf,Pengn,Pcock
441-121↓ Wolf,Pengn,Sable
442-111 Pengn,Wolf
442-322↓ Wolf,Sable,W.Dog
443-111↓ Pengn,Owl,Wolf
443-132 Owl,Wolf,W.Dog
443-211 Wolf,Pengn,Owl

(243 cont'd)
443-212↓ Wolf,W.Dog,Owl
443-311↓ Wolf,W.Dog,Sable

244-
111-111↓ Croc,Porcp
111-121↓ Croc,Porcp,Weasel
111-231↓ Weasel,Croc,Eagle
111-331↓ Eagle,Weasel,W.Dog
112-111↓ Croc,Porcp
112-121↓ Croc,Porcp,Weasel
112-231↓ Weasel,Croc,Eagle
112-331↓ Eagle,W.Dog,Weasel
113-111↓ Croc,Porcp
113-121↓ Croc,Porcp,Weasel
113-131↓ W.Dog,Porcp,Baboon
113-211↓ Croc,Weasel,Warthg
113-231↓ W.Dog,Baboon,Weasel
113-321↓ W.Dog,Croc,Weasel
113-331↓ W.Dog,Eagle
121-111↓ Porcp,Eagle
121-132↓ Porcp,Eagle,Rooster
121-211↓ Porcp,Croc,Eagle
121-221↓ Porcp,Eagle,Warthg
121-231 Eagle,Rooster,Porcp
121-232 Eagle,Rooster,W.Dog
121-311↓ Eagle,SeaLn,W.Dog
122-111↓ Porcp,Baboon
122-132 Porcp,Eagle,Rooster
122-211↓ Porcp,Croc,Warthg
122-221↓ Porcp,Eagle,Warthg
122-231 Eagle,W.Dog,Baboon
122-232 Eagle,W.Dog,Baboon
122-311↓ Eagle,W.Dog,SeaLn
123-111↓ Porcp,Warthg,Baboon
123-131↓ Baboon,W.Dog,Porcp
123-211↓ Warthg,W.Dog,Baboon
123-332↓ W.Dog,Eagle,Baboon
131-111↓ Porcp,Baboon,Walrus
131-122↓ Porcp,Baboon,W.Dog
131-231↓ W.Dog,Baboon,Eagle
132-111↓ Porcp,Baboon,Eagle
132-332 W.Dog,Eagle,Baboon
133-111↓ Baboon,W.Dog,Porcp
133-131↓ Baboon,W.Dog,Lion
141-111↓ W.Dog,Sheep
142-111↓ Wild Dog
143-111↓ Wild Dog
211-111↓ Weasel,Eagle
212-111↓ Weasel,Eagle,Rooster
212-312↓ Weasel,Eagle,W.Dog
213-111↓ Weasel,W.Dog
213-231↓ W.Dog,Weasel,Baboon
213-232↓ W.Dog,Weasel,Eagle
221-111↓ Eagle,Rooster,Weasel
221-131↓ Eagle,Rooster,Baboon
221-211↓ Eagle,Rooster,Weasel
221-232↓ Eagle,Rooster,W.Dog
222-111↓ Eagle,Rooster,Weasel
222-121↓ Eagle,Rooster,Baboon
222-211 Eagle,Rooster,Weasel
222-212↓ Eagle,Rooster,W.Dog
222-311↓ Eagle,W.Dog,SeaLn
222-331↓ Eagle,W.Dog,Rooster
223-111↓ Baboon,W.Dog,Lion

223-312↓ W.Dog,Eagle,Dolphin
223-321↓ W.Dog,Eagle,Baboon
231-111 Baboon,Walrus,W.Dog
231-112 Baboon,W.Dog,Lion
231-121 Baboon,W.Dog,Walrus
231-122↓ Baboon,W.Dog,Lion
231-322↓ W.Dog,Eagle,Baboon
232-111 Baboon,W.Dog,Walrus
232-112↓ Baboon,W.Dog,Lion
232-312↓ W.Dog,Eagle,Baboon
233-111↓ Baboon,W.Dog,Lion
241-111↓ W.Dog,Sheep,Dog
241-222↓ W.Dog,Wolf,Dog
242-111↓ W.Dog,Dog
242-211↓ W.Dog,Sheep
243-111↓ Wild Dog
311-111↓ Weasel,Eagle
311-132↓ Weasel,Eagle,Rooster
311-222↓ Weasel,Eagle,Shrew
311-231↓ Weasel,Eagle,Rooster
312-111↓ Weasel,Shrew
312-122↓ Weasel,Shrew,Eagle
312-131↓ Weasel,Eagle,Rooster
312-212↓ Weasel,Shrew,Eagle
312-332↓ Eagle,Weasel,Rooster
313-111↓ Weasel,Lion,Eagle
313-132↓ Weasel,Eagle,Rooster
313-222↓ Weasel,Eagle,Shrew
313-231 Weasel,Eagle,Lion
313-322↓ Weasel,Eagle,W.Dog
321-111↓ Eagle,Rooster,Weasel
321-231↓ Eagle,Rooster,Lion
321-312↓ Eagle,SeaLn,Rooster
322-111↓ Eagle,Rooster,Weasel
322-131↓ Eagle,Rooster,Lion
322-211↓ Eagle,Rooster,Weasel
322-231↓ Eagle,Rooster,Lion
322-311 Eagle,SeaLn,Zebra
322-312↓ Eagle,SeaLn,Rooster
323-111↓ Lion,Eagle,Rooster
323-312 Eagle,Dolphin,W.Dog
323-321 Eagle,W.Dog,SeaLn
323-322 Eagle,W.Dog,Dolphin
323-331↓ Eagle,W.Dog,Lion
331-111↓ Lion,Eagle,Rooster
331-321↓ Eagle,Wolf,W.Dog
332-111↓ Lion,Eagle,Rooster
332-311 Eagle,W.Dog,SeaLn
332-312 Eagle,W.Dog,Wolf
332-321 Eagle,W.Dog,Lion
332-322 Eagle,W.Dog,Wolf
332-331 Eagle,W.Dog,Lion
332-332 Eagle,W.Dog,Wolf
333-111 Lion,Baboon
333-112↓ Lion,Baboon,W.Dog
333-311↓ W.Dog,Lion,Eagle
341-111↓ Dog,Wolf,W.Dog
341-332↓ Wolf,W.Dog,Eagle
342-111 Dog,W.Dog,Wolf
342-231↓ W.Dog,Wolf,Pr.Dog
342-311↓ W.Dog,Wolf,Dog
343-111↓ W.Dog,Pengn,Pr.Dog
343-212↓ W.Dog,Pr.Dog,Wolf
343-221 W.Dog,Pr.Dog,Lion
343-222 W.Dog,Pr.Dog,Wolf

343-231 W.Dog,Pr.Dog,Lion
343-232↓ W.Dog,Pr.Dog,Wolf
411-111 Pcock,Weasel
411-132↓ Pcock,Weasel,SeaLn
411-331↓ SeaLn,Pcock,Eagle
412-111↓ Weasel,SeaLn,Pcock
412-322↓ SeaLn,Weasel,Eagle
413-111↓ Weasel,SeaLn,Dolphin
413-132 Weasel,Dolphin,W.Cat
413-211↓ Weasel,SeaLn,Dolphin
413-331↓ SeaLn,Dolphin,Eagle
421-111↓ SeaLn,Eagle
421-131↓ SeaLn,Eagle,Rooster
421-222 SeaLn,Eagle,Dolphin
421-231↓ SeaLn,Eagle,Rooster
421-332↓ SeaLn,Eagle,Dolphin
422-111↓ SeaLn,Dolphin
422-122↓ SeaLn,W.Cat,Eagle
422-131↓ SeaLn,Eagle,Rooster
422-212↓ SeaLn,Dolphin,Eagle
422-231↓ SeaLn,Eagle,Rooster
422-311↓ SeaLn,Dolphin,Eagle
423-111↓ SeaLn,Dolphin,W.Cat
423-231 SeaLn,Dolphin,Lion
423-312↓ Dolphin,SeaLn,Eagle
431-111↓ SeaLn,Lion,Eagle
431-322↓ SeaLn,Eagle,Dolphin
432-111 SeaLn,Lion
432-112↓ SeaLn,Lion,Dolphin
432-121↓ SeaLn,Lion,W.Cat
432-131↓ Lion,SeaLn,Eagle
432-212 SeaLn,Dolphin
432-222↓ SeaLn,Lion,Eagle
432-312↓ SeaLn,Dolphin,Eagle
433-111↓ Lion,SeaLn,Dolphin
433-232 Lion,Dolphin,W.Dog
433-322↓ Dolphin,SeaLn,W.Dog
433-331 SeaLn,Lion,Dolphin
433-332 Dolphin,W.Dog,SeaLn
441-111 Dog,Wolf,SeaLn
441-112↓ Dog,Wolf,W.Dog
441-211 Dog,Wolf,SeaLn
441-212↓ Wolf,Dog,W.Dog
441-311↓ Wolf,SeaLn,W.Dog
442-111↓ Dog,Wolf,W.Dog
442-131↓ Wolf,W.Dog,Pr.Dog
442-211↓ Dog,Wolf,W.Dog
442-332↓ Wolf,W.Dog,Sable
443-111 W.Dog,Pengn,Pr.Dog
443-112 W.Dog,Pr.Dog,Lion
443-121 W.Dog,Pengn,Pr.Dog
443-232↓ W.Dog,Pr.Dog,Wolf

251-
111-111↓ Croc,Warthg
112-111↓ Croc,Warthg
113-111↓ Croc,Warthg
121-111↓ Croc,Warthg,Porcp
122-111↓ Croc,Warthg
123-111↓ Warthg,Croc
131-111↓ Croc,Warthg,Porcp
132-111↓ Croc,Warthg
133-111↓ Warthg,Croc
141-111↓ Croc,Warthg
142-111↓ Croc,Warthg

(252 cont'd)

233-131   Warthg,Badger
233-132   Warthg,Tiger
233-211↓ Warthg,Croc,Bear
233-221   Warthg,Bear,Badger
233-222   Warthg,Bear,Tiger
233-231↓ Warthg,Badger,Tiger
241-111   Croc,Bear,Pengn
241-112   Croc,Bear,Warthg
241-121   Bear,Pengn,Croc
241-122   Bear,Warthg,Croc
241-131↓ Badger,Bear,Wolf
241-211↓ Croc,Bear,Badger
241-221   Bear,Badger,Warthg
241-231   Badger,Bear,Wolf
241-232   Badger,Wolf,W.Dog
241-311   Badger,Croc,Bear
241-312   Badger,Croc,Wolf
241-321↓ Badger,Wolf,W.Dog
242-111   Croc,Bear,Pengn
242-112   Croc,Bear,Warthg
242-121   Bear,Pengn,Warthg
242-122   Bear,Warthg,Croc
242-131↓ Badger,Bear,W.Dog
242-211↓ Croc,Bear,Warthg
242-221↓ Bear,Badger,Warthg
242-231   Badger,W.Dog,Bear
242-232   Badger,W.Dog,Wolf
242-311↓ Badger,W.Dog,Croc
242-321↓ Badger,W.Dog,Wolf
243-111   Pengn,Warthg,Croc
243-112↓ Warthg,W.Dog,Pengn
243-132   W.Dog,Warthg,Tiger
243-211↓ Warthg,W.Dog,Croc
243-221↓ Warthg,W.Dog,Bear
243-311↓ W.Dog,Warthg,Badger
243-312   W.Dog,Warthg,Tiger
243-321   W.Dog,Badger,Warthg
243-322   W.Dog,Warthg,Tiger
243-331↓ W.Dog,Badger,Tiger
311-111↓ Croc,Weasel
312-111↓ Croc,Weasel
312-331↓ Weasel,Croc,Badger
313-111↓ Croc,Weasel
313-121↓ Weasel,Croc,Warthg
313-331   Weasel,Croc,Badger
313-332   Weasel,Tiger,Warthg
321-111   Croc,Bear,Weasel
321-112   Croc,Bear,Warthg
321-121↓ Bear,Weasel,Warthg
321-131   Badger,Bear,Weasel
321-132   Badger,Bear,Rooster
321-211   Croc,Bear,Weasel
321-212   Croc,Bear,Warthg
321-221   Bear,Badger,Weasel
321-222   Bear,Warthg,Badger
321-231   Bear,Badger,Weasel
321-232   Badger,Bear,Rooster
321-311↓ Badger,Croc,Bear
322-111↓ Croc,Bear,Warthg
322-121   Bear,Warthg,Weasel
322-132   Badger,Warthg,Bear
322-211↓ Croc,Bear,Warthg
322-221↓ Bear,Warthg,Badger
322-311   Badger,Croc,Bear

322-312   Badger,Croc,Warthg
322-321↓ Badger,Bear,Warthg
322-331   Badger,Tiger,Bear
322-332   Badger,Tiger,Warthg
323-111↓ Warthg,Croc
323-121↓ Warthg,Bear
323-131   Warthg,Badger
323-132   Warthg,Tiger
323-211↓ Warthg,Croc,Bear
323-221   Warthg,Bear,Badger
323-222   Warthg,Bear,Tiger
323-231↓ Warthg,Badger,Tiger
331-111↓ Bear,Badger
332-111↓ Bear,Badger
332-132↓ Badger,Bear,Tiger
332-222↓ Bear,Badger,Warthg
332-312↓ Badger,Bear,Tiger
333-111   Bear,Warthg,Badger
333-112   Bear,Warthg,Tiger
333-121   Bear,Warthg,Badger
333-122   Bear,Warthg,Tiger
333-131   Badger,Tiger,Bear
333-212   Bear,Warthg,Tiger
333-221   Bear,Badger,Warthg
333-222   Bear,Warthg,Tiger
333-231   Badger,Tiger,Bear
341-111↓ Bear,Pengn,Badger
341-222↓ Bear,Badger,Wolf
342-111   Bear,Pengn
342-131↓ Badger,Bear,Pengn
342-332↓ Badger,Wolf,Tiger
343-111   Pengn,Bear
343-122↓ Pengn,Bear,Warthg
343-131↓ Pengn,Badger,Tiger
343-211   Bear,Pengn,Badger
343-212   Bear,Tiger,Warthg
343-221   Bear,Pengn,Badger
343-222↓ Bear,Tiger,Badger
343-232   Tiger,Badger,W.Dog
343-311   Badger,Tiger,Bear
343-312   Tiger,Badger,W.Dog
411-111↓ Croc,Weasel
411-321↓ Weasel,Croc,Tiger
412-111↓ Croc,Weasel
412-321↓ Weasel,Croc,Tiger
413-111   Croc,Weasel
413-212↓ Croc,Weasel,Tiger
413-231↓ Tiger,Weasel,W.Cat
413-311↓ Croc,Tiger,Weasel
421-111↓ Croc,Bear,W.Cat
421-121↓ Bear,W.Cat,Tiger
421-131↓ Tiger,W.Cat,Badger
421-211↓ Croc,Bear,Tiger
421-221↓ Tiger,Bear,W.Cat
421-231↓ Tiger,Badger,W.Cat
421-311↓ Tiger,Badger,SeaLn
422-111   Croc,W.Cat,Bear
422-112   W.Cat,Tiger,Croc
422-121   W.Cat,Tiger,Bear
422-122   W.Cat,Tiger,Warthg
422-211↓ Tiger,Croc,W.Cat
422-221   Tiger,W.Cat,Bear
422-222   Tiger,W.Cat,Warthg
422-322↓ Tiger,Badger,W.Cat
423-111↓ Tiger,Warthg,W.Cat

431-111↓ Bear,Tiger,Badger
432-111   Bear,Tiger
432-221↓ Tiger,Bear,Badger
433-111↓ Bear,Tiger,Pengn
441-111   Bear,Tiger,Pengn
441-112   Bear,Tiger,Badger
441-121   Bear,Tiger,Pengn
441-122↓ Tiger,Bear,Badger
441-312↓ Tiger,Badger,Sable
442-111↓ Bear,Tiger,Pengn
442-131↓ Tiger,Badger,Bear
443-111↓ Tiger,Pengn,Bear

253-

111-111↓ Crocodile
112-111↓ Crocodile
113-111↓ Croc,Warthg
121-111↓ Croc,Warthg
122-111↓ Croc,Warthg
123-111↓ Warthg,Croc
131-111↓ Croc,Warthg
131-331↓ Warthg,Croc,Badger
132-111↓ Croc,Warthg
132-331↓ Warthg,Croc,Badger
133-111↓ Warthg,Croc
141-111↓ Croc,Warthg
142-111↓ Croc,Warthg
142-331↓ W.Dog,Warthg,Wolf
143-111↓ Warthg,Croc
143-311↓ Warthg,W.Dog,Croc
211-111↓ Croc,Weasel
212-111↓ Croc,Weasel
212-232↓ Croc,Weasel,Warthg
213-111↓ Croc,Warthg
221-111↓ Croc,Bear,Warthg
221-132   Warthg,Bear,Rooster
221-211↓ Croc,Bear,Warthg
221-232   Warthg,Bear,Rooster
221-311↓ Croc,Bear,Warthg
221-332   Badger,Warthg,Bear
222-111↓ Croc,Warthg,Bear
222-131↓ Warthg,Bear,Rooster
222-211↓ Croc,Warthg,Bear
222-231↓ Warthg,Bear,Rooster
222-311↓ Croc,Warthg,Bear
222-331↓ Badger,Warthg,Bear
223-111↓ Warthg,Croc
223-221↓ Warthg,Bear,Croc
223-332↓ Warthg,Tiger,Badger
231-111↓ Bear,Croc
231-311↓ Bear,Badger,Croc
232-111   Bear,Croc
232-112↓ Bear,Croc,Warthg
232-132↓ Bear,Badger,Warthg
232-212↓ Bear,Croc,Warthg
232-232↓ Bear,Badger,Warthg
232-332↓ Badger,Bear,Tiger
233-111↓ Warthg,Bear,Croc
233-222↓ Warthg,Bear,Tiger
233-231   Warthg,Bear,Badger
233-232   Warthg,Bear,Tiger
233-311   Warthg,Bear,Badger
233-312   Warthg,Bear,Tiger
233-321   Warthg,Bear,Badger
233-322   Warthg,Bear,Tiger

233-331   Badger,Tiger,W.Dog
241-111↓ Bear,Croc
241-131↓ Bear,Wolf,W.Dog
241-211↓ Bear,Croc
241-222↓ Bear,Wolf,W.Dog
241-331↓ Wolf,W.Dog,Badger
242-111↓ Bear,Croc
242-131↓ Bear,W.Dog,Wolf
242-331↓ W.Dog,Wolf,Badger
243-111   Bear,W.Dog,Pengn
243-112   W.Dog,Bear,Warthg
243-121   W.Dog,Bear,Pengn
243-211↓ W.Dog,Bear,Warthg
243-332   W.Dog,Wolf
311-111↓ Croc,Weasel
312-111↓ Croc,Weasel
313-111↓ Croc,Weasel
313-121↓ Weasel,Croc,Warthg
313-331   Weasel,Croc,Badger
313-332   Weasel,Tiger,Warthg
321-111↓ Bear,Rhino,Croc
321-131↓ Bear,Rooster,Rhino
321-231↓ Bear,Rooster,Badger
321-311↓ Bear,Badger,Rhino
321-331↓ Badger,Bear,Eagle
322-111↓ Bear,Rhino,Croc
322-122↓ Bear,Rhino,Warthg
322-131↓ Bear,Rooster,Rhino
322-211↓ Bear,Rhino,Croc
322-221↓ Bear,Rhino,Warthg
322-231↓ Bear,Rooster,Badger
322-311↓ Bear,Badger,Rhino
322-331↓ Badger,Bear,Eagle
323-111↓ Warthg,Bear,Rhino
323-131↓ Warthg,Bear,Rooster
323-211↓ Warthg,Bear,Rhino
323-231↓ Warthg,Bear,Rooster
323-311   Warthg,Bear,Badger
323-312   Warthg,Bear,Tiger
323-321   Warthg,Bear,Badger
323-322   Warthg,Bear,Tiger
323-331   Badger,Tiger,Warthg
331-111↓ Bear,Badger
332-111↓ Bear,Badger
332-322↓ Bear,Badger,Tiger
333-111↓ Bear,Warthg
333-132↓ Bear,Tiger,Badger
333-212   Bear,Warthg,Tiger
333-221   Bear,Badger,Warthg
333-222   Bear,Warthg,Tiger
333-231↓ Bear,Badger,Tiger
341-111↓ Bear,Wolf,Badger
342-111↓ Bear,Wolf,Badger
342-332   Wolf,Badger,W.Dog
343-111↓ Bear,Pengn
343-121↓ Bear,Pengn,Owl
343-132↓ Bear,Owl,W.Dog
343-222   Bear,W.Dog,Wolf
343-231   Bear,W.Dog,Owl
343-232↓ W.Dog,Wolf,Bear
343-331   W.Dog,Wolf,Badger
343-332   W.Dog,Wolf,Tiger
411-111↓ Croc,Weasel
411-321↓ Weasel,Croc,SeaLn
411-322↓ Weasel,Croc,Tiger

412-111↓ Croc,Weasel
412-321↓ Weasel,Croc,Tiger
413-111↓ Croc,Weasel
413-121↓ Weasel,Croc,Warthg
413-131↓ Tiger,Weasel,W.Cat
413-212↓ Croc,Weasel,Tiger
413-231↓ Tiger,Weasel,W.Cat
413-311↓ Croc,Tiger,Weasel
421-111↓ Bear,Rhino,Croc
421-122↓ Bear,Rhino,W.Cat
421-131↓ Bear,Tiger,Rooster
421-211   Bear,Rhino,Croc
421-212↓ Bear,Rhino,Tiger
421-231↓ Tiger,Bear,Rooster
421-311   SeaLn,Tiger,Bear
421-332   Tiger,Badger
422-111   Bear,Rhino,Croc
422-112↓ Bear,Rhino,W.Cat
422-122↓ Bear,W.Cat,Tiger
422-211↓ Bear,Rhino,Tiger
422-221↓ Bear,Tiger,W.Cat
422-311↓ Tiger,SeaLn,Bear
422-331↓ Tiger,Badger
423-111↓ Tiger,Warthg,Bear
423-122↓ Tiger,Warthg,W.Cat
423-211↓ Tiger,Warthg,Bear
423-222↓ Tiger,Warthg,W.Cat
431-111↓ Bear,Tiger
431-231↓ Tiger,Bear,Badger
432-111↓ Bear,Tiger
432-332↓ Tiger,Badger,Bear
433-111↓ Tiger,Bear
441-111↓ Bear,Tiger
442-111↓ Bear,Tiger
442-331↓ Tiger,Wolf,Badger
443-111↓ Tiger,Bear,Pengn

254-

111-111↓ Crocodile
112-111↓ Crocodile
113-111↓ Croc,Warthg
121-111↓ Croc,Warthg
122-111↓ Croc,Warthg
123-111↓ Warthg,Croc
131-111↓ Croc,Warthg
131-331↓ Warthg,W.Dog,Croc
132-111↓ Croc,Warthg
133-111↓ Warthg,Croc
141-111↓ Croc,Warthg,W.Dog
142-111↓ Croc,Warthg,W.Dog
143-111↓ Warthg,W.Dog,Croc
211-111↓ Croc,Weasel
211-331↓ Croc,Eagle,Weasel
212-111↓ Croc,Weasel
212-331↓ Croc,Eagle,Weasel
212-332↓ Croc,Eagle,W.Dog
213-111↓ Croc,Warthg
213-231↓ Croc,Warthg,W.Dog
221-111↓ Croc,Bear,Warthg
221-131↓ Bear,Warthg,Eagle
221-211↓ Croc,Bear,Warthg
221-231↓ Eagle,Bear,Warthg
221-311↓ Croc,Eagle,Bear
221-321↓ Eagle,Bear,Warthg
221-331↓ Eagle,Badger,W.Dog

222-111↓ Croc,Warthg,Bear
222-131↓ Warthg,Bear,Eagle
222-211↓ Croc,Warthg,Bear
222-231↓ Warthg,Eagle,Bear
222-311↓ Croc,Warthg,Eagle
222-321↓ Eagle,Warthg,Bear
222-331↓ Eagle,W.Dog,Badger
223-111↓ Warthg,Croc
223-131↓ Warthg,Baboon
223-211↓ Warthg,Croc
223-231↓ Warthg,Baboon,W.Dog
223-321↓ Warthg,W.Dog,Eagle
231-111↓ Bear,Baboon
231-231↓ Bear,Badger,Baboon
231-232↓ Bear,W.Dog,Badger
232-111↓ Bear,Baboon
232-132↓ Bear,Baboon,W.Dog
232-222   Bear,Warthg,W.Dog
232-231↓ Bear,Baboon,W.Dog
232-311↓ Bear,W.Dog,Badger
233-111   Bear,Warthg,Baboon
233-132   Baboon,W.Dog,Warthg
233-211   Bear,Warthg,Baboon
233-212   Warthg,Bear,W.Dog
233-221   Bear,Baboon,Warthg
233-222   Warthg,W.Dog,Bear
233-231   Baboon,W.Dog,Lion
233-232   W.Dog,Baboon,Warthg
233-311↓ W.Dog,Bear,Warthg
233-321↓ W.Dog,Bear,Baboon
241-111↓ Bear,W.Dog
242-111↓ W.Dog,Bear
243-111↓ Wild Dog
311-111↓ Croc,Weasel
311-121↓ Weasel,Croc,Bear
311-231↓ Weasel,Eagle,Croc
312-111↓ Croc,Weasel
312-121↓ Weasel,Croc,Bear
312-312↓ Croc,Weasel,Eagle
313-111↓ Croc,Weasel
313-121↓ Weasel,Croc,Warthg
313-231   Weasel,Eagle,Croc
313-232   Weasel,Eagle,Warthg
313-311↓ Croc,Weasel,Eagle
313-331↓ Eagle,Weasel,W.Dog
321-111↓ Bear,Rhino
321-122↓ Bear,Rhino,Eagle
321-131↓ Bear,Eagle,Rooster
321-212↓ Bear,Rhino,Eagle
321-231↓ Eagle,Bear,Rooster
321-311↓ Eagle,Bear,SeaLn
321-321↓ Eagle,Bear,Badger
322-111↓ Bear,Rhino
322-131↓ Bear,Eagle,Rooster
322-212↓ Bear,Rhino,Eagle
322-231↓ Eagle,Bear,Rooster
322-311↓ Eagle,Bear,SeaLn
322-332↓ Eagle,Badger,Bear
323-111   Bear,Warthg,Rhino
323-132   Warthg,Lion,Bear
323-211   Bear,Warthg,Rhino
323-232   Eagle,Warthg,Lion
323-311↓ Eagle,Bear,Warthg
323-331   Eagle,Badger,W.Dog
323-332   Eagle,W.Dog,Tiger

(254 cont'd)

331-111↓ Bear,Badger
331-322↓ Bear,Badger,Eagle
332-111↓ Bear,Badger
332-322↓ Bear,Badger,Eagle
333-111↓ Bear,Lion
333-231↓ Lion,Bear,Badger
333-232 Lion,Bear,W.Dog
333-311 Bear,Badger,W.Dog
333-312 Bear,W.Dog,Tiger
333-321 Bear,Badger,W.Dog
333-322 Bear,W.Dog,Tiger
333-331↓ Badger,W.Dog,Tiger
341-111↓ Bear,Wolf,W.Dog
341-331↓ Wolf,W.Dog,Badger
342-111↓ Bear,W.Dog
342-131↓ Bear,W.Dog,Wolf
342-331↓ W.Dog,Wolf,Badger
343-111↓ Bear,W.Dog,Pengn
343-332 W.Dog,Wolf
411-111↓ Croc,Weasel,SeaLn
411-231↓ Weasel,SeaLn,Eagle
411-311↓ SeaLn,Croc
411-332↓ SeaLn,Eagle,Tiger
412-111↓ Croc,Weasel,SeaLn
412-231↓ Weasel,SeaLn,Eagle
412-312↓ SeaLn,Croc,Dolphin
412-321↓ SeaLn,Weasel
412-331↓ SeaLn,Eagle,Tiger
413-111 Croc,Weasel,SeaLn
413-112 Croc,Weasel,Dolphin
413-121 Weasel,Croc,SeaLn
413-122 Weasel,Dolphin,Croc
413-131 Tiger,Weasel,SeaLn
413-132 Tiger,Weasel,Dolphin
413-211 Croc,Weasel,SeaLn
413-212 Croc,Dolphin,Weasel
413-221↓ Weasel,SeaLn,Dolphin
413-231 Tiger,Weasel,SeaLn
413-232 Tiger,Dolphin,Weasel
413-311 SeaLn,Dolphin,Croc
413-312↓ Dolphin,SeaLn,Tiger
421-111↓ SeaLn,Bear,Rhino
421-131↓ SeaLn,Bear,Eagle
421-232↓ SeaLn,Eagle,Tiger
422-111↓ SeaLn,Bear,Rhino
422-122 SeaLn,Bear,W.Cat
422-131↓ SeaLn,Bear,Tiger
422-231↓ SeaLn,Tiger,Eagle
422-322↓ SeaLn,Tiger,Dolphin
422-331↓ SeaLn,Tiger,Eagle
423-111 SeaLn,Dolphin,Bear
423-112↓ Dolphin,Tiger,SeaLn
423-132 Tiger,Dolphin,W.Cat
423-211↓ SeaLn,Dolphin,Tiger
431-111↓ Bear,Tiger,Badger
431-211↓ Bear,SeaLn
431-231↓ Bear,Tiger,Badger
431-312↓ SeaLn,Tiger,Bear
431-332 Tiger,Badger
432-111↓ Bear,Tiger
432-221↓ Bear,Tiger,SeaLn
432-331↓ Tiger,Badger
433-111↓ Bear,Tiger,Lion
441-111↓ Bear,Wolf,Tiger

441-331↓ Wolf,Tiger,W.Dog
442-111↓ Bear,Tiger
442-131↓ Bear,Tiger,Wolf
443-111 Bear,Tiger,Pengn
443-112↓ Tiger,Bear,W.Dog

311-

111-111↓ Mole
112-111↓ Mole
113-111↓ Mole
121-111↓ Mole
122-111↓ Mole
123-111↓ Mole
131-111↓ Mole
132-111↓ Mole
132-221↓ Mole,Mouse
133-111↓ Mole
141-111↓ Mole
141-332↓ Mole,Mouse,Beaver
142-111↓ Mole,Beaver
142-332↓ Mole,Beaver,Mouse
143-111↓ Mole,Beaver
143-322↓ Mole,Beaver,Mouse
143-332 Beaver,Mole,Owl
211-111 Mole,MGoat
211-312↓ MGoat,Mole,Vultre
211-321 Mole,MGoat,Mouse
211-322 Mole,MGoat,Vultre
211-331 Mole,MGoat,Mouse
211-332↓ Mole,Vultre,MGoat
212-111 Mole,MGoat
212-321↓ Mole,MGoat,Mouse
212-322 Mole,MGoat,Vultre
212-331 Mole,MGoat,Mouse
212-332↓ Mole,Vultre,MGoat
213-111 Mole,MGoat
213-312↓ MGoat,Mole,Vultre
213-321 Mole,MGoat,Mouse
213-322 Mole,MGoat,Vultre
213-331 Mole,MGoat,Mouse
213-332↓ Mole,Vultre,MGoat
221-111↓ Mole,MGoat
221-311↓ MGoat,Mole,Mouse
222-111↓ Mole,MGoat
222-321↓ Mole,MGoat,Mouse
223-111↓ Mole,MGoat
223-311↓ MGoat,Mole,Mouse
231-111 Mole,Mouse
232-111↓ Mole,Mouse,MGoat
233-111↓ Mole,Mouse
241-111↓ Mole,Mouse,MGoat
241-122↓ Mole,Mouse,Beaver
241-311↓ Mouse,MGoat,Sheep
241-322↓ Mouse,Beaver,Sheep
241-332 Mouse,Beaver,Sable
242-111 Mole,Mouse,MGoat
242-122↓ Mole,Mouse,Beaver
242-211 Mouse,MGoat,Mole
242-212 Mouse,Beaver,MGoat
242-222↓ Mouse,Beaver,Mole
242-332↓ Beaver,Mouse,Sable
243-111 Mole,Mouse,Pengn
243-112 Mole,Mouse,Beaver
243-121 Mole,Mouse,Pengn
243-122 Mole,Beaver,Mouse

243-211 Mouse,MGoat,Beaver
243-212 Mouse,Beaver,Owl
243-221 Mouse,Beaver,Mole
243-222↓ Beaver,Mouse,Owl
243-311 Mouse,MGoat,Beaver
243-322↓ Beaver,Mouse,Owl
311-111 Mole,MGoat
311-312↓ MGoat,Mole,Vultre
311-321 Mole,MGoat,Mouse
311-322 Mole,MGoat,Vultre
311-331 Mole,MGoat,Mouse
311-332↓ Mole,Vultre,MGoat
312-111 Mole,MGoat
312-321↓ Mole,MGoat,Mouse
312-322 Mole,MGoat,Vultre
312-331 Mole,MGoat,Mouse
312-332↓ Mole,Vultre,MGoat
313-111 Mole,MGoat
313-312↓ MGoat,Mole,Vultre
313-321 Mole,MGoat,Mouse
313-322 Mole,MGoat,Vultre
313-331 Mole,MGoat,Mouse
313-332↓ Mole,Vultre,MGoat
321-111↓ Mole,MGoat
321-311↓ MGoat,Mole,Mouse
322-111↓ Mole,MGoat
322-212↓ MGoat,Mole,Mouse
323-111↓ Mole,MGoat
323-211↓ MGoat,Mole,Mouse
323-232 Mole,Fox,Mouse
323-311↓ MGoat,Mole,Mouse
323-332↓ Mole,Fox,Mouse
331-111 Mole,Mouse
331-311↓ Mouse,MGoat,Mole
331-312↓ Mouse,MGoat,Swan
332-111↓ Mouse,Mouse,MGoat
332-312↓ Mouse,MGoat,Swan
332-321 Mouse,Mole
332-332↓ Mouse,Swan,Sable
333-111 Mole,Mouse
333-132↓ Mole,Fox,Mouse
333-311 Mouse,MGoat,Mole
333-312↓ Mouse,MGoat,Swan
333-322 Mouse,Swan,Fox
333-331 Mouse,Fox,Mole
333-332 Fox,Mouse,Swan
341-111 Mole,Mouse,Pengn
341-112 Mole,Mouse,Dog
341-121 Mole,Mouse,Pengn
341-122 Mole,Mouse,Dog
341-131 Mole,Mouse,Pengn
341-132 Mole,Mouse,Beaver
341-211 Mouse,MGoat,Mole
341-212 Mouse,Dog,MGoat
341-221 Mouse,Mole,Dog
341-222 Mouse,Dog,Sable
341-231↓ Mouse,Beaver,Sable
341-311 Mouse,Sable,MGoat
341-312 Sable,Mouse,Dog
341-331↓ Sable,Mouse,Beaver
342-111↓ Mole,Mouse,Pengn
342-132 Beaver,Owl,Mole
342-211 Mouse,MGoat,Mole
342-212 Mouse,Dog,Beaver
342-221 Mouse,Mole,Dog

342-222	Mouse,Dog,Beaver
342-231	Mouse,Beaver,Owl
342-232	Beaver,Owl,Sable
342-311	Mouse,Sable,MGoat
342-312	Sable,Mouse,Dog
342-331	Sable,Mouse,Beaver
342-332	Sable,Beaver,Owl
343-111↓	Pengn,Mole,Owl
343-122↓	Pengn,Owl,Pr.Dog
343-212↓	Owl,Pengn,Mouse
343-222↓	Owl,Pr.Dog,Beaver
343-311	Owl,Mouse,Pengn
343-312	Owl,Sable,Mouse
343-321	Owl,Mouse,Pengn
343-322↓	Owl,Sable,Pr.Dog
411-111	Mole,Pcock
411-132↓	Mole,Pcock,Giraf
411-311	Pcock,Giraf,MGoat
411-312	Pcock,Swan,Giraf
411-321	Pcock,Giraf,Deer
411-322	Pcock,Swan,Giraf
411-331	Pcock,Giraf,Deer
411-332	Pcock,Swan,Giraf
412-111↓	Mole,Giraf,Vultre
412-211	Mole,Giraf,MGoat
412-212	Giraf,Mole,Pcock
412-311	Giraf,MGoat,Deer
412-312↓	Swan,Giraf,Deer
413-111↓	Mole,Giraf,Vultre
413-132	Mole,Giraf,W.Cat
413-211	Mole,Giraf,MGoat
413-222↓	Giraf,W.Cat,Mole
413-311	Giraf,MGoat,Deer
413-312	Swan,Giraf,Dolphin
413-321	Giraf,Deer,Swan
413-322	Swan,Giraf,Dolphin
413-331	Giraf,Deer,Swan
413-332	Swan,Giraf,Dolphin
421-111↓	Mole,Giraf
421-211↓	Mole,Giraf,MGoat
421-232↓	Giraf,Mole,Swan
421-311	Swan,Giraf,MGoat
421-312↓	Swan,Giraf,Deer
422-111↓	Mole,Giraf
422-211↓	Mole,Giraf,MGoat
422-232↓	Giraf,Mole,W.Cat
422-311	Swan,Giraf,MGoat
422-312↓	Swan,Giraf,Deer
423-111↓	Mole,Giraf
423-132↓	Mole,Giraf,W.Cat
423-211	Mole,Giraf,MGoat
423-212	Giraf,Mole,Swan
423-221↓	Mole,Giraf,W.Cat
423-311	Swan,Giraf,MGoat
423-312	Swan,Giraf,Dolphin
423-321	Swan,Giraf,Deer
423-322	Swan,Giraf,Dolphin
423-331	Swan,Giraf,Deer
423-332	Swan,Giraf,Dolphin
431-111	Mole,Mouse
431-112	Mole,Swan,Giraf
431-121	Mole,Mouse
431-122	Mole,Swan,Giraf
431-131	Mole,Mouse
431-132	Mole,Swan,Giraf

431-211	Swan,Mouse,Mole
431-212	Swan,Giraf
431-221	Swan,Mouse,Mole
431-222	Swan,Giraf
431-231	Swan,Mouse,Mole
431-232↓	Swan,Sable,Giraf
432-111	Mole,Mouse,Swan
432-112	Mole,Swan,Giraf
432-121	Mole,Mouse
432-122	Mole,Swan,Giraf
432-131	Mole,Mouse,Swan
432-132	Mole,Swan,Giraf
432-211	Swan,Mouse,Mole
432-212	Swan,Giraf
432-221	Swan,Mouse,Mole
432-222	Swan,Giraf
432-231	Swan,Mouse,Mole
432-232↓	Swan,Sable,Giraf
433-111	Mole,Mouse
433-112	Mole,Swan,Giraf
433-121	Mole,Mouse
433-122	Mole,Swan,Giraf
433-131	Mole,Mouse
433-132	Mole,Swan,Fox
433-211	Swan,Mouse,Mole
433-212	Swan,Giraf
433-221	Swan,Mouse,Mole
433-222	Swan,Giraf
433-231	Swan,Mouse,Mole
433-232↓	Swan,Sable,Fox
441-111	Mole,Sable,Mouse
441-112	Sable,Swan,Mole
441-121	Sable,Mouse,Mole
441-122↓	Sable,Swan,Mole
441-221↓	Sable,Swan,Mouse
442-111	Mole,Sable,Pengn
442-112	Sable,Swan,Mole
442-121	Sable,Mole,Pengn
442-122↓	Sable,Swan,Mole
442-221↓	Sable,Swan,Mouse
443-111	Pengn,Mole
443-112↓	Pengn,Sable,Owl
443-212	Sable,Swan,Owl
443-221	Sable,Owl,Pengn
443-222	Sable,Owl,Swan
443-231↓	Sable,Owl,Pr.Dog
443-311↓	Sable,Swan

312-

111-111↓	Mole
112-111↓	Mole
113-111↓	Mole
121-111↓	Mole
122-111↓	Mole
123-111↓	Mole
131-111↓	Mole
132-111↓	Mole
133-111↓	Mole,Beaver
141-111↓	Mole,Beaver
141-222↓	Mole,Sheep,Beaver
141-312	Mole,Sheep,Bison
141-321	Mole,Sheep,Mouse
141-322↓	Mole,Sheep,Beaver
141-332↓	Beaver,Sable,Mole
142-111↓	Mole,Beaver

142-212↓	Mole,Beaver,Sheep
142-332	Beaver,Sable
143-111↓	Mole,Beaver
143-132↓	Beaver,Mole,Owl
143-211↓	Mole,Sheep,Beaver
143-232	Beaver,Owl
143-311↓	Mole,Sheep,Beaver
143-332	Beaver,Owl
211-111↓	Vultre,Mole
211-231↓	Vultre,Mole,MGoat
212-111↓	Vultre,Mole,MGoat
213-111↓	Vultre,Mole,Gorlla
213-231↓	Vultre,Mole,MGoat
221-111↓	MGoat,Mole
221-232↓	Mole,Mouse,MGoat
222-111↓	Mole,MGoat
222-312↓	MGoat,Mole,Mouse
223-111↓	Mole,Gorlla
223-211↓	MGoat,Mole,Gorlla
223-221↓	Mole,MGoat,Mouse
223-232	Mole,Fox,Beaver
223-311	MGoat,Mole,Mouse
223-312	MGoat,Mole,Gorlla
223-321↓	Mole,MGoat,Mouse
223-332	Mole,Fox,Beaver
231-111↓	Mole,Mouse,MGoat
231-232↓	Mouse,Mole,Beaver
231-312↓	Mouse,MGoat,Mole
231-332	Mouse,Beaver,Sable
232-111↓	Mole,Mouse,MGoat
232-132↓	Mole,Mouse,Beaver
233-111↓	Mole,Mouse,Gorlla
233-131	Mole,Mouse,Beaver
233-132	Mole,Fox,Beaver
233-222↓	Mouse,Fox,Mole
233-231	Mouse,Beaver,Mole
233-232	Fox,Beaver,Mouse
233-312↓	Mouse,MGoat,Fox
233-321	Mouse,Mole
233-322↓	Mouse,Fox,Beaver
241-111	Sheep,Mole,Mouse
241-112	Sheep,Bison,Beaver
241-121	Sheep,Mole,Mouse
241-122	Sheep,Beaver,Bison
241-131	Beaver,Sheep,Mole
241-132	Beaver,Sheep,Bison
241-211	Sheep,Mouse
241-212	Sheep,Bison,Beaver
241-221	Sheep,Mouse,Beaver
241-222	Sheep,Beaver,Bison
241-311↓	Sheep,Mouse,Beaver
241-312	Sheep,Bison,Beaver
241-321	Sheep,Mouse,Beaver
241-322	Sheep,Beaver,Bison
241-331↓	Beaver,Sheep,Sable
242-111	Sheep,Mole,Beaver
242-112	Beaver,Sheep,Bison
242-121	Sheep,Beaver,Mole
242-122↓	Sheep,Beaver,Mouse
242-212	Beaver,Sheep,Bison
242-221↓	Sheep,Beaver,Mouse
242-312	Beaver,Sheep,Bison
242-321	Sheep,Beaver,Mouse
242-322	Beaver,Sheep,Bison
242-331↓	Beaver,Sheep,Sable

(312 cont'd)

243-111	Pengn,Sheep,Beaver
243-112	Beaver,Pengn,Owl
243-121	Pengn,Beaver,Sheep
243-211↓	Sheep,Beaver,Owl
311-111↓	Vultre,Mole
311-211↓	MGoat,Vultre,Mole
311-212	Vultre,Pcock,MGoat
311-221↓	Vultre,Mole,Pcock
311-311↓	MGoat,Pcock,Vultre
311-321	Pcock,Vultre,Mole
311-322	Vultre,Pcock,Deer
311-331	Pcock,Vultre,Mole
311-332	Vultre,Pcock,Deer
312-111↓	Vultre,Mole,MGoat
312-312	Vultre,MGoat,Deer
312-321	Vultre,Mole,MGoat
312-322	Vultre,Deer,Giraf
312-331	Vultre,Mole,Deer
312-332	Vultre,Deer,Giraf
313-111↓	Vultre,Mole,Gorlla
313-231↓	Vultre,Mole,Fox
313-311	MGoat,Vultre,Mole
313-312	Vultre,MGoat,Deer
313-321	Vultre,Mole,MGoat
313-322	Vultre,Deer,Giraf
313-331	Vultre,Mole,Fox
313-332	Vultre,Fox,Deer
321-111↓	Mole,MGoat
321-212↓	MGoat,Mole,Giraf
321-221	Mole,MGoat,Mouse
321-222	Mole,Giraf,MGoat
321-231↓	Mole,Mouse,Giraf
321-311	MGoat,Mole,Deer
321-312	MGoat,Deer,Swan
321-321	Mole,MGoat,Deer
321-322	Deer,Swan,Giraf
321-331	Mole,Deer,Mouse
321-332	Deer,Swan,Giraf
322-111↓	Mole,MGoat
322-211↓	MGoat,Mole,Mouse
322-212	MGoat,Mole,Giraf
322-221	Mole,MGoat,Mouse
322-222	Mole,Giraf,MGoat
322-231	Mole,Mouse,Giraf
322-232	Mole,Giraf,Fox
322-311	MGoat,Mole,Deer
322-312	MGoat,Deer,Swan
322-321	Mole,MGoat,Deer
322-322	Deer,Swan,Giraf
322-331	Mole,Deer,Mouse
322-332	Deer,Swan,Giraf
323-111↓	Mole,Gorlla,MGoat
323-132	Mole,Fox
323-211↓	MGoat,Mole,Gorlla
323-221	Mole,MGoat,Mouse
323-222	Fox,Mole,Giraf
323-231↓	Mole,Fox,Mouse
323-311	MGoat,Mole,Deer
323-312	MGoat,Deer,Swan
323-321	Mole,MGoat,Deer
323-322	Fox,Deer,Swan
323-331↓	Fox,Mole,Deer
331-111↓	Mole,Mouse,MGoat
331-132↓	Mole,Mouse,Fox

331-211	Mouse,MGoat,Mole
331-212	Mouse,Swan,MGoat
331-222↓	Mouse,Swan,Mole
331-232	Mouse,Swan,Fox
331-331↓	Mouse,Swan,Sable
332-111	Mole,Mouse
332-132↓	Mole,Fox,Mouse
332-211	Mouse,MGoat,Mole
332-212	Mouse,Swan,MGoat
332-222↓	Mouse,Swan,Mole
332-231	Mouse,Mole,Fox
332-232	Fox,Mouse,Beaver
332-331↓	Mouse,Swan,Sable
332-332	Swan,Sable,Fox
333-111	Mole,Pengn,Mouse
333-112	Fox,Mole,Gorlla
333-121	Mole,Pengn,Mouse
333-122↓	Fox,Mole,Pengn
333-132	Fox,Owl
333-211	Mouse,Fox,MGoat
333-212	Fox,Mouse,Horse
333-231↓	Fox,Owl,Mouse
333-311↓	Mouse,Swan,Fox
333-322	Fox,Swan,Owl
333-331↓	Fox,Owl,Mouse
341-111↓	Pengn,Sheep,Dog
341-131	Pengn,Beaver,Sheep
341-132	Beaver,Owl,Sable
341-211	Sheep,Dog,Mouse
341-212	Dog,Sheep,Sable
341-221	Sheep,Dog,Mouse
341-222	Dog,Sable,Sheep
341-231	Beaver,Sheep,Sable
341-232	Sable,Beaver,Owl
341-311	Sheep,Sable,Dog
341-312	Sable,Dog,Swan
341-321↓	Sable,Sheep,Dog
341-331↓	Sable,Beaver
342-111	Pengn,Sheep,Dog
342-112	Pengn,Dog,Owl
342-121	Pengn,Sheep,Dog
342-122	Pengn,Dog,Owl
342-131↓	Pengn,Owl,Beaver
342-211	Sheep,Dog,Pengn
342-212	Dog,Owl,Beaver
342-221	Sheep,Dog,Owl
342-222	Dog,Owl,Beaver
342-231	Owl,Beaver,Sheep
342-232	Owl,Beaver,Sable
342-311	Sheep,Sable,Dog
342-312	Sable,Dog,Owl
342-321	Sable,Sheep,Dog
342-322	Sable,Dog,Owl
342-331↓	Sable,Owl,Beaver
343-111↓	Pengn,Owl
343-332	Owl,Sable
411-111	Pcock,Giraf,Mole
411-112	Pcock,Giraf,Vultre
411-121	Pcock,Giraf,Mole
411-122	Pcock,Giraf,Vultre
411-131	Pcock,Giraf,Mole
411-311↓	Pcock,Deer,Giraf
411-312	Pcock,Deer,Swan
411-321	Pcock,Deer,Giraf
411-322	Pcock,Deer,Swan

411-331	Pcock,Deer,Giraf
411-332	Pcock,Deer,Swan
412-111	Giraf,Mole,Vultre
412-112	Giraf,Vultre,Pcock
412-121	Giraf,Mole,Vultre
412-122	Giraf,Vultre,Pcock
412-131	Giraf,Mole,Vultre
412-132	Giraf,Vultre,Pcock
412-222↓	Giraf,Pcock,Deer
412-231↓	Giraf,Pcock,W.Cat
412-311↓	Deer,Giraf,Swan
413-111	Giraf,Mole,Vultre
413-112	Giraf,Vultre,W.Cat
413-121	Giraf,Mole,Vultre
413-122	Giraf,Vultre,W.Cat
413-131	Giraf,Mole,W.Cat
413-132	Giraf,W.Cat,Vultre
413-211	Giraf,Pcock,Deer
413-231↓	Giraf,W.Cat,Pcock
413-311↓	Deer,Giraf,Swan
421-111↓	Giraf,Mole
421-311↓	Swan,Deer,Giraf
422-111↓	Giraf,Mole
422-131↓	Giraf,Mole,W.Cat
422-212↓	Giraf,Swan,Deer
422-232	Giraf,W.Cat,Swan
422-311↓	Swan,Deer,Giraf
423-111	Giraf,Mole
423-112↓	Giraf,W.Cat,Mole
423-221↓	Giraf,W.Cat,Swan
423-311↓	Swan,Deer,Giraf
431-111↓	Swan,Giraf,Mole
431-231↓	Swan,Giraf,Sable
432-111↓	Swan,Giraf,Mole
432-231↓	Swan,Giraf,Sable
433-111↓	Swan,Giraf,Mole
433-122↓	Swan,Giraf,Fox
441-111↓	Sable,Pengn,Swan
441-112	Sable,Swan,Dog
442-111↓	Sable,Pengn,Swan
443-111	Pengn,Owl
443-112↓	Pengn,Owl,Sable
443-311↓	Sable,Swan,Owl

313-

111-111↓	Mole
112-111↓	Mole
113-111↓	Mole
121-111↓	Mole
122-111↓	Mole
123-111↓	Mole
131-111↓	Mole
132-111↓	Mole
133-111↓	Mole,Fox
133-332↓	Mole,Fox,Beaver
141-111	Mole,Sheep
141-222↓	Sheep,Bison,Mole
141-231	Sheep,Mole,Beaver
141-232	Sheep,Bison,Beaver
141-311↓	Sheep,Mole,Bison
141-331	Sheep,Mole,Beaver
141-332	Sheep,Bison,Beaver
142-111	Mole,Sheep
142-222↓	Sheep,Bison,Mole
142-231	Sheep,Mole,Beaver

142-232	Beaver,Sheep,Bison	
142-312↓	Sheep,Bison,Mole	
142-322	Sheep,Bison,Beaver	
142-331	Sheep,Beaver,Mole	
142-332	Beaver,Sheep,Bison	
143-111	Mole,Sheep	
143-122↓	Mole,Owl,Sheep	
143-131↓	Mole,Owl,Beaver	
143-211	Sheep,Mole,Owl	
143-212	Sheep,Owl,Bison	
143-221	Sheep,Mole,Owl	
143-222↓	Owl,Sheep,Beaver	
143-311	Sheep,Owl,Mole	
143-312	Sheep,Owl,Bison	
143-321	Sheep,Owl,Mole	
143-322↓	Owl,Sheep,Beaver	
211-111↓	Vultre,Mole,MGoat	
211-212	Vultre,MGoat,Pcock	
211-221↓	Vultre,Mole,Pcock	
211-311	MGoat,Vultre,Mole	
211-312	Vultre,MGoat,Pcock	
211-321↓	Vultre,Mole,Pcock	
212-111↓	Vultre,Mole,MGoat	
213-111↓	Vultre,Mole,Gorlla	
213-211↓	MGoat,Vultre,Mole	
213-231↓	Vultre,Mole,Fox	
221-111↓	Mole,MGoat	
221-311↓	MGoat,Mole,Mouse	
221-312	MGoat,Mole,Deer	
221-321	Mole,MGoat,Mouse	
221-322	Mole,Deer,MGoat	
221-331	Mole,Mouse,MGoat	
221-332↓	Mole,Deer,Mouse	
222-111↓	MGoat,Mole	
222-312↓	MGoat,Mole,Deer	
222-321	Mole,MGoat,Mouse	
222-322	Mole,Deer,MGoat	
222-331	Mole,Mouse,MGoat	
222-332	Mole,Deer,Mouse	
223-111	Mole,Gorlla	
223-112↓	Mole,Gorlla,MGoat	
223-132	Mole,Fox	
223-211↓	MGoat,Mole,Gorlla	
223-221	Mole,MGoat,Mouse	
223-222	Mole,Fox,MGoat	
223-231↓	Mole,Fox,Mouse	
223-311	MGoat,Mole,Mouse	
223-312	MGoat,Mole,Gorlla	
223-321	Mole,MGoat,Mouse	
223-322	Mole,Fox,Deer	
223-331↓	Mole,Fox,Mouse	
231-111	Mole,Mouse	
231-112↓	Mole,Mouse,MGoat	
231-211↓	Mouse,MGoat,Sheep	
231-221↓	Mouse,Sheep,Mole	
231-332↓	Mouse,Sheep,Bison	
232-111↓	Mole,Mouse,MGoat	
232-132↓	Mole,Mouse,Fox	
232-211↓	Mouse,MGoat,Sheep	
232-221↓	Mouse,Sheep,Mole	
232-232	Mouse,Fox,Beaver	
232-311↓	Mouse,MGoat,Sheep	
232-321	Mouse,Sheep,Mole	
232-322↓	Mouse,Sheep,Bison	
232-332	Mouse,Fox,Beaver	
233-111	Mole,Mouse,Gorlla	
233-112	Mole,Gorlla,Fox	
233-121↓	Mole,Mouse,Fox	
233-132	Fox,Owl,Mole	
233-211	Mouse,MGoat,Sheep	
233-212	Fox,Mouse,MGoat	
233-221	Mouse,Fox,Sheep	
233-222↓	Fox,Mouse,Owl	
233-311	Mouse,MGoat,Sheep	
233-312	Fox,Mouse,MGoat	
233-321	Mouse,Fox,Sheep	
233-322↓	Fox,Mouse,Owl	
241-111↓	Sheep,Bison,Dog	
241-132↓	Sheep,Bison,Beaver	
241-212↓	Sheep,Bison,Dog	
241-232↓	Sheep,Bison,Beaver	
241-312↓	Sheep,Bison,Dog	
241-332↓	Sheep,Bison,Beaver	
242-111↓	Sheep,Bison,Beaver	
242-131	Sheep,Beaver,Owl	
242-212↓	Sheep,Bison,Beaver	
242-231	Sheep,Beaver,Owl	
242-312↓	Sheep,Bison,Beaver	
242-331	Sheep,Beaver,Owl	
243-111	Sheep,Owl,Pengn	
243-112	Owl,Sheep,Bison	
243-121	Sheep,Owl,Pengn	
243-122↓	Owl,Sheep,Beaver	
243-212	Owl,Sheep,Bison	
243-311↓	Sheep,Owl,Beaver	
243-312	Owl,Sheep,Bison	
243-321↓	Sheep,Owl,Beaver	
311-111↓	Vultre,Mole,Pcock	
311-311	Pcock,Deer,MGoat	
311-332↓	Pcock,Deer,Vultre	
312-111↓	Vultre,Mole,Pcock	
312-212	Vultre,Pcock,MGoat	
312-221↓	Vultre,Mole,Pcock	
312-311	Deer,MGoat,Vultre	
312-312	Deer,Vultre,Pcock	
312-321	Deer,Vultre,Mole	
312-322	Deer,Vultre,Pcock	
312-331	Deer,Vultre,Mole	
312-332	Deer,Vultre,Pcock	
313-111↓	Vultre,Mole,Gorlla	
313-131↓	Vultre,Mole,Fox	
313-211	MGoat,Vultre,Mole	
313-212	Vultre,Fox,MGoat	
313-231↓	Fox,Vultre,Mole	
313-311	Deer,MGoat,Dolphin	
313-312	Deer,Dolphin,Vultre	
313-321↓	Deer,Fox,Dolphin	
321-111↓	Mole,MGoat	
321-212↓	MGoat,Mole,Giraf	
321-221	Mole,MGoat,Mouse	
321-222	Mole,Giraf,Deer	
321-231	Mole,Mouse,Giraf	
321-232	Mole,Giraf,Deer	
321-311↓	Deer,MGoat,Mole	
322-111↓	Mole,MGoat	
322-132	Mole,Fox	
322-211	MGoat,Mole,Mouse	
322-212	MGoat,Mole,Giraf	
322-221	Mole,MGoat,Mouse	
322-222	Mole,Giraf,Deer	
322-231	Mole,Fox,Mouse	
322-232	Fox,Mole,Giraf	
322-321↓	Deer,Mole,MGoat	
322-331↓	Deer,Mole,Fox	
323-111	Mole,Gorlla	
323-122↓	Mole,Fox,Gorlla	
323-212	Fox,MGoat,Horse	
323-221↓	Fox,Mole,Horse	
323-311	Deer,MGoat,Fox	
323-312↓	Deer,Fox,Dolphin	
331-111	Mole,Mouse	
331-122↓	Mole,Mouse,Dog	
331-131↓	Mole,Mouse,Fox	
331-211	Mouse,MGoat,Sheep	
331-212	Mouse,Dog,Swan	
331-221	Mouse,Sheep,Mole	
331-222	Mouse,Dog,Fox	
331-231	Mouse,Fox,Sheep	
331-232	Fox,Mouse,Dog	
331-311↓	Mouse,Swan,Deer	
331-331	Mouse,Swan,Fox	
331-332	Swan,Fox,Sable	
332-111	Mole,Mouse,MGoat	
332-122↓	Mole,Fox,Mouse	
332-132	Fox,Mole,Owl	
332-211	Mouse,MGoat,Sheep	
332-212	Fox,Mouse,Dog	
332-221	Mouse,Sheep,Mole	
332-222	Fox,Mouse,Dog	
332-231↓	Fox,Mouse,Owl	
332-311	Mouse,Swan,Deer	
332-312	Swan,Deer,Fox	
332-321	Mouse,Swan,Deer	
332-322	Swan,Fox,Deer	
332-331	Fox,Mouse,Swan	
332-332	Fox,Swan,Sable	
333-111	Fox,Mole,Pengn	
333-112	Fox,Horse,Owl	
333-121	Fox,Mole,Pengn	
333-211↓	Fox,Horse,Owl	
341-111	Sheep,Dog,Pengn	
341-112	Dog,Sheep,Bison	
341-121	Sheep,Dog,Pengn	
341-122↓	Dog,Sheep,Owl	
341-132	Owl,Dog,Pr.Dog	
341-212↓	Dog,Sheep,Bison	
341-221	Sheep,Dog,Owl	
341-232	Owl,Dog,Pr.Dog	
341-311↓	Sheep,Dog,Sable	
341-331	Sable,Sheep,Owl	
341-332	Sable,Owl,Dog	
342-111	Sheep,Dog,Pengn	
342-112	Dog,Owl,Sheep	
342-121	Sheep,Dog,Pengn	
342-122	Dog,Owl,Sheep	
342-131	Owl,Sheep,Pr.Dog	
342-132	Owl,Pr.Dog,Dog	
342-211↓	Sheep,Dog,Owl	
342-231	Owl,Sheep,Pr.Dog	
342-232	Owl,Pr.Dog,Dog	
342-311↓	Sheep,Dog,Owl	
342-322	Dog,Owl,Sable	
342-331	Owl,Sable,Sheep	
342-332	Owl,Sable,Pr.Dog	
343-111↓	Owl,Pengn	

223-122↓	Mole,Horse
223-132	Mole,Baboon,Fox
223-211↓	MGoat,Mole,Horse
223-222	Horse,Mole,Baboon
223-231	Mole,Baboon,Pr.Dog
223-232	Baboon,Fox,Pr.Dog
223-311	MGoat,Dolphin,Mole
223-312	Dolphin,MGoat,Horse
223-321	Dolphin,Mole,Horse
223-322	Dolphin,Horse,Baboon
223-331	Baboon,Dolphin,Pr.Dog
223-332	Dolphin,Baboon,Fox
231-111↓	Walrus,Mole,Mouse
231-211	Mouse,MGoat,Walrus
231-212	Mouse,Dog,MGoat
231-221	Mouse,Walrus,Sheep
231-222	Mouse,Dog,Walrus
231-231	Mouse,Walrus,Sheep
231-232	Mouse,Dog,Baboon
231-311	Mouse,MGoat,Sheep
231-312	Mouse,Dog,MGoat
231-321↓	Mouse,Sheep,Dog
231-332	Mouse,Dog,Baboon
232-111↓	Walrus,Mole,Mouse
232-132	Walrus,Mole,Baboon
232-211	Mouse,MGoat,Walrus
232-212	Mouse,Dog,Horse
232-221	Mouse,Walrus,Sheep
232-222	Mouse,Dog,Horse
232-231	Mouse,Baboon,Walrus
232-232	Baboon,Pr.Dog,Mouse
232-311	Mouse,MGoat,Sheep
232-312	Mouse,Dog,Horse
232-321	Mouse,Sheep,Dog
232-322	Mouse,Dog,Horse
232-331	Mouse,Baboon,Sheep
232-332	Baboon,Pr.Dog,Mouse
233-111↓	Walrus,Mole,Horse
233-122	Horse,Baboon,Walrus
233-131	Baboon,Walrus,Pr.Dog
233-132	Baboon,Fox,Pr.Dog
233-211	Horse,Mouse,Baboon
233-212	Horse,Baboon,Fox
233-221	Horse,Mouse,Baboon
233-222	Horse,Baboon,Fox
233-231↓	Baboon,Pr.Dog,Fox
233-311	Horse,Mouse,Baboon
233-312	Horse,Baboon,Fox
233-321	Horse,Mouse,Baboon
233-322	Horse,Baboon,Fox
233-331↓	Baboon,Pr.Dog,Fox
241-111	Sheep,Dog,Walrus
241-122↓	Dog,Sheep,Bison
241-131	Sheep,Dog,Pr.Dog
241-222↓	Dog,Sheep,Bison
241-231↓	Sheep,Dog,Pr.Dog
241-311	Sheep,Dog,Bison
241-332↓	Dog,Pr.Dog,Sheep
242-111	Sheep,Dog
242-112↓	Dog,Sheep,Bison
242-121	Sheep,Dog,Pr.Dog
242-122	Dog,Sheep,Bison
242-131	Sheep,Pr.Dog,Dog
242-132	Pr.Dog,Dog,Beaver
242-212↓	Dog,Sheep,Bison
242-221	Sheep,Dog,Pr.Dog
242-222	Dog,Sheep,Bison
242-231	Sheep,Pr.Dog,Dog
242-232	Pr.Dog,Dog,Beaver
242-312↓	Dog,Sheep,Bison
242-321	Sheep,Dog,Pr.Dog
242-322	Dog,Sheep,Bison
242-331	Sheep,Pr.Dog,Dog
242-332	Pr.Dog,Dog,Beaver
243-111	Sheep,Pr.Dog,Dog
243-112	Pr.Dog,Dog,Owl
243-121	Pr.Dog,Sheep,Owl
243-122↓	Pr.Dog,Owl,Dog
243-211	Sheep,Pr.Dog,Dog
243-212	Pr.Dog,Dog,Owl
243-221	Pr.Dog,Sheep,Owl
243-222↓	Pr.Dog,Owl,Dog
243-311	Sheep,Pr.Dog,Dog
243-312	Pr.Dog,Dog,Owl
243-321	Pr.Dog,Sheep,Owl
243-322↓	Pr.Dog,Owl,Dog
311-111↓	Mole,Vultre,Pcock
311-211	Pcock,MGoat,Mole
311-212	Pcock,Vultre,Dog
311-221	Pcock,Mole,Dog
311-222	Pcock,Vultre,Dog
311-231	Pcock,Mole,Dog
311-232	Pcock,Vultre,Dog
311-311	Pcock,Deer,MGoat
311-312↓	Pcock,Deer,SeaLn
312-111↓	Mole,Vultre,MGoat
312-211	MGoat,Mole,Dog
312-212	Vultre,Dog,Pcock
312-221	Mole,Dog,Vultre
312-222	Vultre,Dog,Pcock
312-231	Mole,Pr.Dog,Dog
312-232	Vultre,Pr.Dog,Dog
312-311	Deer,MGoat,SeaLn
312-312↓	Dolphin,Deer,SeaLn
313-111↓	Mole,Vultre,Horse
313-131	Pr.Dog,Mole,Vultre
313-132	Vultre,Pr.Dog,Fox
313-211	Horse,MGoat,Dolphin
313-212	Horse,Dolphin,Vultre
313-221↓	Horse,Pr.Dog,Dolphin
313-231↓	Pr.Dog,Fox,Horse
313-321↓	Dolphin,Horse,Pr.Dog
313-331↓	Dolphin,Pr.Dog,Fox
321-111	Mole,MGoat
321-132↓	Mole,Dog,Pr.Dog
321-211↓	MGoat,Mole,Dog
321-222	Dog,Mole,Horse
321-231↓	Mole,Dog,Pr.Dog
321-311	Deer,MGoat,SeaLn
321-312	Deer,SeaLn,Dolphin
321-321	Deer,SeaLn,Dog
321-322	Deer,SeaLn,Dolphin
321-331	Deer,SeaLn,Dog
321-332	Deer,SeaLn,Dolphin
322-111↓	Mole,Dog,Horse
322-132	Mole,Pr.Dog,Dog
322-211	MGoat,Mole,Dog
322-212	Dog,Horse,MGoat
322-221↓	Mole,Dog,Horse
322-231	Mole,Pr.Dog,Dog
322-232	Pr.Dog,Dog,Horse
322-311	Deer,MGoat,SeaLn
322-312↓	Dolphin,Deer,SeaLn
323-111	Mole,Horse,MGoat
323-112	Horse,Mole,Gorlla
323-121	Mole,Horse,Pr.Dog
323-122	Horse,Mole,Fox
323-131	Pr.Dog,Mole,Fox
323-132	Fox,Pr.Dog,Horse
323-211	Horse,MGoat,Dolphin
323-212	Horse,Dolphin,Fox
323-221	Horse,Pr.Dog,Fox
323-222	Horse,Fox,Dolphin
323-231	Pr.Dog,Fox,Horse
323-321↓	Dolphin,Horse,Pr.Dog
323-331↓	Dolphin,Pr.Dog,Fox
331-111	Dog,Walrus,Mole
331-112	Dog,Horse
331-121	Dog,Walrus,Mole
331-122	Dog,Horse,Walrus
331-131	Dog,Walrus,Mole
331-132↓	Dog,Pr.Dog,Horse
331-321↓	Dog,Horse,Mouse
331-322	Dog,Horse,Swan
331-331↓	Dog,Pr.Dog,Horse
332-111	Dog,Walrus,Mole
332-112	Dog,Horse,Walrus
332-121	Dog,Walrus,Mole
332-122	Dog,Horse,Pr.Dog
332-131	Pr.Dog,Dog,Walrus
332-132	Pr.Dog,Dog,Horse
332-221↓	Dog,Horse,Mouse
332-222↓	Dog,Horse,Pr.Dog
332-311	Dog,Horse,Mouse
332-312	Dog,Horse,Swan
332-321	Dog,Horse,Mouse
332-322↓	Dog,Horse,Pr.Dog
333-111	Horse,Pr.Dog
333-112↓	Horse,Fox,Pr.Dog
341-111↓	Dog,Pr.Dog
342-111↓	Dog,Pr.Dog
342-331↓	Pr.Dog,Dog,Owl
343-111↓	Pr.Dog,Dog,Owl
411-111↓	Pcock,Deer,SeaLn
412-111	Pcock,Mole,Giraf
412-112	Pcock,Giraf,Dolphin
412-121	Pcock,Mole,Giraf
412-122	Pcock,Giraf,Dolphin
412-131	Pcock,Mole,Giraf
412-132	Pcock,Giraf,Dolphin
412-211	Pcock,Deer,SeaLn
412-212	Pcock,Dolphin,Deer
412-221	Pcock,Deer,SeaLn
412-222	Pcock,Dolphin,Deer
412-231	Pcock,Deer,SeaLn
412-232	Pcock,Dolphin,Deer
412-311↓	Deer,SeaLn,Dolphin
413-111↓	Dolphin,Pcock,Mole
413-112↓	Dolphin,Pcock,Deer
421-111	Mole,Giraf,Deer
421-112	Giraf,Deer,SeaLn
421-121	Mole,Giraf,Deer
421-122	Giraf,Deer,SeaLn
421-131	Mole,Giraf,Deer
421-132↓	Giraf,Deer,SeaLn

(314 cont'd)

421-311↓ Deer,SeaLn,Dolphin
422-111 Mole,Giraf,Deer
422-112 Giraf,Dolphin,Deer
422-121 Mole,Giraf,Deer
422-122 Giraf,Dolphin,Deer
422-131 Mole,Giraf,Deer
422-132 Giraf,Dolphin,Deer
422-211 Deer,SeaLn,Giraf
422-212 Dolphin,Deer,SeaLn
422-221 Deer,SeaLn,Giraf
422-222 Dolphin,Deer,SeaLn
422-231 Deer,SeaLn,Giraf
422-232↓ Dolphin,Deer,SeaLn
423-111↓ Dolphin,Mole,Giraf
423-131 Dolphin,Pr.Dog,Mole
423-132 Dolphin,Fox
423-211↓ Dolphin,Deer
431-111 Cottn,Dog,Swan
431-112 Swan,Dog,Giraf
431-121 Cottn,Dog,Swan
431-122 Swan,Dog,Giraf
431-131 Cottn,Dog,Swan
431-132 Swan,Dog,Giraf
431-211 Swan,Cottn,Dog
431-212 Swan,Dog,Deer
431-221 Swan,Cottn,Dog
431-222 Swan,Dog,Deer
431-231 Swan,Cottn,Dog
431-232 Swan,Dog,Deer
431-311↓ Swan,Deer,SeaLn
431-332 Swan,Deer,Sable
432-111 Cottn,Dog,Swan
432-112 Swan,Dog,Horse
432-121 Cottn,Dog,Swan
432-122 Swan,Dog,Horse
432-131 Cottn,Pr.Dog,Dog
432-132 Swan,Pr.Dog,Dog
432-211 Swan,Cottn,Dog
432-212 Swan,Dolphin,Dog
432-221 Swan,Cottn,Dog
432-222 Swan,Dolphin,Dog
432-231 Swan,Cottn,Pr.Dog
432-232 Swan,Pr.Dog,Dolphin
432-311 Swan,Deer,SeaLn
432-312 Swan,Dolphin,Deer
432-321 Swan,Deer,SeaLn
432-322 Swan,Dolphin,Deer
432-331 Swan,Deer,SeaLn
432-332 Swan,Dolphin,Deer
433-111 Horse,Dolphin,Cottn
433-112 Horse,Dolphin,Fox
433-121 Horse,Dolphin,Pr.Dog
433-122 Horse,Dolphin,Fox
433-131 Pr.Dog,Fox,Horse
433-212 Dolphin,Horse,Swan
433-221 Horse,Dolphin,Pr.Dog
433-222 Dolphin,Horse,Swan
433-231 Pr.Dog,Fox,Horse
433-232 Fox,Pr.Dog,Dolphin
433-331↓ Dolphin,Swan,Pr.Dog
433-332 Dolphin,Swan,Fox
441-111↓ Dog,Pr.Dog,Sable
441-311↓ Dog,Sable,Swan
442-111↓ Dog,Pr.Dog

442-222↓ Dog,Pr.Dog,Sable
442-322 Sable,Dog,Swan
442-331↓ Sable,Pr.Dog,Dog
443-111↓ Pr.Dog,Dog,Owl
443-312 Pr.Dog,Dog,Sable
443-321 Pr.Dog,Owl,Dog
443-322↓ Pr.Dog,Sable,Owl

321-

111-111↓ MGoat,Vultre,Porcp
111-131↓ Vultre,Porcp,Mole
111-221↓ MGoat,Vultre,Porcp
112-111 MGoat,Vultre,Porcp
112-131↓ Vultre,Porcp,Mole
112-221↓ MGoat,Vultre,Porcp
113-111 MGoat,Vultre,Porcp
113-131↓ Vultre,Porcp,Mole
113-221↓ MGoat,Vultre,Porcp
121-111↓ MGoat,Porcp,Mole
122-111↓ MGoat,Porcp,Mole
123-111↓ MGoat,Porcp,Mole
123-112 Porcp,MGoat,Gorlla
131-111↓ MGoat,Porcp,Mole
131-332↓ MGoat,Porcp,Beaver
132-111↓ MGoat,Porcp,Mole
132-332↓ MGoat,Beaver,Porcp
133-111 MGoat,Porcp,Mole
133-112 Bat,Porcp,MGoat
133-121 Porcp,Mole,MGoat
133-122↓ Bat,Porcp,Mole
133-222↓ MGoat,Bat,Porcp
133-231 MGoat,Beaver,Porcp
133-232 Beaver,Bat,Porcp
133-311↓ MGoat,Bat,Porcp
133-332↓ Beaver,MGoat,Fox
141-111↓ MGoat,Sheep,Porcp
141-121 Sheep,Porcp,Mole
141-122↓ Porcp,Beaver,Sheep
141-211↓ MGoat,Sheep,Beaver
141-222↓ Beaver,Sheep,Bison
141-312↓ MGoat,Sheep,Beaver
141-322↓ Beaver,Sheep,Sable
142-111 MGoat,Sheep,Beaver
142-112 Beaver,Porcp,MGoat
142-121 Sheep,Beaver,Porcp
142-211↓ MGoat,Sheep,Beaver
142-322↓ Beaver,Sheep,Sable
143-111 Pengn,MGoat,Beaver
143-112 Beaver,Bat,Porcp
143-121 Beaver,Pengn,Sheep
143-122 Beaver,Bat,Porcp
143-131↓ Beaver,Pengn,Owl
143-211↓ MGoat,Beaver,Sheep
143-331↓ Beaver,Owl
211-111↓ MGoat,Vultre
211-232↓ Vultre,MGoat,Pcock
212-111↓ MGoat,Vultre,Snake
213-111↓ MGoat,Vultre
221-111↓ MGoat,Snake
221-122↓ MGoat,Vultre
222-111↓ MGoat,Snake
222-122↓ MGoat,Vultre,Snake
222-132↓ MGoat,Vultre,Porcp
223-111↓ MGoat,Snake,Gorlla
223-122↓ MGoat,Bat,Gorlla

223-232↓ MGoat,Beaver
231-111↓ MGoat,Bat
231-132↓ MGoat,Bat,Beaver
232-111 MGoat,Snake
232-112↓ MGoat,Bat,Snake
232-122 MGoat,Bat,Vultre
232-131↓ MGoat,Beaver,Bat
233-111 MGoat,Bat
233-122↓ Bat,MGoat,Horse
233-131↓ Bat,MGoat,Beaver
233-211↓ MGoat,Bat,Horse
233-231 MGoat,Beaver,Horse
233-232 Beaver,Fox,Bat
233-311↓ MGoat,Horse,Bat
233-331 MGoat,Beaver,Horse
233-332 Beaver,Fox,MGoat
241-111↓ MGoat,Sheep,Beaver
241-122↓ Beaver,Sheep,Bison
241-212↓ MGoat,Sheep,Beaver
241-322↓ Beaver,Sheep,Sable
242-111↓ MGoat,Sheep,Beaver
242-322↓ Beaver,Sheep,Sable
243-111 Pengn,MGoat,Beaver
243-112 Beaver,Bat,Pengn
243-121 Pengn,Beaver,Sheep
243-122 Beaver,Bat,Pengn
243-131↓ Beaver,Pengn,Owl
243-211 MGoat,Beaver,Sheep
243-212 Beaver,Owl,MGoat
243-221 Beaver,Sheep,Owl
243-232↓ Beaver,Owl,Pr.Dog
243-311 MGoat,Beaver,Sheep
243-312 Beaver,Owl,MGoat
243-321↓ Beaver,Sheep,Owl
311-111↓ MGoat,Vultre,Pcock
312-111↓ MGoat,Vultre
312-222↓ Vultre,MGoat,Pcock
313-111↓ MGoat,Vultre
313-232↓ Vultre,MGoat,Fox
321-111↓ MGoat,Giraf
321-132↓ MGoat,Giraf,Vultre
321-322↓ MGoat,Zebra,Swan
322-111↓ MGoat,Snake
322-122↓ MGoat,Giraf,Vultre
322-322↓ MGoat,Zebra,Swan
323-111↓ MGoat,Gorlla
323-122 MGoat,Horse,Bat
323-131 MGoat,Horse,Fox
323-222↓ MGoat,Horse,Giraf
323-231↓ MGoat,Horse,Fox
323-322 MGoat,Horse,Zebra
323-331↓ MGoat,Horse,Fox
331-111↓ MGoat,Horse,Bat
331-332↓ Swan,Sable,MGoat
332-111↓ MGoat,Horse
332-122↓ MGoat,Horse,Bat
332-131 MGoat,Horse,Pengn
332-132↓ Horse,MGoat,Fox
332-222↓ MGoat,Horse,Swan
332-231 MGoat,Horse,Beaver
332-232↓ Horse,MGoat,Fox
332-321↓ MGoat,Swan,Horse
332-332 Swan,Sable,Horse
333-111 MGoat,Horse,Pengn
333-112 Horse,Bat,MGoat

333-121   Horse,Pengn,MGoat
333-122   Horse,Bat,Fox
333-131   Horse,Fox,Pengn
333-132   Fox,Horse,Bat
333-212↓ Horse,MGoat,Fox
333-231   Horse,Fox,Owl
333-312↓ Horse,MGoat,Swan
333-322   Horse,Swan,Fox
333-331   Horse,Fox,Owl
333-332   Fox,Horse,Swan
341-111↓ Pengn,MGoat,Dog
341-121   Pengn,Dog,Sheep
341-122↓ Dog,Pengn,Beaver
341-132   Beaver,Dog,Sable
341-211   MGoat,Dog,Sheep
341-222↓ Dog,Sable,Beaver
341-312   Sable,Dog,Swan
341-321   Sable,Dog,Sheep
341-322   Sable,Dog,Swan
341-331↓ Sable,Beaver
342-111   Pengn,MGoat,Dog
342-112   Pengn,Dog,Beaver
342-121   Pengn,Dog,Sheep
342-122   Pengn,Dog,Beaver
342-131   Pengn,Beaver,Owl
342-132   Beaver,Owl,Pr.Dog
342-211   MGoat,Dog,Sheep
342-212   Dog,Beaver,MGoat
342-221   Dog,Sheep,Beaver
342-222   Dog,Beaver,Owl
342-231↓ Beaver,Owl,Sable
342-311   MGoat,Sable,Dog
342-312   Sable,Dog,Beaver
342-321   Sable,Dog,Sheep
342-322   Sable,Dog,Beaver
342-331↓ Sable,Beaver,Owl
343-111↓ Pengn,Owl
343-122↓ Pengn,Owl,Pr.Dog
343-222↓ Owl,Pr.Dog,Beaver
343-311   Owl,Pengn,Pr.Dog
343-312   Owl,Sable,Pr.Dog
343-321   Owl,Pengn,Pr.Dog
343-322   Owl,Sable,Pr.Dog
343-331   Owl,Pr.Dog,Beaver
343-332   Owl,Sable,Pr.Dog
411-111↓ Pcock,Giraf
412-111↓ Pcock,Giraf,MGoat
412-132↓ Pcock,Giraf,Vultre
412-311↓ Pcock,Giraf,MGoat
412-312   Pcock,Swan,Giraf
412-321   Pcock,Giraf,Deer
412-322   Pcock,Swan,Giraf
412-331   Pcock,Giraf,Deer
412-332   Pcock,Swan,Giraf
413-111   Pcock,Giraf,MGoat
413-112↓ Pcock,Giraf,Vultre
413-131↓ Pcock,Giraf,W.Cat
413-211↓ Pcock,Giraf,MGoat
413-221↓ Pcock,Giraf,W.Cat
413-311   Pcock,Giraf,MGoat
413-312   Swan,Pcock,Giraf
413-321   Pcock,Giraf,Deer
413-322   Swan,Pcock,Giraf
413-331   Pcock,Giraf,Deer
413-332   Swan,Pcock,Giraf

421-111↓ Giraf,MGoat,Pcock
421-232↓ Giraf,Pcock,Swan
421-311   Swan,Giraf,MGoat
421-312↓ Swan,Giraf,Deer
422-111↓ Giraf,MGoat
422-122↓ Giraf,Swan,W.Cat
422-211↓ Giraf,MGoat,Swan
422-232↓ Giraf,Swan,W.Cat
422-311   Swan,Giraf,MGoat
422-312↓ Swan,Giraf,Deer
423-111↓ Giraf,MGoat
423-122↓ Giraf,W.Cat
423-212↓ Giraf,Swan,MGoat
423-232↓ Giraf,W.Cat,Swan
423-311   Swan,Giraf,MGoat
423-312↓ Swan,Giraf,Deer
431-111   Swan,Giraf,MGoat
431-112↓ Swan,Giraf,Pcock
431-131↓ Swan,Giraf,Sable
432-111↓ Swan,Giraf,MGoat
432-131↓ Swan,Giraf,Sable
433-111   Swan,Giraf,MGoat
433-112↓ Swan,Giraf,Horse
433-132   Swan,Giraf,Fox
433-211   Swan,Giraf,MGoat
433-212↓ Swan,Giraf,Horse
433-231   Swan,Giraf,Sable
441-111↓ Sable,Swan,Pengn
442-111↓ Sable,Pengn,Swan
443-111   Pengn,Owl
443-112↓ Pengn,Sable,Owl
443-132   Sable,Owl,Pr.Dog
443-211   Sable,Pengn,Owl
443-212   Sable,Swan,Owl
443-221   Sable,Owl,Pengn
443-222   Sable,Owl,Swan
443-231↓ Sable,Owl,Pr.Dog
443-311↓ Sable,Swan

322-

111-111↓ Vultre,MGoat
111-211↓ MGoat,Vultre,Pcock
112-111↓ Vultre,MGoat
113-111↓ Vultre,Gorlla,MGoat
113-331↓ Vultre,MGoat,Beaver
121-111   MGoat,Porcp,Mole
121-112   Porcp,MGoat,Vultre
121-121   Porcp,Mole,MGoat
121-122   Porcp,Vultre,Mole
121-131   Porcp,Mole,MGoat
121-132   Porcp,Vultre,Mole
121-211↓ MGoat,Porcp,Vultre
121-231   MGoat,Porcp,Mole
121-232↓ Porcp,MGoat,Vultre
121-322↓ MGoat,Porcp,Deer
122-111   MGoat,Porcp,Mole
122-112   Porcp,MGoat,Vultre
122-121   Porcp,Mole,MGoat
122-122   Porcp,Vultre,Mole
122-131   Porcp,Mole,MGoat
122-132   Porcp,Vultre,Mole
122-221↓ MGoat,Porcp,Mole
122-222   MGoat,Porcp,Vultre
122-231   MGoat,Porcp,Mole
122-232↓ Porcp,MGoat,Beaver

122-322   MGoat,Porcp,Deer
122-332↓ MGoat,Beaver,Porcp
123-111↓ Gorlla,MGoat,Porcp
123-121   Porcp,Mole,Gorlla
123-122   Porcp,Gorlla,Vultre
123-131   Porcp,Mole,Gorlla
123-132   Porcp,Gorlla,Vultre
123-222↓ MGoat,Porcp,Gorlla
123-231↓ MGoat,Beaver,Porcp
123-322↓ MGoat,Porcp,Gorlla
123-332↓ Beaver,MGoat,Fox
131-111   MGoat,Porcp,Mole
131-112   Porcp,MGoat,Vultre
131-121   Porcp,Mole,MGoat
131-122   Porcp,Vultre,Mole
131-131   Porcp,Mole,Beaver
131-132   Porcp,Beaver,Vultre
131-211↓ MGoat,Sheep,Porcp
131-231   Beaver,Sheep,MGoat
131-232   Beaver,Sheep,Porcp
131-322↓ MGoat,Sheep,Beaver
131-332   Beaver,Sable,Sheep
132-111   MGoat,Porcp,Mole
132-112   Porcp,MGoat,Vultre
132-121   Porcp,Mole,MGoat
132-122   Porcp,Vultre,Beaver
132-131   Beaver,Porcp,Mole
132-132   Beaver,Porcp,Vultre
132-221↓ MGoat,Sheep,Beaver
132-332   Beaver,Sable
133-111   Gorlla,MGoat,Porcp
133-112   Gorlla,Bat,Porcp
133-121   Porcp,Mole,Gorlla
133-122   Bat,Porcp,Gorlla
133-131   Beaver,Fox,Porcp
133-132   Beaver,Fox,Bat
133-212↓ MGoat,Horse,Gorlla
133-221   MGoat,Horse,Beaver
133-222↓ Horse,Beaver,Fox
133-312↓ MGoat,Horse,Beaver
133-322↓ Horse,Beaver,Fox
141-111   Sheep,Beaver
141-331↓ Beaver,Sheep,Sable
142-111   Sheep,Beaver
142-222↓ Beaver,Sheep,Bison
142-332   Beaver,Sable
143-111↓ Sheep,Pengn,Beaver
143-311↓ Sheep,Beaver,Owl
211-111↓ Vultre,MGoat
211-211↓ MGoat,Vultre,Pcock
212-111↓ Vultre,MGoat
213-111↓ Vultre,Gorlla,MGoat
213-331↓ Vultre,MGoat,Beaver
221-111   MGoat,Vultre,Snake
221-211↓ MGoat,Vultre,Giraf
221-322↓ MGoat,Deer,Zebra
222-111↓ MGoat,Gorlla,Vultre
222-132↓ Vultre,MGoat,Beaver
222-212↓ MGoat,Vultre,Gorlla
222-222   MGoat,Vultre,Giraf
222-231↓ MGoat,Beaver,Vultre
222-322↓ MGoat,Deer,Zebra
222-332↓ MGoat,Beaver,Deer
223-111↓ Gorlla,MGoat,Vultre
223-132   Gorlla,Vultre,Fox

(322 cont'd)

223-212↓ MGoat,Gorlla,Horse	312-331 Pcock,Vultre,Deer	341-131 Pengn,Beaver,Sheep
223-231↓ MGoat,Beaver,Fox	313-111↓ Vultre,Gorlla,MGoat	341-132 Beaver,Owl,Dog
223-322↓ MGoat,Horse,Gorlla	313-211↓ MGoat,Vultre,Pcock	341-211 Sheep,Dog,Pengn
223-331↓ MGoat,Beaver,Fox	313-222 Vultre,Pcock,Horse	341-212 Dog,Sheep,Sable
231-111↓ MGoat,Vultre,Gorlla	313-231↓ Vultre,Fox,Pcock	341-221 Sheep,Dog,Beaver
231-121↓ MGoat,Sheep,Vultre	313-311↓ MGoat,Vultre,Pcock	341-222 Dog,Sheep,Sable
231-131 Beaver,Sheep,MGoat	313-322 Vultre,Pcock,Horse	341-231 Beaver,Sheep,Sable
231-132 Beaver,Vultre,Sheep	313-331↓ Vultre,Fox,Pcock	341-232 Sable,Beaver,Owl
231-222↓ MGoat,Sheep,Beaver	321-111 MGoat,Giraf	341-311 Sheep,Sable,Dog
231-332 Beaver,Sable,Sheep	321-112↓ MGoat,Giraf,Vultre	341-312 Sable,Dog,Swan
232-111 MGoat,Sheep,Gorlla	321-122 Giraf,Vultre,Pcock	341-321 Sable,Sheep,Dog
232-112 MGoat,Vultre,Gorlla	321-131 Giraf,MGoat,Vultre	341-322 Sable,Dog,Swan
232-121 MGoat,Sheep,Vultre	321-132 Giraf,Vultre,Pcock	341-331 Sable,Beaver,Sheep
232-122 Vultre,Beaver,MGoat	321-212↓ MGoat,Giraf,Pcock	341-332 Sable,Beaver,Owl
232-131 Beaver,Sheep,MGoat	321-311↓ MGoat,Deer,Zebra	342-111 Pengn,Sheep,Dog
232-132 Beaver,Vultre,Fox	321-322 Deer,Zebra,Swan	342-112 Pengn,Dog,Beaver
232-211 MGoat,Sheep,Beaver	321-331 Deer,Zebra,Giraf	342-121 Pengn,Sheep,Dog
232-212 MGoat,Beaver,Horse	321-332 Deer,Zebra,Swan	342-122 Pengn,Dog,Beaver
232-221 MGoat,Sheep,Beaver	322-111 MGoat,Giraf,Gorlla	342-131 Pengn,Beaver,Owl
232-222 Beaver,MGoat,Horse	322-112↓ MGoat,Giraf,Vultre	342-132 Beaver,Owl,Pr.Dog
232-231 Beaver,Sheep,MGoat	322-132 Giraf,Vultre,Fox	342-211 Sheep,Dog,Pengn
232-232 Beaver,Fox,Horse	322-212↓ MGoat,Giraf,Horse	342-212 Dog,Beaver,Owl
232-311 MGoat,Sheep	322-311↓ MGoat,Deer,Zebra	342-221 Sheep,Dog,Beaver
232-312 MGoat,Beaver,Horse	322-322 Deer,Zebra,Swan	342-222 Dog,Beaver,Owl
232-321 MGoat,Sheep,Beaver	322-331 Deer,Zebra,Giraf	342-231 Beaver,Owl,Sheep
232-322 Beaver,MGoat,Horse	322-332 Deer,Zebra,Swan	342-232 Beaver,Owl,Sable
232-331 Beaver,Sheep,MGoat	323-111↓ Gorlla,MGoat,Horse	342-311 Sheep,Sable,Dog
232-332 Beaver,Sable,Fox	323-121 Horse,Pengn,Gorlla	342-312 Sable,Dog,Beaver
233-111 Gorlla,MGoat,Horse	323-122 Horse,Gorlla,Fox	342-321 Sable,Sheep,Dog
233-112 Gorlla,Horse,Bat	323-131 Fox,Horse,Pengn	342-322 Sable,Dog,Beaver
233-121 Horse,Pengn,Gorlla	323-132 Fox,Horse,Gorlla	342-331↓ Sable,Beaver,Owl
233-122 Horse,Bat,Gorlla	323-211 MGoat,Horse,Gorlla	343-111 Pengn,Owl
233-131 Beaver,Fox,Horse	323-222 Horse,Fox,Giraf	343-112↓ Pengn,Owl,Pr.Dog
233-212 Horse,MGoat,Gorlla	323-312↓ Horse,MGoat,Deer	343-211 Owl,Pengn,Sheep
233-221 Horse,MGoat,Beaver	323-322 Horse,Fox,Deer	343-212↓ Owl,Pr.Dog,Pengn
233-222↓ Horse,Fox,Beaver	331-111 MGoat,Horse,Pengn	343-222↓ Owl,Pr.Dog,Beaver
233-312 Horse,MGoat,Fox	331-112 Horse,MGoat,Swan	343-311 Owl,Pengn,Sheep
233-321 Horse,MGoat,Beaver	331-121 Horse,Pengn,MGoat	343-312 Owl,Sable,Pr.Dog
233-322↓ Horse,Fox,Beaver	331-122 Horse,Swan,Giraf	343-321 Owl,Pengn,Pr.Dog
241-111 Sheep,Beaver	331-131 Horse,Pengn,Giraf	343-322 Owl,Sable,Pr.Dog
241-322↓ Sheep,Beaver,Bison	331-132 Horse,Fox,Swan	343-331 Owl,Pr.Dog,Beaver
241-331↓ Beaver,Sheep,Sable	331-211↓ MGoat,Horse,Swan	343-332 Owl,Sable,Pr.Dog
242-111 Sheep,Beaver,Pengn	331-231 Horse,Swan,Giraf	411-111↓ Pcock,Giraf
242-112 Beaver,Sheep,Bison	331-232 Swan,Horse,Fox	412-111↓ Pcock,Giraf
242-121 Sheep,Beaver,Pengn	331-322↓ Swan,Horse,Sable	412-232↓ Pcock,Giraf,W.Cat
242-122 Beaver,Sheep,Bison	332-111 MGoat,Horse,Pengn	412-311 Pcock,Deer,Giraf
242-131 Beaver,Sheep,Owl	332-112 Horse,MGoat,Swan	412-312 Pcock,Deer,Swan
242-132 Beaver,Sheep,Owl	332-121 Horse,Pengn,MGoat	412-321 Pcock,Deer,Giraf
242-312↓ Beaver,Sheep,Bison	332-122 Horse,Swan,Giraf	412-322 Pcock,Deer,Swan
242-331↓ Beaver,Sheep,Sable	332-131 Horse,Fox,Pengn	412-331 Pcock,Deer,Giraf
243-111 Pengn,Sheep,Beaver	332-132 Fox,Horse,Beaver	412-332 Pcock,Deer,Swan
243-112 Beaver,Pengn,Owl	332-211↓ MGoat,Horse,Swan	413-111↓ Pcock,Giraf,Vultre
243-121 Pengn,Beaver,Sheep	332-222 Horse,Swan,Giraf	413-222↓ Pcock,Giraf,W.Cat
243-122↓ Beaver,Owl,Pengn	332-231 Horse,Fox,Beaver	413-311 Pcock,Deer,Giraf
243-132 Beaver,Owl,Pr.Dog	332-312↓ Swan,Horse,MGoat	413-312 Pcock,Deer,Swan
243-211↓ Sheep,Beaver,Owl	332-322↓ Swan,Horse,Sable	413-321 Pcock,Deer,Giraf
243-232 Beaver,Owl,Pr.Dog	332-332 Swan,Sable,Fox	413-322 Pcock,Deer,Swan
243-311↓ Sheep,Beaver,Owl	333-111 Horse,Pengn,Gorlla	413-331 Pcock,Deer,Giraf
243-332 Beaver,Owl,Sable	333-112 Horse,Fox,Gorlla	413-332 Pcock,Deer,Swan
311-111↓ Vultre,Pcock,MGoat	333-121↓ Horse,Pengn,Fox	421-111↓ Giraf,Pcock
312-111 Vultre,MGoat	333-211 Horse,Fox,MGoat	421-211↓ Giraf,Pcock,Swan
312-211↓ MGoat,Vultre,Pcock	333-212↓ Horse,Fox,Owl	421-311↓ Swan,Deer,Giraf
312-222↓ Vultre,Pcock,Giraf	333-321↓ Horse,Fox,Swan	422-111↓ Giraf,Swan,Deer
312-311↓ MGoat,Pcock,Vultre	333-331↓ Fox,Horse,Owl	422-132↓ Giraf,W.Cat,Swan
	341-111↓ Pengn,Sheep,Dog	422-211↓ Giraf,Swan,Deer

422-232 Giraf,Swan,W.Cat
422-311↓ Swan,Deer,Giraf
423-111↓ Giraf,W.Cat
423-122↓ Giraf,W.Cat,Swan
423-211↓ Giraf,Swan,Deer
423-221↓ Giraf,W.Cat,Swan
423-311↓ Swan,Deer,Giraf
431-111↓ Swan,Giraf,Pcock
431-132 Swan,Giraf,Sable
431-211↓ Swan,Giraf,Pcock
431-231↓ Swan,Giraf,Sable
431-321↓ Swan,Deer,Sable
432-111↓ Swan,Giraf,Cottn
432-122 Swan,Giraf,W.Cat
432-131↓ Swan,Giraf,Sable
432-221↓ Swan,Giraf,Cottn
432-222↓ Swan,Giraf,Sable
432-321↓ Swan,Deer,Sable
433-111↓ Swan,Giraf,Horse
433-131↓ Swan,Giraf,Fox
433-211↓ Swan,Giraf,Horse
433-231 Swan,Giraf,Fox
433-232↓ Swan,Fox,Sable
433-321 Swan,Deer,Sable
433-332↓ Swan,Sable,Fox
441-111 Sable,Swan,Pengn
441-112 Sable,Swan,Dog
442-111↓ Sable,Pengn,Swan
442-212↓ Sable,Swan,Dog
442-231↓ Sable,Swan,Owl
443-111 Pengn,Owl
443-122↓ Owl,Sable,Pengn
443-212 Sable,Owl,Swan
443-221 Sable,Owl,Pengn
443-222 Sable,Owl,Swan
443-231↓ Sable,Owl,Pr.Dog
443-321↓ Sable,Swan,Owl

323-

111-111↓ Vultre,Pcock,MGoat
112-111↓ Vultre,MGoat
112-331↓ Vultre,Pcock,MGoat
112-332 Vultre,Pcock,Deer
113-111↓ Vultre,Gorlla,MGoat
113-312↓ Vultre,MGoat,Pcock
113-322 Vultre,Pcock,Deer
113-331 Vultre,MGoat,Pcock
113-332 Vultre,Pcock,Fox
121-111 MGoat,Porcp,Mole
121-112 Porcp,MGoat,Vultre
121-121 Porcp,Mole,MGoat
121-122 Porcp,Vultre,Mole
121-131 Porcp,Mole,MGoat
121-132 Porcp,Vultre,Mole
121-211↓ MGoat,Sheep
121-222 MGoat,Porcp,Pcock
121-231 MGoat,Sheep,Porcp
121-232↓ Porcp,Pcock,MGoat
121-321↓ MGoat,Deer,Sheep
121-322 Deer,MGoat,Pcock
121-331 MGoat,Deer,Sheep
121-332 Deer,Pcock,MGoat
122-111 MGoat,Porcp,Mole
122-112 Porcp,MGoat,Vultre
122-121 Porcp,Mole,MGoat

122-122 Porcp,Vultre,Mole
122-131 Porcp,Mole,MGoat
122-132 Porcp,Vultre,Mole
122-211↓ MGoat,Sheep
122-222 MGoat,Porcp,Vultre
122-231 MGoat,Sheep,Porcp
122-232↓ Porcp,MGoat,Beaver
122-321↓ MGoat,Deer,Sheep
122-322 Deer,MGoat,Porcp
122-331 MGoat,Deer,Sheep
122-332 Deer,MGoat,Beaver
123-111↓ Gorlla,MGoat,Porcp
123-121 Porcp,Mole,Gorlla
123-122 Porcp,Gorlla,Vultre
123-131 Porcp,Mole,Gorlla
123-132 Porcp,Fox,Gorlla
123-211↓ MGoat,Gorlla,Horse
123-221 MGoat,Horse,Sheep
123-222↓ Horse,MGoat,Fox
123-232 Fox,Horse,Beaver
123-311↓ MGoat,Horse,Gorlla
123-321↓ MGoat,Horse,Deer
123-331 MGoat,Fox,Horse
123-332 Fox,Horse,Deer
131-111 MGoat,Sheep,Walrus
131-112 Porcp,MGoat,Sheep
131-121 Sheep,Walrus,Porcp
131-122 Porcp,Sheep,Vultre
131-131 Sheep,Walrus,Porcp
131-132 Porcp,Sheep,Beaver
131-212↓ MGoat,Sheep,Bison
131-222 Sheep,Bison,Horse
131-232↓ Sheep,Beaver,Bison
131-312↓ MGoat,Sheep,Bison
131-322 Sheep,Bison,Deer
131-331 Sheep,Beaver,MGoat
131-332 Sheep,Beaver,Bison
132-111 MGoat,Sheep,Walrus
132-112 Porcp,MGoat,Sheep
132-121 Sheep,Walrus,Porcp
132-122 Porcp,Sheep,Vultre
132-131 Sheep,Beaver,Walrus
132-132 Beaver,Porcp,Sheep
132-212↓ MGoat,Sheep,Horse
132-222 Sheep,Horse,Bison
132-232↓ Beaver,Sheep,Fox
132-312↓ MGoat,Sheep,Horse
132-322 Sheep,Horse,Bison
132-332↓ Beaver,Sheep,Fox
133-111 Horse,Gorlla,MGoat
133-112 Horse,Gorlla,Fox
133-121 Horse,Sheep,Fox
133-122 Horse,Fox,Bat
133-131↓ Fox,Horse,Beaver
133-211 Horse,MGoat,Sheep
133-212 Horse,Fox,MGoat
133-231↓ Fox,Horse,Beaver
133-311 Horse,MGoat,Sheep
133-312 Horse,Fox,MGoat
133-331↓ Fox,Horse,Beaver
141-111↓ Sheep,Bison
141-332↓ Sheep,Beaver,Bison
142-111↓ Sheep,Bison,Beaver
143-111 Sheep,Owl
143-112↓ Sheep,Owl,Bison

143-121↓ Sheep,Owl,Beaver
143-212↓ Sheep,Owl,Bison
143-321 Sheep,Owl,Beaver
211-111↓ Vultre,Pcock,MGoat
212-111↓ Vultre,MGoat
212-311↓ MGoat,Vultre,Pcock
212-322 Vultre,Pcock,Deer
212-331 Vultre,Pcock,MGoat
212-332 Vultre,Pcock,Deer
213-111↓ Vultre,Gorlla,MGoat
213-312↓ Vultre,MGoat,Pcock
213-322 Vultre,Pcock,Horse
213-331 Vultre,MGoat,Fox
213-332 Vultre,Fox,Pcock
221-111↓ MGoat,Vultre,Gorlla
221-121 MGoat,Vultre,Sheep
221-122 Vultre,MGoat,Pcock
221-131 MGoat,Vultre,Sheep
221-221↓ MGoat,Sheep,Pcock
221-222 MGoat,Pcock,Vultre
221-231 MGoat,Sheep,Pcock
221-232↓ Pcock,MGoat,Vultre
221-321↓ MGoat,Deer,Sheep
221-322 Deer,MGoat,Pcock
221-331 MGoat,Deer,Sheep
221-332 Deer,Pcock,MGoat
222-111↓ MGoat,Gorlla,Vultre
222-121 MGoat,Vultre,Sheep
222-122 Vultre,MGoat,Gorlla
222-131 MGoat,Vultre,Sheep
222-132↓ Vultre,MGoat,Beaver
222-212 MGoat,Vultre,Horse
222-221 MGoat,Sheep,Horse
222-222 MGoat,Vultre,Horse
222-231 MGoat,Sheep,Beaver
222-232 MGoat,Beaver,Fox
222-321↓ MGoat,Deer,Sheep
222-322 Deer,MGoat,Horse
222-331 MGoat,Deer,Sheep
222-332 Deer,MGoat,Beaver
223-111 Gorlla,MGoat
223-112↓ Gorlla,MGoat,Horse
223-122 Gorlla,Horse,Vultre
223-131↓ Fox,Horse,Gorlla
223-211↓ MGoat,Horse,Gorlla
223-221 MGoat,Horse,Sheep
223-222↓ Horse,Fox,MGoat
223-312 MGoat,Horse,Gorlla
223-321 MGoat,Horse,Deer
223-322 Horse,Fox,Deer
223-331↓ Fox,Horse,MGoat
231-111 MGoat,Sheep,Walrus
231-112 MGoat,Sheep,Vultre
231-121 Sheep,Walrus,MGoat
231-122 Sheep,Vultre,Horse
231-131 Sheep,Walrus,Beaver
231-132 Sheep,Beaver,Vultre
231-212↓ MGoat,Sheep,Horse
231-222 Sheep,Beaver,Horse
231-312↓ MGoat,Sheep,Horse
231-322 Sheep,Horse,Bison
231-332↓ Sheep,Beaver,Horse
232-111 MGoat,Sheep,Walrus
232-112 MGoat,Horse,Sheep
232-121 Sheep,Walrus,Horse

(323 cont'd)

232-122	Horse,Sheep,Vultre
232-131	Sheep,Beaver,Walrus
232-132	Beaver,Fox,Horse
232-211↓	MGoat,Sheep,Horse
232-222	Horse,Sheep,Bison
232-231	Sheep,Beaver,Horse
232-232	Beaver,Fox,Horse
232-311↓	MGoat,Sheep,Horse
232-322	Horse,Sheep,Bison
232-331	Sheep,Beaver,Horse
232-332	Beaver,Fox,Horse
233-111	Horse,Gorlla,MGoat
233-112	Horse,Gorlla,Fox
233-121	Horse,Sheep,Fox
233-122	Horse,Fox,Bat
233-131↓	Fox,Horse,Owl
233-211	Horse,MGoat,Sheep
233-212	Horse,Fox,MGoat
233-221↓	Horse,Sheep,Fox
233-322	Horse,Fox,Owl
241-111↓	Sheep,Bison,Dog
241-132↓	Sheep,Beaver,Bison
241-211↓	Sheep,Bison,Dog
241-231↓	Sheep,Beaver,Bison
241-322↓	Sheep,Bison,Dog
241-332↓	Sheep,Beaver,Bison
242-111↓	Sheep,Bison,Beaver
242-131↓	Sheep,Beaver,Owl
243-111	Sheep,Owl,Pengn
243-112	Owl,Sheep,Bison
243-121	Sheep,Owl,Pengn
243-122↓	Owl,Sheep,Beaver
243-132	Owl,Beaver,Pr.Dog
243-211	Sheep,Owl,Beaver
243-212	Owl,Sheep,Bison
243-221	Sheep,Owl,Beaver
243-232	Owl,Beaver,Pr.Dog
243-312↓	Owl,Sheep,Bison
243-321	Sheep,Owl,Beaver
243-332	Owl,Beaver,Pr.Dog
311-111↓	Pcock,Vultre
312-111↓	Vultre,Pcock,MGoat
312-322↓	Pcock,Deer,Vultre
313-111↓	Vultre,Pcock,Horse
313-131↓	Vultre,Fox,Pcock
313-211	Pcock,Horse,MGoat
313-212↓	Pcock,Horse,Vultre
313-231↓	Fox,Pcock,Horse
313-311↓	Pcock,Horse,Deer
313-331↓	Fox,Pcock,Horse
321-111↓	MGoat,Pcock,Giraf
321-132	Pcock,Giraf,Vultre
321-212↓	Pcock,MGoat,Giraf
321-222↓	Pcock,Giraf,Deer
321-311	Deer,MGoat,Pcock
321-322↓	Deer,Pcock,Zebra
322-111↓	MGoat,Horse,Giraf
322-131	Horse,Fox,Giraf
322-221	Horse,MGoat,Giraf
322-222	Horse,Giraf,Deer
322-231	Horse,Fox,Giraf
322-321	Deer,Horse,MGoat
322-332↓	Deer,Fox,Horse
323-111	Horse,Gorlla,MGoat

323-132↓	Fox,Horse,Pr.Dog
323-211↓	Horse,MGoat,Fox
323-222	Horse,Fox,Giraf
323-231↓	Fox,Horse,Pr.Dog
323-311	Horse,Deer,MGoat
323-312↓	Horse,Deer,Fox
331-111	Horse,MGoat,Sheep
331-112	Horse,Dog,Pcock
331-121	Horse,Sheep,Dog
331-122	Horse,Dog,Pcock
331-131	Horse,Fox,Sheep
331-132	Horse,Fox,Dog
331-211	Horse,MGoat,Sheep
331-212	Horse,Dog,Pcock
331-221	Horse,Sheep,Dog
331-222	Horse,Dog,Pcock
331-231	Horse,Fox,Sheep
331-232	Horse,Fox,Dog
331-311	Horse,Swan,Deer
331-332	Swan,Horse,Fox
332-111	Horse,MGoat,Sheep
332-112	Horse,Fox,Dog
332-121	Horse,Sheep,Fox
332-122	Horse,Fox,Dog
332-131	Horse,Fox,Owl
332-212	Horse,Fox,Dog
332-221	Horse,Sheep,Fox
332-222	Horse,Fox,Dog
332-231	Horse,Fox,Owl
332-331	Horse,Fox,Swan
333-111	Horse,Fox,Pengn
333-112	Horse,Fox,Owl
333-121	Horse,Fox,Pengn
333-122	Horse,Fox,Owl
333-312	Horse,Fox,Swan
333-321↓	Horse,Fox,Owl
341-111	Sheep,Dog,Pengn
341-112	Dog,Sheep,Bison
341-121	Sheep,Dog,Pengn
341-122↓	Dog,Sheep,Owl
341-132	Owl,Dog,Pr.Dog
341-212↓	Dog,Sheep,Bison
341-221	Sheep,Dog,Owl
341-232	Owl,Dog,Pr.Dog
341-312↓	Dog,Sheep,Sable
341-331	Sheep,Sable,Owl
341-332	Sable,Owl,Dog
342-111	Sheep,Dog,Pengn
342-112	Dog,Owl,Sheep
342-121	Sheep,Dog,Pengn
342-122	Dog,Owl,Sheep
342-131	Owl,Sheep,Pr.Dog
342-132	Owl,Pr.Dog,Dog
342-211↓	Sheep,Dog,Owl
342-231	Owl,Sheep,Pr.Dog
342-232	Owl,Pr.Dog,Dog
342-311↓	Sheep,Dog,Owl
342-322	Dog,Owl,Sable
342-331	Owl,Sheep,Sable
342-332	Owl,Sable,Pr.Dog
343-111	Owl,Pengn,Sheep
343-112↓	Owl,Pengn,Pr.Dog
343-211↓	Owl,Sheep,Pr.Dog
343-212	Owl,Pr.Dog,Horse
343-221↓	Owl,Pr.Dog,Sheep

343-312	Owl,Pr.Dog,Horse
343-321	Owl,Pr.Dog,Sheep
343-322↓	Owl,Pr.Dog,Horse
411-111↓	Pcock,Deer
412-111↓	Pcock,Giraf
413-111↓	Pcock,Giraf,Deer
413-311↓	Pcock,Deer,Dolphin
421-111↓	Pcock,Giraf,Deer
421-311↓	Deer,Pcock,Swan
422-111↓	Giraf,Deer,Pcock
422-311↓	Deer,Swan,Giraf
423-111↓	Giraf,Deer,Horse
423-122	Giraf,Deer,W.Cat
423-131	Giraf,Deer,Fox
423-132	Giraf,Fox,W.Cat
423-211↓	Giraf,Deer,Dolphin
423-231↓	Giraf,Deer,Fox
423-311↓	Deer,Dolphin,Swan
431-111	Pcock,Cottn,Swan
431-112	Pcock,Swan,Giraf
431-121	Pcock,Cottn,Swan
431-122	Pcock,Swan,Giraf
431-131	Pcock,Cottn,Swan
431-132	Pcock,Swan,Giraf
431-211	Pcock,Swan,Cottn
431-212	Swan,Pcock,Giraf
431-221	Pcock,Swan,Cottn
431-222	Pcock,Swan,Giraf
431-231	Pcock,Swan,Cottn
431-232	Swan,Pcock,Sable
431-312↓	Swan,Deer,Pcock
431-331↓	Swan,Deer,Sable
432-111	Cottn,Swan,Giraf
432-112	Swan,Giraf,Deer
432-121	Cottn,Swan,Giraf
432-122	Swan,Giraf,Deer
432-131	Cottn,Swan,Giraf
432-132	Swan,Giraf,Sable
432-211	Swan,Cottn,Giraf
432-212	Swan,Giraf,Deer
432-221	Swan,Cottn,Giraf
432-222	Swan,Giraf,Deer
432-231	Swan,Cottn,Giraf
432-232	Swan,Sable,Giraf
432-331↓	Swan,Deer,Sable
433-111	Horse,Cottn,Swan
433-112	Horse,Swan,Fox
433-121	Horse,Cottn,Swan
433-122	Horse,Swan,Fox
433-131	Fox,Horse,Owl
433-132	Fox,Horse,Swan
433-211	Horse,Swan,Cottn
433-212	Swan,Horse,Fox
433-221	Horse,Swan,Cottn
433-222↓	Swan,Horse,Fox
433-311↓	Swan,Deer,Horse
433-331	Swan,Deer,Fox
433-332	Swan,Fox,Sable
441-111	Dog,Pcock,Sheep
441-112↓	Sable,Dog,Pcock
441-131↓	Sable,Owl,Dog
441-211	Sable,Dog,Pcock
441-212	Sable,Swan,Dog
441-221	Sable,Dog,Pcock
441-222↓	Sable,Swan,Dog

442-111	Dog,Sheep,Sable
442-112	Sable,Dog,Swan
442-121	Sable,Dog,Sheep
442-122	Sable,Dog,Owl
442-131↓	Sable,Owl,Pr.Dog
442-211	Sable,Dog,Sheep
442-212	Sable,Swan,Dog
442-221	Sable,Dog,Sheep
442-222	Sable,Swan,Dog
442-231	Sable,Owl,Pr.Dog
442-322↓	Sable,Swan,Dog
442-331↓	Sable,Swan,Owl
443-111↓	Owl,Pengn,Pr.Dog
443-132↓	Owl,Pr.Dog,Sable
443-311↓	Sable,Owl,Swan
443-331↓	Sable,Owl,Pr.Dog

324-

111-111↓	Vultre,Pcock,MGoat
112-111↓	Vultre,MGoat
112-311↓	MGoat,Vultre,Pcock
112-322	Vultre,Pcock,Deer
112-331	Vultre,Pcock,MGoat
112-332	Vultre,Pcock,Eagle
113-111↓	Vultre,MGoat,Gorlla
113-211↓	MGoat,Horse,Vultre
113-231	Horse,Vultre,Baboon
113-312↓	Horse,Dolphin,Vultre
113-331	Horse,Dolphin,Baboon
113-332	Horse,Dolphin,Vultre
121-111↓	MGoat,Walrus,Porcp
121-121	Walrus,Porcp,Mole
121-122	Porcp,Walrus,Vultre
121-131	Walrus,Porcp,Mole
121-132	Porcp,Walrus,Vultre
121-221↓	MGoat,Horse,Sheep
121-222	Horse,MGoat,Porcp
121-231	MGoat,Horse,Sheep
121-232	Horse,Porcp,Pcock
121-311↓	MGoat,Deer,Horse
121-332	Eagle,Deer,Horse
122-111	MGoat,Walrus,Porcp
122-112	Porcp,MGoat,Horse
122-121	Walrus,Porcp,Mole
122-122	Porcp,Horse,Walrus
122-131	Walrus,Porcp,Mole
122-132	Porcp,Horse,Walrus
122-221↓	MGoat,Horse,Sheep
122-222	Horse,MGoat,Porcp
122-231	MGoat,Horse,Sheep
122-232	Horse,Baboon,Porcp
122-311↓	MGoat,Horse,Deer
122-322	Horse,Deer,Dolphin
122-331	MGoat,Horse,Deer
122-332	Horse,Eagle,Deer
123-111	Horse,MGoat,Gorlla
123-112	Horse,Gorlla,Porcp
123-121↓	Horse,Walrus,Porcp
123-131	Horse,Baboon,Walrus
123-132	Horse,Baboon,Porcp
123-211↓	Horse,MGoat
123-232↓	Horse,Baboon,Pr.Dog
123-331	Horse,MGoat,Dolphin
123-331↓	Horse,Baboon,Dolphin
131-111	Walrus,MGoat,Horse

131-122↓	Walrus,Horse,Dog
131-131	Walrus,Horse,Sheep
131-132	Walrus,Horse,Baboon
131-211	MGoat,Horse,Sheep
131-212	Horse,Dog,MGoat
131-221	Horse,Sheep,Walrus
131-222	Horse,Dog,Sheep
131-231	Horse,Sheep,Walrus
131-232	Horse,Baboon,Dog
131-311	MGoat,Horse,Sheep
131-312	Horse,Dog,MGoat
131-321	Horse,Sheep,Walrus
131-322	Horse,Dog,Sheep
131-331	Horse,Sheep,Baboon
131-332	Horse,Baboon,Dog
132-111↓	Walrus,Horse,MGoat
132-211	Horse,MGoat,Sheep
132-212	Horse,Dog
132-221↓	Horse,Sheep,Walrus
132-231	Horse,Sheep,Baboon
132-232	Horse,Baboon,Pr.Dog
132-311↓	Horse,MGoat,Sheep
132-322	Horse,Dog
132-331↓	Horse,Sheep,Baboon
133-111↓	Horse,Walrus
133-232↓	Horse,Baboon,Pr.Dog
141-111	Sheep,Dog
141-122↓	Dog,Sheep,Bison
141-131	Sheep,Dog,Pr.Dog
141-222↓	Dog,Sheep,Bison
141-231	Sheep,Dog,Pr.Dog
141-322↓	Dog,Sheep,Bison
141-331↓	Sheep,Dog,Pr.Dog
142-111	Sheep,Dog
142-122↓	Dog,Sheep,Bison
142-131	Sheep,Pr.Dog,Dog
142-132	Pr.Dog,Dog,Beaver
142-222↓	Dog,Sheep,Bison
142-231	Sheep,Pr.Dog,Dog
142-232	Pr.Dog,Dog,Beaver
142-322↓	Dog,Sheep,Bison
142-331	Sheep,Pr.Dog,Dog
142-332	Pr.Dog,Dog,Beaver
143-111	Sheep,Pr.Dog,Horse
143-112	Pr.Dog,Horse,Dog
143-121	Sheep,Pr.Dog,Horse
143-122	Pr.Dog,Horse,Dog
143-131	Pr.Dog,Owl,Sheep
143-132	Pr.Dog,Owl,Beaver
143-211	Sheep,Pr.Dog,Horse
143-212	Pr.Dog,Horse,Dog
143-221	Sheep,Pr.Dog,Horse
143-222	Pr.Dog,Horse,Dog
143-231	Pr.Dog,Owl,Sheep
143-232	Pr.Dog,Owl,Beaver
143-311	Sheep,Pr.Dog,Horse
143-312	Pr.Dog,Horse,Dog
143-321	Sheep,Pr.Dog,Horse
143-322	Pr.Dog,Horse,Dog
143-331	Pr.Dog,Owl,Sheep
143-332	Pr.Dog,Owl,W.Dog
211-111↓	Vultre,Pcock,MGoat
212-111↓	Vultre,MGoat
212-211↓	MGoat,Vultre,Pcock
212-222	Vultre,Pcock,Horse

212-231	Vultre,Pcock,MGoat
212-232	Vultre,Pcock,Horse
212-311	MGoat,Vultre,Pcock
212-322	Vultre,Pcock,Horse
212-331	Vultre,Pcock,MGoat
212-332	Vultre,Pcock,Eagle
213-111↓	Vultre,Horse,MGoat
213-231↓	Horse,Vultre,Pr.Dog
213-311	Horse,MGoat,Dolphin
213-322↓	Horse,Dolphin,Vultre
213-331↓	Horse,Pr.Dog,Dolphin
221-111	MGoat,Walrus
221-112↓	MGoat,Horse,Walrus
221-122	Horse,Walrus,Vultre
221-131	Walrus,MGoat,Horse
221-132	Horse,Walrus,Vultre
221-221↓	MGoat,Horse,Sheep
221-222	Horse,MGoat,Dog
221-231	MGoat,Horse,Sheep
221-232	Horse,Dog,Pcock
221-311↓	MGoat,Horse,Deer
221-331	MGoat,Horse,Eagle
221-332	Eagle,Horse,Deer
222-111↓	MGoat,Walrus,Horse
222-122	Horse,Walrus,Vultre
222-131	Walrus,Horse,MGoat
222-132	Horse,Walrus,Vultre
222-212↓	MGoat,Horse,Dog
222-221	Horse,MGoat,Sheep
222-222	Horse,MGoat,Dog
222-231	Horse,MGoat,Sheep
222-232	Horse,Baboon,Pr.Dog
222-312↓	MGoat,Horse,Deer
222-331	Horse,MGoat,Eagle
222-332	Horse,Eagle,Deer
223-111↓	Horse,MGoat,Gorlla
223-131↓	Horse,Baboon,Pr.Dog
223-211↓	Horse,MGoat
223-231↓	Horse,Baboon,Pr.Dog
223-311↓	Horse,MGoat,Dolphin
223-331	Horse,Baboon,Pr.Dog
223-332	Horse,Dolphin,Baboon
231-111	Walrus,Horse,MGoat
231-112	Horse,Walrus,Dog
231-121	Walrus,Horse,Sheep
231-122	Horse,Walrus,Dog
231-131	Walrus,Horse,Sheep
231-132	Horse,Walrus,Dog
231-211	Horse,MGoat,Sheep
231-212	Horse,Dog
231-221	Horse,Sheep,Walrus
231-222	Horse,Dog,Sheep
231-231	Horse,Sheep,Walrus
231-232	Horse,Dog,Baboon
231-311	Horse,MGoat,Sheep
231-331↓	Horse,Sheep,Dog
231-332	Horse,Dog,Baboon
232-111	Walrus,Horse,MGoat
232-112	Horse,Walrus,Dog
232-121	Walrus,Horse,Sheep
232-122	Horse,Walrus,Dog
232-131	Walrus,Horse,Sheep
232-132	Horse,Walrus,Baboon
232-211	Horse,MGoat,Sheep
232-212	Horse,Dog,MGoat

(324 cont'd)

232-221 Horse,Sheep,Walrus
232-222 Horse,Dog,Sheep
232-231 Horse,Sheep,Baboon
232-232 Horse,Baboon,Pr.Dog
232-311 Horse,MGoat,Sheep
232-321↓ Horse,Sheep,Dog
232-331 Horse,Sheep,Baboon
232-332 Horse,Baboon,Pr.Dog
233-111↓ Horse,Walrus
233-131↓ Horse,Baboon,Pr.Dog
241-111 Sheep,Dog
241-122↓ Dog,Sheep,Bison
241-131 Sheep,Dog,Pr.Dog
241-222↓ Dog,Sheep,Bison
241-231 Sheep,Dog,Pr.Dog
241-322↓ Dog,Sheep,Bison
241-331↓ Sheep,Dog,Pr.Dog
242-111 Sheep,Dog
242-112↓ Dog,Sheep,Bison
242-121 Sheep,Dog,Pr.Dog
242-132 Pr.Dog,Dog,Beaver
242-211 Sheep,Dog,Pr.Dog
242-212 Dog,Sheep,Bison
242-221 Sheep,Dog,Pr.Dog
242-232 Pr.Dog,Dog,Beaver
242-312↓ Dog,Sheep,Bison
242-321 Sheep,Dog,Pr.Dog
242-332 Pr.Dog,Dog,Beaver
243-111 Sheep,Pr.Dog,Horse
243-112 Pr.Dog,Horse,Dog
243-121 Pr.Dog,Sheep,Horse
243-122 Pr.Dog,Horse,Dog
243-131 Pr.Dog,Owl,Sheep
243-132 Pr.Dog,Owl,Horse
243-211 Sheep,Pr.Dog,Horse
243-212 Pr.Dog,Horse,Dog
243-221 Pr.Dog,Sheep,Horse
243-222 Pr.Dog,Horse,Dog
243-231 Pr.Dog,Owl,Sheep
243-232 Pr.Dog,Owl,Horse
243-311 Sheep,Pr.Dog,Horse
243-312 Pr.Dog,Horse,Dog
243-321 Pr.Dog,Sheep,Horse
243-322 Pr.Dog,Horse,Dog
243-331 Pr.Dog,Owl,Sheep
243-332 Pr.Dog,Owl,W.Dog
311-111↓ Pcock,Vultre
312-111↓ Vultre,Pcock,Horse
312-211 Pcock,Horse,MGoat
312-212 Pcock,Horse,Vultre
312-221 Pcock,Horse,Dog
312-222 Pcock,Horse,Vultre
312-231 Pcock,Horse,Pr.Dog
312-232 Pcock,Horse,Vultre
312-311↓ Pcock,Horse,Deer
312-331↓ Pcock,Horse,Eagle
313-111↓ Horse,Vultre
313-232↓ Horse,Pr.Dog,Fox
313-331↓ Horse,Pr.Dog,Dolphin
321-111 Horse,MGoat,Dog
321-112↓ Horse,Dog,Pcock
321-211 Horse,MGoat,Dog
321-212↓ Horse,Dog,Pcock
321-311 Horse,Deer,MGoat

321-312↓ Horse,Deer,SeaLn
321-331 Horse,Eagle,Deer
322-111↓ Horse,MGoat,Dog
322-131↓ Horse,Pr.Dog,Dog
322-211 Horse,MGoat,Dog
322-231↓ Horse,Pr.Dog,Dog
322-311 Horse,Deer,MGoat
322-312 Horse,Deer,Dolphin
322-321 Horse,Deer,SeaLn
322-322 Horse,Deer,Dolphin
322-331↓ Horse,Eagle,Deer
323-111↓ Horse,Pr.Dog,Fox
323-331↓ Horse,Pr.Dog,Dolphin
331-111↓ Horse,Dog
331-332↓ Horse,Dog,Pr.Dog
332-111↓ Horse,Dog,Walrus
332-331↓ Horse,Pr.Dog,Dog
333-111↓ Horse,Pr.Dog,Fox
341-111↓ Dog,Pr.Dog,Horse
341-221 Dog,Pr.Dog,Sheep
341-232↓ Dog,Pr.Dog,Owl
342-111↓ Dog,Pr.Dog,Horse
342-131↓ Pr.Dog,Dog,Owl
342-211↓ Dog,Pr.Dog,Horse
342-231↓ Pr.Dog,Dog,Owl
342-311↓ Dog,Pr.Dog,Horse
342-331↓ Pr.Dog,Dog,Owl
343-111↓ Pr.Dog,Horse,Dog
343-131↓ Pr.Dog,Owl,Horse
343-211↓ Pr.Dog,Horse,Dog
343-231↓ Pr.Dog,Owl,Horse
343-311↓ Pr.Dog,Horse,Dog
343-331↓ Pr.Dog,Owl,Horse
411-111↓ Peacock
412-111↓ Peacock
412-222↓ Pcock,Deer,Dolphin
412-311 Pcock,Deer,SeaLn
412-312 Pcock,Deer,Dolphin
412-321 Pcock,Deer,SeaLn
412-322 Pcock,Deer,Dolphin
412-331 Pcock,Deer,SeaLn
412-332 Pcock,Deer,Dolphin
413-111↓ Pcock,Dolphin,Horse
413-331↓ Dolphin,Pcock,Deer
421-111 Pcock,Giraf
421-132↓ Pcock,Giraf,Deer
421-311↓ Deer,SeaLn,Pcock
422-111↓ Giraf,Deer,Horse
422-211 Deer,Giraf,SeaLn
422-212 Deer,Dolphin,Giraf
422-221 Deer,Giraf,SeaLn
422-222 Deer,Dolphin,Giraf
422-231 Deer,Giraf,SeaLn
422-232 Deer,Dolphin,Giraf
422-311↓ Deer,SeaLn,Dolphin
423-111↓ Horse,Dolphin,Giraf
423-332↓ Dolphin,Deer,SeaLn
431-111 Pcock,Horse,Cottn
431-112 Pcock,Horse,Swan
431-121 Pcock,Horse,Cottn
431-122 Pcock,Horse,Swan
431-131 Pcock,Horse,Cottn
431-132↓ Pcock,Horse,Swan
431-311↓ Swan,Deer,SeaLn
431-332 Swan,Deer,Sable

432-111 Horse,Cottn,Dog
432-112 Horse,Swan
432-121 Horse,Cottn
432-122 Horse,Swan,Dog
432-131 Horse,Cottn,Pr.Dog
432-211↓ Horse,Swan,Cottn
432-212 Horse,Swan,Dog
432-221 Horse,Swan,Cottn
432-222 Horse,Swan,Dog
432-231 Horse,Swan,Cottn
432-232 Horse,Swan,Pr.Dog
432-311↓ Swan,Deer,Horse
433-111↓ Horse,Dolphin
433-132↓ Horse,Pr.Dog,Fox
433-222↓ Horse,Dolphin,Swan
433-231↓ Horse,Pr.Dog,Fox
433-311↓ Horse,Dolphin,Swan
441-111↓ Dog,Pr.Dog,Sable
441-311↓ Dog,Sable,Swan
442-111↓ Dog,Pr.Dog
442-222↓ Dog,Pr.Dog,Sable
442-322 Sable,Dog,Swan
442-331↓ Sable,Pr.Dog,Dog
443-111↓ Pr.Dog,Horse,Dog
443-131↓ Pr.Dog,Owl
443-211↓ Pr.Dog,Horse,Dog
443-231↓ Pr.Dog,Owl,Horse
443-311↓ Pr.Dog,Horse,Dog
443-322 Pr.Dog,Sable,Horse
443-331↓ Pr.Dog,Owl,Sable

331-

111-111↓ Vultre,Porcp
112-111↓ Vultre,Porcp
113-111↓ Vultre,Porcp,Gorlla
113-311↓ Croc,Vultre,Porcp
121-111↓ Porcp,MGoat
122-111↓ Porcp,MGoat
123-111↓ Porcp,Gorlla
123-211↓ Porcp,MGoat,Gorlla
123-212↓ Porcp,Gorlla,Warthg
123-311 Porcp,MGoat,Gorlla
123-312 Porcp,Gorlla,Warthg
123-321↓ Porcp,MGoat,Warthg
131-111↓ Porcp,MGoat
131-331↓ Porcp,Sable
132-111↓ Porcp,MGoat
132-331↓ Porcp,Sable
133-111↓ Porcp,Gorlla
133-211↓ Porcp,MGoat,Gorlla
133-231↓ Porcp,Fox,Baboon
133-311↓ Porcp,MGoat,Gorlla
133-312 Porcp,Gorlla,Warthg
133-321 Porcp,MGoat,Warthg
133-322 Porcp,Warthg,Fox
133-331 Porcp,Fox,Baboon
133-332 Fox,Porcp,Sable
141-111↓ Porcp,Bison,Pengn
141-132↓ Porcp,Bison,Sable
142-111↓ Porcp,Pengn,Bison
142-132 Porcp,Bison,Owl
142-221↓ Bison,Porcp,Pengn
142-222 Bison,Porcp,Sable
142-231↓ Bison,Sable,Owl
142-311↓ Bison,Sable,Porcp

143-111	Pengn,Porcp
143-112↓	Porcp,Pengn,Owl
143-211	Pengn,Owl,Bison
143-212	Owl,Bison,Porcp
143-311↓	Owl,Pengn,Bison
143-312	Owl,Bison,Sable
143-321	Owl,Sable,Pengn
143-322↓	Owl,Sable,Bison
211-111↓	Vultre,MGoat
212-111↓	Vultre,MGoat
213-111↓	Vultre,Gorlla
213-211↓	Vultre,MGoat,Gorlla
221-111↓	MGoat,Vultre,Porcp
221-332↓	Zebra,Vultre,MGoat
222-111	MGoat,Gorlla,Vultre
222-112	Vultre,Gorlla,Porcp
222-121	Vultre,Porcp,MGoat
222-122	Vultre,Porcp,Gorlla
222-131	Vultre,Porcp,MGoat
222-132	Vultre,Porcp,Gorlla
222-212↓	MGoat,Vultre,Gorlla
222-221↓	MGoat,Vultre,Porcp
222-312↓	MGoat,Zebra,Vultre
223-111	Gorlla,MGoat,Vultre
223-112↓	Gorlla,Vultre,Porcp
223-212↓	Gorlla,MGoat,Vultre
223-231	MGoat,Fox,Gorlla
223-232	Fox,Gorlla,Vultre
223-312↓	Gorlla,MGoat,Zebra
223-331	MGoat,Fox,Zebra
223-332	Fox,Zebra,Gorlla
231-111↓	MGoat,Vultre,Porcp
231-131↓	Vultre,Porcp,Hippo
231-211↓	MGoat,Vultre,Bison
231-231	MGoat,Vultre,Porcp
231-232	Vultre,Bison,Sable
231-311↓	MGoat,Zebra,Bison
231-321↓	MGoat,Zebra,Sable
232-111	MGoat,Gorlla,Vultre
232-112	Vultre,Gorlla,Porcp
232-121	Vultre,Porcp,Hippo
232-122	Vultre,Porcp,Gorlla
232-131	Vultre,Porcp,Hippo
232-132	Vultre,Porcp,Fox
232-212↓	MGoat,Vultre,Gorlla
232-221	MGoat,Vultre,Porcp
232-222	Vultre,MGoat,Bison
232-231	MGoat,Fox,Vultre
232-232	Fox,Vultre,Bison
232-322↓	Zebra,Sable,MGoat
232-332	Sable,Fox,Zebra
233-111	Gorlla,Pengn,MGoat
233-112	Gorlla,Vultre,Horse
233-121	Pengn,Gorlla,Vultre
233-122	Gorlla,Vultre,Fox
233-131	Fox,Pengn,Gorlla
233-132	Fox,Gorlla,Vultre
233-211	MGoat,Gorlla,Horse
233-212	Gorlla,Horse,Fox
233-221	Horse,Fox,MGoat
233-222	Fox,Horse,Gorlla
233-231↓	Fox,Owl,Horse
233-311	MGoat,Horse,Gorlla
233-312	Horse,Gorlla,Fox
233-321	Horse,Fox,MGoat

233-322↓	Fox,Horse,Owl
233-332	Fox,Owl,Sable
241-111	Pengn,Bison
241-122↓	Bison,Pengn,Vultre
241-131	Pengn,Bison,Owl
241-132	Bison,Sable,Owl
241-211↓	Bison,MGoat,Pengn
241-231↓	Bison,Sable,Owl
241-311↓	Bison,Sable,MGoat
242-111	Pengn,Bison
242-122↓	Bison,Pengn,Owl
242-211	Bison,Pengn,MGoat
242-212	Bison,Owl,Sable
242-221	Bison,Pengn,Owl
242-332↓	Sable,Owl,Bison
243-111	Pengn,Owl
243-132↓	Owl,Pengn,Beaver
243-211↓	Pengn,Owl,Bison
243-231	Owl,Pengn,Beaver
243-232	Owl,Beaver,Bison
243-311	Owl,Pengn,Bison
243-312	Owl,Bison,Sable
243-321	Owl,Pengn,Sable
243-332↓	Owl,Sable,W.Dog
311-111↓	Vultre,Pcock
311-311↓	Pcock,Zebra,Vultre
312-111↓	Vultre,MGoat,Weasel
312-222↓	Vultre,Weasel,Pcock
312-311	Zebra,Vultre,MGoat
312-312	Vultre,Zebra,Weasel
313-111↓	Vultre,Gorlla
313-231↓	Vultre,Fox,Weasel
313-311	Zebra,Vultre,MGoat
313-312	Vultre,Zebra,Weasel
313-331	Zebra,Vultre,Fox
321-111↓	MGoat,Vultre,Porcp
321-132	Vultre,Porcp,Rooster
321-222↓	Zebra,Vultre,MGoat
321-231	Zebra,MGoat,Rooster
321-232	Zebra,Rooster,Vultre
321-311↓	Zebra,MGoat
321-332	Zebra,Sable
322-111	MGoat,Gorlla,Vultre
322-112	Vultre,Gorlla,Porcp
322-121	Vultre,Porcp,MGoat
322-122	Vultre,Porcp,Gorlla
322-131	Vultre,Porcp,MGoat
322-132	Vultre,Porcp,W.Cat
322-211	MGoat,Zebra,Gorlla
322-212	MGoat,Zebra,Vultre
322-221	MGoat,Zebra,W.Cat
322-222	Zebra,W.Cat,Vultre
322-231	Zebra,MGoat,W.Cat
322-232	Zebra,W.Cat,Fox
322-311↓	Zebra,MGoat
322-332↓	Zebra,Sable,Eagle
323-111	Gorlla,Pengn,MGoat
323-112	Gorlla,Vultre,Horse
323-121	Pengn,Gorlla,Vultre
323-122	Gorlla,Vultre,Fox
323-131	Fox,Pengn,Gorlla
323-132	Fox,Gorlla,Vultre
323-211	MGoat,Gorlla,Horse
323-212	Gorlla,Horse,Fox
323-221	Horse,Fox,MGoat

323-222	Fox,Horse,Zebra
323-231↓	Fox,Horse,W.Cat
323-311	Zebra,MGoat,Horse
323-312	Zebra,Dolphin,Horse
323-321	Zebra,Horse,Fox
323-322	Zebra,Fox,Dolphin
323-331	Fox,Zebra,Horse
323-332	Fox,Zebra,Dolphin
331-111	MGoat,Pengn,Vultre
331-112	Vultre,Porcp,MGoat
331-121	Pengn,Vultre,Porcp
331-122	Vultre,Porcp,Horse
331-131	Pengn,Fox,Vultre
331-132	Fox,Vultre,Sable
331-211↓	MGoat,Horse,Zebra
331-231↓	Sable,Fox,Horse
331-311↓	Zebra,MGoat,Sable
331-321↓	Zebra,Sable,Horse
332-111	Pengn,MGoat,Horse
332-112	Vultre,Horse,Gorlla
332-121↓	Pengn,Horse,Vultre
332-131	Pengn,Fox,Horse
332-132	Fox,Vultre,Horse
332-211	MGoat,Horse,Pengn
332-212	Horse,MGoat,Fox
332-221	Horse,Fox,Pengn
332-222	Horse,Fox,Zebra
332-231↓	Fox,Horse,Sable
332-311	Zebra,MGoat,Horse
332-312↓	Zebra,Sable,Horse
332-331↓	Sable,Zebra,Fox
333-111	Pengn,Horse,Gorlla
333-112	Horse,Gorlla,Fox
333-121↓	Pengn,Horse,Fox
333-131	Fox,Pengn,Owl
333-132	Fox,Owl,Horse
333-211	Horse,Fox,Pengn
333-212	Horse,Fox,Owl
333-221	Horse,Fox,Pengn
333-222↓	Fox,Horse,Owl
333-311↓	Horse,Fox,Zebra
333-321	Horse,Fox,Owl
333-332	Fox,Owl,Sable
341-111↓	Pengn,Bison,Sable
341-122↓	Pengn,Sable,Owl
341-212	Sable,Bison,Owl
341-221	Pengn,Sable,Owl
341-222	Sable,Owl,Bison
341-332↓	Sable,Wolf,Owl
342-111↓	Pengn,Owl
342-122↓	Pengn,Owl,Sable
342-322↓	Sable,Owl,Wolf
343-111↓	Pengn,Owl
343-311↓	Owl,Pengn,Sable
411-111↓	Pcock,Vultre
412-111↓	Pcock,Vultre
412-122↓	Vultre,Pcock,W.Cat
412-232↓	Pcock,W.Cat,Sable
413-111↓	Vultre,Pcock,W.Cat
413-232↓	W.Cat,Pcock,Dolphin
413-331↓	Dolphin,W.Cat,Sable
421-111↓	Pcock,Giraf,W.Cat
421-131	Pcock,W.Cat,Sable
421-212↓	Pcock,W.Cat,Giraf
421-231↓	Pcock,W.Cat,Sable

(331 cont'd)

421-311↓ Pcock,SeaLn,Sable
421-322↓ Sable,Pcock,W.Cat
422-111↓ W.Cat,Giraf,MGoat
422-131↓ W.Cat,Sable
422-211 W.Cat,Giraf,MGoat
422-212↓ W.Cat,Giraf,Sable
422-311 SeaLn,Sable,Dolphin
422-312 Sable,Dolphin,W.Cat
422-321 W.Cat,Sable,SeaLn
422-332↓ Sable,W.Cat,Dolphin
423-111 W.Cat,Gorlla,Pengn
423-221↓ W.Cat,Dolphin,Giraf
423-322↓ Dolphin,W.Cat,Sable
431-111↓ Pcock,Sable,Swan
432-111 Sable,Pengn,W.Cat
432-112 Sable,W.Cat,Swan
432-121 W.Cat,Sable,Pengn
432-211↓ Sable,Swan,W.Cat
433-111 Pengn,Horse,W.Cat
433-112 W.Cat,Horse,Fox
433-121 Pengn,W.Cat,Horse
433-122 W.Cat,Fox,Horse
433-131 Fox,Pengn,W.Cat
433-132 Fox,W.Cat,Sable
433-211↓ Horse,W.Cat,Sable
433-222↓ W.Cat,Sable,Fox
433-311↓ Sable,Dolphin,Swan
433-332↓ Sable,Tiger,Fox
441-111↓ Sable,Pengn
442-111↓ Sable,Pengn
443-111↓ Pengn,Sable,Owl

332-

111-111↓ Vultre,Croc
112-111↓ Vultre,Croc
112-121↓ Vultre,Porcp
112-211↓ Vultre,Croc
113-111 Vultre,Gorlla
113-112↓ Vultre,Gorlla,Croc
113-222↓ Vultre,Croc,Warthg
113-311↓ Croc,Vultre,Gorlla
121-111↓ Porcp,Vultre,Gorlla
121-211↓ Porcp,MGoat,Vultre
121-212↓ Porcp,Vultre,Gorlla
121-311 Porcp,MGoat,Zebra
121-312↓ Porcp,Zebra,Vultre
122-111↓ Porcp,Gorlla,Vultre
122-211 Porcp,MGoat,Gorlla
122-212 Porcp,Vultre,Gorlla
122-232↓ Porcp,Vultre,Warthg
122-311 Porcp,MGoat,Zebra
122-312↓ Porcp,Zebra,Vultre
123-111 Gorlla,Porcp
123-112↓ Gorlla,Porcp,Vultre
123-221↓ Warthg,Porcp,Gorlla
123-232 Warthg,Porcp,Fox
123-311↓ Gorlla,Warthg,Porcp
123-331↓ Warthg,Fox,Porcp
131-111 Porcp,Vultre,Hippo
131-112 Porcp,Vultre,Gorlla
131-131↓ Porcp,Vultre,Hippo
131-211 Porcp,MGoat,Bison
131-212↓ Porcp,Bison,Vultre
131-311 Porcp,MGoat,Bison

131-312 Bison,Porcp,Zebra
131-331↓ Sable,Porcp,Bison
132-111↓ Porcp,Gorlla,Vultre
132-121 Porcp,Vultre,Hippo
132-122 Porcp,Vultre,Gorlla
132-131↓ Porcp,Vultre,Hippo
132-211 Porcp,MGoat,Gorlla
132-212↓ Porcp,Bison,Vultre
132-231↓ Porcp,Fox,Bison
132-311 Porcp,MGoat,Bison
132-312 Bison,Porcp,Zebra
132-331 Sable,Porcp,Fox
132-332 Sable,Fox,Bison
133-111↓ Gorlla,Porcp
133-121↓ Porcp,Gorlla,Pengn
133-122 Porcp,Gorlla,Vultre
133-131↓ Fox,Porcp,Gorlla
133-211 Gorlla,Warthg,Horse
133-212 Gorlla,Warthg,Fox
133-221↓ Fox,Warthg,Horse
133-231↓ Fox,Owl,Baboon
133-311 Gorlla,Warthg,Horse
133-312 Gorlla,Warthg,Fox
133-321↓ Fox,Warthg,Horse
133-331↓ Fox,Owl,Baboon
141-111↓ Bison,Pengn
141-121↓ Bison,Pengn,Sheep
141-131 Bison,Pengn,Sable
141-132 Bison,Sable,Owl
141-321↓ Bison,Sable,Sheep
142-111↓ Pengn,Bison,Sheep
142-131↓ Pengn,Bison,Owl
142-132↓ Bison,Owl,Beaver
142-222↓ Bison,Sable,Owl
143-111 Pengn,Owl
143-221↓ Owl,Pengn,Bison
143-232 Owl,Bison,Beaver
143-311 Owl,Bison,Pengn
143-312↓ Owl,Bison,Sable
211-111↓ Vultre,Pcock
212-111↓ Vultre,Zebra
213-111↓ Vultre,Gorlla
221-111↓ Vultre,Gorlla,MGoat
221-221 Vultre,MGoat,Zebra
221-222 Vultre,Zebra,Gorlla
221-231 Vultre,Zebra,MGoat
221-232 Vultre,Zebra,Rooster
221-311 Zebra,MGoat,Vultre
221-331↓ Zebra,Vultre,Sable
222-111↓ Gorlla,Vultre,MGoat
222-222 Vultre,Gorlla,Zebra
222-231 Vultre,Zebra,MGoat
222-232 Vultre,Fox,Zebra
222-311 Zebra,MGoat,Gorlla
222-312 Zebra,Vultre,Gorlla
222-321 Zebra,Vultre,MGoat
222-322 Zebra,Vultre,Gorlla
222-331↓ Zebra,Vultre,Sable
223-111↓ Gorlla,Vultre
223-121↓ Gorlla,Vultre,Pengn
223-122↓ Gorlla,Vultre,Fox
223-311 Gorlla,Zebra,MGoat
223-312 Gorlla,Zebra,Vultre
223-321↓ Zebra,Gorlla,Fox
231-111 Vultre,Hippo,Gorlla

231-112 Vultre,Gorlla,Bison
231-121 Vultre,Hippo,Walrus
231-122 Vultre,Bison,Hippo
231-131 Vultre,Hippo,Walrus
231-132 Vultre,Bison,Hippo
231-211 MGoat,Bison,Vultre
231-212 Bison,Vultre,Gorlla
231-221 Bison,Vultre,Hippo
231-222 Bison,Vultre,Horse
231-231↓ Bison,Vultre,Fox
231-311 Zebra,MGoat,Bison
231-312↓ Zebra,Bison,Sable
232-111 Gorlla,Vultre,Hippo
232-112 Vultre,Gorlla,Bison
232-121 Vultre,Hippo,Walrus
232-122 Vultre,Gorlla,Bison
232-131 Vultre,Hippo,Walrus
232-132 Vultre,Fox,Bison
232-211 MGoat,Gorlla,Bison
232-212 Bison,Vultre,Gorlla
232-221 Bison,Vultre,Horse
232-222↓ Bison,Vultre,Fox
232-311 Zebra,MGoat,Bison
232-312↓ Zebra,Bison,Sable
232-331↓ Sable,Fox,Zebra
233-111 Gorlla,Pengn,Vultre
233-112 Gorlla,Vultre,Fox
233-121 Pengn,Gorlla,Fox
233-122 Gorlla,Fox,Vultre
233-131 Fox,Pengn,Owl
233-132 Fox,Owl,Gorlla
233-211↓ Gorlla,Horse,Fox
233-221↓ Fox,Horse,Owl
233-311↓ Horse,Gorlla,Fox
233-321↓ Fox,Horse,Owl
233-332 Fox,Owl,Sable
241-111 Pengn,Bison
241-122↓ Bison,Pengn,Vultre
241-131 Pengn,Bison,Owl
241-132 Bison,Owl,Sable
241-211 Bison,Sheep
241-212 Bison,Sable
241-221 Bison,Sheep,Pengn
241-322↓ Bison,Sable,Wolf
241-331 Sable,Bison,Owl
241-332 Sable,Bison,Wolf
242-111↓ Pengn,Bison,Owl
242-212 Bison,Owl,Sable
242-221 Bison,Owl,Pengn
242-222↓ Bison,Owl,Sable
243-111↓ Pengn,Owl,Bison
243-312 Owl,Bison,Sable
243-321 Owl,Pengn,Bison
243-322 Owl,Bison,Sable
243-331 Owl,Sable,Pengn
243-332 Owl,Sable,Bison
311-111↓ Vultre,Pcock
311-211↓ Pcock,Vultre,Weasel
311-312↓ Pcock,Vultre,Zebra
312-111↓ Vultre,Weasel,Pcock
312-311 Zebra,Vultre,Weasel
313-111↓ Vultre,Gorlla
313-121↓ Vultre,Pengn,Gorlla
313-132 Vultre,Fox
313-211↓ Vultre,Weasel,Gorlla

313-221↓	Vultre,Weasel,Fox
313-311	Zebra,Vultre,Weasel
313-332	Vultre,Fox,Zebra
321-111↓	Vultre,Gorlla,Zebra
321-121↓	Vultre,Zebra,Pcock
321-131↓	Vultre,Rooster,Zebra
321-211	Zebra,Pcock,MGoat
321-212↓	Zebra,Vultre,Pcock
321-231	Zebra,Rooster,Pcock
321-232↓	Zebra,Rooster,Vultre
321-332↓	Zebra,Sable,Eagle
322-111	Gorlla,Vultre,Pengn
322-112	Vultre,Gorlla,Zebra
322-121	Vultre,Pengn,Gorlla
322-122	Vultre,Gorlla,Zebra
322-131↓	Vultre,Fox,Rooster
322-211	Zebra,MGoat,Gorlla
322-212	Zebra,Vultre,Gorlla
322-221↓	Zebra,W.Cat,Vultre
322-231	Zebra,Fox,Rooster
322-331↓	Zebra,Sable,Fox
323-111	Gorlla,Pengn,Vultre
323-112	Gorlla,Vultre,Fox
323-121	Pengn,Gorlla,Fox
323-122	Gorlla,Fox,Vultre
323-131	Fox,Pengn,Gorlla
323-132	Fox,Gorlla,Vultre
323-211↓	Gorlla,Horse,Fox
323-221↓	Fox,Horse,Zebra
323-231↓	Fox,Horse,W.Cat
323-311	Zebra,Horse,Gorlla
323-312	Zebra,Fox,Dolphin
323-321	Zebra,Fox,Horse
323-322	Zebra,Fox,Dolphin
323-331	Fox,Zebra,Horse
323-332	Fox,Zebra,Dolphin
331-111	Pengn,Vultre,Horse
331-112	Vultre,Horse,Gorlla
331-121↓	Pengn,Vultre,Horse
331-131	Pengn,Fox,Vultre
331-132	Fox,Vultre,Sable
331-211	Horse,Zebra,Pengn
331-221↓	Horse,Zebra,Fox
331-231↓	Fox,Sable,Horse
331-311↓	Zebra,Sable,Horse
331-331↓	Sable,Zebra,Fox
332-111	Pengn,Horse,Gorlla
332-112	Vultre,Horse,Gorlla
332-121	Pengn,Horse,Fox
332-122	Fox,Vultre,Horse
332-131	Fox,Pengn,Owl
332-132	Fox,Owl,Vultre
332-211	Horse,Fox,Pengn
332-212	Horse,Fox,Zebra
332-221	Horse,Fox,Pengn
332-222	Fox,Horse,Zebra
332-231	Fox,Owl,Horse
332-232	Fox,Sable,Owl
332-311↓	Zebra,Horse,Sable
332-322↓	Zebra,Sable,Fox
333-111	Pengn,Horse,Gorlla
333-112	Fox,Horse,Gorlla
333-121↓	Pengn,Fox,Horse
333-131	Fox,Pengn,Owl
333-132	Fox,Owl,Horse

333-211	Horse,Fox,Pengn
333-212↓	Fox,Horse,Owl
333-332	Fox,Owl,Sable
341-111↓	Pengn,Bison,Owl
341-131↓	Pengn,Owl,Sable
341-212	Sable,Bison,Owl
341-221	Pengn,Sable,Owl
341-222	Sable,Owl,Bison
341-231	Sable,Owl,Pengn
341-232↓	Sable,Owl,Bison
341-312	Sable,Bison,Wolf
341-321↓	Sable,Owl,Wolf
342-111	Pengn,Owl
342-122↓	Pengn,Owl,Bison
342-131	Pengn,Owl,Sable
342-212	Owl,Sable,Bison
342-221	Owl,Pengn,Sable
342-222	Owl,Sable,Bison
342-231	Owl,Sable,Pengn
342-232	Owl,Sable,Eleph
342-311	Sable,Owl,Pengn
342-312	Sable,Owl,Bison
342-321	Sable,Owl,Pengn
342-322↓	Sable,Owl,Wolf
343-111↓	Pengn,Owl
343-311↓	Owl,Pengn,Sable
411-111↓	Pcock,Vultre
411-332	Pcock,Sable
412-111↓	Pcock,Vultre
412-121↓	Pcock,Vultre,W.Cat
412-231↓	Pcock,W.Cat,Sable
412-312	Pcock,Sable,Dolphin
412-321↓	Pcock,W.Cat,Sable
413-111↓	Pcock,Vultre,W.Cat
413-211↓	Pcock,W.Cat,Dolphin
413-331↓	Dolphin,W.Cat,Sable
421-111↓	Pcock,W.Cat,Giraf
421-131↓	Pcock,W.Cat,Sable
421-211↓	Pcock,Giraf,W.Cat
421-231↓	Pcock,W.Cat,Sable
421-311↓	Pcock,SeaLn,Sable
421-322↓	Sable,Pcock,W.Cat
422-111↓	W.Cat,Giraf,Pcock
422-131↓	W.Cat,Sable,Giraf
422-211↓	W.Cat,Giraf,Pcock
422-222↓	W.Cat,Giraf,Sable
422-311	SeaLn,Sable,Dolphin
422-312	Sable,Dolphin,W.Cat
422-321	W.Cat,Sable,SeaLn
422-322	W.Cat,Sable,Dolphin
422-331	Sable,W.Cat,SeaLn
422-332	Sable,W.Cat,Dolphin
423-111	W.Cat,Gorlla,Pengn
423-112	W.Cat,Gorlla,Dolphin
423-121	W.Cat,Pengn,Dolphin
423-132↓	W.Cat,Fox,Dolphin
423-211↓	W.Cat,Dolphin,Giraf
423-222↓	W.Cat,Dolphin,Fox
423-311	Dolphin,W.Cat,SeaLn
423-312↓	Dolphin,W.Cat,Sable
431-111↓	Pcock,Sable,Swan
431-121	Pcock,Sable,W.Cat
431-212↓	Sable,Pcock,Swan
431-231↓	Sable,Pcock,W.Cat
431-312↓	Sable,Swan,Pcock

432-111	Sable,Pengn,W.Cat
432-112	Sable,W.Cat,Swan
432-121	W.Cat,Sable,Pengn
432-122	W.Cat,Sable,Swan
432-131↓	Sable,W.Cat,Fox
432-211↓	Sable,Swan,W.Cat
432-231↓	Sable,W.Cat,Fox
432-312↓	Sable,Swan,Dolphin
432-321↓	Sable,Swan,W.Cat
433-111	Pengn,Horse,Fox
433-112	Fox,W.Cat,Horse
433-121	Pengn,Fox,W.Cat
433-122	Fox,W.Cat,Horse
433-131	Fox,Pengn,W.Cat
433-132	Fox,W.Cat,Sable
433-211	Horse,Fox,W.Cat
433-212↓	Fox,W.Cat,Sable
433-311↓	Sable,Dolphin,Swan
433-321↓	Sable,Dolphin,Tiger
433-331↓	Sable,Tiger,Fox
441-111↓	Sable,Pengn
442-111↓	Sable,Pengn
443-111↓	Pengn,Owl,Sable

333-

111-111↓	Vultre,Croc,Pcock
112-111	Vultre,Croc
112-222↓	Vultre,Croc,Pcock
113-111↓	Vultre,Gorlla
113-331↓	Vultre,Fox,Croc
121-111↓	Porcp,Vultre,Gorlla
121-211↓	Porcp,MGoat,Vultre
121-212	Porcp,Vultre,Gorlla
121-221	Porcp,Vultre,Pcock
121-222	Porcp,Vultre,Bison
121-231	Porcp,Vultre,Pcock
121-232	Porcp,Vultre,Rooster
121-311	Porcp,MGoat,Zebra
121-312	Porcp,Zebra,Vultre
121-321	Porcp,Zebra,Pcock
121-322	Porcp,Zebra,Vultre
121-331	Porcp,Zebra,Pcock
121-332	Porcp,Zebra,Eagle
122-111↓	Porcp,Gorlla,Vultre
122-211	Porcp,MGoat,Gorlla
122-222↓	Porcp,Vultre,Bison
122-231↓	Porcp,Vultre,Fox
122-311	Porcp,MGoat,Zebra
122-312↓	Porcp,Zebra,Vultre
122-331↓	Porcp,Zebra,Fox
123-111	Gorlla,Porcp
123-112↓	Gorlla,Porcp,Vultre
123-132	Porcp,Fox,Gorlla
123-211↓	Gorlla,Warthg,Porcp
123-222	Warthg,Fox,Porcp
123-321↓	Warthg,Fox,Dolphin
123-331	Fox,Warthg,Baboon
123-332	Fox,Warthg,Dolphin
131-111	Walrus,Porcp,Vultre
131-112	Porcp,Vultre,Bison
131-121	Walrus,Porcp,Vultre
131-122	Porcp,Vultre,Bison
131-131	Walrus,Porcp,Vultre
131-132	Porcp,Vultre,Bison
131-231↓	Bison,Walrus,Porcp

(333 cont'd)

131-232 Bison,Fox,Porcp
131-311↓ Bison,Walrus,Porcp
131-331↓ Bison,Sable,Fox
132-111 Walrus,Porcp,Gorlla
132-112 Porcp,Vultre,Gorlla
132-121 Walrus,Porcp,Vultre
132-122 Porcp,Vultre,Bison
132-131 Walrus,Porcp,Fox
132-132 Porcp,Fox,Vultre
132-211 Bison,Walrus,Porcp
132-212 Bison,Porcp,Horse
132-221 Bison,Walrus,Porcp
132-222 Bison,Porcp,Fox
132-231↓ Fox,Bison,Baboon
132-321↓ Bison,Horse,Walrus
132-322 Bison,Fox,Horse
132-331↓ Fox,Bison,Sable
133-111 Gorlla,Walrus,Porcp
133-112 Gorlla,Fox,Porcp
133-121 Fox,Walrus,Porcp
133-122 Fox,Porcp,Horse
133-131↓ Fox,Owl,Baboon
133-211 Horse,Fox,Gorlla
133-231↓ Fox,Owl,Baboon
133-311 Horse,Fox,Owl
133-312 Fox,Horse,Bison
133-321↓ Fox,Horse,Owl
133-331↓ Fox,Owl,Baboon
141-111↓ Bison,Sheep
141-331↓ Bison,Sable,Owl
141-332 Bison,Sable,Wolf
142-111↓ Bison,Sheep,Pengn
142-232↓ Bison,Owl,Sable
142-311↓ Bison,Sheep
142-322↓ Bison,Sable,Owl
143-111↓ Owl,Pengn,Bison
143-332↓ Owl,Bison,W.Dog
211-111↓ Vultre,Pcock
212-111↓ Vultre,Pcock
213-111↓ Vultre,Gorlla
213-231↓ Vultre,Fox
213-311↓ Vultre,Gorlla
213-322↓ Vultre,Fox,Dolphin
221-111↓ Vultre,Gorlla,Walrus
221-122 Vultre,Gorlla,Bison
221-131 Vultre,Walrus
221-132 Vultre,Rooster
221-211 MGoat,Vultre,Gorlla
221-212 Vultre,Gorlla,Bison
221-221↓ Vultre,Pcock,Bison
221-231 Vultre,Rooster,Pcock
221-232 Vultre,Rooster,Bison
221-311 Zebra,MGoat,Pcock
221-312 Zebra,Vultre,Bison
221-321 Zebra,Pcock,Vultre
221-322 Zebra,Vultre,Bison
221-331↓ Zebra,Eagle,Rooster
222-111 Gorlla,Vultre,Walrus
222-112 Vultre,Gorlla,Bison
222-121 Vultre,Gorlla,Walrus
222-122 Vultre,Gorlla,Bison
222-131 Vultre,Walrus,Gorlla
222-132 Vultre,Fox,Rooster
222-211 MGoat,Gorlla,Vultre

222-212 Vultre,Gorlla,Bison
222-221 Vultre,Bison,MGoat
222-222 Vultre,Bison,Fox
222-231↓ Fox,Vultre,Rooster
222-311 Zebra,MGoat,Gorlla
222-312 Zebra,Vultre,Gorlla
222-321↓ Zebra,Vultre,Bison
222-331↓ Zebra,Fox,Eagle
223-111↓ Gorlla,Vultre
223-121↓ Gorlla,Vultre,Fox
223-211↓ Gorlla,Horse,Fox
223-231↓ Fox,Horse,Baboon
223-311 Gorlla,Horse,Fox
223-312 Gorlla,Fox,Dolphin
223-321↓ Fox,Horse,Dolphin
223-331 Fox,Horse,Baboon
223-332 Fox,Dolphin,Horse
231-111↓ Walrus,Vultre,Bison
231-132 Vultre,Bison,Fox
231-211 Bison,Walrus,Horse
231-212 Bison,Horse,Vultre
231-221 Bison,Walrus,Horse
231-222 Bison,Horse,Fox
231-231 Bison,Fox,Walrus
231-232 Bison,Fox,Horse
231-311↓ Bison,Horse,Zebra
231-331↓ Bison,Fox,Sable
232-111 Walrus,Gorlla,Vultre
232-112 Vultre,Gorlla,Bison
232-121↓ Walrus,Vultre,Bison
232-131 Walrus,Fox,Vultre
232-132 Fox,Vultre,Bison
232-211 Bison,Horse,Walrus
232-212 Bison,Horse,Fox
232-221 Bison,Walrus,Horse
232-222 Bison,Fox,Horse
232-231↓ Fox,Bison,Owl
232-311↓ Bison,Horse,Fox
232-331 Fox,Bison,Owl
232-332 Fox,Bison,Sable
233-111↓ Gorlla,Horse,Fox
233-121 Fox,Horse,Walrus
233-122↓ Fox,Horse,Owl
241-111↓ Bison,Sheep,Pengn
241-231↓ Bison,Owl,Sheep
241-232↓ Bison,Owl,Sable
241-312 Bison,Sable,Wolf
241-321 Bison,Sheep,Sable
241-322 Bison,Sable,Wolf
241-331 Bison,Sable,Owl
241-332 Bison,Sable,Wolf
242-111↓ Bison,Pengn,Owl
242-132 Owl,Bison,Eleph
242-231↓ Owl,Bison,Sheep
242-232 Owl,Bison,Sable
242-311 Bison,Owl,Sheep
242-312 Bison,Owl,Sable
242-321 Bison,Owl,Sheep
242-322 Bison,Owl,Sable
243-111↓ Owl,Pengn,Bison
311-111↓ Pcock,Vultre
312-111↓ Vultre,Pcock
313-111 Vultre,Gorlla
313-112↓ Vultre,Gorlla,Fox
313-211 Vultre,Pcock,Horse

313-212↓ Vultre,Fox,Pcock
313-312 Dolphin,Vultre,Fox
313-321 Fox,Dolphin,Zebra
313-332↓ Fox,Dolphin,Vultre
321-111 Pcock,Vultre,Gorlla
321-122↓ Vultre,Pcock,Rooster
321-211 Pcock,Zebra,Horse
321-212↓ Pcock,Zebra,Rooster
321-231↓ Rooster,Pcock,Fox
321-312↓ Zebra,Pcock,SeaLn
321-322 Zebra,Pcock,Eagle
321-331↓ Zebra,Eagle,Rooster
322-111 Gorlla,Vultre,Horse
322-122↓ Vultre,Fox,Rooster
322-211↓ Horse,Zebra,Fox
322-222↓ Fox,Rooster,Horse
322-311 Zebra,Horse,SeaLn
322-312 Zebra,Dolphin,Horse
322-321 Zebra,Horse,SeaLn
322-322↓ Zebra,Fox,Eagle
323-111↓ Gorlla,Horse,Fox
323-121 Fox,Horse,Pengn
323-122↓ Fox,Horse,Gorlla
323-222↓ Fox,Horse,Dolphin
331-111 Horse,Walrus,Pengn
331-112 Horse,Fox,Vultre
331-121 Horse,Walrus,Pengn
331-122 Horse,Fox,Vultre
331-131 Fox,Horse,Walrus
331-132 Fox,Horse,Owl
331-211 Horse,Fox,Pcock
331-212 Horse,Fox,Bison
331-221 Horse,Fox,Pcock
331-222 Horse,Fox,Bison
331-231↓ Fox,Horse,Owl
331-311↓ Horse,Zebra,Fox
331-331↓ Fox,Sable,Wolf
332-111 Horse,Pengn,Fox
332-112 Horse,Fox,Vultre
332-121 Horse,Fox,Pengn
332-122↓ Fox,Horse,Owl
332-311↓ Horse,Fox,Zebra
332-332 Fox,Sable,Owl
333-111 Horse,Fox,Pengn
333-112 Fox,Horse,Owl
333-121 Fox,Horse,Pengn
333-122↓ Fox,Horse,Owl
341-111↓ Pengn,Owl,Bison
341-132 Owl,Bison,Sable
341-211 Owl,Bison,Pengn
341-212 Bison,Owl,Sable
341-221 Owl,Bison,Pengn
341-222↓ Owl,Bison,Sable
341-321↓ Sable,Owl,Wolf
342-111↓ Pengn,Owl,Bison
342-131 Owl,Pengn,Eleph
342-132 Owl,Eleph,Bison
342-211 Owl,Bison,Pengn
342-212 Owl,Bison,Sable
342-221 Owl,Bison,Pengn
342-222 Owl,Bison,Sable
342-231↓ Owl,Eleph,Sable
342-311↓ Owl,Sable,Bison
342-321↓ Owl,Sable,Wolf
343-111↓ Owl,Pengn

411-111↓ Peacock
412-111 Peacock
412-132↓ Pcock,Vultre,W.Cat
412-312↓ Pcock,Dolphin,SeaLn
412-332↓ Pcock,Sable,Dolphin
413-111↓ Pcock,Vultre
413-132↓ Pcock,W.Cat,Vultre
413-221↓ Pcock,Dolphin,W.Cat
421-111↓ Pcock,W.Cat
421-222↓ Pcock,W.Cat,SeaLn
421-231↓ Pcock,W.Cat,Sable
421-311↓ Pcock,SeaLn,Dolphin
421-331↓ Pcock,Sable,SeaLn
422-111 Pcock,W.Cat,SeaLn
422-112 Pcock,W.Cat,Dolphin
422-121 W.Cat,Pcock,SeaLn
422-122 W.Cat,Pcock,Dolphin
422-131↓ W.Cat,Pcock,Sable
422-211 Pcock,W.Cat,SeaLn
422-212 Pcock,W.Cat,Dolphin
422-221 W.Cat,Pcock,SeaLn
422-222 W.Cat,Pcock,Dolphin
422-231↓ W.Cat,Pcock,Sable
422-311 SeaLn,Dolphin,Deer
422-332 Sable,Dolphin,SeaLn
423-111 Dolphin,W.Cat,Gorlla
423-112 Dolphin,W.Cat,Fox
423-211 Dolphin,W.Cat,Horse
423-212↓ Dolphin,W.Cat,Fox
423-321↓ Dolphin,SeaLn,W.Cat
423-331↓ Dolphin,Fox,W.Cat
431-111↓ Pcock,Sable
431-131↓ Pcock,Sable,Fox
431-332↓ Sable,Pcock,Swan
432-111↓ Horse,Pcock,Sable
432-121 Horse,W.Cat,Sable
432-122↓ W.Cat,Sable,Fox
432-211 Sable,Horse,Pcock
432-212 Sable,Horse,Swan
432-221 Sable,Horse,W.Cat
432-222↓ Sable,W.Cat,Fox
432-311 Sable,Swan,SeaLn
432-312 Sable,Swan,Dolphin
432-321 Sable,Swan,SeaLn
432-322 Sable,Swan,Dolphin
432-331↓ Sable,Swan,Fox
433-111 Horse,Fox,Pengn
433-112 Fox,Horse,Owl
433-121 Fox,Horse,Pengn
433-122↓ Fox,Horse,Owl
433-211 Horse,Fox,Dolphin
433-232 Fox,Owl,Sable
433-311 Dolphin,Horse,Fox
433-312↓ Dolphin,Fox,Sable
441-111↓ Sable,Pengn,Pcock
441-121↓ Sable,Pengn,Owl
442-111↓ Sable,Pengn,Owl
442-212↓ Sable,Owl,Bison
443-111 Owl,Pengn
443-112↓ Owl,Pengn,Sable
443-132 Owl,Sable,Fox
443-221↓ Owl,Sable,Pengn

334-
111-111↓ Vultre,Pcock,Croc
111-331↓ Pcock,Vultre,Eagle

112-111↓ Vultre,Croc
112-312↓ Vultre,Croc,Dolphin
112-321 Vultre,Croc,SeaLn
112-322 Vultre,Dolphin,Croc
112-331 Vultre,Eagle,SeaLn
112-332 Vultre,Eagle,Dolphin
113-111↓ Vultre,Gorlla
113-231↓ Vultre,Baboon,Horse
113-311 Dolphin,Croc,Vultre
113-321↓ Dolphin,Vultre,Horse
113-331↓ Dolphin,Baboon,Vultre
121-111 Walrus,Porcp
121-132↓ Porcp,Walrus,Vultre
121-211 Walrus,Porcp,MGoat
121-212↓ Porcp,Horse,Walrus
121-231 Walrus,Porcp,Baboon
121-232 Porcp,Baboon,Eagle
121-311 SeaLn,Walrus,Dolphin
121-312 SeaLn,Dolphin,Eagle
121-321 SeaLn,Walrus,Eagle
121-322 SeaLn,Eagle,Dolphin
121-331 Eagle,SeaLn,Baboon
121-332 Eagle,SeaLn,Dolphin
122-111 Walrus,Porcp,Gorlla
122-122↓ Porcp,Walrus,Vultre
122-211↓ Walrus,Porcp,Horse
122-231 Baboon,Walrus,Porcp
122-232 Baboon,Porcp,Horse
122-311 SeaLn,Dolphin,Horse
122-322 Dolphin,SeaLn,Eagle
122-331 Eagle,Baboon,SeaLn
122-332 Eagle,Dolphin,Baboon
123-111 Gorlla,Walrus,Porcp
123-112 Gorlla,Porcp,Horse
123-121 Walrus,Porcp,Horse
123-122 Porcp,Horse,Gorlla
123-131 Baboon,Walrus,Porcp
123-132 Baboon,Porcp,Horse
123-211 Horse,Gorlla,Baboon
123-212 Horse,Gorlla,Dolphin
123-221↓ Horse,Baboon,Dolphin
123-231 Baboon,Horse,Lion
123-232 Baboon,Horse,Fox
123-331↓ Baboon,Dolphin,Horse
131-111↓ Walrus,Porcp,Horse
131-132↓ Walrus,Baboon,Porcp
131-222↓ Horse,Walrus,Bison
131-231↓ Walrus,Baboon,Horse
131-311↓ Walrus,Horse,Bison
131-331 Baboon,Walrus,Horse
131-332 Baboon,Horse,Eagle
132-111↓ Walrus,Horse,Porcp
132-212↓ Horse,Walrus,Bison
132-221 Walrus,Horse,Baboon
132-232 Baboon,Horse,Lion
132-311 Horse,Walrus,Baboon
132-312 Horse,Bison,Baboon
132-321 Horse,Walrus,Baboon
132-322 Horse,Baboon,Bison
132-331 Baboon,Horse,Walrus
132-332 Baboon,Horse,Lion
133-111↓ Walrus,Horse,Baboon
133-222 Horse,Baboon,Fox
133-231 Baboon,Horse,Lion
133-322↓ Horse,Baboon,Fox

133-331 Baboon,Horse,Lion
133-332 Baboon,Horse,Fox
141-111 Walrus,Bison
141-132↓ Bison,Walrus,Owl
141-231↓ Bison,Owl,Sheep
141-331↓ Bison,W.Dog,Sable
142-111↓ Walrus,Bison,Sheep
142-131↓ Walrus,Bison,Owl
142-331↓ W.Dog,Bison,Owl
143-111 Owl,Walrus,Pengn
143-112 Owl,Bison,Horse
143-121 Owl,Walrus,Pengn
143-122↓ Owl,Bison,Horse
143-232↓ Owl,W.Dog,Bison
211-111↓ Vultre,Pcock
212-111↓ Vultre,Walrus
212-311↓ Vultre,SeaLn,Pcock
212-312 Vultre,Dolphin
212-321 Vultre,SeaLn,Pcock
212-322 Vultre,Eagle,Dolphin
212-331 Vultre,Eagle,SeaLn
212-332 Vultre,Eagle,Dolphin
213-111↓ Vultre,Gorlla
213-222↓ Vultre,Horse,Dolphin
213-231↓ Vultre,Horse,Baboon
213-311↓ Dolphin,Horse,Vultre
213-331 Dolphin,Horse,Baboon
213-332 Dolphin,Vultre,Eagle
221-111↓ Walrus,Vultre,Gorlla
221-122↓ Walrus,Vultre,Horse
221-211 Walrus,Horse,MGoat
221-222↓ Horse,Walrus,Vultre
221-231 Walrus,Horse,Eagle
221-232 Eagle,Horse,Baboon
221-311 SeaLn,Horse,Eagle
221-312 SeaLn,Eagle,Dolphin
221-321 SeaLn,Eagle,Horse
221-322↓ Eagle,SeaLn,Dolphin
222-111↓ Walrus,Gorlla,Vultre
222-121↓ Walrus,Vultre,Horse
222-211 Horse,Walrus,MGoat
222-212 Horse,Walrus,Vultre
222-221 Horse,Walrus,Baboon
222-222 Horse,Walrus,Vultre
222-231 Horse,Baboon,Walrus
222-232 Horse,Baboon,Eagle
222-311↓ Horse,SeaLn,Dolphin
222-321 Horse,SeaLn,Eagle
222-322 Eagle,Dolphin,Horse
222-331 Eagle,Horse,Baboon
222-332 Eagle,Dolphin,Horse
223-111↓ Gorlla,Horse,Walrus
223-122 Horse,Gorlla,Baboon
223-131 Horse,Baboon,Walrus
223-132 Horse,Baboon,Fox
223-211 Horse,Gorlla,Baboon
223-212 Horse,Gorlla,Dolphin
223-221 Horse,Baboon,Lion
223-222 Horse,Baboon,Fox
223-231 Horse,Baboon,Lion
223-232 Horse,Baboon,Fox
223-312↓ Dolphin,Horse,Baboon
231-111↓ Walrus,Horse
231-122↓ Walrus,Horse,Bison

(334 cont'd)

231-231 Walrus,Horse,Baboon
231-232 Horse,Baboon,Lion
231-311↓ Horse,Walrus,Bison
231-331 Horse,Baboon,Walrus
231-332 Horse,Baboon,Eagle
232-111 Walrus,Horse
232-122↓ Walrus,Horse,Baboon
232-232 Horse,Baboon,Lion
232-311 Horse,Walrus
232-312 Horse,Bison,Baboon
232-321 Horse,Walrus,Baboon
232-322 Horse,Baboon,Bison
232-331↓ Horse,Baboon,Lion
233-111↓ Horse,Walrus,Baboon
233-132 Horse,Baboon,Fox
233-211 Horse,Baboon,Walrus
233-212 Horse,Baboon,Fox
233-221 Horse,Baboon,Lion
233-222 Horse,Baboon,Fox
233-231 Horse,Baboon,Lion
233-232 Horse,Baboon,Fox
233-311 Horse,Baboon,Lion
233-312 Horse,Baboon,Fox
233-321 Horse,Baboon,Lion
233-322 Horse,Baboon,Fox
233-331 Horse,Baboon,Lion
233-332 Horse,Baboon,Fox
241-111↓ Walrus,Bison
241-132 Bison,Owl
241-211 Bison,Sheep
241-212 Bison,Dog
241-221 Bison,Sheep,Walrus
241-222 Bison,Dog,Owl
241-231 Bison,Owl,Sheep
241-331↓ Bison,W.Dog,Owl
241-332 Bison,W.Dog,Wolf
242-111 Walrus,Bison,Pengn
242-112↓ Bison,Walrus,Owl
242-211 Bison,Owl,Sheep
242-212 Bison,Owl,Horse
242-221 Bison,Owl,Sheep
242-222 Bison,Owl,Horse
242-231↓ Owl,Bison,W.Dog
243-111 Owl,Pengn,Horse
243-112 Owl,Horse,Bison
243-121 Owl,Pengn,Horse
243-122 Owl,Horse,Bison
243-131 Owl,Pengn,Horse
243-132↓ Owl,Horse,Bison
243-311↓ Owl,W.Dog,Horse
311-111↓ Pcock,Vultre
311-232↓ Pcock,Vultre,Eagle
312-111↓ Vultre,Pcock
312-211↓ Pcock,Vultre,Horse
312-232 Vultre,Pcock,Eagle
312-311↓ SeaLn,Pcock,Dolphin
312-321 SeaLn,Pcock,Eagle
312-322 Eagle,Dolphin,SeaLn
312-331 Eagle,SeaLn,Pcock
312-332 Eagle,Dolphin,SeaLn
313-111↓ Horse,Vultre,Gorlla
313-131↓ Horse,Vultre,Lion
313-132 Vultre,Horse,Fox
313-222↓ Horse,Dolphin,Vultre

313-231↓ Horse,Lion,Fox
313-322↓ Dolphin,Horse,Eagle
321-111↓ Horse,Walrus,Pcock
321-131 Horse,Walrus,Lion
321-132 Horse,Eagle,Rooster
321-211↓ Horse,Pcock,SeaLn
321-222 Horse,Eagle,Pcock
321-231 Horse,Eagle,Lion
321-232 Eagle,Horse,Rooster
321-311 SeaLn,Horse,Eagle
321-312 SeaLn,Eagle,Dolphin
321-321 SeaLn,Eagle,Horse
321-332↓ Eagle,SeaLn,Dolphin
322-111 Horse,Walrus
322-112↓ Horse,Walrus,Vultre
322-121 Horse,Walrus,Lion
322-122 Horse,Walrus,Vultre
322-131 Horse,Lion,Walrus
322-132 Horse,Lion,Fox
322-211↓ Horse,SeaLn,Dolphin
322-221 Horse,SeaLn,Lion
322-222 Horse,Eagle,Dolphin
322-231↓ Horse,Lion,Eagle
322-311↓ Horse,SeaLn,Dolphin
322-321 Horse,SeaLn,Eagle
322-322 Eagle,Dolphin,Horse
322-331 Eagle,Horse,SeaLn
322-332 Eagle,Dolphin,Horse
323-111 Horse,Gorlla,Lion
323-112 Horse,Gorlla,Fox
323-121↓ Horse,Lion,Fox
323-211 Horse,Dolphin,Lion
323-212 Horse,Dolphin,Fox
323-221 Horse,Lion,Fox
323-222 Horse,Fox,Dolphin
323-231↓ Horse,Lion,Fox
323-311 Horse,Dolphin,SeaLn
323-312 Dolphin,Horse,Fox
323-321 Horse,Dolphin,Lion
323-322 Dolphin,Horse,Fox
323-331 Horse,Dolphin,Lion
323-332 Dolphin,Horse,Fox
331-111↓ Horse,Walrus
331-122↓ Horse,Walrus,Lion
331-132 Horse,Lion,Fox
331-221↓ Horse,Walrus,Lion
331-222↓ Horse,Lion,Fox
331-322 Horse,Eagle,SeaLn
331-331↓ Horse,Lion,Eagle
332-111↓ Horse,Walrus,Lion
332-322↓ Horse,Lion,Fox
333-111↓ Horse,Lion,Fox
333-312 Horse,Fox,Dolphin
333-321↓ Horse,Lion,Fox
341-111 Dog,Pengn,Horse
341-112 Dog,Bison,Horse
341-121 Dog,Pengn,Owl
341-122 Dog,Owl,Bison
341-131 Owl,Dog,Pengn
341-132 Owl,Dog,Bison
341-211 Dog,Horse,Owl
341-212 Dog,Bison,Horse
341-221 Dog,Owl,Horse
341-222 Dog,Owl,Bison
341-231 Owl,Dog,Horse

341-232 Owl,Dog,Bison
341-311 Dog,Horse,Owl
341-312 Dog,Bison,Wolf
341-321 Dog,Owl,Wolf
341-322 Wolf,Sable,Dog
341-331↓ Owl,Wolf,Sable
342-111 Pengn,Owl,Horse
342-112 Owl,Horse,Dog
342-121 Owl,Pengn,Horse
342-122 Owl,Horse,Dog
342-131 Owl,Pengn,Horse
342-132 Owl,Horse,Pr.Dog
342-211↓ Owl,Horse,Dog
342-231↓ Owl,Horse,Pr.Dog
342-311↓ Owl,Horse,Dog
342-322 Owl,Horse,Wolf
342-331↓ Owl,Wolf,Sable
343-111↓ Owl,Pengn,Horse
343-331↓ Owl,Horse,Pr.Dog
411-111↓ Pcock,SeaLn,Dolphin
412-111↓ Pcock,Dolphin
412-211↓ Pcock,SeaLn,Dolphin
413-111↓ Dolphin,Pcock,Horse
421-111↓ Pcock,SeaLn,Dolphin
422-111 SeaLn,Dolphin,Horse
422-132 Dolphin,SeaLn,W.Cat
422-211 SeaLn,Dolphin,Horse
422-332↓ Dolphin,SeaLn,Eagle
423-111 Dolphin,Horse
423-132↓ Dolphin,Horse,Fox
423-211↓ Dolphin,Horse,SeaLn
423-232 Dolphin,Horse,Fox
423-311↓ Dolphin,SeaLn
431-111 Pcock,Horse,Walrus
431-112 Pcock,Horse,SeaLn
431-121 Pcock,Horse,Walrus
431-122 Pcock,Horse,SeaLn
431-131 Pcock,Horse,Lion
431-132 Pcock,Horse,Sable
431-211↓ Pcock,Horse,SeaLn
431-232 Sable,Pcock,Horse
431-322↓ SeaLn,Dolphin,Sable
432-111 Horse,Walrus,SeaLn
432-112 Horse,Dolphin,SeaLn
432-121 Horse,Walrus,SeaLn
432-122 Horse,Dolphin,SeaLn
432-131↓ Horse,Lion,Fox
432-211↓ Horse,SeaLn,Dolphin
432-231 Horse,Lion,SeaLn
432-232 Horse,Dolphin,Sable
432-311 SeaLn,Dolphin,Horse
432-332 Dolphin,Sable,SeaLn
433-111 Horse,Dolphin
433-112↓ Horse,Dolphin,Fox
433-121 Horse,Dolphin,Lion
433-122 Horse,Dolphin,Fox
433-131↓ Horse,Lion,Fox
433-211 Horse,Dolphin,Lion
433-212 Horse,Dolphin,Fox
433-221 Horse,Dolphin,Lion
433-222 Horse,Dolphin,Fox
433-231 Horse,Lion,Fox
433-232 Horse,Fox,Dolphin
433-311↓ Dolphin,Horse,SeaLn
433-331 Dolphin,Horse,Lion

433-332 Dolphin,Horse,Fox
441-111 Sable,Dog,Pengn
441-112 Sable,Dog,Pcock
441-121 Sable,Dog,Pengn
441-122↓ Sable,Dog,Owl
441-211↓ Sable,Dog,Pcock
442-111↓ Sable,Pengn,Owl
442-112 Sable,Owl,Horse
442-121 Sable,Owl,Pengn
442-211↓ Sable,Owl,Horse
442-312 Sable,Dolphin
442-321 Sable,Owl
442-322 Sable,Dolphin
442-331↓ Sable,Owl
443-111↓ Owl,Pengn,Horse
443-122↓ Owl,Horse,Sable
443-311 Owl,Sable,Dolphin

341-
111-111 Croc,Vultre
111-231↓ Croc,Vultre,Porcp
111-332↓ Croc,Zebra,Vultre
112-111↓ Croc,Vultre,Porcp
112-331↓ Croc,Zebra
113-111 Croc,Vultre
113-112↓ Croc,Vultre,Porcp
113-132 Vultre,Porcp,Warthg
113-331↓ Croc,Warthg,Zebra
121-111↓ Porcp,Croc,MGoat
121-212 Porcp,Croc,Warthg
121-232↓ Porcp,Warthg,Zebra
122-111↓ Porcp,Warthg
122-211↓ Porcp,Croc,Warthg
122-221↓ Porcp,Warthg,Zebra
122-311 Zebra,Croc,Porcp
122-312 Zebra,Croc,Warthg
122-321↓ Zebra,Porcp,Warthg
123-111↓ Porcp,Warthg,Gorlla
123-211↓ Warthg,Porcp,Croc
123-311↓ Warthg,Zebra,Croc
131-111↓ Porcp,Hippo
131-211↓ Porcp,Hippo,Croc
131-212 Porcp,Croc,Warthg
131-221↓ Porcp,Hippo,Warthg
131-311↓ Zebra,Croc,Porcp
131-321 Zebra,Porcp,Hippo
131-322 Zebra,Porcp,Warthg
131-331 Zebra,Porcp,Hippo
131-332 Zebra,Porcp,Wolf
132-111↓ Porcp,Hippo
132-211↓ Porcp,Hippo,Croc
132-212 Porcp,Croc,Warthg
132-221↓ Porcp,Hippo,Warthg
132-232 Porcp,Warthg,Lion
132-311 Zebra,Croc,Porcp
132-312 Zebra,Croc,Warthg
132-321 Zebra,Porcp,Hippo
132-322 Zebra,Warthg,Porcp
132-331 Zebra,Porcp,Hippo
132-332 Zebra,Warthg,Porcp
133-111 Porcp,Hippo,Warthg
133-112 Porcp,Warthg,Gorlla
133-121↓ Porcp,Hippo,Warthg
133-132↓ Porcp,Warthg,Lion
133-311↓ Warthg,Zebra,Croc

133-331↓ Warthg,Lion,Tiger
141-111 Hippo,Porcp
141-132↓ Porcp,Hippo,Bison
141-211 Hippo,Bison,Croc
141-212 Bison,Croc,Porcp
141-221 Hippo,Bison,Porcp
141-222 Bison,Wolf,Porcp
141-231 Wolf,Hippo,Bison
141-232↓ Wolf,Bison,Sable
141-331↓ Wolf,Sable,W.Dog
142-111 Hippo,Porcp,Pengn
142-112 Porcp,Hippo,Bison
142-121 Hippo,Porcp,Pengn
142-122 Porcp,Hippo,Bison
142-131 Hippo,Porcp,Pengn
142-132 Porcp,Hippo,Bison
142-211 Hippo,Bison,Croc
142-212 Bison,Croc,Porcp
142-221 Hippo,Bison,Porcp
142-222 Bison,Wolf,Porcp
142-231 Wolf,W.Dog,Hippo
142-232↓ Wolf,W.Dog,Bison
142-321↓ Wolf,W.Dog,Sable
143-111 Pengn,Hippo,Porcp
143-112 Porcp,Pengn,Warthg
143-121 Pengn,Hippo,Porcp
143-122 Porcp,Pengn,Warthg
143-131 Pengn,Owl,Hippo
143-132 Owl,W.Dog,Porcp
143-211 Warthg,Pengn,Owl
143-212↓ Warthg,W.Dog,Owl
143-231 Owl,W.Dog,Lion
143-232↓ W.Dog,Owl,Warthg
143-312 W.Dog,Warthg,Wolf
143-331↓ W.Dog,Owl,Wolf
211-111↓ Weasel,Vultre,Croc
211-222 Vultre,Weasel,Zebra
211-311 Zebra,Weasel,Croc
211-312↓ Zebra,Weasel,Vultre
212-111↓ Vultre,Weasel
212-211↓ Weasel,Vultre,Croc
212-222 Vultre,Weasel,Zebra
212-311 Zebra,Weasel,Croc
212-312↓ Zebra,Weasel,Vultre
213-111↓ Vultre,Gorlla
213-211 Weasel,Vultre,Croc
213-222 Vultre,Weasel,Zebra
213-311 Zebra,Weasel,Croc
213-312↓ Zebra,Weasel,Vultre
221-111 Hippo,MGoat,Zebra
221-112 Vultre,Zebra,Porcp
221-121 Hippo,Zebra,Vultre
221-122 Vultre,Zebra,Porcp
221-131 Hippo,Zebra,Vultre
221-132 Vultre,Rooster,Zebra
221-221↓ Zebra,Hippo,MGoat
221-231↓ Zebra,Rooster,Hippo
221-232↓ Zebra,Rooster,Eagle
222-111 Hippo,MGoat,Gorlla
222-112 Vultre,Gorlla,Zebra
222-121 Hippo,Zebra,Vultre
222-122 Vultre,Zebra,Porcp
222-131 Hippo,Zebra,Vultre
222-132 Vultre,Rooster,Zebra
222-211 Zebra,MGoat,Hippo

222-212 Zebra,MGoat,Vultre
222-221 Zebra,Hippo,MGoat
222-222 Zebra,Rooster,Vultre
222-231 Zebra,Rooster,Hippo
222-232 Zebra,Rooster,Eagle
222-311↓ Zebra,MGoat
222-332↓ Zebra,Eagle,Rooster
223-111↓ Gorlla,Hippo
223-121↓ Hippo,Gorlla,Zebra
223-122 Gorlla,Vultre,Zebra
223-131 Hippo,Lion,Gorlla
223-132 Lion,Gorlla,Vultre
223-211 Zebra,Gorlla,MGoat
223-212 Zebra,Gorlla,Warthg
223-221↓ Zebra,Warthg,Lion
223-231↓ Zebra,Lion,Rooster
223-332 Zebra,Eagle
231-111↓ Hippo,Zebra,MGoat
231-222 Zebra,Hippo,Bear
231-231↓ Hippo,Zebra,Lion
231-332 Zebra,Wolf
232-111↓ Hippo,Vultre,Zebra
232-132 Hippo,Lion
232-211 Hippo,Zebra,MGoat
232-222↓ Zebra,Hippo,Lion
232-332 Zebra,Wolf,Lion
233-111 Hippo,Gorlla
233-112↓ Gorlla,Hippo,Lion
233-132↓ Lion,Hippo,Fox
233-211 Hippo,Lion,Zebra
233-212 Lion,Zebra,Gorlla
233-221↓ Lion,Hippo,Zebra
233-232 Lion,Fox
233-321↓ Zebra,Lion,Hippo
233-322 Zebra,Lion,Tiger
241-111 Hippo,Pengn
241-112↓ Hippo,Bison,Pengn
241-122 Hippo,Bison,Wolf
241-131 Hippo,Wolf,Pengn
241-132↓ Wolf,Hippo,Bison
241-222 Bison,Wolf,Sable
241-231 Wolf,Hippo,Bison
241-232 Wolf,Bison,Sable
241-311↓ Wolf,Zebra,Bison
241-321 Wolf,Zebra,Sable
241-332↓ Wolf,Sable,W.Dog
242-111 Hippo,Pengn
242-122↓ Hippo,Bison,Pengn
242-131 Hippo,Pengn,Wolf
242-132 Wolf,Hippo,Owl
242-211↓ Hippo,Bison,Wolf
242-222 Bison,Wolf,W.Dog
242-231↓ Wolf,Owl,W.Dog
242-311 Wolf,Zebra,W.Dog
242-312 Wolf,W.Dog,Bison
242-321 Wolf,W.Dog,Zebra
242-322↓ Wolf,W.Dog,Sable
243-111 Pengn,Hippo
243-112↓ Pengn,Owl,Hippo
243-132↓ Owl,W.Dog,Pengn
243-212 Owl,W.Dog,Bison
243-221 Owl,Pengn,W.Dog
243-232↓ Owl,W.Dog,Wolf
311-111↓ Weasel,Vultre
311-132↓ Weasel,Vultre,Rooster

(341 cont'd)

311-332↓ Zebra,Weasel,Eagle
312-111↓ Weasel,Vultre
312-132↓ Weasel,Vultre,Rooster
312-212↓ Weasel,Zebra,Vultre
312-221 Weasel,Zebra,Shrew
312-332↓ Zebra,Weasel,Eagle
313-111↓ Weasel,Vultre
313-132↓ Weasel,Vultre,Rooster
313-332↓ Zebra,Weasel,Eagle
321-111↓ Zebra,Hippo
321-332↓ Zebra,Eagle,Rooster
322-111 Zebra,Hippo
322-121↓ Zebra,Hippo,Rooster
322-122 Zebra,Rooster,Weasel
322-131 Zebra,Rooster,Lion
322-212↓ Zebra,Rooster,Weasel
322-231 Zebra,Rooster,Lion
322-232↓ Zebra,Rooster,Eagle
323-111↓ Zebra,Gorlla,Lion
323-121 Zebra,Lion,Pengn
323-122↓ Zebra,Lion,Rooster
323-331↓ Zebra,Lion,Eagle
331-111 Hippo,Zebra
331-122↓ Zebra,Hippo,Bear
331-131 Hippo,Lion,Zebra
331-132 Lion,Rooster,Zebra
331-221↓ Zebra,Hippo,Bear
331-222 Zebra,Bear,Lion
331-231↓ Zebra,Lion,Rooster
331-332↓ Zebra,Wolf,Eagle
332-111 Hippo,Zebra
332-112↓ Zebra,Hippo,Lion
332-132 Lion,Rooster,Zebra
332-211 Zebra,Lion,Hippo
332-212 Zebra,Lion,Bear
332-221 Zebra,Lion,Hippo
332-222 Zebra,Lion,Bear
332-231↓ Lion,Zebra,Rooster
332-331↓ Zebra,Lion,Wolf
333-111 Lion,Pengn,Hippo
333-112 Lion,Zebra,Gorlla
333-212↓ Lion,Zebra,Fox
333-321↓ Zebra,Lion,Tiger
341-111 Pengn,Hippo
341-112↓ Pengn,Wolf,Hippo
341-122 Wolf,Pengn,Sable
341-131 Wolf,Pengn,Owl
341-132 Wolf,Sable,Owl
341-211 Wolf,Pengn,Zebra
341-212 Wolf,Zebra,Sable
341-221 Wolf,Pengn,Zebra
341-222↓ Wolf,Sable,Zebra
342-111 Pengn,Hippo
342-112↓ Pengn,Wolf,Owl
342-212 Wolf,Owl,Zebra
342-221 Wolf,Pengn,Owl
342-222↓ Wolf,Owl,Sable
342-311↓ Wolf,Zebra,Sable
342-332↓ Wolf,Sable,Owl
343-111↓ Pengn,Owl
343-131↓ Pengn,Owl,Lion
343-222↓ Owl,Wolf,Pengn
343-231 Owl,Lion,Pengn
343-232 Owl,Wolf,Lion

343-311 Owl,Wolf,Pengn
343-312 Wolf,Owl,Zebra
343-321 Owl,Wolf,Pengn
343-322 Wolf,Owl,Sable
411-111 Pcock,Weasel
411-311↓ Zebra,Pcock,Weasel
412-111↓ Weasel,Vultre,Pcock
412-132 Weasel,Vultre,W.Cat
412-211↓ Weasel,Zebra,Pcock
412-332↓ Zebra,Weasel,Sable
413-111↓ Weasel,Vultre
413-121↓ Weasel,Vultre,W.Cat
413-221↓ Weasel,Zebra,W.Cat
413-231↓ Weasel,W.Cat,Tiger
413-311↓ Zebra,Weasel,Dolphin
413-321↓ Zebra,Weasel,Tiger
421-111 Zebra,Pcock
421-112↓ Zebra,Pcock,W.Cat
421-122↓ Zebra,W.Cat,Rooster
421-332↓ Zebra,Sable,Tiger
422-111↓ Zebra,W.Cat
422-121↓ Zebra,W.Cat,Rooster
422-332↓ Zebra,Tiger,Sable
423-111 Zebra,W.Cat,Gorlla
423-112↓ Zebra,W.Cat,Tiger
423-311↓ Zebra,Tiger,Dolphin
431-111 Hippo,Zebra,Bear
431-112 Zebra,Sable,Tiger
431-121 Hippo,Zebra,Sable
431-122 Zebra,Sable,Tiger
431-131↓ Sable,Tiger,Lion
431-211↓ Zebra,Sable,Tiger
432-111 Hippo,Zebra,Tiger
432-112 Zebra,Tiger,Sable
432-121 Hippo,Zebra,Tiger
432-122 Tiger,Zebra,W.Cat
432-131↓ Tiger,Lion,Sable
432-211↓ Zebra,Tiger,Sable
433-111↓ Tiger,Lion,Pengn
433-232↓ Tiger,Lion,Sable
433-322↓ Tiger,Zebra,Sable
441-111↓ Sable,Pengn
442-111↓ Sable,Pengn
442-232↓ Sable,Wolf
443-111 Pengn,Owl
443-112↓ Pengn,Sable,Owl
443-132 Sable,Owl,Tiger
443-211 Sable,Pengn,Owl
443-212 Sable,Owl,Tiger
443-221 Sable,Owl,Pengn
443-222↓ Sable,Owl,Tiger

342-

111-111↓ Croc,Vultre
111-331↓ Croc,Zebra
112-111↓ Croc,Vultre
112-332↓ Croc,Zebra,Vultre
113-111↓ Croc,Vultre
113-121↓ Vultre,Croc,Warthg
113-331↓ Croc,Warthg,Zebra
121-111 Croc,Porcp,Hippo
121-112 Croc,Porcp,Warthg
121-121 Porcp,Hippo,Warthg
121-122 Porcp,Warthg,Vultre
121-131 Porcp,Hippo,Warthg

121-132 Porcp,Warthg,Vultre
121-211↓ Croc,Warthg,Zebra
121-231↓ Warthg,Zebra,Rooster
121-332↓ Zebra,Warthg,Eagle
122-111 Croc,Porcp,Hippo
122-112 Croc,Warthg,Porcp
122-121 Porcp,Hippo,Warthg
122-122 Warthg,Porcp,Vultre
122-131 Porcp,Hippo,Warthg
122-132 Warthg,Porcp,Vultre
122-211↓ Croc,Warthg,Zebra
122-231↓ Warthg,Zebra,Rooster
122-322↓ Zebra,Warthg,Croc
123-111↓ Warthg,Gorlla,Croc
123-122↓ Warthg,Porcp,Gorlla
123-212↓ Warthg,Croc,Gorlla
123-311↓ Warthg,Zebra,Croc
131-111↓ Hippo,Croc,Porcp
131-112↓ Hippo,Porcp,Warthg
131-211↓ Hippo,Croc,Warthg
131-221 Hippo,Warthg,Zebra
131-312 Zebra,Croc,Warthg
131-321↓ Zebra,Hippo,Warthg
131-331 Zebra,Hippo,Wolf
131-332 Zebra,Wolf,Warthg
132-111↓ Hippo,Croc,Warthg
132-122↓ Hippo,Warthg,Porcp
132-211 Hippo,Croc,Warthg
132-222↓ Warthg,Hippo,Zebra
132-231↓ Warthg,Hippo,Lion
132-311 Zebra,Croc,Hippo
132-312 Zebra,Croc,Warthg
132-331↓ Zebra,Hippo,Warthg
132-332 Zebra,Warthg,Wolf
133-111 Hippo,Warthg,Gorlla
133-132↓ Warthg,Lion,Hippo
133-211↓ Warthg,Hippo,Croc
133-231↓ Warthg,Lion,Hippo
133-232 Warthg,Lion,Fox
133-311↓ Warthg,Zebra,Croc
133-331↓ Warthg,Lion,Tiger
141-111 Hippo,Bison
141-132↓ Bison,Wolf,Hippo
141-211 Bison,Hippo,Croc
141-212 Bison,Croc,Wolf
141-231↓ Wolf,Bison,Hippo
141-232↓ Wolf,Bison,Sable
141-331↓ Wolf,Sable,W.Dog
142-111 Hippo,Pengn,Bison
142-112 Bison,Hippo,Croc
142-121 Hippo,Pengn,Bison
142-122 Bison,Hippo,Wolf
142-131 Hippo,Pengn,Bison
142-132 Bison,Wolf,Hippo
142-211 Bison,Hippo,Croc
142-212 Bison,Croc,Wolf
142-231↓ Wolf,Bison,Owl
142-232↓ Wolf,Bison,W.Dog
142-331↓ Wolf,W.Dog,Sable
143-111 Hippo,Pengn,Owl
143-112 Pengn,Warthg,Owl
143-121 Pengn,Hippo,Owl
143-122 Owl,Pengn,Warthg
143-131 Owl,Pengn,Hippo
143-132 Owl,W.Dog

143-211	Owl,Warthg,Pengn
143-212	Warthg,Owl,Bison
143-232↓	Owl,W.Dog,Wolf
211-111↓	Vultre,Weasel,Croc
211-222	Vultre,Weasel,Zebra
211-311	Zebra,Weasel,Croc
211-312↓	Zebra,Weasel,Vultre
212-111↓	Vultre,Weasel,Croc
212-222	Vultre,Weasel,Zebra
212-311	Zebra,Weasel,Croc
212-312↓	Zebra,Weasel,Vultre
213-111	Vultre,Gorlla
213-211↓	Weasel,Vultre,Croc
213-222	Vultre,Weasel,Zebra
213-311	Zebra,Weasel,Croc
213-312↓	Zebra,Weasel,Vultre
221-111↓	Hippo,Zebra,Vultre
221-131	Hippo,Rooster,Zebra
221-132	Rooster,Vultre,Zebra
221-211	Zebra,Hippo
221-212	Zebra,Rooster,Vultre
221-221	Zebra,Hippo,Rooster
221-222	Zebra,Rooster,Vultre
221-231	Zebra,Rooster,Hippo
221-232↓	Zebra,Rooster,Eagle
222-111	Hippo,Gorlla,Zebra
222-112	Vultre,Gorlla,Zebra
222-121↓	Hippo,Zebra,Vultre
222-131	Hippo,Rooster,Zebra
222-132	Rooster,Vultre,Zebra
222-211	Zebra,Hippo,Gorlla
222-212	Zebra,Rooster,Vultre
222-221	Zebra,Hippo,Rooster
222-222	Zebra,Rooster,Vultre
222-231	Zebra,Rooster,Hippo
222-232↓	Zebra,Rooster,Eagle
223-111	Gorlla,Hippo,Zebra
223-112	Gorlla,Vultre,Zebra
223-121	Hippo,Gorlla,Zebra
223-122	Gorlla,Vultre,Zebra
223-131	Hippo,Lion,Gorlla
223-132	Rooster,Lion,Gorlla
223-211↓	Zebra,Gorlla,Warthg
223-221	Zebra,Warthg,Lion
223-222	Zebra,Warthg,Rooster
223-231↓	Zebra,Lion,Rooster
223-311	Zebra,Gorlla
223-331	Zebra,Lion,Eagle
223-332	Zebra,Eagle,Rooster
231-111↓	Hippo,Vultre,Zebra
231-132	Hippo,Rooster
231-212↓	Zebra,Hippo,Bear
231-231	Hippo,Zebra,Lion
231-232	Zebra,Rooster,Lion
231-331↓	Zebra,Wolf,Hippo
231-332	Zebra,Wolf,Eagle
232-111↓	Hippo,Vultre,Gorlla
232-122	Hippo,Vultre,Zebra
232-132↓	Hippo,Lion,Rooster
232-211	Hippo,Zebra,Bear
232-222↓	Zebra,Hippo,Lion
232-232	Lion,Zebra,Rooster
232-311↓	Zebra,Hippo
232-331↓	Zebra,Wolf,Lion
233-111↓	Hippo,Gorlla,Lion

233-131	Hippo,Lion,Fox
233-212	Lion,Zebra,Gorlla
233-221	Lion,Hippo,Zebra
233-222	Lion,Fox,Zebra
233-231	Lion,Fox,Hippo
233-232	Lion,Fox,Owl
233-311	Zebra,Lion,Hippo
233-312	Zebra,Lion,Tiger
233-321	Zebra,Lion,Hippo
233-322	Zebra,Lion,Tiger
241-111	Hippo,Pengn,Bison
241-112	Bison,Hippo,Wolf
241-121	Hippo,Pengn,Bison
241-122	Bison,Hippo,Wolf
241-131	Hippo,Wolf,Pengn
241-132↓	Wolf,Bison,Hippo
241-232↓	Wolf,Bison,Sable
241-332	Wolf,Sable,W.Dog
242-111↓	Hippo,Pengn,Bison
242-122	Bison,Hippo,Wolf
242-131	Hippo,Pengn,Wolf
242-132	Wolf,Owl,Bison
242-211	Bison,Hippo,Wolf
242-212	Bison,Wolf,Owl
242-221	Bison,Wolf,Hippo
242-222↓	Bison,Wolf,Owl
242-311	Wolf,Bison,Zebra
242-312↓	Wolf,Bison,W.Dog
242-331↓	Wolf,W.Dog,Sable
243-111	Pengn,Hippo,Owl
243-112	Pengn,Owl,Bison
243-121	Pengn,Owl,Hippo
243-122	Owl,Pengn,Bison
243-131	Owl,Pengn,Hippo
243-132	Owl,W.Dog,Pengn
243-211	Owl,Pengn,Bison
243-212	Owl,Bison,W.Dog
243-221	Owl,Pengn,W.Dog
243-222	Owl,W.Dog,Bison
243-231↓	Owl,W.Dog,Wolf
311-111↓	Weasel,Vultre
311-132↓	Weasel,Vultre,Rooster
311-212↓	Weasel,Zebra,Vultre
311-221	Weasel,Zebra,Shrew
311-222	Weasel,Zebra,Vultre
311-332↓	Zebra,Weasel,Eagle
312-111↓	Weasel,Vultre,Zebra
312-131↓	Weasel,Vultre,Rooster
312-211	Weasel,Zebra,Shrew
312-212	Weasel,Zebra,Vultre
312-221	Weasel,Zebra,Shrew
312-222	Weasel,Zebra,Vultre
312-331↓	Zebra,Weasel,Eagle
313-111↓	Weasel,Vultre
313-132↓	Weasel,Vultre,Rooster
313-212↓	Weasel,Zebra,Vultre
313-221	Weasel,Zebra,Shrew
313-222	Weasel,Zebra,Vultre
313-332↓	Zebra,Weasel,Eagle
321-111	Zebra,Hippo
321-112	Zebra,Rooster,Weasel
321-121	Zebra,Rooster,Hippo
321-132↓	Rooster,Zebra,Eagle
321-211↓	Zebra,Rooster,Weasel
321-231↓	Zebra,Rooster,Eagle

322-111	Zebra,Hippo,Rooster
322-112	Zebra,Rooster,Weasel
322-121	Zebra,Rooster,Hippo
322-122	Zebra,Rooster,Weasel
322-131↓	Rooster,Zebra,Lion
322-211↓	Zebra,Rooster,Weasel
322-231	Zebra,Rooster,Lion
322-232↓	Zebra,Rooster,Eagle
323-111	Zebra,Gorlla,Lion
323-112	Zebra,Gorlla,Rooster
323-121↓	Zebra,Lion,Rooster
323-331	Zebra,Lion,Eagle
323-332	Zebra,Eagle,Rooster
331-111	Hippo,Zebra,Bear
331-132	Rooster,Lion,Zebra
331-211	Zebra,Bear,Hippo
331-212	Zebra,Bear,Rooster
331-221	Zebra,Bear,Hippo
331-222	Zebra,Bear,Rooster
331-231↓	Zebra,Lion,Rooster
331-331↓	Zebra,Wolf,Lion
331-332	Zebra,Wolf,Eagle
332-111	Hippo,Zebra,Bear
332-122	Zebra,Hippo,Lion
332-131	Lion,Hippo,Rooster
332-132	Lion,Rooster,Zebra
332-211↓	Zebra,Bear,Lion
332-231↓	Lion,Zebra,Rooster
332-331↓	Zebra,Wolf,Lion
333-111	Lion,Pengn,Hippo
333-112	Lion,Fox,Zebra
333-121	Lion,Pengn,Hippo
333-122	Lion,Fox,Zebra
333-131	Lion,Fox,Pengn
333-132	Lion,Fox,Owl
333-211↓	Lion,Zebra,Fox
333-231↓	Lion,Fox,Owl
333-311↓	Zebra,Lion,Tiger
341-111	Pengn,Hippo,Wolf
341-112	Wolf,Pengn,Bison
341-121	Pengn,Wolf,Hippo
341-122↓	Wolf,Pengn,Owl
341-211	Wolf,Pengn,Zebra
341-212	Wolf,Zebra,Sable
341-221	Wolf,Pengn,Zebra
341-222	Wolf,Sable,Zebra
341-231↓	Wolf,Sable,Owl
341-312↓	Wolf,Zebra,Sable
342-111	Pengn,Hippo
342-112↓	Pengn,Wolf,Owl
342-212	Wolf,Owl,Zebra
342-221	Wolf,Owl,Pengn
342-222↓	Wolf,Owl,Sable
342-311↓	Wolf,Zebra,Sable
342-331↓	Wolf,Sable,Owl
343-111↓	Pengn,Owl
343-122↓	Owl,Pengn,Lion
343-211↓	Owl,Pengn,Wolf
343-231↓	Owl,Wolf,Lion
343-311	Owl,Wolf,Pengn
343-312	Wolf,Owl,Zebra
343-321	Owl,Wolf,Pengn
343-322	Wolf,Owl,Sable
411-111↓	Pcock,Weasel
411-311↓	Pcock,Zebra,Weasel

(342 cont'd)

412-111↓ Weasel,Pcock,Vultre
412-211↓ Weasel,Pcock,Zebra
412-331↓ Zebra,Weasel,Sable
413-111　Weasel,Vultre
413-112↓ Weasel,Vultre,Pcock
413-121↓ Weasel,Vultre,W.Cat
413-222↓ Weasel,Zebra,W.Cat
413-231↓ Weasel,W.Cat,Tiger
413-311↓ Zebra,Weasel,Dolphin
413-321↓ Zebra,Weasel,Tiger
421-111　Zebra,Pcock
421-112↓ Zebra,Pcock,Rooster
421-131↓ Rooster,Zebra,W.Cat
421-222↓ Zebra,Rooster,Pcock
421-231↓ Zebra,Rooster,W.Cat
421-332↓ Zebra,Sable,Tiger
422-111↓ Zebra,W.Cat,Rooster
422-322↓ Zebra,Tiger,W.Cat
422-331↓ Zebra,Tiger,Sable
423-111　Zebra,W.Cat,Gorlla
423-112　Zebra,W.Cat,Tiger
423-132　W.Cat,Tiger,Rooster
423-211↓ Zebra,W.Cat,Tiger
423-311↓ Zebra,Tiger,Dolphin
431-111　Hippo,Zebra,Bear
431-112　Zebra,Bear,Sable
431-121　Hippo,Zebra,Bear
431-122　Zebra,Sable,Tiger
431-131　Sable,Tiger,Lion
431-132　Sable,Tiger,Rooster
431-211　Zebra,Sable,Bear
431-212↓ Zebra,Sable,Tiger
432-111　Hippo,Zebra,Bear
432-112　Zebra,Tiger,Bear
432-121　Hippo,Zebra,Tiger
432-122　Tiger,Zebra,W.Cat
432-131↓ Tiger,Lion,Sable
432-211↓ Zebra,Tiger,Sable
433-111　Tiger,Lion,Pengn
433-112　Tiger,Lion,Fox
433-121　Tiger,Lion,Pengn
433-122↓ Tiger,Lion,Fox
433-211↓ Tiger,Lion,Zebra
433-222↓ Tiger,Lion,Fox
433-312↓ Tiger,Zebra,Sable
433-331↓ Tiger,Sable,Lion
441-111↓ Sable,Pengn
441-222↓ Sable,Wolf
442-111↓ Sable,Pengn
442-231↓ Sable,Wolf,Owl
443-111　Pengn,Owl
443-122↓ Owl,Sable,Pengn
443-132　Owl,Sable,Tiger
443-211　Sable,Owl,Pengn
443-212　Sable,Owl,Tiger
443-221　Sable,Owl,Pengn
443-321↓ Sable,Tiger,Owl
443-322　Sable,Tiger,Wolf
443-331　Sable,Tiger,Owl
443-332　Sable,Tiger,Wolf

343-

111-111↓ Croc,Vultre
111-332↓ Croc,Zebra,Eagle

112-111↓ Croc,Vultre
112-232↓ Croc,Vultre,Rooster
112-332↓ Croc,Zebra,Eagle
113-111↓ Croc,Vultre
113-121↓ Vultre,Croc,Warthg
113-331↓ Croc,Warthg,Zebra
121-111　Croc,Porcp,Hippo
121-112　Croc,Porcp,Warthg
121-121　Porcp,Hippo,Warthg
121-122　Porcp,Warthg,Vultre
121-131　Rooster,Porcp,Hippo
121-132　Rooster,Porcp,Warthg
121-211↓ Croc,Warthg,Zebra
121-222　Warthg,Rooster,Zebra
121-312↓ Zebra,Croc,Warthg
121-322　Zebra,Warthg,Eagle
121-331↓ Zebra,Eagle,Rooster
122-111　Croc,Porcp,Hippo
122-112　Croc,Warthg,Porcp
122-121　Porcp,Hippo,Warthg
122-122　Warthg,Porcp,Vultre
122-131　Rooster,Porcp,Hippo
122-132　Rooster,Warthg,Porcp
122-211↓ Croc,Warthg,Zebra
122-322↓ Zebra,Warthg,Eagle
122-331↓ Zebra,Eagle,Rooster
123-111↓ Warthg,Gorlla,Croc
123-131↓ Warthg,Lion,Rooster
123-211↓ Warthg,Croc
123-232↓ Warthg,Rooster,Lion
123-331↓ Warthg,Zebra,Lion
123-332　Warthg,Zebra,Eagle
131-111↓ Hippo,Croc,Porcp
131-122↓ Hippo,Porcp,Warthg
131-132　Hippo,Rooster,Lion
131-211　Hippo,Croc,Bear
131-212　Croc,Warthg,Bear
131-221↓ Hippo,Bear,Warthg
131-231　Hippo,Lion,Rooster
131-232　Rooster,Lion,Wolf
131-311　Zebra,Croc,Hippo
131-312　Zebra,Croc,Wolf
131-321　Zebra,Hippo,Wolf
131-322　Zebra,Wolf,Warthg
131-331　Wolf,Zebra,Lion
131-332　Wolf,Zebra,Eagle
132-111↓ Hippo,Croc,Warthg
132-122　Hippo,Warthg,Porcp
132-132↓ Hippo,Lion,Rooster
132-211　Hippo,Croc,Warthg
132-212　Croc,Warthg,Bear
132-221　Hippo,Warthg,Lion
132-222　Warthg,Lion,Bear
132-231　Lion,Hippo,Rooster
132-232　Lion,Rooster,Warthg
132-311　Zebra,Croc,Hippo
132-312　Zebra,Croc,Warthg
132-321　Zebra,Hippo,Wolf
132-322　Zebra,Wolf,Warthg
132-331↓ Wolf,Lion,Zebra
133-111　Hippo,Warthg,Gorlla
133-112　Warthg,Gorlla,Lion
133-121↓ Hippo,Warthg,Lion
133-132　Lion,Warthg,Fox
133-221↓ Warthg,Lion,Hippo

133-222　Warthg,Lion,Fox
133-312↓ Warthg,Lion,W.Dog
141-111↓ Bison,Hippo
141-231↓ Wolf,Bison,W.Dog
142-111↓ Bison,Hippo,Pengn
142-231↓ Wolf,Bison,Owl
142-232↓ Wolf,Bison,W.Dog
143-111　Owl,Pengn,Bison
143-112　Owl,Bison,W.Dog
143-121　Owl,Pengn,Bison
143-211↓ Owl,Bison,W.Dog
143-232↓ Owl,W.Dog,Wolf
211-111↓ Vultre,Weasel
211-132　Vultre,Rooster
211-211　Weasel,Vultre,Croc
211-222　Vultre,Weasel,Rooster
211-311　Zebra,Weasel,Croc
211-312↓ Zebra,Weasel,Vultre
211-331　Zebra,Eagle,Weasel
211-332　Zebra,Eagle,Rooster
212-111　Vultre,Weasel
212-131↓ Vultre,Weasel,Rooster
212-211　Weasel,Vultre,Croc
212-222　Vultre,Weasel,Rooster
212-311　Zebra,Weasel,Croc
212-312↓ Zebra,Weasel,Vultre
212-331　Zebra,Eagle,Weasel
212-332　Zebra,Eagle,Rooster
213-111↓ Vultre,Gorlla
213-122↓ Vultre,Weasel
213-132　Vultre,Rooster
213-211　Weasel,Vultre,Croc
213-222　Vultre,Weasel,Rooster
213-311　Zebra,Weasel,Croc
213-312↓ Zebra,Weasel,Vultre
213-331　Zebra,Eagle,Weasel
213-332　Zebra,Eagle,Rooster
221-111　Hippo,Zebra,Vultre
221-112　Vultre,Rooster,Zebra
221-121　Hippo,Rooster,Zebra
221-122　Rooster,Vultre,Zebra
221-131　Rooster,Hippo
221-132　Rooster,Vultre
221-221↓ Zebra,Rooster,Hippo
221-222↓ Rooster,Zebra,Eagle
222-111　Hippo,Gorlla,Zebra
222-112　Vultre,Rooster,Gorlla
222-121　Hippo,Rooster,Zebra
222-122　Rooster,Vultre,Zebra
222-131　Rooster,Hippo,Lion
222-132　Rooster,Vultre,Lion
222-211　Zebra,Rooster,Hippo
222-212　Zebra,Rooster,Eagle
222-221　Zebra,Rooster,Hippo
222-222　Rooster,Zebra,Eagle
222-231　Rooster,Zebra,Lion
222-232↓ Rooster,Zebra,Eagle
223-111　Gorlla,Hippo
223-112　Gorlla,Vultre,Rooster
223-121　Hippo,Gorlla,Lion
223-122　Gorlla,Rooster,Lion
223-131　Lion,Rooster,Hippo
223-132　Rooster,Lion,Fox
223-211　Zebra,Gorlla,Lion
223-212　Zebra,Gorlla,Rooster

223-221↓ Lion,Zebra,Rooster
223-231 Lion,Rooster,Fox
223-312 Zebra,Eagle,Rooster
223-321 Zebra,Lion,Eagle
223-322 Zebra,Eagle,Rooster
223-331 Zebra,Lion,Eagle
223-332 Zebra,Eagle,Rooster
231-111↓ Hippo,Bear
231-121↓ Hippo,Walrus,Bear
231-122 Hippo,Bear,Rooster
231-132↓ Rooster,Hippo,Lion
231-211 Hippo,Bear,Zebra
231-212 Bear,Zebra,Rooster
231-221 Hippo,Bear,Zebra
231-222 Bear,Rooster,Zebra
231-231 Lion,Rooster,Hippo
231-232 Rooster,Lion,Wolf
231-311↓ Zebra,Bear,Wolf
231-331 Wolf,Zebra,Lion
231-332 Wolf,Zebra,Eagle
232-111 Hippo,Walrus,Bear
232-112 Hippo,Bear,Lion
232-121 Hippo,Walrus,Lion
232-122 Hippo,Lion,Bear
232-131↓ Hippo,Lion,Rooster
232-211 Hippo,Bear,Lion
232-212 Bear,Lion,Zebra
232-221 Hippo,Lion,Bear
232-222 Lion,Bear,Rooster
232-231 Lion,Rooster,Hippo
232-232 Lion,Rooster,Wolf
232-311↓ Zebra,Bear,Wolf
232-321↓ Zebra,Wolf,Lion
233-111↓ Hippo,Lion,Gorlla
233-121↓ Hippo,Lion,Fox
233-132 Lion,Fox,Owl
233-211 Lion,Hippo,Fox
233-212 Lion,Fox,Bear
233-221 Lion,Fox,Hippo
233-222 Lion,Fox,Bear
233-231↓ Lion,Fox,Owl
233-311↓ Lion,Zebra,W.Dog
233-331↓ Lion,W.Dog,Fox
241-111↓ Bison,Hippo,Wolf
241-222↓ Bison,Wolf,W.Dog
241-231 Wolf,Bison,Owl
241-322↓ Wolf,Bison,W.Dog
242-111 Bison,Hippo,Pengn
242-121↓ Bison,Hippo,Wolf
242-122↓ Bison,Wolf,Owl
242-311↓ Wolf,Bison,W.Dog
242-331↓ Wolf,W.Dog,Owl
243-111↓ Owl,Pengn,Bison
243-122 Owl,Bison,W.Dog
243-131 Owl,W.Dog,Pengn
243-132 Owl,W.Dog,Lion
243-211↓ Owl,Bison,W.Dog
243-231↓ Owl,W.Dog,Wolf
311-111↓ Weasel,Vultre,Pcock
311-122↓ Weasel,Vultre,Rooster
311-222↓ Weasel,Rooster,Pcock
311-322↓ Zebra,Weasel,Eagle
311-332 Zebra,Eagle,Rooster
312-111 Weasel,Vultre
312-112↓ Weasel,Vultre,Rooster

312-222↓ Weasel,Rooster,Zebra
312-312↓ Zebra,Weasel,Eagle
312-332 Zebra,Eagle,Rooster
313-111 Weasel,Vultre
313-112↓ Weasel,Vultre,Rooster
313-131 Weasel,Rooster,Lion
313-132 Rooster,Weasel,Vultre
313-212↓ Weasel,Zebra,Rooster
313-231 Weasel,Rooster,Lion
313-322↓ Zebra,Weasel,Eagle
313-332 Zebra,Eagle,Rooster
321-111↓ Zebra,Rooster,Bear
321-131 Rooster,Zebra,Lion
321-132 Rooster,Zebra,Eagle
321-211 Zebra,Rooster,Bear
321-212↓ Zebra,Rooster,Eagle
322-111 Zebra,Rooster,Bear
322-131↓ Rooster,Lion,Zebra
322-211 Zebra,Rooster,Bear
322-212 Zebra,Rooster,Eagle
322-221 Zebra,Rooster,Lion
322-222 Rooster,Zebra,Eagle
322-231 Rooster,Zebra,Lion
322-232↓ Rooster,Zebra,Eagle
323-111↓ Lion,Zebra,Rooster
323-131 Lion,Rooster,Fox
323-212↓ Zebra,Rooster,Lion
323-231 Lion,Rooster,Fox
323-312 Zebra,Eagle,Rooster
323-321 Zebra,Lion,Eagle
323-322 Zebra,Eagle,Rooster
323-331 Zebra,Lion,Eagle
323-332 Zebra,Eagle,Rooster
331-111 Bear,Hippo,Lion
331-112 Bear,Rooster,Lion
331-121 Bear,Hippo,Lion
331-122↓ Bear,Rooster,Lion
331-212 Bear,Zebra,Rooster
331-221 Bear,Zebra,Lion
331-222 Bear,Rooster,Zebra
331-231 Lion,Rooster,Bear
331-232 Rooster,Lion,Wolf
331-311↓ Zebra,Bear,Wolf
331-331 Wolf,Zebra,Lion
331-332 Wolf,Zebra,Eagle
332-111 Bear,Hippo,Lion
332-112 Bear,Lion,Rooster
332-121 Lion,Bear,Hippo
332-122↓ Lion,Bear,Rooster
332-132 Lion,Rooster,Fox
332-211↓ Bear,Lion,Zebra
332-231 Lion,Rooster,Bear
332-232 Lion,Rooster,Wolf
332-311↓ Zebra,Bear,Wolf
332-321↓ Zebra,Wolf,Lion
333-111↓ Lion,Fox,Bear
333-131↓ Lion,Fox,Owl
333-211↓ Lion,Fox,Bear
333-231↓ Lion,Fox,Owl
333-311↓ Lion,Zebra,Fox
333-331↓ Lion,Fox,Wolf
341-111 Wolf,Pengn,Owl
341-112 Wolf,Bison,Owl
341-121 Wolf,Pengn,Owl
341-212↓ Wolf,Bison,Owl

342-111↓ Pengn,Wolf,Owl
342-112 Wolf,Owl,Bison
342-121 Wolf,Pengn,Owl
342-122 Wolf,Owl,Bison
342-131 Wolf,Owl,Pengn
342-132 Wolf,Owl,Lion
342-211↓ Wolf,Owl,Bison
342-221 Wolf,Owl,Lion
342-222 Wolf,Owl,Bison
342-231↓ Wolf,Owl,Lion
342-311↓ Wolf,Owl,Zebra
343-111 Owl,Pengn
343-112↓ Owl,Pengn,Lion
343-132 Owl,Lion,Wolf
343-211 Owl,Wolf,Pengn
343-312↓ Wolf,Owl,W.Dog
411-111↓ Pcock,Weasel
411-232↓ Pcock,Rooster
411-322↓ Pcock,Zebra
412-111 Pcock,Weasel
412-122↓ Pcock,Weasel,Vultre
412-131↓ Pcock,Weasel,Rooster
412-311↓ Zebra,Pcock,Weasel
412-331↓ Zebra,Pcock,Eagle
413-111↓ Weasel,Pcock,Vultre
413-131↓ Weasel,Rooster,Pcock
413-331↓ Tiger,Dolphin,Zebra
421-111↓ Pcock,Zebra,Rooster
421-322↓ Zebra,Eagle,Rooster
422-111 Zebra,Rooster,W.Cat
422-132 Rooster,W.Cat,Lion
422-212↓ Zebra,Rooster,W.Cat
422-232 Rooster,Zebra,Eagle
422-311↓ Zebra,SeaLn,Dolphin
422-321 Zebra,SeaLn,Eagle
422-322 Zebra,Eagle,Dolphin
422-331↓ Zebra,Eagle,Rooster
423-111 Lion,Dolphin,Zebra
423-112 Dolphin,Rooster,Lion
423-121 Lion,Rooster,W.Cat
423-132 Rooster,Lion,Fox
423-211 Dolphin,Zebra,Lion
423-212 Dolphin,Zebra,Rooster
423-221 Lion,Dolphin,Zebra
423-222 Dolphin,Rooster,Lion
423-231 Lion,Rooster,Tiger
423-331↓ Tiger,Dolphin,Zebra
431-111 Bear,Pcock,Hippo
431-112 Bear,Pcock,Rooster
431-121 Bear,Pcock,Lion
431-122 Bear,Rooster,Pcock
431-131 Lion,Rooster,Bear
431-132 Rooster,Lion,Sable
431-211↓ Bear,Pcock,Zebra
431-222 Bear,Rooster,Pcock
431-231 Lion,Rooster,Sable
431-331↓ Sable,Tiger,Wolf
432-111 Bear,Lion,Hippo
432-112 Bear,Lion,Rooster
432-211↓ Bear,Lion,Zebra
432-231↓ Lion,Tiger,Rooster
432-311↓ Zebra,Tiger,Sable
433-111↓ Lion,Fox,Tiger
433-311↓ Tiger,Lion,Dolphin
433-331↓ Tiger,Lion,Fox

(343 cont'd)
441-111↓ Sable,Wolf,Pengn
442-111↓ Sable,Pengn,Wolf
442-112   Sable,Wolf,Owl
442-121   Sable,Wolf,Pengn
442-331↓ Sable,Wolf,Owl
443-111↓ Owl,Pengn
443-212↓ Owl,Sable,Wolf

344-
111-111↓ Croc,Vultre
111-231↓ Croc,Eagle,Vultre
112-111↓ Croc,Vultre
112-231↓ Croc,Eagle,Vultre
113-111↓ Croc,Vultre
113-121↓ Vultre,Croc,Warthg
113-131   Lion,Vultre,Croc
113-132   Vultre,Lion,Warthg
113-211↓ Croc,Warthg,Lion
113-321↓ Croc,Warthg,Eagle
113-331↓ Eagle,W.Dog,Lion
121-111   Walrus,Porcp,Croc
121-112   Porcp,Croc,Warthg
121-121   Walrus,Porcp,Hippo
121-122   Porcp,Eagle,Warthg
121-131   Lion,Eagle,Walrus
121-132   Eagle,Rooster,Lion
121-211↓ Croc,Eagle,Warthg
121-221   Eagle,Lion,Warthg
121-222   Eagle,Warthg,Rooster
121-231↓ Eagle,Lion,Rooster
121-311↓ Eagle,Zebra,Croc
122-111   Walrus,Porcp,Croc
122-112   Porcp,Croc,Warthg
122-121   Walrus,Porcp,Lion
122-122   Porcp,Warthg,Lion
122-131   Lion,Eagle,Walrus
122-132   Lion,Eagle,Rooster
122-211   Croc,Warthg,Lion
122-212   Croc,Warthg,Eagle
122-221↓ Lion,Eagle,Warthg
122-231   Lion,Eagle,Rooster
122-321↓ Eagle,Zebra
123-111↓ Warthg,Lion,Gorlla
123-312↓ Warthg,Eagle,Lion
123-331   Lion,Eagle,W.Dog
131-111↓ Walrus,Hippo,Lion
131-311↓ Lion,Eagle,Zebra
131-312   Eagle,Lion,W.Dog
132-111↓ Walrus,Hippo,Lion
132-311↓ Lion,W.Dog,Eagle
133-111↓ Lion,Walrus
133-232↓ Lion,W.Dog,Baboon
141-111   Walrus,Bison,Hippo
141-112↓ Bison,W.Dog,Walrus
141-122   Bison,W.Dog,Wolf
141-131   W.Dog,Lion,Walrus
141-132   W.Dog,Bison,Wolf
141-231   W.Dog,Wolf,Lion
141-232↓ W.Dog,Wolf,Bison
142-111   Walrus,Bison,W.Dog
142-112   Bison,W.Dog,Lion
142-121   W.Dog,Walrus,Bison
142-122   W.Dog,Bison,Lion
142-131   W.Dog,Lion,Walrus

142-132↓ W.Dog,Lion,Bison
142-212   W.Dog,Bison,Wolf
142-221↓ W.Dog,Bison,Lion
142-231↓ W.Dog,Lion,Wolf
143-111↓ W.Dog,Lion,Owl
211-111↓ Vultre,Eagle,Rooster
211-211   Weasel,Vultre,Croc
211-212   Vultre,Weasel,Eagle
211-231   Eagle,Rooster,Weasel
211-232   Eagle,Rooster,Vultre
211-321↓ Eagle,Zebra,Weasel
212-111↓ Vultre,Lion,Eagle
212-132   Vultre,Eagle,Rooster
212-211   Weasel,Vultre,Croc
212-212   Vultre,Weasel,Eagle
212-231↓ Eagle,Lion,Rooster
212-311↓ Eagle,Zebra,Weasel
213-111↓ Vultre,Lion,Gorlla
213-211↓ Lion,Weasel,Vultre
213-311↓ Eagle,Lion,Zebra
213-322↓ Eagle,Lion,W.Dog
221-111   Walrus,Hippo,Lion
221-112   Eagle,Rooster,Lion
221-121   Walrus,Lion,Hippo
221-122↓ Eagle,Rooster,Lion
221-211   Eagle,Zebra,Lion
221-212   Eagle,Rooster,Zebra
221-221↓ Eagle,Lion,Rooster
221-322↓ Eagle,Zebra,Rooster
222-111   Walrus,Lion,Hippo
222-112   Lion,Eagle,Rooster
222-121   Walrus,Lion,Hippo
222-122↓ Lion,Eagle,Rooster
222-211   Lion,Eagle,Zebra
222-212   Eagle,Lion,Rooster
222-312↓ Eagle,Zebra,Lion
222-332   Eagle,Lion,Rooster
223-111↓ Lion,Gorlla
223-122↓ Lion,Horse,Eagle
223-132↓ Lion,Eagle,Rooster
223-311   Lion,Eagle,Zebra
223-322   Eagle,Lion,W.Dog
231-111↓ Walrus,Hippo,Lion
231-212   Lion,Eagle,Bear
231-221   Lion,Walrus
231-232↓ Lion,Eagle,Rooster
231-311   Lion,Eagle,Zebra
231-322   Eagle,Lion,W.Dog
232-111   Walrus,Lion,Hippo
232-211   Lion,Horse,Horse
232-212   Lion,Horse,Eagle
232-221   Lion,Walrus,Horse
232-311↓ Lion,Eagle,Zebra
232-312↓ Lion,Eagle,W.Dog
233-111↓ Lion,Walrus,Horse
233-311↓ Lion,W.Dog,Horse
233-331↓ Lion,W.Dog,Eagle
241-111   Walrus,Bison,Hippo
241-112   Bison,W.Dog,Wolf
241-121   Walrus,Bison,W.Dog
241-122   Bison,W.Dog,Wolf
241-131↓ W.Dog,Lion,Wolf
241-211↓ Bison,W.Dog,Wolf
242-111   Walrus,Bison,W.Dog
242-112   Bison,W.Dog,Lion

242-121   W.Dog,Walrus,Lion
242-122   W.Dog,Bison,Lion
242-131↓ W.Dog,Lion,Wolf
242-211   W.Dog,Bison,Lion
242-212   W.Dog,Bison,Wolf
242-221   W.Dog,Lion,Bison
242-222   W.Dog,Bison,Wolf
242-231   W.Dog,Lion,Wolf
242-312↓ W.Dog,Wolf,Bison
242-321   W.Dog,Wolf,Lion
242-322   W.Dog,Wolf,Bison
242-331↓ W.Dog,Wolf,Lion
243-111↓ W.Dog,Lion,Owl
311-111↓ Weasel,Vultre,Pcock
311-122   Weasel,Vultre,Eagle
311-131↓ Eagle,Rooster,Weasel
311-211↓ Weasel,Pcock,Eagle
311-222↓ Eagle,Weasel,Rooster
311-321↓ Eagle,Zebra,Weasel
312-111   Weasel,Vultre,Lion
312-112   Weasel,Vultre,Eagle
312-121   Weasel,Vultre,Lion
312-122   Weasel,Vultre,Eagle
312-131↓ Lion,Eagle,Rooster
312-211   Weasel,Eagle,Zebra
312-212   Weasel,Eagle,Rooster
312-221   Weasel,Eagle,Lion
312-222   Eagle,Weasel,Rooster
312-231↓ Eagle,Lion,Rooster
312-311↓ Eagle,Zebra,Weasel
312-331   Eagle,Zebra,Lion
312-332   Eagle,Rooster
313-111↓ Lion,Weasel,Vultre
313-211↓ Lion,Weasel,Eagle
313-232↓ Lion,Eagle,Rooster
321-111↓ Lion,Eagle,Rooster
321-211   Eagle,Zebra,Lion
321-212   Eagle,Rooster,Zebra
321-221↓ Eagle,Lion,Rooster
321-312↓ Eagle,Zebra,Rooster
321-331↓ Eagle,Zebra,Lion
322-111↓ Lion,Eagle,Rooster
322-211   Lion,Eagle,Zebra
322-212   Eagle,Lion,Rooster
322-311↓ Eagle,Zebra,Lion
323-111   Lion,Horse
323-132↓ Lion,Eagle,Rooster
323-211   Lion,Horse,Eagle
323-232↓ Lion,Eagle,Rooster
323-311↓ Lion,Eagle,Zebra
331-111↓ Lion,Walrus,Bear
331-122↓ Lion,Bear,Eagle
331-132   Lion,Eagle,Rooster
331-212↓ Lion,Eagle,Bear
331-231↓ Lion,Eagle,Rooster
331-311   Lion,Eagle,Zebra
331-332   Eagle,Lion,Wolf
332-111   Lion,Horse,Walrus
332-112   Lion,Horse,Bear
332-121   Lion,Horse,Walrus
332-122↓ Lion,Horse,Bear
332-132   Lion,Eagle
332-211   Lion,Horse,Bear
332-212↓ Lion,Horse,Eagle
332-311↓ Lion,Eagle,Zebra

332-331↓ Lion,Eagle,Wolf
333-111↓ Lion,Horse
333-311↓ Lion,Horse,Eagle
341-111 Lion,Wolf,Pengn
341-112 Wolf,Lion,Bison
341-121 Lion,Wolf,Pengn
341-122 Wolf,Lion,Owl
341-212 Wolf,Lion,Bison
341-231↓ Wolf,Lion,Owl
341-232↓ Wolf,Lion,W.Dog
342-111 Lion,Wolf,Pengn
342-112↓ Lion,Wolf,Owl
343-111↓ Lion,Owl,Pengn
343-122↓ Lion,Owl,W.Dog
343-312 W.Dog,Lion,Wolf
343-321 W.Dog,Lion,Owl
343-322 W.Dog,Lion,Wolf
343-331 W.Dog,Lion,Owl
343-332 W.Dog,Lion,Wolf
411-111↓ Pcock,Eagle
411-312↓ Pcock,SeaLn,Eagle
412-111 Pcock,Weasel
412-122↓ Pcock,Weasel,Eagle
412-131 Pcock,Lion,Eagle
412-132 Pcock,Eagle,Rooster
412-211 Pcock,Weasel,SeaLn
412-212 Pcock,Dolphin,Weasel
412-221 Pcock,Weasel,SeaLn
412-222 Pcock,Eagle,Dolphin
412-231 Eagle,Pcock,Lion
412-232 Eagle,Pcock,Rooster
412-311↓ SeaLn,Dolphin,Eagle
413-111↓ Dolphin,Lion,Pcock
413-132↓ Lion,Dolphin,Eagle
421-111 Pcock,SeaLn,Lion
421-112 Pcock,SeaLn,Eagle
421-121 Pcock,SeaLn,Lion
421-122 Eagle,Rooster,Pcock
421-131↓ Lion,Eagle,Rooster
421-211 SeaLn,Pcock,Eagle
421-212 SeaLn,Eagle,Dolphin
421-221 SeaLn,Eagle,Pcock
421-222 Eagle,SeaLn,Dolphin
421-231↓ Eagle,Lion,Rooster
421-311↓ SeaLn,Eagle,Dolphin
422-111↓ Lion,SeaLn,Dolphin
422-121 Lion,SeaLn,Eagle
422-122 Lion,Eagle,Dolphin
422-131↓ Lion,Eagle,Rooster
422-211 SeaLn,Dolphin,Lion
422-212 Dolphin,SeaLn,Eagle
422-221 SeaLn,Lion,Eagle
422-222 Eagle,Dolphin,SeaLn
422-231 Lion,Eagle,Rooster
422-312↓ Dolphin,SeaLn,Eagle
423-111↓ Lion,Dolphin
423-231↓ Lion,Dolphin,Eagle
423-312 Dolphin,SeaLn,Eagle
423-321 Dolphin,Lion,SeaLn
423-322↓ Dolphin,Eagle,Lion
431-111↓ Lion,Bear
431-211↓ Lion,SeaLn,Bear
431-311↓ SeaLn,Lion,Eagle
431-312 SeaLn,Eagle,Dolphin
431-321↓ SeaLn,Lion,Eagle

432-111↓ Lion,Dolphin,Horse
432-222↓ Lion,Eagle,Dolphin
432-311↓ Lion,SeaLn,Dolphin
432-321 Lion,SeaLn,Eagle
432-322 Lion,Eagle,Dolphin
432-331↓ Lion,Eagle,Tiger
433-111↓ Lion,Horse,Dolphin
433-312↓ Dolphin,Lion,Tiger
441-111↓ Lion,Wolf,Sable
442-111↓ Lion,Wolf,Sable
443-111↓ Lion,Owl,Pengn
443-232↓ Lion,Owl,Wolf
443-312 Lion,Wolf,W.Dog
443-321 Lion,Wolf,Owl
443-322 Lion,Wolf,W.Dog
443-331 Lion,Owl,Wolf
443-332 Lion,Wolf,W.Dog

351-

111-111↓ Croc,Warthg
112-111↓ Croc,Warthg
113-111↓ Croc,Warthg
121-111↓ Croc,Warthg
122-111↓ Croc,Warthg
123-111↓ Warthg,Croc
131-111↓ Croc,Warthg
131-331↓ Warthg,Croc,Tiger
132-111↓ Croc,Warthg
133-111↓ Warthg,Croc
141-111↓ Croc,Warthg
141-321↓ Croc,Warthg,Bear
141-332↓ Warthg,Tiger,Croc
142-111↓ Croc,Warthg
142-331↓ Warthg,Tiger,Croc
143-111↓ Warthg,Croc
143-321↓ Warthg,Tiger
211-111↓ Croc,Vultre
212-111↓ Croc,Vultre
213-111↓ Croc,Warthg
213-331↓ Croc,Warthg,Tiger
221-111↓ Croc,Bear,Warthg
221-132 Warthg,Bear,Rhino
221-211↓ Croc,Bear,Warthg
221-232 Warthg,Bear,Rhino
221-311 Croc,Bear,Zebra
221-312 Croc,Warthg,Bear
221-321↓ Bear,Zebra,Warthg
221-331 Tiger,Bear,Zebra
221-332 Tiger,Warthg,Bear
222-111↓ Croc,Warthg,Bear
222-231 Warthg,Bear,Rhino
222-232 Warthg,Bear,Tiger
222-311↓ Croc,Warthg,Bear
222-321↓ Warthg,Bear,Zebra
222-331↓ Tiger,Warthg,Bear
223-111↓ Warthg,Croc
223-311↓ Warthg,Tiger,Croc
231-111↓ Bear,Croc
231-121↓ Bear,Hippo
231-211↓ Bear,Croc
231-331↓ Tiger,Bear,Badger
232-111↓ Bear,Croc,Hippo
232-122 Bear,Warthg
232-131↓ Bear,Tiger,Hippo

232-232↓ Bear,Tiger,Warthg
233-111↓ Warthg,Bear,Tiger
241-111↓ Bear,Croc,Hippo
241-311↓ Bear,Croc,Tiger
241-322↓ Bear,Tiger,Wolf
242-111↓ Bear,Croc,Hippo
242-131↓ Bear,Tiger,Hippo
242-211↓ Bear,Croc
242-322↓ Bear,Tiger,Wolf
243-111 Bear,Pengn,Warthg
243-112 Bear,Warthg,Tiger
243-121 Bear,Pengn,Warthg
243-122 Bear,Warthg,Tiger
243-131 Tiger,Bear,Pengn
243-132↓ Tiger,Bear,Warthg
311-111↓ Croc,Bear,Weasel
311-321↓ Croc,Zebra,Bear
311-331↓ Croc,Zebra,Tiger
312-111↓ Croc,Bear
312-231↓ Croc,Bear,Weasel
312-321↓ Croc,Zebra,Bear
312-331↓ Croc,Tiger,Zebra
313-111↓ Croc,Warthg,Bear
313-131 Croc,Warthg,Tiger
313-221 Croc,Warthg,Bear
313-222↓ Croc,Warthg,Tiger
321-111↓ Bear,Rhino,Croc
321-231↓ Bear,Rhino,Tiger
321-311↓ Bear,Zebra,Rhino
321-322↓ Bear,Zebra,Tiger
322-111↓ Bear,Rhino,Croc
322-122↓ Bear,Rhino,Warthg
322-131↓ Bear,Rhino,Tiger
322-211↓ Bear,Rhino,Croc
322-221 Bear,Rhino,Zebra
322-222 Bear,Rhino,Warthg
322-231↓ Bear,Rhino,Tiger
322-311 Bear,Zebra,Rhino
322-312↓ Bear,Zebra,Tiger
323-111↓ Warthg,Bear,Rhino
323-122↓ Warthg,Bear,Tiger
331-111↓ Bear,Tiger
332-111↓ Bear,Tiger
332-322↓ Bear,Tiger,Zebra
332-331↓ Tiger,Bear,Badger
333-111↓ Bear,Tiger
341-111↓ Bear,Tiger
341-322↓ Bear,Tiger,Wolf
342-111↓ Bear,Tiger
342-322↓ Bear,Tiger,Wolf
343-111↓ Bear,Pengn,Tiger
343-221↓ Bear,Tiger,Owl
411-111↓ Croc,Tiger,Bear
412-111↓ Croc,Tiger,Bear
413-111↓ Croc,Tiger
421-111↓ Bear,Tiger,Rhino
422-111↓ Tiger,Bear,Rhino
423-111↓ Bear,Tiger
431-111↓ Bear,Tiger
432-111↓ Tiger,Bear
433-111↓ Bear,Tiger
441-111↓ Bear,Tiger
442-111↓ Tiger,Bear
443-111↓ Tiger

352-

111-111↓	Croc,Warthg
112-111↓	Croc,Warthg
113-111↓	Croc,Warthg
121-111↓	Croc,Warthg
122-111↓	Croc,Warthg
123-111↓	Warthg,Croc
131-111↓	Croc,Warthg
131-321	Warthg,Croc,Bear
131-331↓	Warthg,Croc,Tiger
132-111	Croc,Warthg
132-112↓	Croc,Warthg,Bear
132-331↓	Warthg,Tiger,Croc
133-111↓	Warthg,Croc
133-312↓	Warthg,Croc,Tiger
141-111↓	Croc,Warthg
141-321↓	Croc,Warthg,Bear
141-332↓	Warthg,Tiger,Croc
142-111↓	Croc,Warthg
142-322↓	Warthg,Croc,Tiger
143-111↓	Warthg,Croc
143-321↓	Warthg,Tiger
211-111↓	Croc,Vultre
212-111↓	Croc,Vultre
213-111↓	Croc,Warthg
213-322↓	Croc,Warthg,Tiger
221-111↓	Croc,Bear,Warthg
221-121↓	Bear,Warthg,Rhino
221-211↓	Croc,Bear,Warthg
221-221↓	Bear,Warthg,Rhino
221-311	Croc,Bear,Zebra
221-312	Croc,Bear,Warthg
221-321↓	Bear,Zebra,Warthg
221-331	Bear,Tiger,Zebra
221-332	Tiger,Bear,Warthg
222-111↓	Croc,Warthg,Bear
222-121↓	Warthg,Bear,Rhino
222-211↓	Croc,Warthg,Bear
222-221↓	Warthg,Bear,Rhino
222-311↓	Croc,Warthg,Bear
222-321↓	Warthg,Bear,Zebra
222-331↓	Tiger,Warthg,Bear
223-111	Warthg,Croc
223-132↓	Warthg,Tiger,Bear
223-311↓	Warthg,Tiger,Croc
223-321↓	Warthg,Tiger,Bear
231-111↓	Bear,Croc
231-212↓	Bear,Croc,Warthg
231-332↓	Tiger,Bear,Warthg
232-111	Bear,Croc,Hippo
232-112	Bear,Croc,Warthg
232-121↓	Bear,Hippo,Warthg
232-131	Bear,Tiger,Hippo
232-132↓	Bear,Tiger,Warthg
232-311↓	Bear,Tiger,Croc
232-321↓	Bear,Tiger,Warthg
232-331↓	Tiger,Bear,Badger
233-111	Bear,Warthg
233-112↓	Warthg,Bear,Tiger
241-111↓	Bear,Tiger
241-322↓	Bear,Tiger,Wolf
242-111↓	Bear,Tiger
242-331↓	Tiger,Bear,Wolf
243-111	Bear,Pengn,Warthg
243-112	Bear,Warthg,Tiger

243-121	Bear,Pengn,Warthg
243-122	Bear,Warthg,Tiger
243-131↓	Tiger,Bear,Owl
243-211↓	Bear,Warthg,Tiger
243-231↓	Tiger,Bear,Owl
243-311↓	Tiger,Bear,Warthg
243-332	Tiger,W.Dog
311-111↓	Croc,Bear,Rhino
311-321↓	Croc,Zebra,Bear
311-332↓	Croc,Tiger,Zebra
312-111↓	Croc,Bear
312-121↓	Croc,Bear,Rhino
312-312↓	Croc,Zebra,Bear
312-331↓	Croc,Tiger,Zebra
313-111↓	Croc,Warthg,Bear
313-131	Croc,Warthg,Tiger
313-212↓	Croc,Warthg,Bear
313-231↓	Tiger,Croc,Warthg
321-111↓	Bear,Rhino
321-211↓	Bear,Rhino,Croc
321-221↓	Bear,Rhino,Zebra
321-231↓	Bear,Rhino,Tiger
321-311↓	Bear,Zebra,Rhino
321-331	Bear,Tiger,Zebra
322-111↓	Bear,Rhino,Croc
322-121↓	Bear,Rhino,Warthg
322-131↓	Bear,Rhino,Tiger
322-211↓	Bear,Rhino,Croc
322-221	Bear,Rhino,Zebra
322-222	Bear,Rhino,Warthg
322-231↓	Bear,Rhino,Tiger
322-311↓	Bear,Zebra,Rhino
322-322↓	Bear,Zebra,Tiger
323-111	Bear,Warthg,Rhino
323-132	Tiger,Warthg,Bear
323-211	Bear,Warthg,Rhino
323-212↓	Warthg,Bear,Tiger
331-111↓	Bear,Tiger
331-331↓	Bear,Tiger,Badger
332-111↓	Bear,Tiger
332-331↓	Tiger,Bear,Badger
333-111↓	Bear,Tiger
341-111↓	Bear,Tiger
341-322↓	Bear,Tiger,Wolf
342-111↓	Bear,Tiger
342-322↓	Bear,Tiger,Wolf
343-111	Bear,Pengn
343-121↓	Bear,Pengn,Tiger
343-122↓	Bear,Tiger,Owl
343-332	Tiger,Bear,Wolf
411-111↓	Croc,Bear,Rhino
412-111↓	Croc,Tiger,Bear
413-111↓	Croc,Tiger
413-112↓	Croc,Tiger,Warthg
421-111↓	Bear,Tiger,Rhino
422-111↓	Bear,Tiger,Rhino
423-111↓	Tiger,Warthg,Bear
431-111↓	Bear,Tiger
432-111↓	Bear,Tiger
433-111↓	Tiger,Bear
441-111↓	Bear,Tiger
442-111↓	Bear,Tiger
442-321↓	Tiger,Sable
443-111↓	Tiger

353-

111-111↓	Crocodile
112-111↓	Crocodile
113-111↓	Croc,Warthg
121-111↓	Croc,Warthg
122-111↓	Croc,Warthg
123-111↓	Warthg,Croc
131-111↓	Croc,Bear,Warthg
131-332	Warthg,Bear,Tiger
132-111↓	Croc,Warthg,Bear
132-331↓	Warthg,Bear,Tiger
133-111↓	Warthg,Croc
133-211↓	Warthg,Croc,Bear
133-232↓	Warthg,Tiger,Bear
133-311↓	Warthg,Croc
133-322↓	Warthg,Tiger,Bear
141-111↓	Croc,Bear,Warthg
141-331↓	Bear,Wolf,Warthg
142-111↓	Croc,Bear,Warthg
142-332	Warthg,Bear,Wolf
143-111↓	Warthg,Croc,Bear
143-231↓	Warthg,Bear,Owl
143-311↓	Warthg,Croc,Bear
143-331↓	Warthg,Tiger,W.Dog
211-111↓	Croc,Bear,Vultre
212-111↓	Croc,Vultre,Bear
212-332↓	Croc,Bear,Rhino
213-111↓	Croc,Warthg
213-131↓	Croc,Warthg,Bear
213-331↓	Croc,Warthg,Tiger
221-111↓	Bear,Rhino,Croc
221-232↓	Bear,Rhino,Warthg
221-332↓	Bear,Rhino,Tiger
222-111↓	Bear,Rhino,Croc
222-121↓	Bear,Rhino,Warthg
222-211↓	Bear,Rhino,Croc
222-221↓	Bear,Rhino,Warthg
222-311↓	Bear,Rhino,Croc
222-321↓	Bear,Rhino,Warthg
222-331↓	Bear,Rhino,Tiger
223-211↓	Warthg,Bear,Rhino
223-232	Warthg,Bear,Tiger
223-311	Warthg,Bear,Rhino
223-312↓	Warthg,Bear,Tiger
231-111↓	Bear,Tiger
232-111↓	Bear,Tiger
233-111↓	Bear,Warthg
233-132↓	Bear,Tiger,Warthg
241-111↓	Bear,Wolf,Tiger
242-111↓	Bear,Wolf
242-322↓	Bear,Wolf,Tiger
243-111↓	Bear,Owl
243-131↓	Bear,Owl,Tiger
243-311↓	Bear,Tiger,W.Dog
311-111↓	Croc,Bear,Rhino
312-111↓	Croc,Bear,Rhino
312-332	Bear,Rhino,Tiger
313-111↓	Croc,Bear,Rhino
313-132	Bear,Rhino,Warthg
313-211↓	Croc,Bear,Rhino
313-231↓	Bear,Rhino,Tiger
313-311↓	Croc,Bear,Rhino
313-321↓	Bear,Rhino,Tiger
321-111↓	Bear,Rhino
321-332↓	Bear,Rhino,Tiger

322-111↓ Bear,Rhino
322-232↓ Bear,Rhino,Rooster
322-311↓ Bear,Rhino,Zebra
322-331↓ Bear,Rhino,Tiger
323-111 Bear,Rhino
323-112↓ Bear,Rhino,Warthg
323-131↓ Bear,Rhino,Tiger
323-211↓ Bear,Rhino,Warthg
323-231↓ Bear,Rhino,Tiger
331-111↓ Bear,Tiger
332-111↓ Bear,Tiger
333-111↓ Bear,Tiger
333-231↓ Bear,Tiger,Lion
341-111↓ Bear,Wolf
341-332↓ Bear,Wolf,Tiger
342-111↓ Bear,Wolf
342-232↓ Bear,Wolf,Tiger
343-111↓ Bear,Owl
343-321↓ Bear,Tiger,Owl
343-322 Bear,Tiger,Wolf
343-331 Tiger,Bear,Owl
343-332 Tiger,Bear,Wolf
411-111↓ Croc,Bear,Rhino
411-131↓ Bear,Rhino,Tiger
411-211↓ Croc,Bear,Rhino
411-231↓ Tiger,Bear,Rhino
411-311↓ Croc,Tiger,Bear
411-321↓ Tiger,Bear,Rhino
412-111↓ Croc,Bear,Rhino
412-131↓ Tiger,Bear,Rhino
412-211↓ Croc,Bear,Rhino
412-222↓ Bear,Rhino,Tiger
413-111↓ Croc,Tiger,Bear
413-121↓ Tiger,Bear,Rhino
413-211↓ Tiger,Croc,Bear
413-221↓ Tiger,Bear,Rhino
421-111↓ Bear,Rhino
421-212↓ Bear,Rhino,Tiger
422-111 Bear,Rhino
422-112↓ Bear,Rhino,Tiger
423-111↓ Tiger,Bear,Rhino
431-111↓ Bear,Tiger
432-111↓ Bear,Tiger
433-111↓ Tiger,Bear
441-111↓ Bear,Tiger
442-111↓ Bear,Tiger
442-332↓ Tiger,Sable,Bear
443-111↓ Tiger,Bear

354-
111-111↓ Crocodile
112-111↓ Crocodile
113-111↓ Croc,Warthg
121-111↓ Croc,Warthg
122-111↓ Croc,Warthg
123-111↓ Warthg,Croc
131-111↓ Croc,Bear,Warthg
131-332 Bear,Warthg,Tiger
132-111↓ Croc,Bear,Warthg
132-332 Warthg,Bear,Tiger
133-111↓ Warthg,Croc
133-121↓ Warthg,Bear
133-211↓ Warthg,Croc
133-222↓ Warthg,Bear
133-311↓ Warthg,Croc

133-321↓ Warthg,Bear
133-331↓ Warthg,Tiger
141-111 Croc,Bear
141-112↓ Croc,Bear,Warthg
141-231↓ Bear,Warthg,W.Dog
141-312↓ Croc,Bear,Warthg
141-321 Bear,W.Dog,Croc
141-322 Bear,W.Dog,Warthg
141-331↓ W.Dog,Bear,Wolf
142-111↓ Croc,Bear,Warthg
142-131↓ Bear,Warthg,W.Dog
142-211↓ Croc,Bear,Warthg
142-231↓ Bear,Warthg,W.Dog
142-311↓ Croc,Bear,Warthg
142-321 Bear,W.Dog,Warthg
143-111↓ Warthg,Croc,Bear
143-131↓ Warthg,W.Dog,Lion
143-211↓ Warthg,Croc,Bear
143-221↓ Warthg,Bear,W.Dog
143-231↓ Warthg,W.Dog,Lion
143-311↓ Warthg,W.Dog,Croc
143-321↓ W.Dog,Warthg,Bear
211-111↓ Croc,Bear,Rhino
211-331↓ Croc,Eagle,Bear
212-111↓ Croc,Bear
212-122↓ Croc,Bear,Vultre
212-131 Croc,Bear,Rhino
212-132↓ Croc,Bear,Vultre
212-322↓ Croc,Bear,Rhino
212-331↓ Croc,Eagle,Bear
213-111↓ Croc,Warthg,Bear
213-131 Croc,Warthg,Lion
213-221↓ Croc,Warthg,Bear
213-231 Croc,Warthg,Lion
213-321↓ Croc,Warthg,Bear
213-331 Croc,Warthg,Tiger
221-111↓ Bear,Rhino,Croc
221-321↓ Bear,Rhino,Eagle
222-111↓ Bear,Rhino,Croc
222-232↓ Bear,Rhino,Warthg
222-311↓ Bear,Rhino,Croc
222-321↓ Bear,Rhino,Eagle
223-111↓ Warthg,Bear,Rhino
223-131↓ Warthg,Lion,Bear
223-211↓ Warthg,Bear,Rhino
223-231↓ Warthg,Lion,Bear
223-311↓ Warthg,Bear,Rhino
223-322 Warthg,Bear,Tiger
223-331 Tiger,Warthg,Lion
223-332 Tiger,Warthg,Eagle
231-111↓ Bear
232-111↓ Bear
232-332↓ Bear,Tiger,Lion
233-111↓ Bear,Lion
233-222↓ Bear,Lion,Warthg
233-321↓ Bear,Tiger,Lion
241-111↓ Bear,W.Dog
241-322↓ Bear,W.Dog,Wolf
242-111↓ Bear,W.Dog
242-322↓ Bear,W.Dog,Wolf
243-111↓ Bear,W.Dog,Lion
311-111↓ Croc,Bear,Rhino
311-231↓ Bear,Rhino,Eagle
311-311↓ Croc,Bear,Rhino
311-321↓ Bear,Rhino,Eagle

312-111↓ Croc,Bear,Rhino
312-231↓ Bear,Rhino,Eagle
312-311↓ Croc,Bear,Rhino
312-321↓ Bear,Rhino,Eagle
313-111↓ Croc,Bear,Rhino
313-131↓ Lion,Bear,Rhino
313-211↓ Croc,Bear,Rhino
313-231↓ Lion,Bear,Rhino
313-311↓ Croc,Bear,Rhino
313-321↓ Bear,Rhino,Tiger
313-331↓ Tiger,Eagle,Lion
321-111↓ Bear,Rhino
321-312↓ Bear,Rhino,Eagle
322-111↓ Bear,Rhino
322-231↓ Bear,Rhino,Lion
322-312↓ Bear,Rhino,Eagle
323-111↓ Bear,Rhino
323-121↓ Bear,Rhino,Lion
323-311↓ Bear,Rhino,Tiger
323-331 Tiger,Lion,Bear
323-332 Tiger,Eagle,Lion
331-111↓ Bear,Lion
331-332↓ Bear,Tiger,Eagle
332-111↓ Bear,Lion
332-331↓ Bear,Tiger,Lion
333-111↓ Bear,Lion
333-221↓ Bear,Lion,Tiger
341-111↓ Bear,Wolf
342-111↓ Bear,Wolf,Lion
342-331↓ Bear,Wolf,Tiger
343-111↓ Bear,Lion,Owl
343-321↓ Bear,Tiger,W.Dog
343-331↓ Tiger,W.Dog,Lion
411-111↓ Croc,Bear,Rhino
411-131↓ Bear,Rhino,Tiger
411-211↓ Croc,Bear,Rhino
411-231↓ Bear,Rhino,Tiger
411-311 Croc,Bear,Rhino
411-312 Croc,Tiger,Bear
411-321↓ Tiger,Bear,Rhino
411-331↓ Tiger,Eagle,Bear
412-111↓ Croc,Bear,Rhino
412-131↓ Bear,Rhino,Tiger
412-211↓ Croc,Bear,Rhino
412-222↓ Bear,Rhino,Tiger
412-311 Croc,Tiger,Bear
412-331↓ Tiger,Eagle
413-111↓ Croc,Bear,Tiger
413-121↓ Tiger,Bear,Rhino
413-131↓ Tiger,Lion,Bear
413-211↓ Tiger,Croc,Bear
413-221↓ Tiger,Bear,Rhino
413-311↓ Tiger,Dolphin
421-111↓ Bear,Rhino
421-131↓ Bear,Rhino,Tiger
421-332 Tiger,Eagle
422-111↓ Bear,Rhino
422-122↓ Bear,Rhino,Tiger
422-332 Tiger,Eagle,Bear
423-111↓ Bear,Tiger,Rhino
423-232 Tiger,Lion,Bear
423-311↓ Tiger,Dolphin
431-111↓ Bear,Tiger
432-111↓ Bear,Tiger
433-111↓ Bear,Tiger

(354 cont'd)
441-111↓ Bear,Tiger
442-111↓ Bear,Tiger
443-111↓ Bear,Tiger,Lion

411-
111-111↓ Mole,Giraf
112-111↓ Mole,Giraf
113-111↓ Mole,Giraf
121-111↓ Mole,Giraf
122-111↓ Mole,Giraf
123-111↓ Mole,Giraf
131-111↓ Mole,Mouse
131-232↓ Mole,Giraf,Mouse
132-111↓ Mole,Mouse
132-232↓ Mole,Giraf,Mouse
133-111↓ Mole,Mouse
133-232↓ Mole,Giraf,Mouse
141-111↓ Mole,Walrus
141-132↓ Mole,Walrus,Eleph
141-211 Mole,Mouse,Walrus
141-212 Mole,Bison,Mouse
141-221 Mole,Mouse,Walrus
141-222 Mole,Bison,Mouse
141-231 Mole,Mouse,Eleph
141-232 Mole,Eleph,Bison
141-311 Mole,Mouse,Giraf
141-312 Mole,Bison,Mouse
141-321 Mole,Mouse,Giraf
141-322 Mole,Bison,Mouse
141-331 Mole,Mouse,Eleph
141-332 Eleph,Mole,Bison
142-111↓ Mole,Walrus
142-132↓ Mole,Eleph,Walrus
142-211 Mole,Mouse,Walrus
142-212 Mole,Bison,Mouse
142-221 Mole,Mouse,Walrus
142-222 Mole,Bison,Mouse
142-231 Mole,Eleph,Mouse
142-232 Eleph,Mole,Bison
142-311 Mole,Mouse,Giraf
142-312 Mole,Bison,Mouse
142-321 Mole,Mouse,Eleph
142-322 Mole,Bison,Mouse
142-331 Mole,Eleph,Mouse
142-332 Eleph,Mole,Bison
143-111 Mole,Walrus
143-211↓ Mole,Eleph,Mouse
143-212 Eleph,Mole,Bison
143-221↓ Mole,Eleph,Mouse
143-312 Eleph,Mole,Bison
143-321 Eleph,Mole,Mouse
143-322↓ Eleph,Mole,Bison
211-111↓ Mole,Giraf,Vultre
212-111↓ Mole,Giraf,Vultre
213-111↓ Mole,Gorlla,Giraf
213-112 Gorlla,Giraf,Vultre
213-121↓ Mole,Giraf,Vultre
213-211 Giraf,MGoat,Mole
213-212 Giraf,Gorlla
213-221↓ Giraf,Mole
213-311↓ Giraf,MGoat
221-111↓ Mole,Giraf,Walrus
221-211↓ Giraf,MGoat,Mole
221-221↓ Giraf,Mole,Mouse

221-311↓ Giraf,MGoat,Mouse
222-111↓ Mole,Giraf,Walrus
222-231↓ Giraf,Mole,Mouse
222-311↓ Giraf,MGoat,Mouse
223-111↓ Mole,Gorlla,Giraf
223-121 Mole,Giraf,Walrus
223-122 Giraf,Mole,Gorlla
223-131 Mole,Giraf,Walrus
223-132 Giraf,Mole,Gorlla
223-211 Giraf,MGoat,Mole
223-212 Giraf,Gorlla
223-221↓ Giraf,Mole,Mouse
223-311↓ Giraf,MGoat,Mouse
231-111 Walrus,Mouse,Mole
231-112 Walrus,Giraf,Mouse
231-121 Walrus,Mouse,Mole
231-122 Walrus,Giraf,Mouse
231-131 Walrus,Mouse,Mole
231-132↓ Walrus,Giraf,Mouse
232-111 Walrus,Mouse,Mole
232-112 Walrus,Giraf,Mouse
232-121 Walrus,Mouse,Mole
232-122 Walrus,Giraf,Mouse
232-131 Walrus,Mouse,Mole
232-132↓ Walrus,Giraf,Mouse
233-111 Walrus,Mouse,Mole
233-112 Walrus,Gorlla,Giraf
233-121 Walrus,Mouse,Mole
233-122 Walrus,Giraf,Mouse
233-131 Walrus,Mouse,Mole
233-132 Walrus,Giraf,Eleph
233-211 Mouse,Giraf,Walrus
233-232 Giraf,Eleph,Mouse
233-321↓ Mouse,Giraf,Walrus
233-322 Giraf,Mouse,Eleph
241-111 Walrus,Mouse
241-112↓ Walrus,Bison,Mouse
241-121 Walrus,Mouse,Mole
241-122 Walrus,Bison,Mouse
241-131 Walrus,Eleph,Mouse
241-132 Eleph,Walrus,Bison
241-211 Mouse,Walrus,Giraf
241-212 Bison,Mouse,Giraf
241-221 Mouse,Walrus,Eleph
241-222 Bison,Mouse,Eleph
241-231 Eleph,Mouse,Walrus
241-232 Eleph,Bison,Mouse
241-311↓ Mouse,Giraf,Bison
241-321 Mouse,Eleph,Giraf
241-322 Bison,Mouse,Eleph
241-331 Eleph,Mouse,Giraf
241-332 Eleph,Bison,Mouse
242-111 Walrus,Mouse
242-112 Walrus,Eleph,Bison
242-121 Walrus,Mouse,Eleph
242-122 Walrus,Eleph,Bison
242-131 Walrus,Eleph,Mouse
242-132 Eleph,Walrus,Bison
242-211 Mouse,Walrus,Eleph
242-212 Eleph,Bison,Mouse
242-221 Mouse,Eleph,Walrus
242-311↓ Mouse,Eleph,Giraf
242-312 Eleph,Bison,Mouse
242-321 Mouse,Eleph,Giraf
243-111↓ Eleph,Walrus,Mouse

311-111↓ Giraffe
312-111↓ Giraffe
313-111↓ Giraffe
321-111↓ Giraffe
322-111↓ Giraffe
323-111↓ Giraffe
331-111↓ Giraf,Walrus,Mouse
332-111↓ Giraf,Walrus,Mouse
333-111↓ Giraf,Walrus,Mouse
341-111↓ Giraf,Walrus,Eleph
341-311↓ Giraf,Eleph,Mouse
341-312 Giraf,Eleph,Sable
341-321 Eleph,Giraf,Mouse
341-332↓ Eleph,Sable,Giraf
342-111↓ Eleph,Giraf,Walrus
342-311↓ Eleph,Giraf,Mouse
343-111↓ Elephant
411-111↓ Giraffe
412-111↓ Giraffe
413-111↓ Giraffe
421-111↓ Giraffe
422-111↓ Giraffe
423-111↓ Giraffe
431-111↓ Giraffe
432-111↓ Giraffe
433-111↓ Giraffe
441-111↓ Giraffe
441-232↓ Giraf,Sable
442-111↓ Giraf,Eleph
442-331↓ Giraf,Sable,Eleph
443-111↓ Giraf,Eleph
443-331↓ Eleph,Giraf,Sable

412-
111-111↓ Mole,Giraf
112-111↓ Mole,Giraf
113-111↓ Mole,Gorlla,Giraf
113-132↓ Mole,Giraf,Vultre
121-111↓ Mole,Giraf
122-111↓ Mole,Giraf
123-111↓ Mole,Gorlla,Giraf
131-111↓ Walrus,Mole,Giraf
132-111↓ Walrus,Mole,Giraf
133-111↓ Walrus,Mole,Gorlla
133-121↓ Walrus,Mole,Giraf
133-232 Giraf,Eleph,Walrus
133-311↓ Giraf,Walrus,Mole
133-331↓ Giraf,Eleph,Walrus
141-111↓ Walrus,Mole,Giraf
141-131 Walrus,Mole,Eleph
141-132 Eleph,Walrus,Bison
141-211 Walrus,Bison,Giraf
141-212 Bison,Giraf,Eleph
141-221 Walrus,Bison,Giraf
141-222 Bison,Giraf,Eleph
141-231 Eleph,Walrus,Bison
141-232 Eleph,Bison,Giraf
141-311 Bison,Giraf,Walrus
141-312↓ Bison,Giraf,Eleph
141-332 Eleph,Bison,Sable
142-111↓ Walrus,Mole,Bison
142-121 Walrus,Mole,Eleph
142-122 Walrus,Bison,Eleph
142-131 Walrus,Eleph,Mole
142-132↓ Eleph,Walrus,Bison

142-212   Bison,Eleph,Giraf
142-221   Eleph,Walrus,Bison
142-222↓ Bison,Eleph,Giraf
143-111   Walrus,Eleph,Mole
143-112   Eleph,Walrus,Bison
143-121   Eleph,Walrus,Mole
143-211↓ Eleph,Walrus,Bison
211-111↓ Giraf,Vultre,Walrus
212-111↓ Giraf,Vultre,Walrus
213-111↓ Gorlla,Giraf,Vultre
213-131   Giraf,Vultre,Walrus
213-132↓ Giraf,Vultre,Gorlla
221-111↓ Giraf,Walrus
222-111↓ Giraf,Walrus
223-111↓ Gorlla,Giraf,Walrus
231-111↓ Walrus,Giraf
231-311↓ Giraf,Walrus,Mouse
232-111↓ Walrus,Giraf
232-311↓ Giraf,Walrus,Mouse
233-111↓ Walrus,Gorlla,Giraf
233-122↓ Walrus,Giraf,Eleph
241-111↓ Walrus,Bison,Eleph
241-212   Bison,Eleph,Giraf
241-221   Eleph,Walrus,Bison
241-222↓ Bison,Eleph,Giraf
242-111   Walrus,Eleph
242-112↓ Walrus,Eleph,Bison
242-311↓ Eleph,Bison,Giraf
243-111↓ Eleph,Walrus
311-111↓ Giraffe
312-111↓ Giraffe
313-111↓ Giraffe
321-111↓ Giraffe
322-111↓ Giraffe
323-111↓ Giraffe
331-111↓ Giraf,Walrus
332-111↓ Giraf,Walrus
333-111↓ Giraf,Walrus,Eleph
341-111↓ Eleph,Giraf,Walrus
342-111↓ Eleph,Giraf,Walrus
343-111↓ Elephant
411-111↓ Giraffe
412-111↓ Giraffe
413-111↓ Giraffe
421-111↓ Giraffe
422-111↓ Giraffe
423-111↓ Giraffe
431-111↓ Giraffe
432-111↓ Giraffe
433-111↓ Giraffe
441-111↓ Giraffe
441-331↓ Giraf,Sable,Eleph
442-111↓ Giraf,Eleph
442-331↓ Giraf,Sable,Eleph
443-111↓ Giraf,Eleph
443-331↓ Eleph,Giraf,Sable

413-
111-111   Mole,Walrus,Giraf
111-112   Mole,Giraf,Vultre
111-121   Mole,Walrus,Giraf
111-122   Mole,Giraf,Vultre
111-131   Mole,Walrus,Giraf
111-132   Mole,Giraf,Vultre
112-111↓ Mole,Walrus,Giraf

112-112   Mole,Giraf,Vultre
112-121   Mole,Walrus,Giraf
112-122   Mole,Giraf,Vultre
112-131   Mole,Walrus,Giraf
112-132   Mole,Giraf,Vultre
112-231↓ Giraf,Mole,Walrus
113-111   Mole,Walrus,Gorlla
113-112   Mole,Gorlla,Giraf
113-121   Mole,Walrus,Giraf
113-122   Mole,Giraf,Vultre
113-131   Mole,Walrus,Giraf
113-132   Mole,Giraf,Vultre
113-211   Giraf,Mole,Walrus
113-212   Giraf,Mole,Gorlla
113-231↓ Giraf,Mole,Eleph
121-111↓ Mole,Walrus,Giraf
122-111↓ Mole,Walrus,Giraf
123-111   Mole,Walrus,Gorlla
123-112   Mole,Gorlla,Giraf
123-121↓ Mole,Walrus,Giraf
123-331↓ Giraf,Mole,Eleph
131-111↓ Walrus,Mole
131-211↓ Walrus,Giraf,Mole
131-232   Walrus,Giraf,Eleph
131-331↓ Walrus,Giraf,Mole
131-332   Giraf,Walrus,Eleph
132-111↓ Walrus,Mole
132-211↓ Walrus,Giraf,Mole
132-232↓ Walrus,Giraf,Eleph
133-111↓ Walrus,Mole
133-131↓ Walrus,Mole,Eleph
133-211   Walrus,Giraf,Mole
133-212↓ Walrus,Giraf,Eleph
141-111   Walrus,Bison
141-112↓ Walrus,Bison,Eleph
142-111   Walrus,Bison
142-122↓ Walrus,Bison,Eleph
143-111↓ Walrus,Eleph,Bison
211-111↓ Walrus,Giraf,Vultre
212-111↓ Walrus,Giraf,Vultre
213-111↓ Walrus,Gorlla,Giraf
213-112   Gorlla,Giraf,Vultre
213-121↓ Giraf,Walrus,Vultre
213-131   Walrus,Giraf,Eleph
213-132   Giraf,Vultre,Eleph
213-231↓ Giraf,Eleph,Walrus
221-111↓ Walrus,Giraf
222-111↓ Walrus,Giraf
223-111↓ Walrus,Gorlla,Giraf
223-131↓ Walrus,Giraf,Eleph
231-111↓ Walrus,Giraf
231-332↓ Giraf,Walrus,Eleph
232-111↓ Walrus,Giraf
232-322↓ Giraf,Walrus,Eleph
233-111↓ Walrus,Eleph
233-211↓ Walrus,Eleph,Giraf
241-111   Walrus,Bison
241-122↓ Walrus,Bison,Eleph
242-111↓ Walrus,Eleph,Bison
243-111↓ Eleph,Walrus
311-111↓ Giraffe
312-111↓ Giraffe
313-111↓ Giraf,Eleph
321-111↓ Giraf,Walrus
322-111↓ Giraf,Walrus

323-111↓ Giraf,Walrus
323-121↓ Giraf,Walrus,Eleph
331-111   Walrus,Giraf
331-331↓ Giraf,Eleph,Walrus
332-111   Walrus,Giraf
332-311↓ Giraf,Walrus,Eleph
333-111↓ Walrus,Eleph,Giraf
341-111↓ Eleph,Walrus
341-212↓ Eleph,Giraf,Bison
342-111↓ Eleph,Walrus
343-111↓ Elephant
411-111↓ Giraffe
412-111↓ Giraffe
413-111↓ Giraffe
421-111↓ Giraffe
422-111↓ Giraffe
423-111↓ Giraffe
431-111↓ Giraffe
432-111↓ Giraffe
433-111↓ Giraf,Eleph
441-111↓ Giraf,Eleph
441-322↓ Giraf,Sable,Eleph
442-111↓ Giraf,Eleph
442-322↓ Giraf,Eleph,Sable
443-111↓ Eleph,Giraf

414-
111-111   Walrus,Mole
111-132↓ Walrus,Mole,Giraf
112-111   Walrus,Mole
112-132↓ Walrus,Mole,Giraf
113-111   Walrus,Mole
113-132↓ Walrus,Mole,Giraf
113-232   Walrus,Giraf,Eleph
113-311   Walrus,Giraf,Mole
113-332   Giraf,Walrus,Eleph
121-111↓ Walrus,Mole
121-211↓ Walrus,Mole,Giraf
122-111↓ Walrus,Mole
122-232↓ Walrus,Giraf,Mole
123-111↓ Walrus,Mole
123-211↓ Walrus,Mole,Giraf
123-232   Walrus,Giraf,Eleph
123-311↓ Walrus,Giraf,Mole
123-332↓ Walrus,Giraf,Eleph
131-111↓ Walrus
132-111↓ Walrus
133-111↓ Walrus,Eleph
141-111↓ Walrus,Bison
141-232↓ Walrus,Eleph,Bison
142-111↓ Walrus,Eleph
142-232↓ Eleph,Walrus,Bison
143-111↓ Walrus,Eleph
143-322↓ Eleph,Walrus,Bison
211-111↓ Walrus,Giraf
212-111↓ Walrus,Giraf
213-111↓ Walrus,Gorlla
213-322↓ Giraf,Walrus,Eleph
221-111↓ Walrus,Giraf
222-111↓ Walrus,Giraf
223-111↓ Walrus,Giraf
223-322↓ Walrus,Giraf,Eleph
231-111↓ Walrus
232-111↓ Walrus
233-111↓ Walrus,Eleph

(414 cont'd)

241-111↓ Walrus,Eleph
241-322↓ Walrus,Bison,Eleph
242-111↓ Walrus,Eleph
243-111↓ Walrus,Eleph
311-111↓ Walrus,Giraf
312-111↓ Walrus,Giraf
313-111↓ Walrus,Giraf
313-231↓ Giraf,Eleph,Walrus
321-111↓ Walrus,Giraf
322-111↓ Walrus,Giraf
323-111↓ Walrus,Giraf
323-331↓ Giraf,Eleph,Walrus
331-111↓ Walrus,Giraf
331-322↓ Walrus,Giraf,Eleph
332-111↓ Walrus,Giraf
332-322↓ Walrus,Giraf,Eleph
333-111↓ Walrus,Eleph
333-311↓ Walrus,Eleph,Giraf
341-111↓ Walrus,Eleph
342-111↓ Walrus,Eleph
343-111↓ Eleph,Walrus
411-111↓ Giraffe
412-111↓ Giraffe
413-111↓ Giraffe
421-111↓ Giraffe
422-111↓ Giraffe
423-111↓ Giraffe
431-111↓ Giraf,Walrus
432-111↓ Giraf,Walrus
433-111↓ Giraf,Walrus
433-131↓ Giraf,Walrus,Eleph
441-111↓ Walrus,Giraf,Eleph
442-111↓ Walrus,Giraf,Eleph
443-111↓ Eleph,Walrus,Giraf

421-

111-111↓ Giraf,Vultre,MGoat
111-131↓ Giraf,Vultre,Walrus
112-111↓ Giraf,Vultre,MGoat
112-131↓ Giraf,Vultre,Walrus
112-211↓ Giraf,MGoat
113-111↓ Gorlla,Giraf,Vultre
113-131 Giraf,Vultre,Walrus
113-132 Giraf,Vultre,Gorlla
121-111↓ Giraf,Walrus,MGoat
121-121↓ Giraf,Walrus,Hippo
122-111↓ Giraf,Walrus,MGoat
122-121↓ Giraf,Walrus,Hippo
122-211↓ Giraf,MGoat
123-111↓ Gorlla,Giraf,Walrus
123-121 Giraf,Walrus,Hippo
123-122 Giraf,Gorlla
123-131 Giraf,Walrus,Hippo
123-211↓ Giraf,MGoat,Gorlla
131-111↓ Walrus,Hippo,Giraf
131-311↓ Giraf,Walrus,MGoat
131-321↓ Giraf,Walrus,Hippo
132-111↓ Walrus,Hippo,Giraf
132-311↓ Giraf,Walrus,MGoat
132-321↓ Giraf,Walrus,Hippo
133-111 Walrus,Hippo,Gorlla
133-112 Walrus,Gorlla,Giraf
133-121↓ Walrus,Hippo,Giraf
133-311↓ Giraf,Walrus,MGoat

133-321↓ Giraf,Walrus,Hippo
133-331↓ Giraf,Eleph,Walrus
141-111 Walrus,Hippo
141-122↓ Walrus,Hippo,Bison
141-131↓ Walrus,Hippo,Eleph
141-211 Walrus,Giraf,Hippo
141-212 Bison,Giraf,Walrus
141-221 Walrus,Giraf,Hippo
141-222 Bison,Giraf,Eleph
141-231 Eleph,Walrus,Giraf
141-232 Eleph,Bison,Giraf
141-311 Giraf,Bison,Walrus
141-312 Bison,Giraf,Eleph
141-321 Giraf,Bison,Walrus
141-322↓ Bison,Giraf,Eleph
142-111 Walrus,Hippo
142-122↓ Walrus,Hippo,Bison
142-131↓ Walrus,Hippo,Eleph
142-211 Walrus,Giraf,Hippo
142-212 Bison,Giraf,Eleph
142-221 Walrus,Giraf,Eleph
142-222 Bison,Giraf,Eleph
142-231 Eleph,Walrus,Giraf
142-232 Eleph,Bison,Giraf
142-311 Giraf,Bison,Walrus
142-312↓ Bison,Giraf,Eleph
143-111 Walrus,Hippo,Eleph
143-211↓ Eleph,Walrus,Giraf
143-212 Eleph,Bison,Giraf
143-221 Eleph,Walrus
143-311↓ Eleph,Giraf,Bison
211-111↓ Giraf,Vultre,MGoat
211-131↓ Giraf,Vultre,Walrus
212-111↓ Giraf,Vultre,MGoat
212-131↓ Giraf,Vultre,Walrus
212-211↓ Giraf,MGoat
213-111↓ Gorlla,Giraf,Vultre
213-131 Giraf,Vultre,Walrus
213-132 Giraf,Vultre,Gorlla
221-111↓ Giraf,Walrus,MGoat
221-121↓ Giraf,Walrus,Hippo
222-111↓ Giraf,Walrus,MGoat
222-121↓ Giraf,Walrus,Hippo
222-211↓ Giraf,MGoat
223-111↓ Gorlla,Giraf,Walrus
223-121 Giraf,Walrus,Hippo
223-122 Giraf,Gorlla
223-131↓ Giraf,Walrus,Hippo
223-211 Giraf,MGoat
223-212↓ Giraf,Gorlla
223-311↓ Giraf,MGoat
231-111↓ Walrus,Hippo,Giraf
231-311↓ Giraf,Walrus,MGoat
231-321↓ Giraf,Walrus,Hippo
232-111↓ Walrus,Hippo,Giraf
232-311↓ Giraf,Walrus,MGoat
232-321↓ Giraf,Walrus,Hippo
233-111 Walrus,Hippo,Gorlla
233-112 Walrus,Gorlla,Giraf
233-121↓ Walrus,Hippo,Giraf
233-231↓ Giraf,Eleph,Walrus
233-311↓ Giraf,Walrus,MGoat
233-321↓ Giraf,Walrus,Hippo
233-331↓ Giraf,Eleph,Walrus
241-111 Walrus,Hippo

241-122↓ Walrus,Hippo,Bison
241-131↓ Walrus,Hippo,Eleph
241-211 Walrus,Giraf,Hippo
241-212 Bison,Giraf,Eleph
241-221 Walrus,Giraf,Eleph
241-222 Bison,Giraf,Eleph
241-231 Eleph,Walrus,Giraf
241-232 Eleph,Bison,Giraf
241-311 Giraf,Bison,Walrus
241-312↓ Bison,Giraf,Eleph
242-111 Walrus,Hippo
242-112↓ Walrus,Hippo,Eleph
242-212 Eleph,Bison,Giraf
242-221 Eleph,Walrus,Giraf
242-222 Eleph,Bison,Giraf
242-231↓ Eleph,Walrus
242-311↓ Eleph,Giraf,Bison
243-111↓ Eleph,Walrus,Hippo
311-111↓ Giraffe
312-111↓ Giraffe
313-111↓ Giraffe
321-111↓ Giraffe
322-111↓ Giraffe
323-111↓ Giraffe
331-111↓ Giraf,Walrus,Hippo
332-111↓ Giraf,Walrus,Hippo
332-232↓ Giraf,Eleph
333-111↓ Giraf,Walrus,Hippo
341-111↓ Giraf,Walrus,Eleph
341-332↓ Eleph,Giraf,Sable
342-111↓ Eleph,Giraf,Walrus
343-111↓ Elephant
411-111↓ Giraffe
412-111↓ Giraffe
413-111↓ Giraffe
421-111↓ Giraffe
422-111↓ Giraffe
423-111↓ Giraffe
431-111↓ Giraffe
432-111↓ Giraffe
433-111↓ Giraffe
441-111↓ Giraffe
441-322↓ Giraf,Sable
442-111↓ Giraf,Eleph
442-331↓ Giraf,Sable,Eleph
443-111↓ Giraf,Eleph
443-322↓ Giraf,Eleph,Sable

422-

111-111↓ Giraf,Vultre,Walrus
112-111↓ Giraf,Vultre,Walrus
113-111↓ Gorlla,Giraf,Vultre
113-131 Giraf,Vultre,Walrus
113-132↓ Giraf,Vultre,Gorlla
121-111↓ Giraf,Walrus,Hippo
122-111↓ Giraf,Walrus,Hippo
123-111↓ Gorlla,Giraf,Walrus
123-121 Giraf,Walrus,Hippo
123-122 Giraf,Gorlla
123-131↓ Giraf,Walrus,Hippo
131-111↓ Walrus,Hippo,Giraf
132-111↓ Walrus,Hippo,Giraf
133-111 Walrus,Hippo,Gorlla
133-112 Walrus,Gorlla,Giraf
133-121↓ Walrus,Hippo,Giraf

133-231↓ Giraf,Walrus,Eleph
133-311↓ Giraf,Walrus,Hippo
133-331↓ Giraf,Eleph,Walrus
141-111 Walrus,Hippo
141-122↓ Walrus,Bison,Hippo
141-131 Walrus,Hippo,Eleph
141-132 Eleph,Walrus,Bison
141-211 Walrus,Bison,Giraf
141-212 Bison,Giraf,Eleph
141-221 Walrus,Bison,Giraf
141-222 Bison,Giraf,Eleph
141-231 Eleph,Walrus,Bison
141-232 Eleph,Bison,Giraf
141-311 Bison,Giraf,Walrus
141-312↓ Bison,Giraf,Eleph
142-111 Walrus,Hippo
142-112↓ Walrus,Bison,Hippo
142-121 Walrus,Hippo,Eleph
142-122 Walrus,Bison,Hippo
142-131 Walrus,Eleph,Hippo
142-132 Eleph,Walrus,Bison
142-211 Walrus,Bison,Giraf
142-212 Bison,Giraf,Eleph
142-221 Eleph,Walrus,Bison
142-222↓ Bison,Eleph,Giraf
143-111 Walrus,Eleph,Hippo
143-112 Eleph,Walrus,Bison
143-121↓ Eleph,Walrus,Hippo
143-212↓ Eleph,Bison
211-111↓ Giraf,Vultre,Walrus
212-111↓ Giraf,Vultre,Walrus
213-111↓ Gorlla,Giraf,Vultre
213-131↓ Giraf,Vultre,Walrus
221-111↓ Giraf,Walrus,Hippo
222-111 Giraf,Walrus,Hippo
222-112↓ Giraf,Gorlla,Walrus
223-111↓ Gorlla,Giraf,Walrus
231-111↓ Walrus,Hippo,Giraf
232-111↓ Walrus,Hippo,Giraf
233-111 Walrus,Hippo,Gorlla
233-112 Walrus,Gorlla,Giraf
233-121↓ Walrus,Hippo,Giraf
233-131 Walrus,Hippo,Eleph
233-132 Walrus,Eleph,Giraf
233-211 Giraf,Walrus,Hippo
233-212 Giraf,Walrus,Eleph
233-221 Giraf,Walrus,Hippo
233-222 Giraf,Eleph,Walrus
233-311↓ Giraf,Walrus,Hippo
233-331↓ Eleph,Giraf,Walrus
241-111 Walrus,Hippo
241-122↓ Walrus,Bison,Hippo
241-131 Walrus,Eleph,Hippo
241-132 Eleph,Walrus,Bison
241-211 Walrus,Bison,Giraf
241-212 Bison,Giraf,Eleph
241-221 Eleph,Walrus,Bison
241-222↓ Bison,Eleph,Giraf
242-111 Walrus,Hippo,Eleph
242-112 Walrus,Eleph,Bison
242-121 Walrus,Hippo,Eleph
242-122↓ Eleph,Walrus,Bison
242-212 Eleph,Bison,Giraf
242-221 Eleph,Walrus,Bison
242-311↓ Eleph,Bison,Giraf

243-111↓ Eleph,Walrus,Hippo
243-222↓ Eleph,Bison
311-111↓ Giraffe
312-111↓ Giraffe
313-111↓ Giraffe
321-111↓ Giraffe
322-111↓ Giraffe
323-111 Giraffe
323-112↓ Giraf,Gorlla
323-132↓ Giraf,Eleph
331-111↓ Giraf,Walrus,Hippo
331-232↓ Giraf,Eleph
332-111↓ Giraf,Walrus,Hippo
333-111↓ Giraf,Walrus,Hippo
333-121↓ Giraf,Walrus,Eleph
341-111↓ Giraf,Eleph,Walrus
342-111↓ Eleph,Giraf,Walrus
343-111↓ Elephant
411-111↓ Giraffe
412-111↓ Giraffe
413-111↓ Giraffe
421-111↓ Giraffe
422-111↓ Giraffe
423-111↓ Giraffe
431-111↓ Giraffe
432-111↓ Giraffe
433-111↓ Giraffe
441-111↓ Giraffe
441-331↓ Giraf,Sable,Eleph
442-111↓ Giraf,Eleph
442-331↓ Giraf,Sable,Eleph
443-111↓ Giraf,Eleph
443-322↓ Giraf,Eleph,Sable

423-

111-111↓ Walrus,Giraf,Vultre
112-111↓ Walrus,Giraf,Vultre
113-111↓ Walrus,Gorlla,Giraf
113-112 Gorlla,Giraf,Vultre
113-121↓ Walrus,Giraf,Vultre
113-231↓ Giraf,Eleph
121-111↓ Walrus,Giraf
122-111↓ Walrus,Giraf
123-111↓ Walrus,Gorlla,Giraf
123-231↓ Giraf,Walrus,Eleph
131-111↓ Walrus,Giraf
131-332↓ Giraf,Walrus,Eleph
132-111↓ Walrus,Giraf
132-332↓ Giraf,Walrus,Eleph
133-111↓ Walrus,Eleph
133-212↓ Walrus,Giraf,Eleph
141-111 Walrus,Bison
141-122↓ Walrus,Bison,Eleph
142-111 Walrus,Bison
142-122↓ Walrus,Bison,Eleph
143-111↓ Walrus,Eleph,Bison
211-111↓ Walrus,Giraf,Vultre
212-111↓ Walrus,Giraf,Vultre
213-111 Walrus,Gorlla,Giraf
213-112 Gorlla,Giraf,Vultre
213-121↓ Walrus,Giraf,Vultre
213-131 Walrus,Giraf,Eleph
213-132↓ Giraf,Vultre,Eleph
221-111↓ Walrus,Giraf
222-111↓ Walrus,Giraf

223-111↓ Walrus,Gorlla,Giraf
223-131 Walrus,Giraf,Eleph
223-212 Giraf,Gorlla
223-222↓ Giraf,Eleph,Walrus
231-111↓ Walrus,Hippo
231-332↓ Giraf,Walrus,Eleph
232-111 Walrus,Hippo
232-221↓ Walrus,Giraf,Hippo
232-322↓ Giraf,Walrus,Eleph
233-111↓ Walrus,Hippo,Eleph
233-211↓ Walrus,Giraf,Eleph
241-111↓ Walrus,Bison,Eleph
242-111 Walrus,Eleph
242-132↓ Eleph,Walrus,Bison
243-111↓ Eleph,Walrus
243-212↓ Eleph,Bison
311-111↓ Giraffe
312-111↓ Giraffe
313-111↓ Giraf,Eleph
321-111↓ Giraf,Walrus
322-111↓ Giraf,Walrus
323-111↓ Giraf,Walrus,Eleph
331-111 Walrus,Giraf
331-222↓ Giraf,Eleph,Walrus
332-111 Walrus,Giraf
332-122↓ Giraf,Walrus,Eleph
333-111↓ Walrus,Giraf,Eleph
341-111↓ Eleph,Walrus,Giraf
341-312↓ Eleph,Giraf,Bison
342-111↓ Eleph,Walrus
342-222↓ Eleph,Giraf,Bison
343-111↓ Elephant
411-111↓ Giraf,Pcock
412-111↓ Giraffe
413-111↓ Giraffe
421-111↓ Giraffe
422-111↓ Giraffe
423-111↓ Giraffe
431-111↓ Giraffe
432-111↓ Giraffe
433-111↓ Giraffe
441-111↓ Giraf,Eleph
441-322↓ Giraf,Sable,Eleph
442-111↓ Giraf,Eleph
442-322↓ Giraf,Eleph,Sable
443-111↓ Eleph,Giraf

424-

111-111↓ Walrus,Giraf
112-111↓ Walrus,Giraf
113-111↓ Walrus,Gorlla,Giraf
113-332↓ Giraf,Walrus,Eleph
121-111↓ Walrus,Giraf
122-111↓ Walrus,Giraf
123-111↓ Walrus,Giraf
123-322↓ Giraf,Walrus,Horse
123-331↓ Walrus,Giraf,Eleph
131-111↓ Walrus
132-111↓ Walrus
133-111↓ Walrus,Eleph
133-332↓ Walrus,Eleph,Horse
141-111↓ Walrus,Bison
141-322↓ Walrus,Bison,Eleph
142-111↓ Walrus,Eleph
142-322↓ Walrus,Bison,Eleph

(424 cont'd)
143-111↓ Walrus,Eleph
143-311↓ Walrus,Eleph,Bison
211-111↓ Walrus,Giraf
212-111↓ Walrus,Giraf
213-111↓ Walrus,Gorlla,Giraf
213-222↓ Giraf,Walrus,Horse
213-231　Walrus,Giraf,Eleph
213-322↓ Giraf,Walrus,Horse
213-331↓ Walrus,Giraf,Eleph
221-111↓ Walrus,Giraf
222-111↓ Walrus,Giraf
223-111↓ Walrus,Giraf
223-322↓ Giraf,Walrus,Horse
223-331↓ Walrus,Giraf,Eleph
231-111↓ Walrus
232-111↓ Walrus
232-222↓ Walrus,Giraf
232-232↓ Walrus,Eleph
233-111↓ Walrus,Horse
233-332↓ Walrus,Eleph,Horse
241-111↓ Walrus,Eleph
241-322↓ Walrus,Bison,Eleph
242-111↓ Walrus,Eleph
243-111↓ Walrus,Eleph
311-111↓ Walrus,Giraf
312-111↓ Walrus,Giraf
313-111↓ Walrus,Giraf
313-122↓ Giraf,Walrus,Horse
313-131↓ Walrus,Giraf,Eleph
313-221↓ Giraf,Walrus,Horse
313-222　Giraf,Horse,Eleph
313-231　Giraf,Eleph,Walrus
313-321↓ Giraf,Horse,Eleph
321-111↓ Walrus,Giraf
322-111↓ Walrus,Giraf
323-111↓ Walrus,Giraf
323-122↓ Giraf,Walrus,Horse
323-131　Walrus,Giraf,Eleph
323-221↓ Giraf,Walrus,Horse
323-222　Giraf,Horse,Eleph
323-231　Giraf,Eleph,Walrus
323-232↓ Giraf,Eleph,Horse
331-111↓ Walrus,Giraf
331-322↓ Giraf,Walrus,Horse
331-331↓ Walrus,Giraf,Eleph
332-111↓ Walrus,Giraf
332-212↓ Walrus,Giraf,Horse
332-231↓ Walrus,Eleph,Giraf
332-311　Walrus,Giraf,Horse
332-332↓ Eleph,Giraf,Walrus
333-111↓ Walrus,Horse
333-132↓ Walrus,Eleph,Horse
333-312　Horse,Eleph,Giraf
333-321　Horse,Walrus,Eleph
333-322　Horse,Eleph,Giraf
333-331↓ Eleph,Horse,Walrus
341-111↓ Walrus,Eleph
341-311↓ Eleph,Walrus,Dog
342-111↓ Walrus,Eleph
343-111↓ Eleph,Walrus
411-111↓ Giraffe
412-111↓ Giraffe
413-111↓ Giraffe
421-111↓ Giraffe

422-111↓ Giraffe
423-111↓ Giraffe
431-111↓ Giraf,Walrus
432-111↓ Giraf,Walrus
433-111↓ Giraf,Walrus
433-131↓ Giraf,Walrus,Eleph
433-222　Giraf,Horse
441-111↓ Giraf,Walrus,Eleph
441-331↓ Eleph,Giraf,Sable
442-111↓ Giraf,Walrus,Eleph
442-322↓ Giraf,Eleph,Sable
443-111↓ Eleph,Giraf,Walrus

431-
111-111↓ Vultre,Hippo,Walrus
111-212　Vultre,Giraf,Croc
111-221　Vultre,Hippo,Walrus
111-222　Vultre,Giraf
111-231　Vultre,Hippo,Walrus
111-311↓ Vultre,Giraf,Hippo
111-312　Vultre,Giraf,Croc
111-331↓ Vultre,Giraf,Hippo
112-111　Vultre,Hippo,Walrus
112-112　Vultre,Gorlla
112-121↓ Vultre,Hippo,Walrus
112-212　Vultre,Giraf,Gorlla
112-221　Vultre,Hippo,Walrus
112-222　Vultre,Giraf
112-231　Vultre,Hippo,Walrus
112-311↓ Vultre,Giraf,Hippo
112-312　Vultre,Giraf,Croc
112-331↓ Vultre,Giraf,Hippo
113-111↓ Gorlla,Vultre,Hippo
113-131　Vultre,Hippo,Walrus
113-211↓ Gorlla,Vultre,Hippo
113-212　Gorlla,Vultre,Giraf
113-221　Vultre,Hippo,Gorlla
113-222　Vultre,Gorlla,Giraf
113-231　Vultre,Hippo,Eleph
113-232　Vultre,Eleph,Gorlla
113-311↓ Gorlla,Vultre,Giraf
113-321　Vultre,Giraf,Hippo
113-322　Vultre,Giraf,Gorlla
113-331↓ Vultre,Eleph,Giraf
121-111↓ Hippo,Walrus,Porcp
121-211↓ Hippo,Walrus,Giraf
122-111↓ Hippo,Walrus,Gorlla
122-121↓ Hippo,Walrus,Porcp
122-211　Hippo,Walrus,Giraf
122-212　Giraf,Hippo,Gorlla
122-221↓ Hippo,Walrus,Giraf
122-312　Giraf,Hippo,Gorlla
122-321↓ Hippo,Walrus,Giraf
123-111↓ Gorlla,Hippo,Walrus
123-222　Gorlla,Giraf,Hippo
123-231　Hippo,Walrus,Eleph
123-232　Eleph,Gorlla,Giraf
123-311　Gorlla,Hippo,Walrus
123-312　Gorlla,Giraf
123-321　Hippo,Walrus,Giraf
123-322　Giraf,Gorlla,Hippo
123-331　Hippo,Eleph,Walrus
123-332　Eleph,Giraf,Gorlla
131-111↓ Hippo,Walrus
131-332↓ Hippo,Walrus,Eleph

132-111↓ Hippo,Walrus
132-332↓ Hippo,Walrus,Eleph
133-111↓ Hippo,Walrus,Gorlla
133-132↓ Hippo,Walrus,Eleph
133-311↓ Hippo,Walrus,Gorlla
133-321↓ Hippo,Walrus,Eleph
141-111　Hippo,Walrus
141-122↓ Hippo,Walrus,Bison
141-131↓ Hippo,Walrus,Eleph
141-211↓ Hippo,Walrus,Bison
141-222　Bison,Eleph,Hippo
141-231　Eleph,Hippo,Walrus
141-232　Eleph,Bison,Hippo
141-311　Hippo,Bison,Walrus
141-312　Bison,Eleph,Hippo
141-321　Hippo,Bison,Walrus
141-322↓ Bison,Eleph,Hippo
141-332　Eleph,Bison,Sable
142-111　Hippo,Walrus
142-122↓ Hippo,Walrus,Bison
142-131↓ Hippo,Walrus,Eleph
142-211　Hippo,Walrus,Bison
142-212　Bison,Eleph,Hippo
142-221　Hippo,Walrus,Eleph
142-222　Bison,Eleph,Hippo
142-231　Eleph,Hippo,Walrus
142-232　Eleph,Bison
142-311　Hippo,Bison,Walrus
142-312↓ Bison,Eleph,Hippo
142-332　Eleph,Bison,Sable
143-111↓ Hippo,Walrus,Eleph
143-212　Eleph,Bison
143-221　Eleph,Hippo
143-222↓ Eleph,Bison
211-111↓ Vultre,Hippo,Walrus
211-212　Vultre,Giraf
211-221　Vultre,Hippo,Walrus
211-222　Vultre,Giraf
211-231　Vultre,Hippo,Walrus
211-331↓ Vultre,Giraf,Hippo
212-111↓ Vultre,Hippo,Walrus
212-212　Vultre,Giraf,Gorlla
212-221　Vultre,Hippo,Walrus
212-222　Vultre,Giraf
212-231　Vultre,Hippo,Walrus
212-311↓ Vultre,Giraf,Hippo
212-312　Vultre,Giraf,Gorlla
212-331↓ Vultre,Giraf,Hippo
213-111↓ Gorlla,Vultre,Hippo
213-131　Vultre,Hippo,Walrus
213-221↓ Vultre,Hippo,Gorlla
213-222　Vultre,Gorlla,Giraf
213-231　Vultre,Eleph,Hippo
213-232　Vultre,Eleph,Gorlla
213-311↓ Gorlla,Vultre,Giraf
213-321　Vultre,Giraf,Hippo
213-322　Vultre,Giraf,Gorlla
213-331↓ Eleph,Vultre,Giraf
221-111　Hippo,Walrus
221-211↓ Hippo,Walrus,Giraf
222-111　Hippo,Walrus,Gorlla
222-132↓ Hippo,Walrus,Giraf
222-212　Giraf,Hippo,Gorlla
222-221↓ Hippo,Walrus,Giraf
222-312　Giraf,Hippo,Gorlla

222-321↓ Hippo,Walrus,Giraf
223-111↓ Gorlla,Hippo,Walrus
223-222 Gorlla,Giraf,Hippo
223-231 Hippo,Eleph,Walrus
223-232 Eleph,Gorlla,Giraf
223-311 Gorlla,Hippo,Walrus
223-312 Gorlla,Giraf
223-321 Hippo,Walrus,Giraf
223-322 Giraf,Gorlla,Eleph
223-331 Eleph,Hippo,Walrus
223-332 Eleph,Giraf
231-111↓ Hippo,Walrus
231-332↓ Hippo,Walrus,Eleph
232-111↓ Hippo,Walrus
232-222↓ Hippo,Walrus,Giraf
232-331↓ Hippo,Walrus,Eleph
233-111↓ Hippo,Walrus,Gorlla
233-221↓ Hippo,Walrus,Eleph
241-111 Hippo,Walrus
241-122↓ Hippo,Walrus,Bison
241-131↓ Hippo,Walrus,Eleph
241-211 Hippo,Walrus,Bison
241-212 Bison,Eleph,Hippo
241-221 Hippo,Walrus,Eleph
241-222 Bison,Eleph,Hippo
241-231 Eleph,Hippo,Walrus
241-232 Eleph,Bison
241-311 Hippo,Bison,Walrus
241-312↓ Bison,Eleph,Hippo
241-332 Eleph,Bison,Sable
242-111 Hippo,Walrus
242-112↓ Hippo,Walrus,Eleph
242-212 Eleph,Bison,Hippo
242-221 Eleph,Hippo,Walrus
242-321↓ Eleph,Hippo,Bison
243-111 Hippo,Eleph,Walrus
243-222↓ Eleph,Bison
311-111↓ Vultre,Giraf,Hippo
311-332↓ Giraf,Vultre,Eleph
312-111↓ Vultre,Giraf,Hippo
312-332↓ Giraf,Eleph,Vultre
313-111↓ Gorlla,Vultre,Giraf
313-121 Vultre,Giraf,Hippo
313-122 Vultre,Giraf,Gorlla
313-131↓ Eleph,Vultre,Giraf
313-211↓ Giraf,Gorlla,Eleph
313-322↓ Giraf,Eleph,Vultre
321-111↓ Hippo,Walrus,Giraf
321-232↓ Giraf,Eleph
322-111 Hippo,Walrus,Giraf
322-112 Giraf,Hippo,Gorlla
322-121↓ Hippo,Walrus,Giraf
322-222 Giraf,Rhino,Eleph
322-231↓ Giraf,Eleph,Hippo
323-111 Gorlla,Hippo,Walrus
323-112 Gorlla,Giraf
323-121 Hippo,Walrus,Giraf
323-122 Giraf,Gorlla,Eleph
323-131 Eleph,Hippo,Walrus
323-211↓ Giraf,Gorlla,Eleph
323-221↓ Giraf,Eleph,Hippo
331-111↓ Hippo,Walrus
331-132↓ Hippo,Walrus,Eleph
331-211↓ Hippo,Walrus,Giraf
331-231 Hippo,Walrus,Eleph

331-232 Eleph,Giraf,Hippo
331-311↓ Hippo,Walrus,Giraf
331-322 Giraf,Eleph,Hippo
331-331 Eleph,Hippo,Walrus
331-332 Eleph,Giraf,Sable
332-111 Hippo,Walrus
332-122↓ Hippo,Walrus,Giraf
332-131↓ Hippo,Walrus,Eleph
332-211↓ Hippo,Walrus,Giraf
332-222 Giraf,Eleph,Hippo
332-231 Eleph,Hippo,Walrus
332-232 Eleph,Giraf,Hippo
332-311 Hippo,Walrus,Giraf
332-312 Giraf,Eleph,Hippo
332-321 Hippo,Walrus,Giraf
332-322 Giraf,Eleph,Hippo
332-331 Eleph,Hippo,Walrus
332-332 Eleph,Giraf
333-111↓ Hippo,Walrus,Eleph
333-212 Eleph,Giraf
333-221 Eleph,Hippo,Walrus
333-222↓ Eleph,Giraf,Hippo
333-232 Eleph,Fox
341-111↓ Hippo,Walrus,Eleph
341-312↓ Eleph,Sable
342-111↓ Eleph,Hippo,Walrus
342-222↓ Eleph,Bison
342-332↓ Eleph,Sable
343-111↓ Elephant
411-111↓ Giraffe
412-111↓ Giraffe
413-111↓ Giraffe
421-111↓ Giraffe
422-111↓ Giraffe
423-111↓ Giraffe
431-111↓ Giraf,Hippo,Walrus
431-331↓ Giraf,Sable
432-111↓ Giraf,Hippo,Walrus
432-331↓ Giraf,Sable
433-111↓ Giraf,Hippo,Walrus
433-331↓ Giraf,Eleph,Sable
441-111 Giraf,Eleph,Hippo
441-112↓ Giraf,Eleph,Sable
442-111 Eleph,Giraf,Hippo
442-211↓ Eleph,Giraf,Sable
443-111↓ Eleph,Sable

432-
111-111↓ Vultre,Hippo,Walrus
111-212 Vultre,Giraf,Croc
111-221 Vultre,Hippo,Walrus
111-222 Vultre,Giraf
111-231 Vultre,Hippo,Walrus
111-311↓ Vultre,Giraf,Hippo
111-312 Vultre,Giraf,Croc
111-331↓ Vultre,Giraf,Hippo
112-111 Vultre,Hippo,Walrus
112-112 Vultre,Gorlla
112-121↓ Vultre,Hippo,Walrus
112-212 Vultre,Giraf,Gorlla
112-221 Vultre,Hippo,Walrus
112-222 Vultre,Giraf
112-231 Vultre,Hippo,Walrus
112-311↓ Vultre,Giraf,Hippo
112-312 Vultre,Giraf,Croc

112-331↓ Vultre,Giraf,Hippo
113-111↓ Gorlla,Vultre,Hippo
113-131 Vultre,Hippo,Walrus
113-221↓ Vultre,Hippo,Gorlla
113-222 Vultre,Gorlla,Giraf
113-231 Vultre,Eleph,Hippo
113-232 Vultre,Eleph,Gorlla
113-311↓ Gorlla,Vultre,Giraf
113-321 Vultre,Giraf,Hippo
113-322 Vultre,Giraf,Gorlla
113-331 Eleph,Vultre,Giraf
121-111 Hippo,Walrus
121-132↓ Hippo,Walrus,Giraf
122-111 Hippo,Walrus,Gorlla
122-132↓ Hippo,Walrus,Giraf
122-212 Giraf,Hippo,Gorlla
122-221↓ Hippo,Walrus,Giraf
122-312 Giraf,Hippo,Gorlla
122-321↓ Hippo,Walrus,Giraf
123-111↓ Gorlla,Hippo,Walrus
123-222 Gorlla,Giraf,Hippo
123-231 Hippo,Walrus,Eleph
123-232 Eleph,Gorlla,Giraf
123-311 Gorlla,Hippo,Walrus
123-312 Gorlla,Giraf
123-321 Hippo,Walrus,Giraf
123-322 Giraf,Gorlla,Eleph
123-331 Eleph,Hippo,Walrus
123-332 Eleph,Giraf,Gorlla
131-111↓ Hippo,Walrus
131-332↓ Hippo,Walrus,Eleph
132-111↓ Hippo,Walrus
132-332↓ Hippo,Walrus,Eleph
133-111↓ Hippo,Walrus,Gorlla
133-132↓ Hippo,Walrus,Eleph
133-211↓ Hippo,Walrus,Gorlla
133-221↓ Hippo,Walrus,Eleph
141-111 Hippo,Walrus
141-122↓ Hippo,Walrus,Bison
141-131↓ Hippo,Walrus,Eleph
141-211 Hippo,Walrus,Bison
141-212 Bison,Eleph,Hippo
141-221 Hippo,Walrus,Bison
141-222 Bison,Eleph,Hippo
141-231 Eleph,Hippo,Walrus
141-232 Eleph,Bison
141-311 Bison,Hippo,Walrus
141-331↓ Eleph,Bison,Hippo
141-332 Eleph,Bison,Sable
142-111 Hippo,Walrus
142-122↓ Hippo,Walrus,Bison
142-131↓ Hippo,Walrus,Eleph
142-211 Hippo,Walrus,Bison
142-212↓ Bison,Eleph,Hippo
143-111↓ Hippo,Walrus,Eleph
143-212↓ Eleph,Bison
211-111↓ Vultre,Hippo,Walrus
211-212 Vultre,Giraf
211-221 Vultre,Hippo,Walrus
211-222 Vultre,Giraf
211-231 Vultre,Hippo,Walrus
211-331↓ Vultre,Giraf,Hippo
212-111 Vultre,Hippo,Walrus
212-112 Vultre,Gorlla
212-121↓ Vultre,Hippo,Walrus

(432 cont'd)

212-212	Vultre,Giraf,Gorlla
212-221	Vultre,Hippo,Walrus
212-222	Vultre,Giraf
212-231	Vultre,Hippo,Walrus
212-311↓	Vultre,Giraf,Hippo
212-312	Vultre,Giraf,Gorlla
212-331↓	Vultre,Giraf,Hippo
212-332	Vultre,Giraf,Eleph
213-111↓	Gorlla,Vultre,Hippo
213-131	Vultre,Hippo,Walrus
213-221↓	Vultre,Hippo,Gorlla
213-222	Vultre,Gorlla,Giraf
213-231	Eleph,Vultre,Hippo
213-232	Vultre,Eleph,Gorlla
213-311↓	Gorlla,Vultre,Giraf
213-321↓	Vultre,Giraf,Eleph
221-111↓	Hippo,Walrus,Gorlla
221-211↓	Hippo,Walrus,Giraf
222-111↓	Hippo,Walrus,Giraf
222-132↓	Hippo,Walrus,Giraf
222-212	Giraf,Hippo,Gorlla
222-221↓	Hippo,Walrus,Giraf
222-312	Giraf,Hippo,Gorlla
222-321↓	Hippo,Walrus,Giraf
222-332	Giraf,Eleph,Hippo
223-111↓	Gorlla,Hippo,Walrus
223-212	Gorlla,Giraf,Hippo
223-221	Hippo,Walrus,Gorlla
223-222	Gorlla,Giraf,Eleph
223-231	Eleph,Hippo,Walrus
223-232	Eleph,Gorlla,Giraf
223-311	Gorlla,Hippo,Walrus
223-312	Gorlla,Giraf,Eleph
223-321	Hippo,Walrus,Giraf
223-322	Giraf,Eleph,Gorlla
223-331	Eleph,Hippo,Walrus
223-332	Eleph,Giraf
231-111↓	Hippo,Walrus
231-222↓	Hippo,Walrus,Giraf
231-331↓	Hippo,Walrus,Eleph
232-111	Hippo,Walrus
232-312↓	Hippo,Walrus,Giraf
232-321↓	Hippo,Walrus,Eleph
233-111↓	Hippo,Walrus,Gorlla
233-122↓	Hippo,Walrus,Eleph
241-111	Hippo,Walrus
241-112↓	Hippo,Walrus,Bison
241-121	Hippo,Walrus,Eleph
241-122	Hippo,Walrus,Bison
241-131↓	Hippo,Walrus,Eleph
241-211	Hippo,Walrus,Bison
241-212	Bison,Eleph,Hippo
241-221	Hippo,Eleph,Walrus
241-222	Bison,Eleph,Hippo
241-231	Eleph,Hippo,Walrus
241-321↓	Eleph,Bison,Hippo
242-111↓	Hippo,Walrus,Eleph
242-332↓	Eleph,Bison,Sable
243-111↓	Eleph,Hippo,Walrus
243-212	Eleph,Bison
243-221	Eleph,Hippo
243-222↓	Eleph,Bison
311-111↓	Vultre,Giraf,Hippo
311-222↓	Giraf,Vultre,Rhino

311-231↓	Giraf,Eleph,Vultre
311-312↓	Giraf,Vultre,Rhino
311-332↓	Giraf,Eleph,Vultre
312-111	Vultre,Giraf,Hippo
312-112	Vultre,Giraf,Gorlla
312-131↓	Vultre,Giraf,Hippo
312-212↓	Giraf,Vultre,Rhino
312-231↓	Giraf,Eleph,Vultre
312-322↓	Giraf,Vultre,Rhino
312-331↓	Giraf,Eleph,Rhino
313-111↓	Gorlla,Vultre,Giraf
313-121↓	Vultre,Giraf,Eleph
313-211↓	Giraf,Eleph,Gorlla
313-321↓	Giraf,Eleph,Rhino
321-111↓	Hippo,Walrus,Giraf
321-212	Giraf,Rhino
321-221	Giraf,Hippo,Walrus
321-222	Giraf,Rhino,Hippo
321-332↓	Giraf,Eleph,Rhino
322-111	Hippo,Walrus,Giraf
322-112	Giraf,Hippo,Gorlla
322-121↓	Hippo,Walrus,Giraf
322-132	Giraf,Eleph,Hippo
322-211	Giraf,Hippo,Walrus
322-212	Giraf,Rhino,Eleph
322-221	Giraf,Hippo,Walrus
322-222	Giraf,Rhino,Eleph
322-231	Giraf,Eleph,Hippo
322-312↓	Giraf,Rhino,Zebra
322-331↓	Giraf,Eleph,Rhino
323-111	Gorlla,Hippo,Walrus
323-112	Gorlla,Giraf,Eleph
323-121	Hippo,Walrus,Giraf
323-122	Giraf,Eleph,Gorlla
323-131	Eleph,Hippo,Walrus
323-132	Eleph,Giraf,Gorlla
323-222	Giraf,Eleph,Rhino
323-231	Eleph,Giraf,Hippo
323-232	Eleph,Giraf,Fox
323-311↓	Giraf,Eleph,Gorlla
323-332↓	Eleph,Giraf,Fox
331-111↓	Hippo,Walrus
331-122↓	Hippo,Walrus,Giraf
331-131↓	Hippo,Walrus,Eleph
331-211↓	Hippo,Walrus,Giraf
331-222	Giraf,Hippo,Eleph
331-231	Eleph,Hippo,Walrus
331-232	Eleph,Giraf,Hippo
331-311	Hippo,Walrus,Giraf
331-312	Giraf,Eleph,Hippo
331-321	Hippo,Walrus,Giraf
331-322	Giraf,Eleph,Hippo
331-331	Eleph,Hippo,Walrus
331-332	Eleph,Giraf
332-111	Hippo,Walrus
332-112↓	Hippo,Walrus,Giraf
332-121↓	Hippo,Walrus,Eleph
332-211	Hippo,Walrus,Giraf
332-212	Giraf,Eleph,Hippo
332-221	Hippo,Walrus,Eleph
332-222	Eleph,Giraf,Hippo
332-231	Eleph,Hippo,Walrus
332-232	Eleph,Giraf,Hippo
332-311	Hippo,Walrus,Giraf
332-312	Giraf,Eleph,Hippo

332-321	Hippo,Eleph,Walrus
332-322	Eleph,Giraf,Hippo
332-331	Eleph,Hippo,Walrus
332-332	Eleph,Giraf,Sable
333-111↓	Hippo,Walrus,Eleph
333-212	Eleph,Giraf,Hippo
333-221	Eleph,Hippo,Walrus
333-222	Eleph,Giraf,Fox
333-321↓	Eleph,Hippo,Walrus
333-322↓	Eleph,Giraf,Fox
341-111↓	Eleph,Hippo,Walrus
341-212↓	Eleph,Bison
341-332	Eleph,Sable
342-111↓	Eleph,Hippo,Walrus
342-212↓	Eleph,Bison
342-322↓	Eleph,Sable
343-111↓	Elephant
411-111↓	Giraf,Pcock
412-111↓	Giraffe
413-111↓	Giraffe
421-111↓	Giraffe
422-111↓	Giraffe
423-111↓	Giraf,Eleph
431-111↓	Giraf,Hippo
431-121↓	Giraf,Hippo,Walrus
431-232↓	Giraf,Eleph
431-331↓	Giraf,Sable
432-111↓	Giraf,Hippo,Walrus
432-332↓	Giraf,Sable,Eleph
433-111	Giraf,Hippo
433-331↓	Eleph,Giraf,Sable
441-111	Giraf,Eleph,Hippo
441-232↓	Eleph,Sable,Giraf
442-111	Eleph,Giraf,Hippo
442-211↓	Eleph,Giraf,Sable
443-111↓	Eleph,Sable

433-

111-111↓	Walrus,Vultre,Hippo
111-212	Vultre,Walrus,Giraf
111-221	Walrus,Vultre,Hippo
111-222	Vultre,Walrus,Giraf
111-231	Walrus,Vultre,Hippo
111-232	Vultre,Walrus,Giraf
112-111	Walrus,Vultre,Hippo
112-112	Vultre,Walrus,Gorlla
112-211↓	Walrus,Vultre,Hippo
112-212	Vultre,Walrus,Giraf
112-221	Walrus,Vultre,Hippo
112-222	Vultre,Walrus,Giraf
112-231	Walrus,Vultre,Hippo
112-232	Vultre,Walrus,Eleph
112-311	Walrus,Vultre,Giraf
112-332	Vultre,Eleph,Walrus
113-111↓	Walrus,Gorlla,Vultre
113-121	Walrus,Vultre,Hippo
113-122	Vultre,Walrus,Gorlla
113-131	Walrus,Vultre,Eleph
113-212	Gorlla,Vultre,Walrus
113-221↓	Walrus,Vultre,Eleph
113-311	Walrus,Gorlla,Eleph
113-312	Gorlla,Vultre,Eleph
113-321↓	Walrus,Eleph,Vultre
121-111↓	Walrus,Hippo
121-232↓	Walrus,Giraf,Hippo

121-312	Walrus,Giraf,Rhino
121-321	Walrus,Hippo
121-322	Walrus,Giraf,Rhino
121-331	Walrus,Hippo
121-332	Walrus,Giraf,Eleph
122-111	Walrus,Hippo
122-222↓	Walrus,Giraf,Hippo
122-232	Walrus,Eleph,Giraf
122-311	Walrus,Hippo
122-312	Walrus,Giraf,Rhino
122-321	Walrus,Hippo
122-322	Walrus,Giraf,Rhino
122-331	Walrus,Hippo,Eleph
122-332	Walrus,Eleph,Giraf
123-111↓	Walrus,Gorlla,Hippo
123-132	Walrus,Eleph,Gorlla
123-211	Walrus,Gorlla,Hippo
123-212	Gorlla,Walrus,Eleph
123-221	Walrus,Hippo,Eleph
123-222↓	Walrus,Eleph,Gorlla
123-322↓	Eleph,Walrus,Giraf
131-111↓	Walrus,Hippo
131-332↓	Walrus,Eleph,Hippo
132-111↓	Walrus,Hippo
132-322↓	Walrus,Hippo,Bison
132-331↓	Walrus,Hippo,Eleph
133-111↓	Walrus,Hippo
133-212↓	Walrus,Eleph,Hippo
141-111	Walrus,Hippo
141-112↓	Walrus,Bison,Hippo
141-122	Walrus,Bison,Eleph
141-131	Walrus,Eleph,Hippo
141-132↓	Eleph,Walrus,Bison
142-111	Walrus,Hippo,Bison
142-112	Walrus,Bison,Eleph
142-121	Walrus,Hippo,Eleph
142-122	Walrus,Bison,Eleph
142-131	Walrus,Eleph,Hippo
142-132↓	Eleph,Walrus,Bison
143-111	Walrus,Eleph,Hippo
143-211↓	Eleph,Walrus,Bison
211-111↓	Walrus,Vultre,Hippo
211-212	Vultre,Walrus,Rhino
211-221	Walrus,Vultre,Hippo
211-222	Vultre,Walrus,Rhino
211-231	Walrus,Vultre,Hippo
211-232	Vultre,Walrus,Eleph
211-311	Walrus,Vultre,Rhino
211-332	Vultre,Eleph,Walrus
212-111↓	Walrus,Vultre,Hippo
212-212	Vultre,Walrus,Rhino
212-221	Walrus,Vultre,Hippo
212-222	Vultre,Walrus,Rhino
212-231↓	Walrus,Vultre,Eleph
212-311	Walrus,Vultre,Rhino
212-332	Eleph,Vultre,Walrus
213-111↓	Walrus,Gorlla,Vultre
213-121	Walrus,Vultre,Hippo
213-122	Vultre,Walrus,Gorlla
213-131↓	Walrus,Eleph,Vultre
213-211	Walrus,Gorlla,Eleph
213-212	Gorlla,Vultre,Eleph
213-221	Walrus,Eleph,Vultre
213-311↓	Walrus,Gorlla,Eleph
213-312	Gorlla,Eleph,Vultre

213-321↓	Eleph,Walrus,Vultre
221-111	Walrus,Hippo
221-112↓	Walrus,Hippo,Gorlla
221-212	Walrus,Rhino,Giraf
221-221	Walrus,Rhino,Hippo
221-222	Walrus,Rhino,Giraf
221-231	Walrus,Hippo
221-232	Walrus,Eleph,Rhino
221-311	Walrus,Hippo
221-312	Walrus,Rhino,Giraf
221-321	Walrus,Hippo
221-322	Walrus,Rhino,Giraf
221-331	Walrus,Hippo,Eleph
221-332	Walrus,Eleph,Rhino
222-111↓	Walrus,Hippo,Gorlla
222-132↓	Walrus,Hippo,Eleph
222-211	Walrus,Hippo,Rhino
222-212	Walrus,Rhino,Giraf
222-221	Walrus,Hippo,Rhino
222-222	Walrus,Rhino,Giraf
222-231	Walrus,Hippo,Eleph
222-232	Walrus,Eleph,Rhino
222-311	Walrus,Hippo
222-312	Walrus,Rhino,Giraf
222-321	Walrus,Hippo,Rhino
222-322	Walrus,Rhino,Giraf
222-331	Walrus,Eleph,Hippo
222-332	Eleph,Walrus,Hippo
223-111↓	Walrus,Gorlla,Hippo
223-131	Walrus,Eleph,Hippo
223-132↓	Walrus,Eleph,Gorlla
223-231	Eleph,Walrus,Hippo
223-232	Eleph,Walrus,Fox
223-311↓	Walrus,Gorlla,Eleph
223-321↓	Walrus,Eleph,Hippo
231-111↓	Walrus,Hippo
231-222↓	Walrus,Hippo,Bison
231-231	Walrus,Hippo,Eleph
231-322↓	Walrus,Hippo,Bison
231-331↓	Walrus,Hippo,Eleph
232-111↓	Walrus,Hippo
232-222↓	Walrus,Hippo,Eleph
233-111	Walrus,Hippo
233-112↓	Walrus,Hippo,Gorlla
233-121↓	Walrus,Hippo,Eleph
233-332	Eleph,Walrus,Fox
241-111	Walrus,Hippo
241-112	Walrus,Bison,Eleph
241-121	Walrus,Hippo,Eleph
241-122	Walrus,Bison,Eleph
241-131	Walrus,Eleph,Hippo
241-132↓	Eleph,Walrus,Bison
242-111	Walrus,Hippo,Eleph
242-112	Walrus,Eleph,Bison
242-121	Walrus,Eleph,Hippo
242-122	Eleph,Walrus,Bison
242-131	Walrus,Eleph,Hippo
242-132↓	Eleph,Walrus,Bison
243-111	Walrus,Eleph,Hippo
243-112	Eleph,Walrus,Bison
243-121	Walrus,Eleph,Hippo
243-211↓	Eleph,Walrus,Bison
311-111	Walrus,Vultre,Rhino
311-132	Vultre,Eleph,Walrus
311-211	Rhino,Giraf,Walrus

311-212	Rhino,Giraf,Pcock
311-221	Rhino,Giraf,Walrus
311-222	Rhino,Giraf,Pcock
311-231↓	Eleph,Rhino,Giraf
311-311↓	Rhino,Giraf,Pcock
311-331↓	Eleph,Rhino,Giraf
312-111	Walrus,Vultre,Rhino
312-132	Eleph,Vultre,Walrus
312-211	Rhino,Giraf,Walrus
312-212↓	Rhino,Giraf,Eleph
313-111	Walrus,Gorlla,Eleph
313-112	Gorlla,Eleph,Vultre
313-121↓	Eleph,Walrus,Vultre
313-211↓	Eleph,Rhino,Giraf
321-111	Walrus,Hippo
321-112	Walrus,Rhino,Giraf
321-121	Walrus,Hippo,Rhino
321-122	Walrus,Rhino,Giraf
321-131	Walrus,Hippo,Eleph
321-132	Walrus,Eleph,Rhino
321-211↓	Walrus,Rhino,Giraf
321-222	Rhino,Giraf,Eleph
321-231	Eleph,Walrus,Rhino
321-232	Eleph,Rhino,Giraf
321-311	Rhino,Giraf,Walrus
321-312	Rhino,Giraf,Eleph
321-321	Rhino,Giraf,Walrus
321-322↓	Rhino,Giraf,Eleph
322-111	Walrus,Hippo,Rhino
322-112	Walrus,Rhino,Giraf
322-121	Walrus,Hippo,Rhino
322-122	Walrus,Rhino,Giraf
322-131	Walrus,Eleph,Hippo
322-132	Eleph,Walrus,Rhino
322-211	Walrus,Rhino,Giraf
322-212	Rhino,Giraf,Eleph
322-221	Walrus,Rhino,Giraf
322-222	Rhino,Giraf,Eleph
322-231	Eleph,Walrus,Rhino
322-232	Eleph,Rhino,Giraf
322-311	Rhino,Giraf,Walrus
322-312↓	Rhino,Giraf,Eleph
323-111↓	Walrus,Gorlla,Eleph
323-121	Walrus,Eleph,Hippo
323-132↓	Eleph,Walrus,Fox
323-211	Eleph,Walrus,Rhino
323-212	Eleph,Rhino,Giraf
323-221	Eleph,Walrus,Rhino
323-222↓	Eleph,Rhino,Giraf
323-232	Eleph,Fox
323-311↓	Eleph,Rhino,Giraf
323-332	Eleph,Fox
331-111	Walrus,Hippo
331-122↓	Walrus,Hippo,Eleph
331-212	Walrus,Eleph,Rhino
331-221	Walrus,Eleph,Hippo
331-222	Eleph,Walrus,Rhino
331-311↓	Walrus,Eleph,Hippo
331-312	Eleph,Walrus,Rhino
331-321↓	Walrus,Eleph,Hippo
332-111↓	Walrus,Hippo,Eleph
332-212	Eleph,Walrus,Rhino
332-221	Walrus,Eleph,Hippo
332-222	Eleph,Walrus,Rhino
332-311↓	Walrus,Eleph,Hippo

(433 cont'd)

332-312 Eleph,Walrus,Rhino
332-321↓ Eleph,Walrus,Hippo
333-111↓ Walrus,Eleph,Hippo
341-111↓ Eleph,Walrus
341-221↓ Eleph,Walrus,Bison
342-111 Eleph,Walrus,Hippo
342-112 Eleph,Walrus,Bison
342-121 Eleph,Walrus,Hippo
342-211↓ Eleph,Walrus,Bison
343-111↓ Elephant
411-111↓ Giraf,Pcock
412-111↓ Giraffe
413-111↓ Giraffe
413-131↓ Giraf,Eleph
421-111↓ Giraffe
422-111↓ Giraffe
422-121↓ Giraf,Walrus
423-111↓ Giraf,Eleph
431-111↓ Walrus,Giraf,Hippo
431-131↓ Walrus,Giraf,Eleph
431-331↓ Giraf,Eleph,Sable
432-111↓ Walrus,Giraf,Hippo
432-231↓ Giraf,Eleph,Walrus
432-322↓ Giraf,Eleph,Sable
433-111↓ Walrus,Giraf,Eleph
441-111↓ Eleph,Walrus,Giraf
441-311↓ Eleph,Sable,Giraf
442-111↓ Eleph,Walrus
443-111↓ Eleph,Sable

434-

111-111↓ Walrus
112-111↓ Walrus
113-111↓ Walrus,Gorlla
113-231↓ Walrus,Eleph
113-312↓ Walrus,Gorlla
113-322↓ Walrus,Eleph
121-111↓ Walrus
122-111↓ Walrus
123-111↓ Walrus,Eleph
131-111↓ Walrus
132-111↓ Walrus
133-111↓ Walrus,Eleph
141-111↓ Walrus,Bison
141-232↓ Walrus,Eleph,Bison
142-111↓ Walrus,Eleph
142-232↓ Eleph,Walrus,Bison
143-111↓ Walrus,Eleph
143-312↓ Eleph,Walrus,Bison
211-111↓ Walrus
212-111↓ Walrus
212-122↓ Walrus,Vultre
212-332↓ Walrus,Eleph
213-111↓ Walrus,Gorlla
213-312↓ Walrus,Eleph,Gorlla
221-111↓ Walrus
222-111↓ Walrus
222-232↓ Walrus,Eleph
223-111↓ Walrus,Gorlla
223-132↓ Walrus,Eleph
223-212↓ Walrus,Gorlla
223-222↓ Walrus,Eleph,Horse
231-111↓ Walrus
232-111↓ Walrus

233-111↓ Walrus,Eleph
241-111↓ Walrus,Bison,Eleph
242-111↓ Walrus,Eleph,Bison
243-111↓ Walrus,Eleph
243-322↓ Eleph,Walrus,Bison
311-111↓ Walrus,Rhino,Giraf
311-232↓ Walrus,Eleph,Rhino
311-311↓ Walrus,Rhino,Giraf
311-331↓ Walrus,Eleph,Rhino
312-111↓ Walrus,Eleph
312-212↓ Walrus,Rhino,Giraf
312-232↓ Eleph,Walrus,Rhino
312-322↓ Walrus,Rhino,Giraf
312-331↓ Walrus,Eleph,Rhino
313-111↓ Walrus,Eleph,Gorlla
313-311↓ Walrus,Eleph,Horse
321-111↓ Walrus,Rhino,Giraf
321-232↓ Walrus,Eleph,Rhino
321-312↓ Walrus,Rhino,Giraf
321-332↓ Walrus,Eleph,Rhino
322-111↓ Walrus,Eleph
322-212↓ Walrus,Rhino,Giraf
322-231↓ Walrus,Eleph,Rhino
322-322↓ Walrus,Rhino,Giraf
322-332↓ Eleph,Walrus,Rhino
323-111↓ Walrus,Eleph
323-212↓ Walrus,Eleph,Horse
331-111↓ Walrus,Eleph
332-111↓ Walrus,Eleph
333-111↓ Walrus,Eleph,Horse
341-111↓ Walrus,Eleph
342-111↓ Walrus,Eleph
343-111↓ Eleph,Walrus
411-111↓ Giraf,Walrus,Pcock
412-111↓ Giraf,Walrus
412-312↓ Giraf,Dolphin
413-111↓ Giraf,Walrus
413-121↓ Giraf,Walrus,Eleph
413-332↓ Dolphin,Giraf,Eleph
421-111↓ Walrus,Giraf
422-111↓ Walrus,Giraf
422-322↓ Giraf,Dolphin
423-111 Walrus,Giraf
423-122↓ Giraf,Walrus,Eleph
423-212 Giraf,Dolphin
423-221 Giraf,Walrus,Eleph
423-222 Giraf,Eleph,Dolphin
423-231 Giraf,Eleph,Walrus
423-332↓ Dolphin,Giraf,Eleph
431-111↓ Walrus,Giraf
431-332↓ Giraf,Eleph,Walrus
432-111↓ Walrus,Giraf
432-222↓ Giraf,Walrus,Eleph
433-111↓ Walrus,Eleph,Horse
433-212 Eleph,Horse,Giraf
433-221 Walrus,Eleph,Horse
433-222 Eleph,Horse,Giraf
433-311↓ Walrus,Eleph,Horse
433-312 Eleph,Dolphin,Horse
433-321 Eleph,Walrus,Horse
433-332↓ Eleph,Dolphin,Horse
441-111↓ Walrus,Eleph
441-321↓ Eleph,Sable,Walrus
442-111 Walrus,Eleph
442-311↓ Eleph,Sable,Walrus
443-111↓ Eleph,Walrus

441-

111-111↓ Hippo,Vultre,Croc
111-322↓ Hippo,Croc,Zebra
112-111↓ Hippo,Vultre,Croc
112-322↓ Hippo,Croc,Zebra
113-111↓ Hippo,Gorlla,Vultre
113-212↓ Croc,Hippo,Gorlla
113-222↓ Hippo,Croc,Vultre
113-232 Hippo,Vultre,Warthg
113-312↓ Croc,Hippo,Warthg
121-111↓ Hippo,Zebra
122-111↓ Hippo
123-111 Hippo
123-312↓ Hippo,Warthg,Gorlla
123-322↓ Hippo,Warthg,Zebra
131-111↓ Hippo
132-111↓ Hippo
133-111↓ Hippo
141-111↓ Hippo
142-111↓ Hippo,Eleph
143-111↓ Hippo,Eleph
211-111↓ Hippo,Vultre
211-212↓ Hippo,Vultre,Rhino
211-332↓ Hippo,Zebra,Rhino
212-111↓ Hippo,Vultre
212-212↓ Hippo,Vultre,Rhino
212-312↓ Hippo,Zebra,Rhino
213-111↓ Hippo,Gorlla,Vultre
213-222↓ Hippo,Vultre,Rhino
213-332↓ Hippo,Zebra,Rhino
221-111↓ Hippo,Zebra,Rhino
222-111↓ Hippo,Rhino
222-312↓ Hippo,Zebra,Rhino
223-111↓ Hippo,Gorlla
223-312↓ Hippo,Zebra,Rhino
231-111↓ Hippo
232-111↓ Hippo
233-111↓ Hippo
241-111↓ Hippo
242-111↓ Hippo,Eleph
243-111↓ Hippo,Eleph
311-111↓ Hippo,Rhino,Vultre
311-232↓ Rhino,Hippo,Zebra
312-111↓ Hippo,Rhino,Vultre
312-232↓ Rhino,Hippo,Zebra
313-111↓ Hippo,Rhino,Gorlla
313-122↓ Hippo,Rhino,Vultre
313-212↓ Rhino,Hippo,Zebra
313-231↓ Hippo,Rhino,Eleph
313-321↓ Zebra,Rhino,Hippo
313-332 Zebra,Rhino,Eleph
321-111↓ Hippo,Rhino
321-232↓ Rhino,Hippo,Zebra
322-111↓ Hippo,Rhino
322-312↓ Zebra,Rhino,Hippo
323-111↓ Hippo,Rhino,Gorlla
323-222↓ Rhino,Hippo,Zebra
323-231 Hippo,Rhino,Eleph
323-312↓ Zebra,Rhino,Hippo
323-332 Zebra,Rhino,Eleph
331-111↓ Hippo,Zebra,Rhino
332-111↓ Hippo,Rhino
332-232↓ Hippo,Rhino,Eleph
332-312↓ Hippo,Zebra,Rhino

333-111↓ Hippo,Eleph
333-232↓ Hippo,Eleph,Lion
333-312↓ Hippo,Zebra,Eleph
333-332↓ Eleph,Hippo,Lion
341-111↓ Hippo,Eleph
341-322↓ Eleph,Hippo,Wolf
341-332 Eleph,Wolf,Sable
342-111↓ Hippo,Eleph
343-111↓ Hippo,Eleph
411-111↓ Giraf,Hippo,Rhino
411-311↓ Giraf,Zebra,Rhino
412-111↓ Giraf,Hippo,Rhino
412-311↓ Giraf,Zebra,Rhino
413-111↓ Giraf,Hippo,Rhino
413-311↓ Giraf,Zebra,Rhino
413-331↓ Giraf,Tiger,Zebra
421-111 Hippo,Giraf
421-231↓ Giraf,Hippo,Rhino
421-311↓ Giraf,Zebra,Rhino
422-111 Hippo,Giraf
422-321↓ Giraf,Zebra,Rhino
423-111 Hippo,Giraf
423-231↓ Giraf,Hippo,Rhino
423-311↓ Giraf,Zebra,Rhino
423-322↓ Giraf,Zebra,Tiger
431-111↓ Hippo,Giraf
431-232↓ Giraf,Hippo,Rhino
431-311 Hippo,Giraf,Zebra
431-332 Giraf,Sable,Tiger
432-111↓ Hippo,Giraf
432-322↓ Giraf,Hippo,Tiger
433-111↓ Hippo,Giraf
433-222↓ Giraf,Hippo,Tiger
433-231 Hippo,Eleph,Tiger
433-232 Tiger,Eleph,Giraf
433-311↓ Hippo,Tiger,Giraf
433-331↓ Tiger,Hippo,Eleph
441-111↓ Hippo,Eleph
441-132↓ Hippo,Eleph,Sable
442-111↓ Hippo,Eleph
442-321↓ Sable,Eleph,Hippo
443-111 Hippo,Eleph
443-332↓ Eleph,Sable,Tiger

442-
111-111↓ Hippo,Vultre,Croc
111-232 Hippo,Vultre,Rhino
111-312↓ Croc,Hippo,Rhino
112-111↓ Hippo,Vultre,Croc
112-232 Hippo,Vultre,Rhino
112-322↓ Hippo,Croc,Rhino
113-111↓ Hippo,Gorlla,Vultre
113-212↓ Croc,Hippo,Gorlla
113-222↓ Hippo,Croc,Vultre
113-232 Hippo,Vultre,Warthg
113-312↓ Croc,Hippo,Warthg
113-332↓ Hippo,Warthg,Rhino
121-111↓ Hippo,Rhino
122-111↓ Hippo,Rhino
123-111↓ Hippo,Gorlla
123-312↓ Hippo,Warthg,Rhino
131-111↓ Hippo
132-111↓ Hippo
133-111↓ Hippo
141-111↓ Hippo

141-332↓ Hippo,Eleph,Bison
142-111↓ Hippo,Eleph
142-332↓ Hippo,Eleph,Bison
143-111↓ Hippo,Eleph
143-312↓ Hippo,Eleph,Bison
211-111↓ Hippo,Vultre
211-332↓ Hippo,Rhino,Zebra
212-111↓ Hippo,Vultre
212-332↓ Hippo,Rhino,Zebra
213-111↓ Hippo,Gorlla,Vultre
213-212↓ Hippo,Rhino,Gorlla
213-332↓ Hippo,Rhino,Zebra
221-111↓ Hippo,Rhino
221-312↓ Hippo,Rhino,Zebra
222-111↓ Hippo,Rhino
222-332↓ Hippo,Rhino,Zebra
223-111↓ Hippo,Gorlla
223-232↓ Hippo,Rhino,Eleph
223-312↓ Hippo,Rhino,Zebra
231-111↓ Hippo
232-111↓ Hippo
233-111↓ Hippo,Eleph
241-111↓ Hippo,Bison
241-332↓ Hippo,Eleph,Bison
242-111↓ Hippo,Eleph
243-111↓ Hippo,Eleph
243-222↓ Eleph,Hippo,Bison
311-111↓ Hippo,Rhino,Vultre
311-331↓ Rhino,Zebra,Hippo
312-111 Hippo,Rhino
312-331↓ Rhino,Zebra,Hippo
313-111↓ Hippo,Rhino,Gorlla
313-122↓ Hippo,Rhino,Vultre
313-231↓ Rhino,Hippo,Eleph
313-331↓ Rhino,Zebra,Eleph
321-111↓ Hippo,Rhino
321-232↓ Rhino,Hippo,Zebra
322-111↓ Hippo,Rhino
322-211↓ Hippo,Rhino,Zebra
323-111 Hippo,Rhino
323-212↓ Rhino,Hippo,Zebra
323-221↓ Hippo,Rhino,Eleph
323-311↓ Rhino,Zebra,Hippo
323-332 Rhino,Zebra,Eleph
331-111↓ Hippo,Rhino
331-232↓ Hippo,Rhino,Eleph
331-312↓ Hippo,Rhino,Zebra
332-111↓ Hippo,Rhino
332-312↓ Hippo,Rhino,Zebra
332-331↓ Hippo,Rhino,Eleph
333-111↓ Hippo,Eleph
333-222↓ Hippo,Eleph,Rhino
333-231↓ Hippo,Eleph,Lion
341-111↓ Hippo,Eleph
342-111↓ Hippo,Eleph
343-111↓ Hippo,Eleph
411-111↓ Giraf,Hippo,Rhino
411-311↓ Giraf,Rhino,Zebra
412-111↓ Giraf,Hippo,Rhino
412-311↓ Giraf,Rhino,Zebra
413-111↓ Giraf,Hippo,Rhino
413-231↓ Giraf,Rhino,Eleph
413-311↓ Giraf,Rhino,Zebra
413-331↓ Giraf,Tiger,Rhino

421-111 Hippo,Giraf
421-132↓ Giraf,Hippo,Rhino
421-311↓ Giraf,Rhino,Zebra
422-111↓ Hippo,Giraf,Rhino
422-311↓ Giraf,Rhino,Zebra
423-111 Hippo,Giraf
423-132↓ Giraf,Hippo,Rhino
423-232 Giraf,Rhino,Eleph
423-311↓ Giraf,Rhino,Zebra
423-331↓ Giraf,Tiger,Rhino
431-111↓ Hippo,Giraf
431-232↓ Giraf,Hippo,Rhino
431-331 Hippo,Giraf,Sable
431-332 Giraf,Sable,Tiger
432-111↓ Hippo,Giraf
432-322↓ Giraf,Hippo,Tiger
433-111↓ Hippo,Giraf
433-222↓ Giraf,Hippo,Eleph
433-231 Hippo,Eleph,Tiger
433-232 Eleph,Tiger,Giraf
433-311↓ Hippo,Tiger,Giraf
433-322 Tiger,Giraf,Eleph
433-331↓ Tiger,Eleph,Hippo
441-111↓ Hippo,Eleph
441-321↓ Sable,Hippo,Eleph
442-111↓ Hippo,Eleph
442-321↓ Sable,Eleph,Hippo
443-111 Hippo,Eleph
443-311↓ Eleph,Sable

443-
111-111↓ Hippo,Vultre,Croc
111-122↓ Hippo,Vultre,Rhino
111-211 Hippo,Croc,Rhino
111-232↓ Rhino,Hippo,Vultre
111-311↓ Hippo,Croc,Rhino
112-111↓ Hippo,Vultre,Croc
112-211 Hippo,Croc,Rhino
112-232↓ Rhino,Hippo,Vultre
112-311↓ Hippo,Croc,Rhino
113-111↓ Hippo,Gorlla,Vultre
113-122↓ Hippo,Vultre,Rhino
113-211↓ Hippo,Croc,Rhino
113-231 Hippo,Rhino,Eleph
113-312↓ Croc,Rhino,Hippo
113-332↓ Rhino,Eleph,Hippo
121-111↓ Hippo,Rhino
122-111↓ Hippo,Walrus
122-212↓ Hippo,Rhino
123-111↓ Hippo,Gorlla
123-322↓ Rhino,Hippo,Warthg
123-331↓ Rhino,Hippo,Eleph
131-111↓ Hippo,Walrus
132-111↓ Hippo,Walrus
133-111↓ Hippo,Walrus
141-111↓ Hippo,Eleph
141-322↓ Hippo,Bison,Eleph
142-111↓ Hippo,Eleph
142-312↓ Hippo,Bison,Eleph
143-111↓ Hippo,Eleph
143-311↓ Eleph,Hippo,Bison
211-111↓ Hippo,Rhino,Vultre
212-111↓ Hippo,Rhino,Vultre
213-111↓ Hippo,Gorlla,Rhino
213-331↓ Rhino,Hippo,Eleph

(443 cont'd)

221-111 Hippo,Walrus
221-222↓ Rhino,Hippo,Walrus
222-111 Hippo,Walrus
222-321↓ Hippo,Rhino,Walrus
222-322↓ Rhino,Hippo,Zebra
223-111 Hippo,Walrus,Gorlla
223-112↓ Hippo,Gorlla,Rhino
223-221 Hippo,Rhino,Walrus
223-332↓ Rhino,Eleph,Hippo
231-111↓ Hippo,Walrus
232-111↓ Hippo,Walrus
232-322↓ Hippo,Rhino,Walrus
232-332 Hippo,Rhino,Eleph
233-111↓ Hippo,Walrus
233-222↓ Hippo,Eleph,Walrus
233-332↓ Eleph,Hippo,Lion
241-111↓ Hippo,Walrus
241-312↓ Hippo,Bison,Eleph
242-111 Hippo,Walrus
242-122↓ Hippo,Eleph,Walrus
242-212 Hippo,Eleph,Bison
242-221 Hippo,Eleph,Walrus
242-222 Hippo,Eleph,Bison
242-231 Hippo,Eleph,Walrus
242-332↓ Eleph,Hippo,Bison
243-111↓ Hippo,Eleph
243-222↓ Eleph,Hippo,Bison
311-111↓ Rhino,Hippo
311-312↓ Rhino,Zebra
312-111↓ Rhino,Hippo
312-311↓ Rhino,Zebra
313-111↓ Rhino,Hippo
313-231↓ Rhino,Eleph,Hippo
313-332↓ Rhino,Eleph,Zebra
321-111 Hippo,Rhino
321-321↓ Rhino,Zebra,Hippo
322-111↓ Hippo,Rhino,Walrus
322-231↓ Rhino,Hippo,Eleph
322-331↓ Rhino,Zebra,Hippo
322-332 Rhino,Zebra,Eleph
323-111 Hippo,Rhino
323-212↓ Rhino,Eleph,Hippo
323-232↓ Rhino,Eleph,Lion
323-321 Rhino,Zebra,Hippo
323-322↓ Rhino,Zebra,Eleph
331-111 Hippo,Walrus
331-332↓ Rhino,Hippo,Eleph
332-111 Hippo,Walrus
332-122↓ Hippo,Rhino,Walrus
332-132 Hippo,Rhino,Eleph
332-211 Hippo,Rhino,Walrus
332-212 Rhino,Hippo,Eleph
332-221 Hippo,Rhino,Walrus
332-322↓ Rhino,Hippo,Eleph
333-111 Hippo,Walrus,Eleph
333-112 Hippo,Eleph,Rhino
333-121 Hippo,Walrus,Eleph
333-122 Hippo,Eleph,Rhino
333-131 Hippo,Eleph,Walrus
333-132 Eleph,Hippo,Lion
333-211↓ Hippo,Eleph,Rhino
333-231 Eleph,Hippo,Lion
333-232 Eleph,Lion,Rhino
333-311↓ Hippo,Eleph,Rhino

333-331 Eleph,Hippo,Lion
333-332 Eleph,Lion,Rhino
341-111↓ Hippo,Eleph
341-332 Eleph,Wolf
342-111↓ Hippo,Eleph
342-221↓ Eleph,Hippo,Rhino
342-322↓ Eleph,Wolf
343-111↓ Eleph,Hippo
411-111 Rhino,Giraf,Hippo
411-112 Rhino,Giraf,Pcock
411-121 Rhino,Giraf,Hippo
411-122 Rhino,Giraf,Pcock
411-131 Rhino,Giraf,Hippo
411-132↓ Rhino,Giraf,Pcock
412-111↓ Rhino,Giraf,Hippo
413-111↓ Rhino,Giraf,Hippo
413-322↓ Rhino,Giraf,Zebra
413-331↓ Rhino,Giraf,Eleph
421-111↓ Rhino,Hippo,Giraf
421-332↓ Rhino,Giraf,Zebra
422-111↓ Rhino,Hippo,Giraf
423-111↓ Rhino,Hippo,Giraf
423-132↓ Rhino,Giraf,Eleph
431-111↓ Hippo,Rhino,Giraf
431-332 Rhino,Giraf,Sable
432-111↓ Hippo,Rhino,Giraf
432-132 Hippo,Rhino,Eleph
432-211↓ Hippo,Rhino,Giraf
432-231 Hippo,Rhino,Eleph
432-232 Rhino,Eleph,Giraf
432-311↓ Rhino,Hippo,Giraf
432-331 Rhino,Hippo,Eleph
432-332 Rhino,Eleph,Tiger
433-111↓ Hippo,Eleph,Rhino
433-132↓ Eleph,Hippo,Lion
433-211 Hippo,Eleph,Rhino
433-212 Eleph,Rhino,Giraf
433-221 Hippo,Eleph,Rhino
433-222 Eleph,Rhino,Giraf
433-231↓ Eleph,Hippo,Lion
433-311 Eleph,Rhino,Hippo
433-332↓ Eleph,Tiger,Lion
441-111↓ Hippo,Eleph
441-311↓ Eleph,Sable,Hippo
441-312 Sable,Eleph,Wolf
441-321 Eleph,Sable,Hippo
441-332↓ Sable,Eleph,Wolf
442-111 Hippo,Eleph
442-311↓ Eleph,Sable
443-111↓ Eleph,Hippo

444-

111-111↓ Walrus,Hippo
111-211↓ Walrus,Hippo,Rhino
111-212 Walrus,Rhino,Croc
111-221↓ Walrus,Hippo,Rhino
111-312 Rhino,Croc,Walrus
111-321↓ Walrus,Hippo,Rhino
111-332 Rhino,Walrus,Eagle
112-111↓ Walrus,Hippo
112-211↓ Walrus,Hippo,Rhino
112-212 Walrus,Rhino,Croc
112-221↓ Walrus,Hippo,Rhino
112-312 Rhino,Croc,Walrus
112-321↓ Walrus,Hippo,Rhino

112-332 Rhino,Walrus,Eagle
113-111 Walrus,Hippo
113-211↓ Walrus,Hippo,Rhino
113-212 Walrus,Rhino,Croc
113-221↓ Walrus,Hippo,Rhino
113-232 Walrus,Rhino,Lion
113-311 Walrus,Hippo,Rhino
113-312 Rhino,Croc,Walrus
113-321↓ Walrus,Hippo,Rhino
113-332 Rhino,Lion,Walrus
121-111↓ Walrus,Hippo
121-232↓ Walrus,Hippo,Rhino
122-111↓ Walrus,Hippo
122-232↓ Walrus,Hippo,Rhino
123-111↓ Walrus,Hippo
123-222↓ Walrus,Hippo,Rhino
123-231↓ Walrus,Hippo,Lion
123-311↓ Walrus,Hippo,Rhino
123-331 Walrus,Hippo,Lion
123-332 Lion,Walrus,Rhino
131-111↓ Walrus,Hippo
132-111↓ Walrus,Hippo
133-111↓ Walrus,Hippo
133-222↓ Walrus,Hippo,Lion
141-111↓ Walrus,Hippo
141-222↓ Walrus,Hippo,Bison
141-231↓ Walrus,Hippo,Eleph
141-311↓ Walrus,Hippo,Bison
141-331 Walrus,Hippo,Eleph
141-332 Eleph,Walrus,Bison
142-111↓ Walrus,Hippo
142-222↓ Walrus,Hippo,Bison
142-231↓ Walrus,Hippo,Eleph
142-311↓ Walrus,Hippo,Bison
142-321 Walrus,Hippo,Eleph
142-322 Walrus,Bison,Eleph
142-331 Walrus,Eleph,Hippo
142-332 Eleph,W.Dog,Walrus
143-111 Walrus,Hippo
143-122↓ Walrus,Hippo,Eleph
143-312 Eleph,W.Dog,Walrus
143-321 Eleph,Walrus,Hippo
143-322↓ Eleph,W.Dog,Walrus
211-111 Walrus,Hippo
211-132↓ Walrus,Hippo,Rhino
212-111 Walrus,Hippo
212-132↓ Walrus,Hippo,Rhino
213-111 Walrus,Hippo
213-132↓ Walrus,Hippo,Rhino
213-232 Rhino,Lion,Walrus
213-311 Walrus,Rhino,Hippo
213-322 Rhino,Walrus,Lion
221-111↓ Walrus,Hippo
221-211↓ Walrus,Hippo,Rhino
221-332 Rhino,Walrus,Eagle
222-111 Walrus,Hippo
222-132↓ Walrus,Hippo,Rhino
222-332 Rhino,Walrus,Eagle
223-111↓ Walrus,Hippo
223-132↓ Walrus,Hippo,Lion
223-211↓ Walrus,Hippo,Rhino
223-231 Walrus,Hippo,Lion
223-232 Lion,Walrus,Rhino
223-311↓ Walrus,Hippo,Rhino
223-322 Rhino,Walrus,Lion

223-331	Walrus,Lion,Hippo
223-332	Lion,Rhino,Walrus
231-111↓	Walrus,Hippo
232-111↓	Walrus,Hippo
232-332↓	Walrus,Hippo,Lion
233-111↓	Walrus,Hippo
233-212↓	Walrus,Hippo,Lion
233-332	Lion,Walrus,Eleph
241-111↓	Walrus,Hippo
241-222↓	Walrus,Hippo,Bison
241-231↓	Walrus,Hippo,Eleph
241-311↓	Walrus,Hippo,Bison
241-321	Walrus,Hippo,Eleph
241-322	Walrus,Bison,Eleph
241-331	Walrus,Eleph,Hippo
241-332	Eleph,Walrus,Bison
242-111↓	Walrus,Hippo
242-212↓	Walrus,Hippo,Eleph
242-312	Walrus,Eleph,Bison
242-321	Walrus,Hippo,Eleph
242-322	Eleph,Walrus,Bison
242-331	Eleph,Walrus,Hippo
242-332	Eleph,W.Dog,Walrus
243-111	Walrus,Hippo
243-112↓	Walrus,Hippo,Eleph
243-312	Eleph,W.Dog,Walrus
243-321	Eleph,Walrus,Hippo
243-322↓	Eleph,W.Dog
311-111↓	Walrus,Rhino,Hippo
311-331↓	Rhino,Eagle
312-111↓	Walrus,Rhino,Hippo
312-331↓	Rhino,Eagle
313-111	Walrus,Rhino,Hippo
313-322↓	Rhino,Lion,Eleph
321-111↓	Walrus,Hippo,Rhino
321-331↓	Rhino,Eagle,Walrus
322-111↓	Walrus,Hippo,Rhino
322-231↓	Rhino,Walrus,Lion
322-332↓	Rhino,Eagle,Lion
323-111↓	Walrus,Hippo,Rhino
323-122	Rhino,Walrus,Lion
323-131	Walrus,Lion,Hippo
323-132↓	Lion,Rhino,Walrus
323-331↓	Lion,Rhino,Eleph
331-111↓	Walrus,Hippo
331-211↓	Walrus,Hippo,Rhino
331-231	Walrus,Hippo,Lion
331-232	Walrus,Lion,Rhino
331-311↓	Walrus,Hippo,Rhino
331-331	Walrus,Lion,Hippo
331-332	Lion,Rhino,Walrus
332-111	Walrus,Hippo
332-122↓	Walrus,Hippo,Rhino
332-131↓	Walrus,Hippo,Lion
332-211↓	Walrus,Hippo,Rhino
332-231	Walrus,Lion,Hippo
332-232	Lion,Walrus,Rhino
332-311	Walrus,Hippo,Rhino
332-312	Rhino,Walrus,Lion
332-321	Walrus,Hippo,Rhino
332-322	Rhino,Walrus,Lion
332-331	Walrus,Lion,Hippo
332-332	Lion,Rhino,Eleph
333-111	Walrus,Hippo
333-112↓	Walrus,Hippo,Lion

333-132	Lion,Walrus,Eleph
333-211	Walrus,Lion,Hippo
333-212	Lion,Walrus,Eleph
333-221	Walrus,Lion,Hippo
333-222↓	Lion,Eleph,Walrus
333-311	Lion,Walrus,Hippo
333-312	Lion,Eleph,Rhino
333-321	Lion,Walrus,Eleph
333-322↓	Lion,Eleph,Rhino
341-111	Walrus,Hippo
341-112↓	Walrus,Hippo,Eleph
341-312	Eleph,Wolf,Walrus
341-321	Eleph,Walrus,Hippo
341-322↓	Eleph,Wolf
342-111↓	Walrus,Hippo,Eleph
343-111↓	Eleph,Walrus,Hippo
343-222↓	Eleph,Lion
411-111	Rhino,Walrus,Giraf
411-112	Rhino,Giraf,Pcock
411-121	Rhino,Walrus,Giraf
411-122	Rhino,Giraf,Pcock
411-131	Rhino,Walrus,Giraf
411-132↓	Rhino,Giraf,Pcock
411-332	Rhino,Eagle,Giraf
412-111↓	Rhino,Walrus,Giraf
412-331↓	Rhino,Giraf,Eagle
413-111↓	Rhino,Walrus,Giraf
413-131	Rhino,Lion,Walrus
413-132	Rhino,Lion,Eleph
413-221↓	Rhino,Giraf,Lion
413-231↓	Rhino,Lion,Eleph
413-311↓	Rhino,Dolphin,Giraf
413-331	Rhino,Lion,Eleph
413-332	Rhino,Dolphin,Lion
421-111	Walrus,Rhino,Hippo
421-112	Rhino,Giraf,Walrus
421-121	Walrus,Rhino,Hippo
421-122	Rhino,Giraf,Walrus
421-131	Walrus,Rhino,Hippo
421-331↓	Rhino,Giraf,Eagle
422-111	Walrus,Rhino,Hippo
422-112	Rhino,Giraf,Walrus
422-121	Walrus,Rhino,Hippo
422-122	Rhino,Giraf,Walrus
422-131	Walrus,Rhino,Hippo
422-231↓	Rhino,Giraf,Walrus
422-331↓	Rhino,Giraf,Eagle
423-111	Walrus,Rhino,Hippo
423-112	Rhino,Giraf,Walrus
423-121	Walrus,Rhino,Hippo
423-122	Rhino,Giraf,Walrus
423-131	Lion,Walrus,Rhino
423-132	Lion,Rhino,Eleph
423-211↓	Rhino,Giraf,Lion
423-231↓	Lion,Rhino,Eleph
423-311↓	Rhino,Dolphin,Giraf
423-331	Lion,Rhino,Eleph
423-332	Lion,Rhino,Dolphin
431-111	Walrus,Hippo
431-132↓	Walrus,Hippo,Lion
431-211	Walrus,Hippo,Rhino
431-212	Rhino,Walrus,Giraf
431-221	Walrus,Hippo,Rhino
431-222	Rhino,Walrus,Giraf
431-231	Walrus,Lion,Hippo

431-232	Lion,Rhino,Walrus
431-311	Walrus,Rhino,Hippo
431-312	Rhino,Giraf,Walrus
431-321	Walrus,Rhino,Hippo
431-322	Rhino,Giraf,Walrus
431-331	Walrus,Lion,Rhino
431-332	Lion,Rhino,Eleph
432-111	Walrus,Hippo
432-122↓	Walrus,Hippo,Rhino
432-131↓	Walrus,Hippo,Lion
432-211	Walrus,Hippo,Rhino
432-212	Rhino,Walrus,Giraf
432-221	Walrus,Hippo,Rhino
432-222	Rhino,Walrus,Lion
432-231	Walrus,Lion,Hippo
432-232	Lion,Rhino,Eleph
432-311	Walrus,Rhino,Hippo
432-312	Rhino,Giraf,Walrus
432-321	Walrus,Rhino,Hippo
432-322	Rhino,Lion,Giraf
432-331	Lion,Walrus,Rhino
432-332	Lion,Rhino,Eleph
433-111↓	Walrus,Hippo,Lion
433-221↓	Lion,Walrus,Eleph
433-312	Lion,Eleph,Rhino
433-321	Lion,Eleph,Walrus
433-332↓	Lion,Eleph,Tiger
441-111↓	Walrus,Hippo,Eleph
441-311	Eleph,Sable,Walrus
441-312	Eleph,Sable,Wolf
441-321	Eleph,Sable,Walrus
441-332↓	Eleph,Sable,Wolf
442-111	Walrus,Hippo,Eleph
442-311↓	Eleph,Sable,Walrus
443-111↓	Eleph,Walrus,Hippo

451-

111-111↓	Croc,Rhino,Hippo
112-111↓	Croc,Rhino,Hippo
113-111↓	Croc,Warthg
113-321↓	Croc,Warthg,Rhino
121-111↓	Rhino,Hippo,Croc
122-111↓	Rhino,Hippo,Croc
123-111↓	Warthg,Rhino,Hippo
123-311↓	Warthg,Rhino,Croc
131-111↓	Hippo,Rhino
131-332↓	Rhino,Hippo,Tiger
132-111↓	Hippo,Rhino
132-211↓	Hippo,Rhino,Croc
132-232↓	Rhino,Hippo,Warthg
132-331↓	Rhino,Hippo,Tiger
133-111↓	Hippo,Warthg,Rhino
133-312	Warthg,Rhino,Tiger
133-321	Warthg,Rhino,Hippo
133-322↓	Warthg,Rhino,Tiger
141-111↓	Hippo,Rhino
142-111↓	Hippo,Rhino
142-211↓	Hippo,Rhino,Croc
142-232↓	Rhino,Hippo,Eleph
142-311	Hippo,Rhino,Croc
142-322	Rhino,Hippo,Warthg
142-331↓	Hippo,Rhino,Tiger
143-111↓	Hippo,Warthg,Rhino
143-132	Hippo,Eleph,Warthg
143-211↓	Hippo,Warthg,Rhino

(451 cont'd)

143-231 Hippo,Eleph,Warthg
143-232 Eleph,Warthg,Rhino
143-311 Hippo,Warthg,Rhino
143-312 Warthg,Rhino,Tiger
143-321 Hippo,Warthg,Rhino
143-322 Warthg,Tiger,Rhino
143-331 Tiger,Eleph,Hippo
143-332 Tiger,Eleph,Warthg
211-111↓ Rhino,Hippo
212-111↓ Rhino,Hippo
213-111↓ Rhino,Hippo
221-111↓ Rhino,Hippo
222-111↓ Rhino,Hippo
223-111↓ Rhino,Hippo
231-111↓ Hippo,Rhino
232-111↓ Hippo,Rhino
233-111↓ Hippo,Rhino
241-111↓ Hippo,Rhino
242-111↓ Hippo,Rhino
243-111↓ Hippo,Rhino
243-312 Rhino,Tiger,Eleph
243-321 Rhino,Hippo,Eleph
243-322↓ Rhino,Tiger,Eleph
311-111↓ Rhinocerous
312-111↓ Rhinocerous
313-111↓ Rhinocerous
321-111↓ Rhinocerous
322-111↓ Rhinocerous
323-111↓ Rhinocerous
331-111↓ Rhino,Hippo
332-111↓ Rhino,Hippo
332-222↓ Rhino,Bear
332-332 Rhino,Tiger
333-111↓ Rhino,Hippo
333-232↓ Rhino,Tiger
341-111↓ Rhino,Hippo
342-111↓ Rhino,Hippo
342-331↓ Rhino,Eleph,Tiger
343-111↓ Rhino,Hippo,Eleph
343-311↓ Rhino,Eleph,Tiger
411-111↓ Rhino,Tiger
412-111↓ Rhino,Tiger
413-111↓ Rhino,Tiger
421-111↓ Rhino,Tiger
422-111↓ Rhino,Tiger
423-111↓ Rhino,Tiger
431-111↓ Rhino,Hippo
431-131↓ Rhino,Hippo,Tiger
432-111↓ Rhino,Hippo
433-111↓ Rhino,Tiger,Hippo
441-111↓ Rhino,Hippo
441-312↓ Tiger,Rhino,Sable
442-111 Rhino,Hippo
442-131↓ Rhino,Tiger,Hippo
443-111↓ Rhino,Tiger,Hippo
443-112 Tiger,Rhino,Eleph
443-121 Tiger,Rhino,Hippo
443-122↓ Tiger,Rhino,Eleph

452-

111-111↓ Croc,Rhino
112-111↓ Croc,Rhino
113-111↓ Croc,Rhino
113-121↓ Croc,Rhino,Warthg

121-111 Rhino,Hippo
122-111↓ Rhino,Hippo,Croc
122-222↓ Rhino,Warthg
122-311↓ Rhino,Croc
123-111↓ Rhino,Warthg,Hippo
123-312↓ Warthg,Rhino,Croc
131-111↓ Hippo,Rhino
132-111↓ Hippo,Rhino
132-332 Rhino,Tiger
133-111↓ Hippo,Warthg,Rhino
133-331↓ Tiger,Rhino,Warthg
141-111↓ Hippo,Rhino
141-331↓ Rhino,Hippo,Tiger
142-111↓ Rhino,Hippo
142-331↓ Rhino,Hippo,Tiger
143-111↓ Hippo,Warthg,Rhino
143-132 Hippo,Eleph,Warthg
143-211↓ Rhino,Hippo,Warthg
143-231 Hippo,Eleph,Rhino
143-232 Eleph,Warthg,Rhino
143-311 Rhino,Hippo,Warthg
143-312 Warthg,Rhino,Tiger
143-321 Rhino,Hippo,Warthg
143-322 Warthg,Rhino,Tiger
143-331 Tiger,Eleph,Rhino
143-332 Tiger,Eleph,Warthg
211-111↓ Rhino,Hippo
212-111↓ Rhino,Hippo
213-111↓ Rhino,Hippo
221-111↓ Rhino,Hippo
222-111↓ Rhino,Hippo
223-111↓ Rhino,Hippo
231-111↓ Rhino,Hippo
232-111↓ Hippo,Rhino
233-111↓ Hippo,Rhino
241-111↓ Hippo,Rhino
242-111↓ Hippo,Rhino
243-111↓ Hippo,Rhino,Eleph
243-312 Rhino,Eleph,Tiger
243-321 Rhino,Hippo,Eleph
243-322↓ Rhino,Eleph,Tiger
311-111↓ Rhinocerous
312-111↓ Rhinocerous
313-111↓ Rhinocerous
321-111↓ Rhinocerous
322-111↓ Rhinocerous
323-111↓ Rhinocerous
323-332 Rhino,Tiger
331-111↓ Rhino,Hippo
332-111↓ Rhino,Hippo
332-132↓ Rhino,Hippo,Bear
332-332↓ Rhino,Tiger,Bear
333-111↓ Rhino,Hippo
333-122↓ Rhino,Hippo,Bear
333-322↓ Rhino,Tiger,Bear
341-111↓ Rhino,Hippo
342-111↓ Rhino,Hippo
342-131↓ Rhino,Hippo,Eleph
342-222 Rhino,Bear
342-332↓ Rhino,Eleph,Tiger
343-111↓ Rhino,Hippo,Eleph
343-331↓ Eleph,Tiger,Rhino
411-111↓ Rhinocerous
412-111↓ Rhinocerous
413-111↓ Rhino,Tiger

421-111↓ Rhino,Tiger
422-111↓ Rhino,Tiger
423-111↓ Rhino,Tiger
431-111↓ Rhino,Hippo
431-132↓ Rhino,Tiger
432-111↓ Rhino,Hippo
433-111↓ Rhino,Tiger
433-121↓ Rhino,Tiger,Hippo
441-111↓ Rhino,Hippo
441-332↓ Tiger,Rhino,Sable
442-111↓ Rhino,Hippo
442-131↓ Rhino,Tiger,Hippo
443-111↓ Rhino,Tiger,Hippo
443-112↓ Rhino,Tiger,Eleph

453-

111-111↓ Croc,Rhino
112-111↓ Croc,Rhino
113-111↓ Croc,Rhino
113-332↓ Rhino,Warthg,Croc
121-111↓ Rhinocerous
122-111↓ Rhinocerous
123-111↓ Rhino,Warthg
131-111↓ Hippo,Rhino
132-111↓ Hippo,Rhino
133-111↓ Hippo,Rhino
133-132↓ Rhino,Hippo,Warthg
133-332↓ Rhino,Tiger,Warthg
141-111↓ Hippo,Rhino
142-111↓ Hippo,Rhino
142-331↓ Rhino,Eleph,Hippo
143-111 Hippo,Rhino
143-112↓ Rhino,Hippo,Eleph
143-212 Rhino,Eleph,Warthg
143-221 Rhino,Eleph,Hippo
143-222 Rhino,Eleph,Warthg
143-311↓ Rhino,Eleph,Hippo
143-312 Rhino,Eleph,Warthg
143-321 Rhino,Eleph,Hippo
143-322 Rhino,Eleph,Warthg
143-331↓ Eleph,Rhino,Tiger
211-111↓ Rhinocerous
212-111↓ Rhinocerous
213-111↓ Rhinocerous
221-111↓ Rhinocerous
222-111↓ Rhino,Hippo
223-111↓ Rhino,Hippo
231-111↓ Rhino,Hippo
232-111↓ Rhino,Hippo
232-121↓ Rhino,Hippo,Walrus
232-321↓ Rhino,Hippo,Bear
233-111↓ Rhino,Hippo
233-221↓ Rhino,Hippo,Bear
233-332 Rhino,Tiger
241-111↓ Hippo,Rhino
242-111↓ Hippo,Rhino
243-111↓ Rhino,Hippo,Eleph
311-111↓ Rhinocerous
312-111↓ Rhinocerous
313-111↓ Rhinocerous
321-111↓ Rhinocerous
322-111↓ Rhinocerous
323-111↓ Rhinocerous
331-111↓ Rhino,Bear
331-121↓ Rhino,Hippo

331-132↓ Rhino,Bear
332-111↓ Rhino,Hippo
333-111↓ Rhino,Bear
333-121↓ Rhino,Hippo
333-332↓ Rhino,Tiger,Bear
341-111↓ Rhinocerous
342-111↓ Rhinocerous
343-111↓ Rhino,Eleph
411-111↓ Rhinocerous
412-111↓ Rhinocerous
413-111↓ Rhino,Tiger
421-111↓ Rhinocerous
422-111↓ Rhinocerous
423-111↓ Rhino,Tiger
431-111↓ Rhino,Tiger
432-111↓ Rhino,Bear
433-111↓ Rhino,Tiger
441-111↓ Rhino,Tiger
442-111↓ Rhino,Eleph
442-231↓ Rhino,Eleph,Tiger
443-111 Rhino,Eleph
443-122↓ Rhino,Eleph,Tiger

454-

111-111↓ Rhino,Croc
112-111↓ Rhino,Croc
113-111↓ Rhino,Croc
113-332↓ Rhino,Warthg,Croc
121-111↓ Rhino,Walrus

122-111↓ Rhino,Walrus
123-111↓ Rhino,Walrus
131-111↓ Walrus,Rhino,Hippo
132-111↓ Walrus,Rhino,Hippo
133-111↓ Walrus,Rhino,Hippo
133-332 Rhino,Tiger
141-111↓ Walrus,Hippo,Rhino
142-111↓ Walrus,Hippo,Rhino
142-331↓ Rhino,Walrus,Eleph
143-111↓ Walrus,Hippo,Rhino
143-131 Walrus,Eleph,Hippo
143-132↓ Eleph,Walrus,Rhino
143-322↓ Rhino,Eleph,W.Dog
211-111↓ Rhinocerous
212-111↓ Rhinocerous
213-111↓ Rhinocerous
221-111↓ Rhinocerous
222-111↓ Rhino,Walrus
223-111↓ Walrus,Rhino,Hippo
231-111↓ Walrus,Rhino,Hippo
232-111↓ Walrus,Rhino,Hippo
233-111↓ Walrus,Rhino,Hippo
241-111↓ Walrus,Rhino,Hippo
242-111↓ Walrus,Rhino,Hippo
243-111↓ Walrus,Rhino,Hippo
243-112 Rhino,Walrus,Eleph
243-121 Walrus,Rhino,Hippo
243-122↓ Rhino,Walrus,Eleph
311-111↓ Rhinocerous

312-111↓ Rhinocerous
313-111↓ Rhinocerous
321-111↓ Rhinocerous
322-111↓ Rhinocerous
323-111↓ Rhinocerous
331-111↓ Rhinocerous
332-111↓ Rhinocerous
332-121↓ Rhino,Walrus
332-211↓ Rhino,Bear
333-111↓ Rhino,Walrus
341-111↓ Rhino,Walrus
342-111↓ Rhino,Walrus
343-111↓ Rhino,Eleph,Walrus
411-111↓ Rhinocerous
412-111↓ Rhinocerous
413-111↓ Rhino,Tiger
421-111↓ Rhinocerous
422-111↓ Rhinocerous
423-111↓ Rhino,Tiger
431-111↓ Rhino,Tiger
432-111↓ Rhino,Tiger
433-111↓ Rhino,Tiger
441-111↓ Rhino,Eleph
441-332↓ Rhino,Tiger,Eleph
442-111↓ Rhino,Eleph
442-331↓ Rhino,Tiger,Eleph
443-111↓ Rhino,Eleph
443-212↓ Rhino,Eleph,Tiger

Joe Mozdzen

ABOUT THE AUTHOR

Born in South Africa, ROY FEINSON studied zoology at the University of Port Elizabeth and has had a lifelong interest in the relationship between animals and humans. Currently he owns a computer software firm in Southern California. Feinson is a *Fox*.